Trafficware®

T5-CVJ-790

Traffic Signal Software - User Guide

Synchro Studio 7
Synchro plus SimTraffic and 3D Viewer

Synchro Studio 7 User Guide

Copyright © 1993 - 2006 Trafficware Ltd. All rights reserved.

International Standard Book Number: 0-9742903-3-5

Printed in the United States of America.

First Printing: June 2006.

Trademarks

Trafficware, Synchro and SimTraffic are registered trademarks or trademarks of Trafficware Ltd. Microsoft and Windows are registered trademarks of Microsoft Corporation. HCS2000 and TRANSYT-7F are trademarks of University of Florida. PASSER is a trademark of Texas Transportation Institute (TTI).

Written By

David Husch

John Albeck

Published By

Trafficware, Ltd.

PO Box 499

Sugar Land, TX 77487-0499

www.trafficware.com

(510) 526-5891

Keeping Up to Date

To keep this information up to date, Trafficware might issue new printings of this manual. New printings reflect minor changes and technical corrections. You can keep this information up to date by visiting and installing the latest revision of the Trafficware software since this User Guide is replicated in the Help Menu of the program. To find out if you have the latest revision or build of the software visit our website at www.trafficware.com.

About the Authors

David Husch is the leading developer of the Synchro and SimTraffic software packages. Mr. Husch has 19 years experience working with Transportation Engineering and Software Development. The Synchro software is used by over 4000 agencies and consultants throughout North America and the world. In the course of supporting and updating the software, Mr. Husch has encountered a huge variety of intersection configurations and special situations.

John Albeck is a Senior Transportation Engineer with 19 years of experience working in Transportation Engineering. Mr. Albeck has gained experience at a state agency, a city and consulting firm. In this capacity, he has instructed numerous classes in the Transportation field, written technical documentation and provided software support. In addition, he has served on a variety of projects involving traffic capacity analysis, traffic operations analysis, traffic forecasting, and traffic signal design.

Table of Contents

Figures

Tables

Chapter 1 – Introduction

Introduction

Synchro Plus is a complete software package for modeling, optimizing, managing and simulating traffic systems.

Synchro Plus is a software suite that includes:

- Synchro, a macroscopic analysis and optimization program;

- SimTraffic, a powerful, easy-to-use traffic simulation software application;

- 3D Viewer, a three-dimensional view of SimTraffic simulations;

- SimTraffic CI, an application that interacts with a controller interface (CI) device connected to a controller to simulate the operation of the controller with simulated traffic.

This User Guide includes instructions for using Synchro Plus and details of the internal traffic models.

The following is a summary of the key features of Synchro Plus.

Capacity Analysis

Synchro implements the Intersection Capacity Utilization (ICU) 2003 method for determining intersection capacity. This method compares the current volume to the intersections ultimate capacity. The method is very straightforward to implement and can be determined with a single page worksheet.

Synchro also implements the methods of the 2000 Highway Capacity Manual, Chapters 15, 16, and 17; Urban Streets, Signalized Intersections, and Unsignalized Intersections. Synchro provides an easy-to-use solution for single intersection capacity analysis and timing optimization.

Synchro includes a term for queue interaction blocking delay. The Total Delay includes the traditional control delay plus the queue delay. Delay calculations are an integral part of the optimization objective in Synchro so this will be directly considered.

In addition to calculating capacity, Synchro can optimize cycle lengths, splits and offsets, eliminating the need to try multiple timing plans in search of the optimum.

All values are entered in easy-to-use forms. Calculations and intermediate results are shown on the same forms.

If the intersection is coordinated, Synchro explicitly calculates the progression factor. With other Highway Capacity Manual (HCM) based software, it is necessary to estimate the effects of coordination. Synchro calculates the effects of coordination automatically and accurately.

Coordinate and Optimize

Synchro allows for quick generation of optimum timing plans. Synchro optimizes cycle length, split times, offsets and phase sequence to minimize driver stops and delay.

Synchro is fully interactive. When input values are changed, the results are updated automatically. Timing plans are shown on easy to comprehend timing diagrams.

Actuated Signals

Synchro provides detailed, automatic modeling of actuated signals. Synchro can model skipping and gapping behavior and apply this information to delay modeling.

Time-Space Diagram

Synchro has colorful, informative Time-Space Diagrams. Splits and offsets can be changed directly on the diagram.

Synchro features two styles of Time-Space Diagrams. The bandwidth style shows how traffic might be able to travel down an entire arterial without stopping. The traffic flow style shows individual vehicles that stop, queue up, and then go. The traffic flow style gives a much clearer picture of what the traffic flow actually looks like.

Time-Space Diagrams can be printed using any Settings compatible printer.

The Time-Space Diagrams also display queue interaction problems with color-coded bars near the intersections.

SimTraffic Simulations

SimTraffic performs micro simulation and animation of vehicle traffic. With SimTraffic, individual vehicles are modeled and displayed traversing a street network. SimTraffic models signalized and unsignalized intersections as well as freeway sections with cars, trucks, pedestrians, and busses. Unlike a number of other modeling applications, SimTraffic animation is displayed while the simulation is performed. Data entry is intuitive and efficient and the same data set created with Synchro can be used to run simulation in SimTraffic.

3D Animations

SimTraffic can create a 3D file which can be viewed with the Trafficware 3D Viewer. The three primary modes of the viewer for playback of SimTraffic data in a 3D environment include scene, ride, and track. The ability to create scenery to enhance the default background is also available in the 3D Viewer.

Controller Interface (CI)

SimTraffic CI simulates vehicles and detector operations. Detector calls are sent to the controller via the controller interface (CI) device. The Controller operates as though it has real traffic. Current phase information is returned from the controller to SimTraffic CI through the CI device.

Data is exchanged between SimTraffic CI and the CI device software 10 times per second.

CORSIM and HCS

Synchro features preprocessors to the CORSIM (TSIS) and HCS (Highway Capacity Software) models.

Synchro data sets can be exported to CORSIM (TSIS) and the HCS to compare measures-of-effectiveness calculated by each model.

Chapter 2 – Map View and Layout

Map View

The **MAP** view (see **Figure 2-1**), includes the drawing area and the map information buttons. The purpose of the drawing area of the **MAP** view is to create the network of links and nodes.

 To activate the **MAP** view, press the *Map View* button or the **[F2]** key from anywhere in the program. By default, Synchro will show the **MAP** view when you start the application.

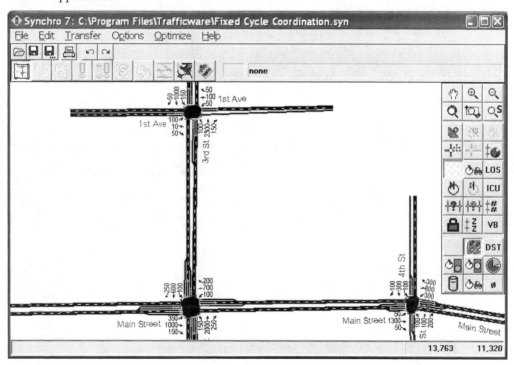

Figure 2-1   MAP View

On the right side of the **MAP** view are the map information buttons. These buttons include the following:

- Intersection information (Node Number, Zone, Cycle Length, Delay and LOS),

- Movement text (Volumes, Splits, Start of Green(s) or Yellow(s), Volume to Capacity Ratio, or Movement Delay).

These are discussed in more detail in the subsequent topics.

The **MAP** view also includes map information buttons to show the following:

- Intersection Capacity Utilization [ICU]

- Show the link distance, speed and travel time on the map [DST]

- Show unbalanced flow [VB]

- Show the movement phase numbers [Ø].

Introduction to Links and Intersections

Synchro models streets and intersections as links and nodes. These links and nodes are created in the **MAP** view. Every intersection to be analyzed in the study area is represented by a node.

 Synchro has the ability to create curved links. See the topic on **How to Add a Link**, page 2-4.

There are two types of links: internal links and external links. Internal links represent a section of street between two intersections. External links indicate an approach to an intersection that does not connect to another signalized intersection.

Bend Nodes

A node with exactly two links is assumed to be a bend node. A bend node is a special case of an unsignalized intersection. Volume and timing data is not entered for a bend node; however, lane data can be entered. Synchro assumes the volumes and lanes from the downstream intersection. The number of lanes on a link approaching a bend node can be changed with the **LANE** settings (see Chapter 5).

Creating bend nodes can be useful to create a taper (lane add or lane drop) within a link.

Bend nodes are not generally needed for roadway curvature. Synchro has the ability to create curved links. Right click on the link and choose Add-Curvature (see page 2-5).

If you plan to use your Synchro network for simulation (SimTraffic or CORSIM), minimize the number of bends that you create. Bend nodes increase the time for calculations. Excessive bends and short links cause SimTraffic to model vehicles at slower speeds.

Unsignalized Intersections

Synchro fully models unsignalized intersections based on Chapter 17 of the 2000 Highway Capacity Manual. Input requirements include turning movement counts, intersection geometry and sign control type for each approach (stop, yield or free flow).

If you are using synchro to optimize a signal system network, it is not necessary to model unsignalized intersections. Keep in mind that every intersection added to the network increases increases the computation time.

Unsignalized intersections can be used to model merging and diverging traffic flows from two or more link segments. In addition, median areas and two-way left-turn lanes can be used to approximate real world applications encountered in the field.

Unsignalized intersections created in Synchro can be simulated using SimTraffic and exported to CORSIM and the HCS. The analysis of unsignalized intersections with SimTraffic is especially helpful for spotting blocking problems and for observing the interaction of signalized intersections and unsignalized intersections.

Mapping out Links and Intersections

It is often helpful to sketch a large network using a photocopy of a detailed map of the study area. The sketch can be used to record intersection numbers, link distances and speeds and lane configurations before coding these details in Synchro.

Another option is to import a base map in DXF, GIS, BMP or JPEG format) into Synchro as base layer. Links and nodes can then be created on top of the graphic layer. For details, see **Background Images**, page 2-22. If you are using accurate basemaps, the distances and angles can be traced on the basemap.

The steps to mapping out links and intersections are as follows:

1. Identify the intersections to be analyzed.

2. Identify the internal links and determine the length and direction of each link. Synchro indicates direction by azimuths (North = 0°, East = 90°, South = 180°, etc.).

3. Identify the external links and determine their direction. If using Synchro only, the length of the external link is not important. If you plan to export the study area to a microscopic simulation model (SimTraffic or CORSIM), then the length of the external link should be long enough to allow vehicles to make a downstream maneuver. While highly dependent on the volume level, an external length of 2000 feet (610 m) typically works well. This should allow vehicles ample time to make decisions regarding their downstream movement. Increase this length if vehicles appear to have difficulties getting into their target lane.

When drawing a link, the angle is shown in the lower left hand corner of the **MAP** view. North is always up (zero degrees). Synchro allows up to eight links per node. Each link is assigned to the closest compass point heading (North, North-west, North-east, etc.).

Chapter 3 explains how to manually change the approach directions assigned by Synchro when links are added to the network. However, the user should refrain from changing the assigned direction as much as possible.

It is not necessary to determine the exact length of the links. It is sufficient to determine the distance to within 20 or 30 feet (6 to 8 meters). The primary use of street lengths is to determine travel times. A car traveling at 30 mph (50 km/h) covers 20 feet (6 meters) in 0.5 seconds. Traveling time less then 1 second is not significant for Synchro's offset calculations. To make a link a precise distance, move the node to an exact coordinate location with the **NODE** settings (see Chapter 4).

Before changing the geometry of an existing network, back up your data files to a different location or filename. Changes to network geometric may cause intersection data to become lost if an intersection is re-configured, for example.

How to Add a Link

To add a link to the map:

1. Select the *Add Link* button  or press the **[A]** key.

2. Position the mouse cursor on the **MAP** view where you want the link to start, and click the left mouse button. The status indicators, at the lower-right corner of the settings, show the East and South coordinates in feet (meters). Note: To cancel adding a link, press [Esc].

3. Release the mouse button and move the cursor to the position on the map where you want the link to end. Click the left mouse button again. Refer to the status bar at the bottom of the settings to see the length and direction of the link.

 Press and hold the [Shift] key while drawing to create a link centered on a 45 degree compass point on the map.

It is not necessary to have the exact distance when adding a link. The distance can be adjusted via the **LANE** settings. However, new links added to the network should be within 50 feet of actual link distances to insure accuracy during simulation.

 It can sometimes be tricky to create short links because Synchro will snap to a nearby node. To reduce the snap distance, reduce the Intersection Radius with the **Options→MAP View** command.

Curved Links

Synchro allows users to add curvature to link segments using Bezier curves which are commonly found in CAD and drawing packages. Bezier curves can be used to approximate any curvature represented on the base drawing.

Simply right-click on a straight link segment and select Add-Curvature. Two squares (curve points) will appear on the curved link which serve as control points. Select and drag a control point to modify the shape of the curve. With a little practice, you can create smooth arcs and curves that represent any geometry found in your street network.

Synchro will calculate the length of the curve. It should be possible to create a 270 degree loop ramp using 2 links with one bend node. Most other alignments should be possible with a single segment. The curvature can be removed by "right clicking" on the link and selecting Remove-Curvature. If two links are joined because an intersection is removed, the links will lose their curvature. The direction of traffic at the intersection (i.e., NB, EB, NE, …) is determined by the direction of the first control point, rather than the direction of the next node. This can be used to increase the angle between diagonals at the intersection.

 The curve points must be placed after any tangents from a right turn Island, otherwise image distortion will occur.

How to Add an Intersection

There is no direct command to add an intersection to the map. Intersections are created automatically when you insert a link that crosses an existing link in the network. Simply, insert a new link over an existing link at the center of the intersection you wish to add to the network. The existing link will be broken into two link segments at the intersection.

Intersections cannot be created from curved links. Therefore, create intersections from straight link segments and then add curvature to the links using Bezier curves.

 Press and hold the [Ctrl] key while drawing to create a link that is grade separated. No intersection is created where the links cross.

How to Draw Closely Spaced Intersections

When adding a link, Synchro will attempt to connect the link to nearby existing points. Make the nodes at least 100 feet (33m) apart and then move them closer together.

 If you are using this file with SimTraffic, your nodes must be at least 70 ft apart. If you are using this file with CORSIM, your nodes must be at least 50 ft apart.

How to Delete a Link

To remove a link from the map:

1. Select the link by clicking on it with the left mouse button. Half the link will become highlighted.

2. Select the *Delete Link* button ![button] or press the [Delete] key.

3. Select [Yes] to the question, "Delete Link, are you sure?"

The link will be removed from the screen. If the link was connected to an intersection with only two links, that intersection will be removed as well.

How to Delete an Intersection

To remove an intersection from the map:

1. Select the intersection by clicking on it with the left mouse button. The node will become highlighted.

2. Select the **Delete Node** button or press the **[Delete]** key.

3. Answer **[Yes]** to the question, "Delete Intersection, are you sure?"

Any through links going through this intersection will be joined together. Any other links going to adjacent intersections will be shortened to preserve data at adjacent intersections. Any joined links will be redrawn.

How to Move an Intersection or External Node

To move an intersection or external node on the map:

1. Select the *Move Node* button or press the **[M]** key.

2. Select an intersection, or the end of an external link, by clicking on it with the left mouse button. Note: You can cancel a move operation by pressing [Esc], or by clicking the original intersection location.

3. Drag the intersection, or node, to the new location and click the left mouse button.

If an external node is moved onto another external node, the two nodes will be combined as a new intersection. However, existing intersections cannot be combined with other intersections or external nodes.

Synchro automatically assigns lane groups that agree with the layout of the network. Therefore, it is possible that a realigned links forces Synchro to adjust the lane group assigned to the link. For example, if the relative angle between two links is changed from 180° to 90°, there will no longer be a through lane group for these links. Synchro preserves the lane group data. If a movement changes from NBL to NBT, for example, the data for NBL will be transferred to NBT.

To move to exact coordinates, see the topic on **Node Coordinates** on page 4-4.

Link Settings

Past versions of Synchro included a LINK setting that was opened by double-clicking on a link. This setting no longer exists in version 7. The data items found in the LINK settings have been moved to the **LANE** (see Chapter 5) and **SIMULATION** settings. Double-click the link to access the LANE settings. Select the SIMULATION button to access the simulation settings for the link.

Zooming and Scrolling

 To scroll around the **MAP** view, choose the *Pan* button or press the **[End]** key. To deactivate, select the button again or press [Esc]. In addition, holding the mouse wheel button down will allow you to drag the map.

 The *Pan* button replaces the option to scroll when the mouse is moved to the edge of the Map in older versions of Synchro. Using the key pad arrows still scrolls the Map view even if the Pan button is not selected.

 To view more of the map, choose the *Zoom Out* button or press **[Page Up]**. The mouse scroll wheel can also be used to change the map view scale. Scrolling up will zoom out and scrolling down will zoom in.

 To view the entire map, choose the *Zoom All* button or press **[Home]**.

 To view the map closer, choose the *Zoom In* button or press **[Page Down]**. It may be necessary to scroll to put the map in the center of the **MAP** view. The mouse scroll wheel can also be used to change the map view scale. Scrolling up will zoom out and scrolling down will zoom in.

 To view a specific section of the map, use the *Zoom Settings* button or press **[W]**. To define the area, click on the upper-left corner of the viewing area then click in the lower-right corner of the viewing area.

 To view the map at a specific scale, use the *Zoom Scale* button or press **[Shift]+[S]**. Enter the desired scale to view the map in feet per inch (meters per inch). This command assumes 100 pixels per inch on your screen.

The command **File→Print-Settings** for both Synchro and SimTraffic will print to the scale specified by Zoom-Scale. The printout will be centered on the center point of the current screen view.

To center the **MAP** view, press **[Ctrl]+[C]** and the click where you want the map to be centered.

Select Intersection

 Use the *Select-Intersection* button or the **[F8]** key to bring up a list of the intersections in your network. This will bring up the **SELECT INTERSECTION** settings.

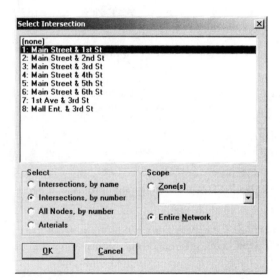

Figure 2-2   Select Intersection Settings

Choosing an intersection from the list and pressing [OK] will switch the current settings to that intersection. The **MAP** view will be centered on the selected intersection.

The **SELECT INTERSECTION** setting is used to select whether intersections or named arterials are displayed. The intersections can be listed by name or node number. All nodes, including bends and external nodes, can be listed by node number.

Selecting a named arterial will bring up a Time-Space diagram showing the arterial. The Named Arterial view can show part of an arterial based on its name, zone, or route #. The Named Arterial view can also show an arterial that turns corners. See the topic **Arterial Route Naming** on page 5-7.

The Scope box can be used to view the list by a named zone or for the entire network.

Intersection and Link Buttons

The buttons below the zooming and scrolling buttons are used to create, delete and move links and nodes. There is alos a button used to transform the Map. The buttons available are listed below.

 Select the *Add Link* button or press **[A]** to create a link on the **MAP** view. Refer to page 2-4 for additional details.

 Select the *Delete Link* button or press **[Del]** to delete the selected link. Refer to page 2-6 for additional details.

 Select the *Lane Settings* button or press **[Enter]** to enter **LANE** settings for the selected link. The side view data window will be displayed. Refer to page 3-4 and page 5-2 for additional details.

 Select the *Move Node* button or press **[M]** to move a node. Refer to page 2-7 for additional details.

 Select the *Delete Node* button or press **[Del]** to delete the node. Refer to page 2-7 for additional details.

 Select the *Transform Map* button to change the network node coordinate, rotate the map or to enter a scaling factor. Refer to page 2-26 for additional details.

Show Information Buttons

The buttons on the right side of the **MAP** view can be used to show information on the **MAP** view. The information buttons available are listed below.

Show Intersection Delays

 Select the *Show Intersection Delays* button or press **[Shift]+[D]** to display the intersection delay for each intersection. This is the **Intersection Delay** shown in the **TIMING** settings (see Chapter 7).

Show Levels of Service

 Select the *Show Levels of Service* button or press the **[O]** key to display the intersection delay for each intersection. This is the **Intersection Level of Service** shown in the **TIMING** settings.

Show Cycle Lengths

 Select the *Show Cycle Lengths* button or press the **[C]** key to display the current cycle length for each intersection. This is the **Cycle Length** shown in the **TIMING** settings. Unsignalized intersections will be displayed with a 'U'.

Show Natural Cycle Lengths

 Select the *Show Natural Cycle Lengths* button or press the **[N]** key to display the natural cycle length for each intersection. This is the **Natural Cycle Length** shown in the **TIMING** settings. Unsignalized intersections will be displayed with a 'U'.

Show Intersection Capacity Utilization

 Select the *Show Intersection Capacity Utilization* button to display the intersections' capacity utilization for each intersection. This is the **Intersection Capacity Utilization** shown in the **TIMING** settings.

Show Coordinatability Factor

 Select the ***Show Coordinatabilty Factor*** button to display the coordinatability factor for each link. For further details, see the topic on **Coordinatabilty Factors** on page 13-22.

Show Natural Coordinatabiltity Factor

 Select the ***Show Natural Coordinatabilty Factor*** button to display the coordinatability factor for each link. For further details, see the topic on **Coordinatabilty Factors** on page 13-22.

Show Node Numbers

 To see the node numbers press the ***Show Node Numbers*** button or the **[#]** key. Node numbers can be changed with the **NODE** settings (see Chapter 4).

Show Locked Timings

 Select the ***Show Locked Timings*** button to display the intersections with locked timings. This is the **Lock Timings** field shown in the **TIMING** settings.

Show Zones

 To see the zone names press the ***Show Intersection Zones*** button or the **[Z]** key. Zone names can be changed with the **NODE** settings. Zone names can include any letter or number up to seven characters.

Show Volume Balancing

 Select the ***Show Volume Balancing*** button to display the unbalance of traffic volumes between intersections. The map can be printed (**File→Print-Settings**) to view the volume unbalance. This can be used in conjunction with volume diagrams for quick editing adjustments. The information is directional, with the incoming volume located on the right side of the link, closest to the downstream intersection. Also, see coding errors 100, 101 and 206 (page 17-1).

Volume Diagrams

 To show volumes on the map, select the *Show Volumes on Map* button to the left of the **MAP** view or press the **[V]** key.

Show Link Distance, Speed and Travel Time

 Select the *Show Link Distance, Speed and Travel Time* button or press the **[T]** key to show link distance, speed and travel time on the **MAP** view. Double clicking on the diagram brings up side view settings. The diagrams will be included on bend and external links.

Show Start of Greens, Start of Yellow

 To see progression quality, press the *Show Start of Greens* button or press the **[G]** key. This option shows the beginning of green time for each movement. The intersection cycle length is also shown. This display shows progression numerically. For permitted plus protected movements, the start of the protected green is shown. For actuated signals, the start is based on maximum green times. Double clicking on the diagram opens the **TIMING** settings.

 The *Show Start of Yellow Times* button shows the beginning of yellow time for each movement. The intersection cycle length is also shown. This display shows progression numerically. For permitted plus protected movements, the end of the protected green is shown. For actuated signals, the end is based on maximum green times. Double clicking on the diagram opens the **TIMING** settings. and brings you to the Total Split row.

Show Maximum Green Times

 Select the *Maximum Green Times* button to show the maximum green time for each phase in seconds. The intersection cycle length is also shown. This display shows green times in a map format. For permitted plus protected movements, only the protected greens are shown. For actuated signals, the time shown is based on maximum green times. Double clicking on the diagram opens the **TIMING** settings.

Show Volume to Capacity Ratios

 Select the **Show Volume to Capacity Ratios** button to display the volume to capacity ratios for each movement. The v/c ratios are based on average green times. The v/c ratios DO NOT show problems with defacto turning lanes. This display can be used to quickly identify capacity problems. Double clicking on the diagram opens the **TIMING** settings.

For unsignalized intersections, this is the volume to capacity for the movement. Unlike signals, the v/c ratio is the maximum for the movement, not lane group. See the Highway Capacity Manual (HCM) Unsignalized report for more details about the capacity and delays by lane.

For roundabouts, the HIGH capacity v/c ratio is shown for the approach. This is the high capacity range of possible v/c ratios for the method. To see the low capacity ratios, see the HCM Unsignalized report. See the Highway Capacity Manual for details on high and low capacity ranges.

Show Movement Delays

 Select the **Show Movement Delays** button or press the **[D]** key to display the delay for each movement. The delay shown will be the **Control Delay** (see page 7-25). Double clicking on the diagram opens the **TIMING** settings.

For unsignalized intersections, the delay is shown for the movement. Unlike signals, the delay is for the movement, not lane group. A value of 9999 indicates no capacity is available. See the HCM Unsignalized report for more details about the capacity and delays by lane.

 Movement delays are not displayed for roundabouts using this method.

Show Phase Numbers

 Select the **Show Phase Numbers** button or press the **[P]** key to show phase numbers for each movement. Permitted phases are shown in parenthesis ( ). Clicking on the diagram opens the **TIMING** settings and brings you to the Protected Phases row.

Hide Information

 To hide the information, select the *No Map Information* [space] or *No Movement Text* buttons or press [Shift]+[space].

 The displayed volumes are adjusted for growth factor (from the **VOLUME** settings but not for peak hour factor).

Use the **File→Print-Settings** command to print the **MAP** view with the lane and/or volume diagram.

MAP View Keyboard Commands
Change Map View Commands

Zoom All	[Home]
Zoom In	[Page Down]
Zoom Out	[Page Up]
Zoom Settings	[W], [Shift]+[W], [Ctrl]+[W]
Zoom Scale	[Shift]+[S]
Zoom Previous	[Ctrl]+[BkSpace]
Zoom Center	[Ctrl]+[C]
Scroll Map	[↑] [↓] [←] [→]
Page Map	[Ctrl]+[↑] [↓] [←] [→]

Link and Intersection Commands

Delete Intersection	[Delete]
Delete Link	[Delete]
Add Link	[A]
Move Intersection	[M]
Link Settings	[Enter]
Cancel Add or Move	[Esc] or [Space]

Intersection Information Commands

No Intersection Information	[Space]
Show Cycle Lengths	[C] A indicates actuated signal, U indicates unsignalized
Show Natural Cycle Length	[N]
Show Zones	[Z]
Show Intersection Delays	[Shift]+[D]
Show Intersection Level of Services	[O]
Node Settings	[Enter]
Show Node Numbers	[#]
Show Volume Diagram	[V]

Movement Text Commands

Movement Volumes	[V]
Show Link Distance, Speed and Travel Time	[T]
Movement and Intersection Delays	[D]
Show Starts of Green	[G]
Show Starts of Yellow	[Y]
Show Split Times	[S]
Show Volume to Capacity	[X]
Show Movement Phase Numbers	[P]

Select Intersection Commands

Select Next Intersection to SW	[1]
Select Next Intersection to S	[2]
Select next intersection to SE	[3]
Select next intersection to W	[4]
Select next intersection to E	[6]
Select next intersection to NW	[7]
Select next intersection to N	[8]
Select next intersection to NE	[9]

File Units

Use the **Options→Convert-to-Metric** command or the **Options→Convert-to-English** command to change the units used for the current file.

Convert to English

Select **Convert to English** command to convert your file to use feet and miles per hour.

Convert to Metric

Select **Convert to Metric** command to convert your file to use meters and kilometers per hour.

 When changing file units, any map background is discarded. You will have to convert your source DXF file to the new units and re-import it.

Map coordinates are scaled by 3.28 about the point (0,0).

Speeds, storage lengths, widths, and other values are similarly converted.

Each file has its own *File Units* setting. New files are created based on the units specified in the *Regional and Language Options*. To change the *Regional Settings*, go to the Control Panel and select *Regional and Language Options*.

Drawing Features

Freeway Links

Freeways can be coded for simulation with SimTraffic using the same links and nodes as surface streets and intersections. Each direction of the freeway can be coded with a one-way link or as a single link with a wide median. For setting the median width, see the discussion on **Median Width** on page 9-4.

Freeways typically have higher speeds and flow rates than signalized intersections. You can set freeway link speeds and headway factors using the **LANES** and **SIMULATION** options (double click on the link to access these settings). When you set the default Saturation Flow (see page 5-11) for the link, the Headway factor (see page 9-8) will be automatically calculated

Freeway Merges

Figure 2-3 shows a freeway merge in SimTraffic. Here are the steps to creating a freeway merge.

1. The merge point is a 3-legged unsignalized intersection.

2. Create a bend node 200 to 1000 ft downstream of the merge. The acceleration lane will end here. The distance from the merge to the lane drop should represent the acceleration lane distance or the distance to where the taper is less than 1/2 of a lane width.

3. Select the **LANE** settings for the acceleration link. Code the number of lanes equal to the sum of the mainline lanes plus the number of ramp lanes. No lanes should merge or cross at the merge point. Set the Saturation Flow to an appropriate value for freeway links (2000 – 2200 vphpl).

4. Select the **TIMING** settings for the merge intersection. Set the control type to *Unsignalized* and all sign control to *Free*. The ramp should not have a stop or yield sign.

5. Select the **SIMULATION OPTIONS** settings for the merge intersection. Set the turning speeds to the speed limit. Do not use the default right turning speed of 9 mph; this will cause unacceptable slowing at the merge. The headway factors headway factor is automatically updated based on the input Saturation Flow. Adjust the Link Offset as described on page 9-6.

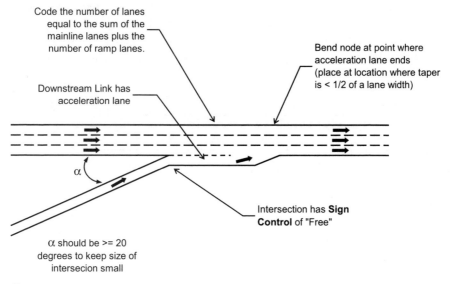

Code the number of lanes equal to the sum of the mainline lanes plus the number of ramp lanes.

Bend node at point where acceleration lane ends (place at location where taper is < 1/2 of a lane width)

Downstream Link has acceleration lane

α

Intersection has **Sign Control** of "Free"

α should be >= 20 degrees to keep size of intersecion small

Notes:
- Set the **Turning Speed** to the appropriate value.
- Change the **Saturation Flow** for freeway links.
- Set the **Link Offset** equal to the width of the mainline

Figure 2-3   Freeway Merge

Freeway Diverges

Figure 2-4 illustrates a freeway diverge. Diverges are coded with a single unsignalized intersection. No deceleration lane is required, but one can be coded similar to the acceleration lane for a two lane on ramp.

Here are the steps to creating a freeway diverge.

1. The diverge point is a 3 legged unsignalized intersection.

2. Select the **TIMING** settings for the diverge intersection. Set the control type to *Unsignalized* and all sign control to *Free*.

3. Select the **LANE** settings and set the Saturation Flow to an appropriate value for freeway links (2000 – 2200 vphpl).

4. Select the **SIMULATION OPTIONS** settings for the diverge intersection. Set the turning speeds to the speed limit. Do not use the default right turning speed of 9 mph, this will cause unacceptable slowing at the merge. The headway factors headway factor is automatically updated based on the input Saturation Flow. Adjust the Link Offset as described on page 9-6.

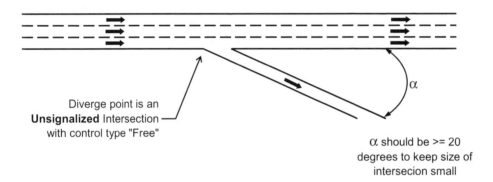

Diverge point is an
Unsignalized Intersection
with control type "Free"

α should be >= 20
degrees to keep size of
intersecion small

Notes:
- Set the **Turning Speed** to the appropriate value.
- Change the **Saturation Flow** for freeway links.
- Set the **Link Offset** to the width of the mainline (use a negative value)

Figure 2-4   Freeway Diverge

Limit of One Link for Each of Eight Directions

The maximum number of links that can meet at each intersection is eight. There can only be one link for each of the eight major directions (North, South, East, West, North-East, North-West, South-East and South-West). This limitation is due to the way that Synchro stores intersections and links. This limitation should not be a problem for the vast majority of intersections, it might be a problem when there are two or more diagonal streets that cross or join.

Map Settings, Color, and Sizes

Use the **Options→Map-Settings** command to change the appearance of the map. This command can change the color and size of the map elements, as well as control the appearance of street names.

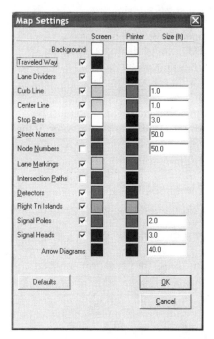

Figure 2-5   Synchro Map Settings

To change a color, click on the *Color* button for the desired element and then select a color from the choices shown.

The sizes for street names, link widths, and intersection radii are in feet (meters). These elements will be scaled when the map is zoomed in and out. The Street Name Height also affects how often the street name is repeated. To have the street names repeat closer together, decrease the height of the street names.

The [**Defaults**] button will return the settings to the default settings (see page 2-27).

Background Images

Synchro supports importing multiple images at the same time for the map background. The file types supported include:

- DXF, CAD vector file. In version 7, the DXF file is referenced as an external file and not embedded in the Synchro file (*.syn).

 When a version 6 or earlier file with a DXF file is opened, you will be prompted to save the DXF as an external file. When this DXF file is saved as an external file, some irregularities in the saved DXF may appear. It is suggested to import the original DXF file instead of saving out the DXF from the old Synchro file.

- SHP, GIS shape files. The shape files come with supporting index files and must be kept together in the same directory. The user will have the option to set the color of the shape file.

- SID, GIS bitmap files. Synchro uses MrSID Decode from www.lizardtech.com to convert SID files from GIS to JPEG format (see next section).

- JPG, JPEG, BMP, bitmap files.

- The background image can be a combination of any of the listed file types.

 JPEG is preferred to BMP due to compression. The JPEG format allows only part of the file to be loaded when zoomed out.

Select Backgrounds settings

To add, remove, or adjust backgrounds; select **File→Select Background** as shown in **Figure 2-6**.

If no files are attached, the user is prompted for a file or multiple file(s). The files can have the extension JPG, JPEG, BMP, DXF, or SHP as defined above.

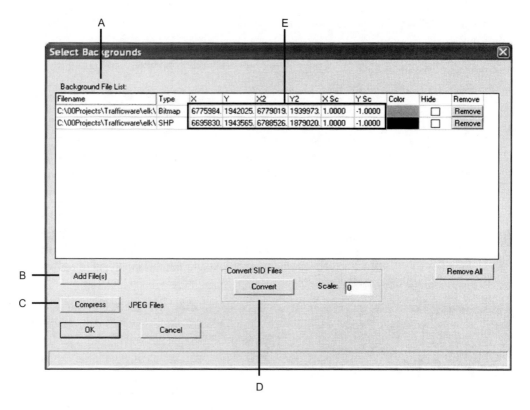

Figure 2-6   Select Backgrounds Settings

The list of files is shown in the **Background File List** as shown as "A" in **Figure 2-6**. This file list includes the following:

- Filename is the background image filename including the path.

- Type is the type of file (Bitmap, SHP, DXF, JPG).

- X, Y is the Synchro coordinate for the upper left hand corner of the image.

- X2, Y2 is the Synchro coordinate for the lower right hand corner of the image.

- X Sc, Y Sc is the image scale factor (see the section "Set Bitmap Scale and Offset" below).

- Color allows you to change the color of a GIS shape file.

- Hide will hide the background image when checked.

- Remove will remove the image from the background.

Use the **[Add File(s)]** button ("B" in **Figure 2-6**) to select one or more files. Read the topic on **Importance of Memory Footprint** on page 2-26).

The **[Compress]** JPEG Files button ("C" in **Figure 2-6**) will prompt you for JPEG files. The selected files will be loaded and resaved with higher compression, but less quality.

 This function will alter your existing JPG files and reduce the image quality. Use this feature to reduce the file size of background bitmaps. You cannot undo this command.

The **Convert SID** files area ("D" in **Figure 2-6**) provides access to the MRSIDDECODE.EXE, freeware utility. This is an unsupported DOS tool to help convert SID files into JPG. Select one or more SID files, a jpg and jgw file will be created with the same base name as the SID file. The jgw file is a text file that contains coordinate and scaling information. Synchro reads this to automatically set the scale for converted SID files.

The **Scale** setting can be used to reduce the scale and size of the converted files; 0 full size, 1 half size, 2 quarter size, 3 1/8 size. Set this number before clicking convert. The resulting JPG must be less than 50M. If the source file is large, use the following scales:

Size of SID File	Use this scale
>200M	3
>100M	2
>40M	1
<=40M	0

Use the **[Remove all]** button to remove all files from list.

Set Bitmap Scale and Offset

When loading a bitmap file (bmp or jpg) it is necessary to set the scale and base point. From the **Select Background** settings, double click the scale settings (are outlined as "E" in **Figure 2-6**) to set the bitmap scale and offset. The **SET BITMAP SCALE AND OFFSET** settings will appear as shown in **Figure 2-7**.

NOTE For converted SID files, the scale is automatically set so you can skip the Set Bitmap Scale and Offset setting.

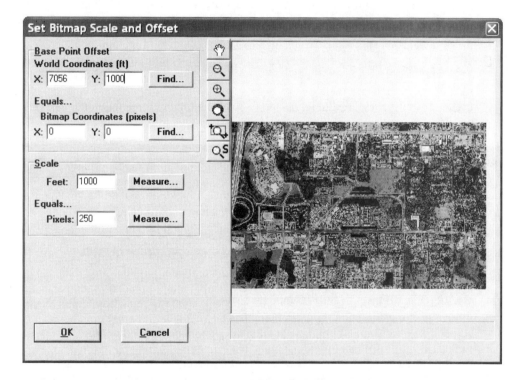

Figure 2-7   Set Bitmap Scale and Offset Settings

The upper-left corner of the bitmap will have bitmap coordinates (0,0) in pixels. In an existing Synchro file, it is necessary to match a point on the bitmap to a node in the Synchro file.

1. Click [**Find**] for world coordinates and select an intersection on the Synchro map. This will set the **World coordinates** for the base point

2. Click [**Find**] for bitmap coordinates and select the point on the bitmap in the center of the previously selected bitmap. This will set the **Bitmap coordinates** for the basepoint. The bitmap will be placed so that the bitmap intersection is coincident with the Synchro intersection.

It is necessary to set the scale of the map. To help set the scale, Synchro allows you to measure distances on the bitmap and in an existing Synchro map.

1. Click [**Measure**] for Feet (or Meters) and select the first point on a link of known length. Within a new file, simply type in the distance of a known street length.

2. Click on the second point of the Synchro point with known length. This will set N in the formula, N feet per M pixels.

3. Click [**Measure**] for Pixels and select the starting point of the same link on the bitmap.

4. Click on the second link point on the bitmap. This will set M in the formula N feet per M pixels.

 ## Importance of memory footprint

It is very important to keep the size of the files used as small as possible. All of the bitmaps and other files are loaded into RAM and accessed whenever the map view changes.

Keep the total size of backgrounds under 100M or 10% of computer's RAM. The limit in Synchro is 200M; this is to prevent a lockup of your computer from overuse of memory.

Some tips to keeping the background file sizes small.

- Use JPEG, not Bitmap, JPEG is compressed, and optimized for viewing when zoomed out.

- Use the scale factor when converting SID to JPEG.

- Load files in a Picture editor such as Microsoft Photo Editor or Adobe Photo Shop, resave with compression on high, and image quality low. Set off network areas to a single color. For extremely large files, resize the image to ½ size or ¼ size.

- Remove tiled bitmaps that are not part of the street network.

Rotate, Scale and Move the Map's Coordinate System

 Use the *Transform Map* button to move, scale, or rotate the entire map. If your map was initially laid out with a different coordinate system, you can change it with this command.

To translate the map, do the following steps:

1. Select the ***Transform-Map*** button command.

2. Click on an intersection that has known coordinates in the new coordinate system.

3. The **TRANSFORM MAP** view will appear with the existing coordinates of the selected intersection. Enter the new coordinates for this intersection and select [OK].

4. Enter a scale factor or rotation angle. The scale and rotation base point will be the selected intersection.

5. The map will be translated. Any background image will be cleared.

6. To change a map between feet and metric units, use the **Options→Convert-to-Metric** or **Options→Convert-to-Feet** command.

Default Settings

The following settings have a [**Default**] button available:

*   Network Settings (Synchro)

*   Report Settings (Synchro and SimTraffic)

*   Map Settings (Synchro and SimTraffic)

*   Driver and Vehicle Parameters (SimTraffic)

*   Interval Parameters (SimTraffic)

Using the [**Default**] button loads in the defaults for the given dialog, window or view.

The defaults are read from a zero intersection file (defaults.syn) in the Trafficware directory. When a user has a file with preferred defaults settings, it can be saved as the "defaults.syn" file and placed in the Trafficware directory (or wherever Synchro is installed). If an organization wants to have standard settings for everyone, they can deploy a defaults.syn to all users.

 Some organizations may lock down the application directory. Therefore, the administrator may need to change or deploy the defaults file.

Chapter 3 – Data Entry Settings

Data can be input, edited and viewed with the data entry setting buttons after links and nodes have been created in the **MAP** view. Refer to Chapter 2 for details on creating links and nodes.

In Synchro, a horizontal row of buttons is always in view. These buttons are used to switch between the various data entry settings.

The data entry buttons are greyed out and not accessible until either a link or node is selected on the map. **Figure 3-1** shows the location of the data entry setting buttons in Synchro.

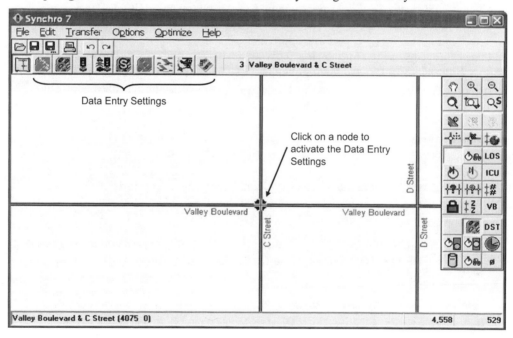

Figure 3-1   Data Entry Settings

Data Entry Setting Buttons

The data entry setting buttons include the following:

 This is the *Lane Settings* button. Use this button or the [**F3**] key to switch to the **LANE** settings. Refer to Chapter 5 for details.

 This is the *Volume Settings* button. Use this button or the [**F4**] key to activate the **VOLUME** settings. Refer to Chapter 6 for details.

 This is the *Timing Settings* button. Use this button or the [**F5**] key to activate the **TIMING** settings. This button is not visible if a signalized intersection is selected. Refer to Chapter 7 for details.

 This is the *Signing Settings* button. Use this button or the [**F5**] key to activate the **SIGNING** settings. This button is not visible if an unsignalized intersection is selected. Refer to Chapter 7 for details.

 This is the *Phasing Settings* button. Use this button or the [**F6**] key to activate the **PHASING** settings. Refer to Chapter 8 for details.

 This is the *Simulation Settings* button. Use this button or the [**F10**] key to activate the **SIMULATION SETTINGS** button. Refer to Chapter 9 for details.

 This is the *Detector Settings* button. Use this button or the [**F11**] key to activate the **DETECTOR** settings. Refer to Chapter 10 for details.

 This is the *Time-Space Diagram* button. Use this button or the [**F7**] key to activate the **TIME-SPACE DIAGRAM**. An intersection or link must be selected for this button to be active. Refer to Chapter 12 for details.

 This is the *Select-Intersection* button. Use this button or the [**F8**] key to bring up a list of the intersections in your network. Choosing an intersection and pressing [OK] will switch the current settings to that intersection. In addition, the **MAP View** will be centered on the selected intersection. This button is always active.

This is the *SimTraffic Animation* button. Use this button or press **[Ctrl]+[G]** to start SimTraffic and load the current file in SimTraffic. This button is always active.

Clicking once on the button described above, or pressing the appropriate **[F]** key, will open to the full view data entry screen. Clicking on the button again will change to a side view data entry view. See the discussion below for details.

Full View Data Entry

Data entry in Synchro can be performed with a traditional full screen view or a **MAP** view side entry. In full view data entry, the **MAP** view will disappear. To activate, highlight an intersection from the **MAP** view and select the desired data entry button along the top of Synchro. **Figure 3-2** illustrates the full view data entry screen for the **LANE** settings. Details on the settings are found in the upcoming chapters.

LANE SETTINGS	EBL	EBT	EBR	WBL	WBT	WBR	NBL	NBT	NBR	SBL	SBT	SBR
Lanes and Sharing (#RL)												
Traffic Volume (vph)	350	1000	150	100	700	200	150	2000	250	100	600	25
Street Name	—	Main Stre	—	—	Main Stre	—	—	3rd St	—	—	3rd St	—
Link Distance (ft)	—	1407	—	—	1345	—	—	1083	—	—	1142	—
Link Speed (mph)	—	40	—	—	40	—	—	45	—	—	45	—
Set Arterial Name and Speed	—	EB	—	—	WB	—	—	NB	—	—	SB	—
Travel Time (s)	—	24.0	—	—	22.9	—	—	16.4	—	—	17.3	—
Ideal Satd. Flow (vphpl)	1900	1900	1900	1900	1900	1900	1900	1900	1900	1900	1900	190
Lane Width (ft)	12	12	12	12	12	12	12	12	12	12	12	1
Grade (%)	—	0	—	—	0	—	—	0	—	—	0	—
Area Type CBD	—	☐	—	—	☐	—	—	☐	—	—	☐	—
Storage Length (ft)	250	—	200	250	—	200	150	—	200	150	—	20
Storage Lanes (#)	2	—	1	1	—	1	1	—	1	1	—	
Right Turn Channelized	—	—	None	—	—	None	—	—	None	—	—	Non
Curb Radius (ft)	—	—	—	—	—	—	—	—	—	—	—	

Synchro 7: C:\Program Files\Trafficware\Fixed Cycle Coordination.syn

File   Edit   Transfer   Options   Optimize   Help

3 Main Street & 3rd St

Main Street & 3rd St (13242 10054)

Figure 3-2   Full View Data Entry, LANES Settings

When in the full view of the **PHASING** and **TIMING** settings, press the [**F9**] key to move focus between blue (directional) and yellow (node) sections.

The full view data entry screens will show all available movement headings. The available movement headings will depend on the layout of the links. For instance, a T-intersection will have 6 columns visible and a 4-leg intersection will have twelve columns visible.

The direction headings are based on the angle of the link as drawn in the **MAP** view (north is always up, or zero degrees).

Side View Data Entry

In addition to a full view data entry screen, data can also be entered with a side view screen. This view displays the data entry rows on the left side of the **MAP** view allowing you to see the data update as you enter. To activate the side view data entry, double click on a link approaching an intersection. **Figure 3-3** illustrates the side view data entry.

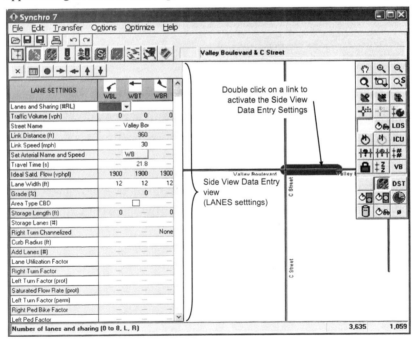

Figure 3-3   Side View Data Entry, LANES Settings

The side view setting that will open is based on the last view edited. By default, the **LANE** settings will appear. To choose a new view, click on the appropriate data entry settings button or press an [**F**] key.

You can toggle between full screen and side view with the [**F**] keys. Press [**F3**] for lanes, [**F4**] for volumes, [**F5**] for timing, [**F6**] for phasing, [**F10**] for simulation settings and [**F11**] for detector settings.

The top of the side view settings contains a series of buttons.

The [**X**] button will close the side view settings. The second button will toggle between full view and side view. The **red circle** will bring up the **NODE** settings and the **arrows** will switch the approach.

When displaying the side view of the **PHASING** settings for a direction, it will show all phases that serve that direction.

Lanes and Volumes Data Rows

Lanes and Sharing (#RL)	↰	↟↟	↱
Traffic Volume (vph)	100	200	300

The first two rows of the **LANE**, **VOLUME**, **TIMING**, **SIMULATION OPTIONS** and **DETECTORS** settings will show the **Lanes and Sharing** row followed by the **Traffic Volume** row. This will reduce the need to switch back and forth between settings.

Details on the **Lanes and Sharing** setting can be found on page 5-2 and for the **Traffic Volume setting** on page 6-2.

Changing the Name of the Approach Direction

To change the name of an approach direction, right click on the column label of the **LANE**, **VOLUME**, **TIMING**, **SIMULATION OPTIONS** or **DETECTORS** settings. Double click on the desired direction name to reassign the direction. To reset to the original map direction, select "Free".

The column label appears in the side view when you double click on a link. The column label displays a directional arrow and a heading name (for instance, NBL, NBT, NBR, SBL, SBT, etc.)

The ability to change the approach heading is intended to reclassify diagonal approaches into orthogonal approaches (NB, SB, EB, WB). This is not intended to rotate an entire intersection or map. North must always be up on the **MAP** view.

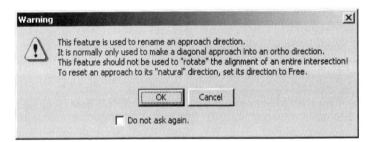

Figure 3-4   Warning Screen

 To navigate between intersections, click on the column heading picture to move in that direction. For instance, click on the EBT column heading arrow to move to the intersection to the east. Clicking on the EBL column heading arrow will move to the intersection to the north.

Approach Movements

Synchro will allow 6 movements per approach. This includes one through, one U-turn, two lefts and two rights. The through is defined as the opposing direction. Consider **Figure 3-5** of the six-leg intersection. Traveling from nodes 1-2-5 is assigned the EBT direction, 1-2-4 is the EBL, 1-2-3 is the EBL2 (hard left), 1-2-1 is the U-turn, 1-2-6 is the EBR and 1-2-7 is the EBR2 (hard right).

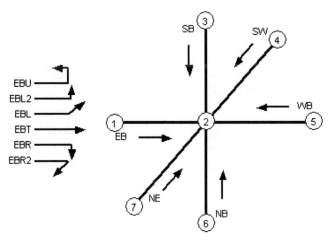

Figure 3-5   Approach Movements

If you do not have two opposing directions that line up (i.e., EB and WB), then there would be no through movement defined. If you want a through movement to be defined, the opposing link must be labeled with the opposing direction. You could change the approach name (as defined above) to create the through movement.

File Command Buttons

Synchro includes buttons that allow the user to save, open a file, create a report, undo and redo. There is also a new box on the Synchro toolbar that shows the node number of the selected intersection that is helpful to see the node number when in a data screen.

This is the Open-File button. Use this button or the [Ctrl]+[O] keys to open a file.

This is the File-Save button. Use this button or the [Ctrl]+[S] keys to save the file.

This is the File-Save As button. Use this button to save the file with a different name.

This is the Create-Report button. Use this button or the [Ctrl]+[R] keys to create a report (opens the **SELECT REPORTS** window).

This is the Undo button. Use this to undo the last 100 commands.

This is the Redo button. Use this to redo the last 100 undone commands.

Summary of Menu Commands

Synchro has a variety of commands that can be accessed with button clicks, left mouse-click commands or menu commands. This section will summarize the available commands (listed in order shown in the menu commands).

Table 3-1   File Commands

Menu Command	Action	Keystrokes
File→New	Start a new file	[Ctrl]+[N]
File→Open	Open an existing file	[Ctrl]+[O]
File→Save	Save the file you are working on	[Ctrl]+[S]
File→Save As...	Save the current file with a new file name or format	-
File→Save Part...	Save a portion of your file to another file	-
File→Merge...	Combine or merge two files	-
File→Select Backgrounds…	Import background images into the Synchro **MAP** settings	-
File→Print Window	Send the contents of the active window to your printer	[Ctrl]+[P]
File→Create Report...	Opens the **SELECT REPORTS** window	-
File→Printer Setup	Opens your default printer set-up window	-
File→'list of files'	Shows the list of the last four files that were opened	-
File→Exit	Exits the program	-

Table 3-2   Edit Commands

Menu Command	Action	Keystrokes
Edit→Undo	Use to undo multiple changes	[Ctrl]+[Z]
Edit→Redo	Use to redo multiple changes	[Ctrl]+[Y]

Table 3-3   Transfer Commands

Menu Command	Action	Keystrokes
Transfer→Data Access...	Opens the UTDF Database Access window to allow you to read/write data to a database file	[Ctrl]+[D]
Transfer→ SimTraffic Simulation	Launches the SimTraffic micro simulation program	[Ctrl]+[G]
Transfer→ CORSIM Analysis...	Creates a CORSIM compatible file	-
Transfer→Save to HCS	Creates a HCS compatible file	-

Table 3-4   Option Commands

Menu Command	Action	Keystrokes
Options→Scenario Manager	Open the Scenario Manager	-
Options→Map Settings...	Use to change the appearance of the map	-
Options→Network Settings...	Allows you to make changes that affect the entire network	-
Options→Time-Space Diagram	Will open the time-space diagram	-
Options→Coding Error Check	To check data for coding errors	-
Options→ Convert to Metric/Feet	Covert between Metric and Feet	-
Options→Phase Templates→ Intersection to East-West	Set the phase template to an east-west template (phase 2/6 east and west)	-
Options→Phase Templates→ Intersection to North-South	Set the phase template to a north-south template (phase 2/6 north and south)	-
Options→Phase Templates→Edit Template Phases	Edit the phase templates	-
Options→Ring-and-Barrier-Designer...	To modify the ring and barriers for phases within Synchro	-
Options→Cluster Editor...	To group multiple intersections on one controller	-

Table 3-5   Optimize Commands

Menu Command	Action	Keystrokes
Optimize→ Intersection Splits	To optimize the splits of the selected intersection	[Ctrl]+[T]
Optimize→ Intersection Cycle Length	To optimize the cycle length of the selected intersection	-
Optimize→ Intersection Offset	To optimize the offset of the selected intersection only	[Ctrl]+[I]
Optimize→ Partition Network	To divide a network into multiple systems (zones)	-
Optimize→Network Cycle Length	To optimize the cycle length for your entire file or selected zone(s)	-
Optimize→Network Offset	To optimize the offsets for your entire file or selected zone(s)	-

Table 3-6   Help Commands

Menu Command	Action	Keystrokes
Help→Contents	Open the Help file	[Shift]+[F1]
Help→About Synchro	Shows the current version, build and copyright	-
Help→Product Key	Shows your Product Key	-
Help→In the Node	Opens the Trafficware Newsletter	-

Chapter 4 – Node Settings

To activate the **NODE** settings, double click on an intersection or select an intersection and press [Enter]. **Figure 4-1** illustrates the **NODE** settings.

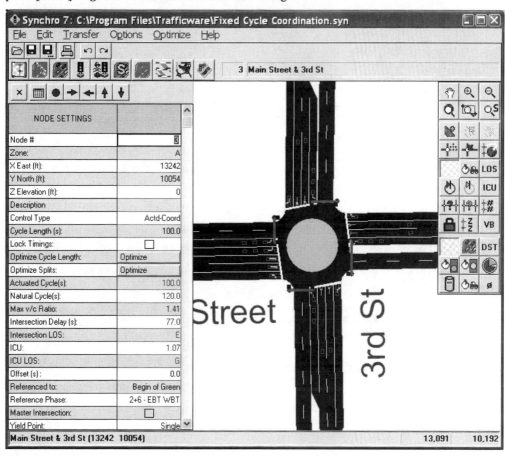

Figure 4-1   NODE Settings

The **NODE** settings allow the following values to be edited:

- Intersection ID or Node Number
- Zone
- Cycle Length, Control Type, Lock Timings and Optimize buttons
- Coordinates (X, Y, Z)
- Description Note box
- Signal Timing data (controller, offset, etc.)

 Synchro 7 no longer contains the **INTERSECTION PROPERTIES** settings of past versions. This has been changed to the **NODE** settings which appears as a side view setting when a node is double clicked.

 The **NODE** settings also appear on the left panel of the **TIMING** and **PHASING** settings.

Selecting Multiple Intersections

Multiple intersections can be selected by dragging a rectangle around the group of intersections.

1. Left-click on the map background being careful not to select a link or node.
2. While holding the button down, drag a rectangle to the opposite corner.
3. When the desired intersections are inside the rectangle, release the mouse button.

Bend nodes are automatically selected if an adjacent intersection is selected.

Additional intersections can be selected or deselected by clicking on them with the mouse while holding down the [Ctrl] key down.

The **NODE** settings can be used with a group of intersections to set the zone, change the control type or cycle length, or lock/unlock the timings.

Node Number

All intersections and external nodes are assigned a unique node number. used to identify the node in reports and data exported to CORSIM, HCS and UTDF files.

If you plan to use a file with CORSIM, keep all node numbers less than 7,000.

Zone

Synchro allows intersections to be assigned to zones. Zones are useful for analyzing a section of a network. Use zones to keep the timings for some intersections constant while the timings for other intersections are changed.

Using zones allows part of a large network to be analyzed with other software (i.e., CORSIM).

The following features can be used on a per-zone basis:

- **Optimize→Network-Cycle-Lengths** (see page 13-11)
- **Optimize→Network-Offsets** (see page 13-18)
- Reports (see page 15-1)
- Universal Traffic Data Format (see page 16-1)
- CORSIM preprocessors (see page 18-1)

Zones with Calculations and Optimizations

If adjacent intersections have the same (or half or double) cycle lengths, they will be modeled as coordinated, even if they are in different zones.

A Time-Space diagram will show all intersections along an arterial even if the arterial crosses several zones.

Offset optimization considers compatible cycle lengths of adjacent intersections even if they are assigned to different zones.

The feature **Optimize→Network-Cycle-Lengths** allows the user to assign a cycle length for the entire network or by zone.

The **Optimize→Partition-Network** command reassigns zones to optimize cycle lengths within each zone while attempting to preserve existing zone assignments as much as possible.

The user may designate an intersection in the zone as a master reference. This master will be used as the time reference for all intersections assigned to the same cycle length. However, if no master is defined, then Synchro will use an arbitrary time reference for the cycle length. Intersections are assigned to a master based on a common cycle length, not by zone.

Using Multiple Zones

Multiple zones may be selected in dialog boxes that request zones by separating the zone numbers with a comma. For example, to select zones N and S under **SELECT REPORTS**, enter "N, S" in teh dialog box.

Node Coordinates

The **NODE** settings allow the X, Y and Z coordinates to be entered exactly. The coordinates of the nodes are used in the layout of the map and the geometry of intersection approaches.

The X, Y and Z coordinate settings provide a convenient method for moving intersections to exact coordinates. The coordinates are for the center point of the intersection. For traffic engineering purposes, it is good enough to have the coordinates to within 20 feet.

To create an overpass, assign a higher Z coordinate elevation to the nodes of the overpass link. The Z elevation is only used for visual purposes.

Description

The **Description** cell is a convenient location to type notes about the intersection. The information will appear at the bottom of the Intersection Reports (see the chapter on **Reports and Printing** on page 15-1).

Controller Type

Timing Settings

Use the **Controller Type** field to indicate what type of controller you are using. The choices are Pretimed, Semi-Actuated-Uncoordinated, Actuated-Uncoordinated, Actuated-Coordinated and Unsignalized. Here is a brief description of each control type.

Pretimed: A pretimed signal has no detector actuations and all phases are set to Maximum recall. The signal is considered coordinated because the cycle length is fixed each cycle.

Semi-Actuated-Uncoordinated: A semi-actuated signal recalls the main street through phases to their Maximum values. Other assigned phases may skip or gap-out based on vehicle detection. This signal is not considered coordinated because the cycle length can vary each cycle.

Actuated-Uncoordinated: All phases are fully actuated and no recalls are set. The cycle length is allowed to vary each cycle (based on detection), so the intersection is considered uncoordinated.

Actuated-Coordinated: In this case, all phases other than the assigned coord phases are fully actuated. The signal operates on a fixed cycle length and any unused time in the cycle is added to the assigned coord phases.

Actuated-Coordinated and **Semi-Actuated-Uncoordinated** are not the same. With coordinated operation, any unused time on minor phases is used by the main street. With semi-actuated operation, any unused time on minor phases shortens the cycle length.

Signing Settings

When you select an unsignalized intersection, the **TIMING** settings button switches to the **SIGNING** settings button. The symbol of the [F5] button also switches from the signal symbol to a stop sign to indicate whether the selected intersection is signalized or unsignalized.

Unsignalized: Traffic movements at unsignalized intersections may be free-flow or controlled by stop or yield signs.

Roundabouts: Synchro models single lane traffic circles or roundabouts using current HCM methods. This method only analyzes single lane roundabouts and the only output is a range of v/c ratios. There is no attempt to produce delays or queues.

Roundabouts are modeled in SimTraffic. The user can input the number of lanes in the roundabout, the inside and outside radius, the speed, sign control to entering the roundabout and the number of exit lanes; this information is ignored by Synchro.

Cycle Length

The cycle length is the total time required to service all competing traffic movements at a signalized or unsignalized intersection. Coordination fixes the cycle length at a constant value and insures that all slack time not utilized by the actuated phases is used by the assigned coord phases.

The user may specify the desired cycle length in seconds for each intersection.

To set a default for newly created intersections or to change all of the Cycle Lengths, use the **Options→Network-Settings** command. The minimum value allowed by Synchro is 3 seconds and the maximum is 900 seconds. Coordinated cycle lengths are typically in the 30 - 180 second range depending on the number of competing phases serviced. However, the Synchro range insures that the capability of any traffic signal controller can be modeled.

Lock Timings

The **Lock Timings** field is used to prevent the timing from changing. To preserve the timing for one or more intersections, click the check box in this field for each of the intersections. If you optimize the network, these intersections' timing plans will not change, but the other intersections will be optimized around them.

This field could be helpful if there are some intersections that are controlled by another agency and you want to coordinate your signals with theirs. To do this, set up the timing for the other agency signals and then lock these timing plans. Enter the timing for your signals and leave them unlocked.

If you have two or more intersections that are close together and require a special type of timing, you can setup their timing manually, lock the intersections, and optimize the intersections around them.

It is advisable that one of the locked intersections be the *Master Intersection* if the master intersection option is used. Otherwise, the offsets for the locked intersections may be changed if the timing for the master intersection changes.

An alternative to locking intersections is to divide the study area into zones, and perform analysis on specific zones. Each zone can be locked after the optimization is complete for that zone.

Optimize Cycle Length

The **Optimize Cycle Length** button will optimize the selected intersection cycle length. Full details on the intersection cycle length optimization can be found on page 13-7.

Optimize Splits

The **Optimize Splits** button will optimize the selected intersection splits. Full details on the intersection split optimization can be found on page 13-4.

Actuated Cycle Length

The Actuated Cycle Length (CL) is the average cycle length for an actuated signal.

> C' = Actuated CL

> C' = C for pretimed and coordinated signals.

Calculation

$$C' = \frac{\sum Ci}{5}$$

> Ci = Percentile Scenario Cycle Length

> C' may not equal the sum of the actuated splits due to skipped phases and dwell time.

HCM Report Calculation

> C' = $\sum$(g' + YAR)

> g' = Actuated Green times

The percentile actuated cycle length is the sum of the actuated splits, subject to ring and barrier rules.

Actuated Cycles by Percentile

 The Actuated Cycles by Percentile are show in the **NODE** settings on the left side of the **PHASING** settings. The Actuated Cycles will not appear in the **NODE** settings in any other location.

To represent a range of volume levels, five percentile scenarios are modeled. They are called the 90th, 70th, 50th, 30th, and 10th percentiles. Traffic volumes for each approach are adjusted up or down to model these percentile scenarios. By adjusting the traffic for different scenarios, the actuated signals can be modeled under a range of traffic conditions.

If traffic is observed for 100 cycles, the 90th percentile would be the 90th busiest, the 10th percentile would be the 10th busiest, and the 50th percentile would represent average traffic.

For each of the percentile scenarios, this is the expected cycle length. This value is the sum of the actuated splits for each phase.

Natural Cycle Length

The Natural Cycle Length is the shortest cycle length that will give acceptable capacity. In general, intersections have an optimum cycle length that provides the best level of service. Using a shorter cycle length will not provide enough green time to clear all of the waiting vehicles causing congestion. Using a longer cycle length increases delays by introducing unused green time. For Natural Cycle Length, enter the shortest cycle length for this intersection only. The Natural Cycle Length is the cycle length this intersection would operate at if it were to operate independently of all other intersections. (For more information about using the Natural Cycle Length, see **Intersection Cycle Length Optimization** on page 13-7)

At congested intersections, no cycle length gives acceptable capacity. In these cases, Synchro uses the cycle length with the lowest combination of stops, delays, and unserved vehicles.

Maximum v/c Ratio

Timing Settings

The **TIMING** setting displays the Volume to Capacity Ratio (v/c) for each traffic movement or lane group (see page 7-23). The **Maximum v/c Ratio** is the highest individual movement or lane group v/c ratio.

The HCM 2000 version added several new features that consider protected-permitted left-turns from shared lanes, saturation flow adjustments for pedestrians and bicycles and queue length estimation. The Volume to Capacity Ratio calculations in Synchro incorporates all these enhancements in HCM 2000.

In addition, Synchro provides an alternate method of evaluating intersection capacity called the ICU (Intersection Capacity Utilization) method. In general, the ICU method is a more direct measure of intersection capacity and easier to calculate. The ICU method also overcame several shortcomings that were corrected in HCM 2000.

Intersection capacity values are summarized in the **NODE SETTINGS** for each node. The Max v/c Ratio is the maximum lane group Volume to Capacity Ratio using the HCM method. The ICU value is also shown with the associated ICU Level of Service (LOS).

Signing Settings

Volume to Capacity Ratios are also provided for 2-way stop and yield sign control. V/c ratios for 4-way stop control are undefined. These results are consistent with HCM 2000. In addition v/c ratios are estimated for the through flows at roundabouts.

Intersection Delay

Timing Settings

The **Intersection Delay** field shows the average Total Delay for the signalized intersection and it is calculated by taking a volume weighted average of all the Total Delays. The Total Delay includes the Queue Delay (see page 7-25) plus the Control Delay (see page 7-25).

Signing Settings

The average intersection delay for unsignalized intersections is based on an average of each movement's delays. The unsignalized intersection delay is strictly based on the methods in the HCM. Therefore, the unsignalized delay does not include Queue Delay.

 Intersection delay and level of service is not defined by the HCM for two-way stop controlled intersections; therefore, it is not shown in the report. The analyst needs to look at the delay and LOS for the individual movements.

Intersection Level of Service

Timing Settings

For signalized intersections, the Level of Service for the intersection is calculated by taking the total Intersection Delay and converting it to a level (A-F) using **Table 4-1**.

Table 4-1   Signalized Intersection Level of Service (2000 HCM)

LOS	Control Delay Per Vehicle (s)
A	≤10
B	>10 and ≤20
C	>20 and ≤35
D	>35 and ≤55
E	>55 and ≤80
F	>80

Signing Settings

For an unsignalized two-way stopped controlled (TWSC) or all-way stop-controlled (AWSC) intersection, the Level of Service for the intersection is calculated by taking the Intersection Delay and converting it to a letter using **Table 4-2**.

Table 4-2   TWSC & AWSC Level of Service Criteria (2000 HCM)

LOS	Control Delay Per Vehicle(s)
A	≤10
B	>10 and ≤15
C	>15 and ≤25
D	>25 and ≤35
E	>35 and ≤50
F	>50

The LOS criteria for TWSC and AWSC intersections are different than that used for a signalized intersection. The primary reason for this is that drivers expect different levels of performance between signalized and unsignalized intersections.

Intersection Capacity Utilization

Intersection Capacity Utilization is the 2003 (ICU 2003) for the intersection. Full details of the ICU 2003 can be found in the topic, Intersection Capacity (ICU) Report (see page 15-11). A full description of ICU 2003 along with commentary and instructions is available in the reference book, **Intersection Capacity Utilization 2003** available from Trafficware.

The ICU is shown for unsignalized intersections because it represents the potential capacity for the intersection if it were to be signalized.

ICU Level of Service

The ICU Level of Service (LOS) gives insight into how an intersection is functioning and how much extra capacity is available to handle traffic fluctuations and incidents. ICU is not a value that can be measured with a stopwatch, but it does give a good reading on the conditions that can be expected at the intersection. Full details of the ICU LOS can be found in the topic, Intersection Capacity (ICU) Report.

Letters A to H are assigned to the intersection based on the Intersection Capacity Utilization using **Table 4-3**. Note that the ICU 2003 includes additional levels past F to further differentiate congested operation.

Table 4-3   Level of Service Criteria for ICU Analysis

ICU	Level of Service
0 to 55%	A
>55% to 64%	B
>64% to 73%	C
>73% to 82%	D
>82% to 91%	E
>91% to 100%	F
>100% to 109%	G
>109%	H

Offset Settings

The settings in the **Offset** settings box specify the phase the offset is reference to and the value of the current offset. Each intersection is given one offset that can be referenced to the beginning of green, yellow or red of the phase. The offset value represents the number of seconds that the reference phase lags the master reference (or arbitrary reference if no master is specified). The master reference synchronizes the intersections sharing a common cycle length to provide a coordinated system.

Please refer to your traffic signal controller manual for the specific settings required by your hardware.

Coordination requires a fixed cycle length and a reference offset for each controller in the system. Therefore, set **Control Type** to Actuated-coordinated or Pretimed if the intersection is coordinated and specify Actuated-uncoordinated for isolated signals without fixed cycle lengths.

Offset Referenced To

Select the point to which you wish to have offsets referenced. Some types of traffic signal controllers allow the offset to be referenced from the beginning of the green time. Other types or controllers require the offset to be referenced to the beginning of yellow, or the end of the yellow plus red.

Some NEMA controllers reference offsets to the last of the coordinated phases to turn green. NEMA TS2 controllers reference offsets to the first of the coordinated phases to turn green. Synchro supports both styles of offset referencing.

With two reference phases and offsets referenced to *Begin of Green*, offsets will be referenced to last phase to turn green.

With two reference phases and offsets referenced to *TS2 - 1st Green*, offsets will be referenced to first phase to turn green.

With two reference phases and offset referencing to the beginning of yellow or beginning of red, offsets will be referenced to first phase to turn yellow or red.

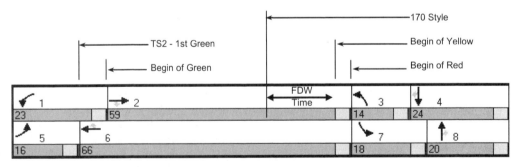

Figure 4-2   Offset Reference

Offset Referenced Phase(s)

The offset reference phase(s) are typically the coordinated phases associated with the arterial street. Selecting two reference phases allows Synchro to optimize phase sequences and select the coord phase based on the optimal phase sequence.

For example, using TS2 - 1st Green, if a leading left-turn sequence is optimal, then Synchro will automatically select the first through phase following the leading lefts as the reference phase. If a lead/lag phase sequence is optimal, Synchro will select the through movement serviced with the leading left-turn as the reference (coord) phase.

You must insure that the reference phase selected by Synchro in the optimization matches the coord phase set in your controller. Some NEMA TS1 controllers reference the offset to the last through phase to turn green. NEMA TS2 references the offset to the first through phase to turn green (TS2 - 1st Green). Still, other controllers give you full control over specifying the coord (reference) phase and synchronizing the offset to the begin-of-green or end-of-green of that phase.

Table 4-4   Reference Point with Multiple Reference Phases

Referenced To	Reference Point
Begin of Green	Referenced to last of phases to turn green
Begin of Yellow	Referenced to first of phases to turn Yellow
Begin of Red	Referenced to first of phases to turn Red
TS2 - 1st Green	Referenced to first of phases to turn green
170 Style	Referenced to start of FDW or start of yellow (see below)

 If the 170 Style reference is used, the reference point will depend on the **Recall Mode** setting. If Coordinated-Max is used, the offset will be referenced to the start of flashing don't walk. If Coordinated-Min is used, the offset will be referenced to the start of yellow.

The reference phases also control which phases are the coordinated phases for an actuated-coordinated signal.

To set a default for newly created intersections or change all of the reference phases, use the **Options→Network Settings** command.

The **Reference Phase** is used to determine the coordinated phase(s) for an actuated signal.

 170 Users — For a 170-type controller, the offset is referenced to the end of phase 2 or phase 6 green. If either phase 1 or 5 is lagging, the offset is referenced to the first phase of 2 and 6 to turn yellow. If the main street has rest-in-walk set, the offset is referenced to the beginning of do not walk.

Current Offset

The intersection **Offset** is the number of seconds that the reference (coord) phase lags after the master offset. The offset may be referenced to the begin-of-green or end-of-green of the reference phase based on the Referenced To value selected.

The Offset begins at zero because the master cycle counter always begins counting at zero. The maximum Offset is one second less than the Cycle length because the master cycle counter always increments to that value, then resets to zero.

The optimum offset can be found by using the optimization commands explained in **Optimize→Intersection Offset**, or by using the time-space diagrams.

Master Intersection

The **Master Intersection** typically has a zero offset value. Synchro allows you to designate an intersection as the Master Intersection to reference offsets to the cycle counter at that intersection. If a master intersection is not specified, then Synchro will choose an arbitrary offset reference as the master reference.

A cycle length of half or double the Master Intersection cycle length is considered compatible. The offset at the half our double cycled intersection will be referenced to the Master Intersection.

 NOTE — If you have a master assigned to your network, then make your cycle length change at the master first, then change the cycle lengths at the other intersections you wish to follow the master cycle reference. This will avoid creating a situation where two or more masters provide the same cycle length. In those cases Synchro assigns the master with the most traffic volume.

Be sure to check for the master intersection after the Cycle Length(s) have been changed, for example using the **Optimize→Network Cycle Lengths** command.

To see which intersection(s) is the master, go to the **MAP** view and choose the *Show Cycle Lengths* button. The master intersection(s) is shown with a * next to the cycle length in the **MAP** view.

Yield Points

The **Yield Point** determines when the Coordinated Phases will "yield" to side street phases. This setting affects whether there is a single yield point for all phases, or multiple yield points.

Figure 4-3 illustrates how a single yield point works. The main street phases have a single scheduled end time. If the next up phases have no calls, the other phases start at this point. If there are no calls for any of the phases 3, 7, 4 and 8; then phases 1 and 5 can start early and the signal will return to the main street phases sooner.

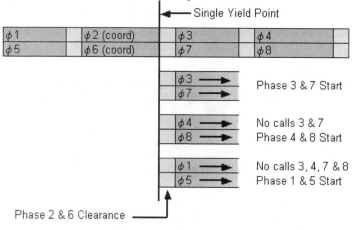

Figure 4-3   Single Yield Point

Figure 4-4 illustrates how yield point by phases works. The main street phases stay on until the scheduled start time of a conflicting phase. If phases 3 and 7 have no calls, the signal will not yield to phases 4 and 8 until their scheduled start times.

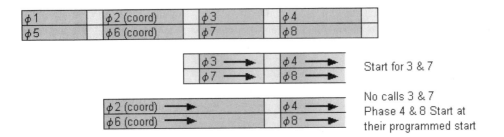

Figure 4-4   Yield Point by Phase

Flexible yield points allow the signal to yield any time between the single point and the phases' scheduled start time. Flexible yield points can be useful with low volume side streets; the side streets have a wider range of time to yield the signal.

Using a single yield point in conjunction with Inhibit Max makes the most time available for side street phases. Yield point by phase extends the green bands for the coordinated movements rather than provide slack time at the beginning of the bands. Either method must be provided as a feature by your controller manufacturer.

Keep in mind that the controller will yield as soon as there is a call on the yield phase. Therefore, even if there is only one call on phase 3 or 7 in the Yield Point by Phase example above, the controller will leave to service the call after the yield point.

If you wish to allow the non-coordinated phases to utilize slack time from preceding actuated phases, then you should select Inhibit Max. This will prevent SimTraffic from terminating the phase if the sum of the slack time and programmed split is greater than the max time.

Synchro does not explicitly model flexible yield point. Synchro will model flexible yield points the same as single yield points. This will be equivalent except for when the first up actuated phases have low volume. With by phase yield points, Synchro models a single yield point for each barrier.

Chapter 5 – Lane Settings

From the **MAP** view, click on the desired intersection with the Right mouse button and select **LANE** settings.

 From anywhere in the program, press **[F8]** and select the desired intersection from the list. Then push the *Lane Settings* button or the **[F3]** key.

The **LANE** settings display a grid in which you can enter lane and geometric information. See Chapter 3 for details on navigating the data entry screens.

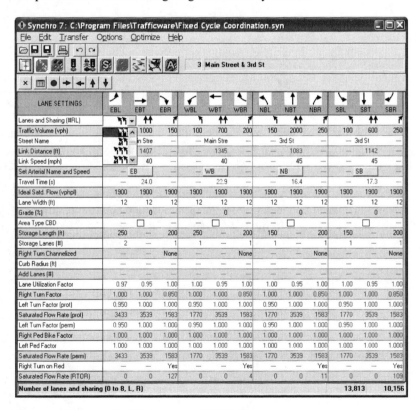

LANE SETTINGS	EBL	EBT	EBR	WBL	WBT	WBR	NBL	NBT	NBR	SBL	SBT	SBR
Lanes and Sharing (#RL)												
Traffic Volume (vph)		1000	150	100	700	200	150	2000	250	100	600	250
Street Name		in Stre	---	---	Main Stre	---	---	3rd St	---	---	3rd St	---
Link Distance (ft)		1407	---	---	1345	---	---	1083	---	---	1142	---
Link Speed (mph)		40	---	---	40	---	---	45	---	---	45	---
Set Arterial Name and Speed	---	EB	---	---	WB	---	---	NB	---	---	SB	---
Travel Time (s)	---	24.0	---	---	22.9	---	---	16.4	---	---	17.3	---
Ideal Satd. Flow (vphpl)	1900	1900	1900	1900	1900	1900	1900	1900	1900	1900	1900	1900
Lane Width (ft)	12	12	12	12	12	12	12	12	12	12	12	12
Grade (%)	---	0	---	---	0	---	---	0	---	---	0	---
Area Type CBD	---	☐	---	---	☐	---	---	☐	---	---	☐	---
Storage Length (ft)	250	---	200	250	---	200	150	---	200	150	---	200
Storage Lanes (#)	2	---	1	1	---	1	1	---	1	1	---	1
Right Turn Channelized	---	---	None	---	---	None	---	---	None	---	---	None
Curb Radius (ft)	---	---	---	---	---	---	---	---	---	---	---	---
Add Lanes (#)	---	---	---	---	---	---	---	---	---	---	---	---
Lane Utilization Factor	0.97	0.95	1.00	1.00	0.95	1.00	1.00	0.95	1.00	1.00	0.95	1.00
Right Turn Factor	1.000	1.000	0.850	1.000	1.000	0.850	1.000	1.000	0.850	1.000	1.000	0.850
Left Turn Factor (prot)	0.950	1.000	1.000	0.950	1.000	1.000	0.950	1.000	1.000	0.950	1.000	1.000
Saturated Flow Rate (prot)	3433	3539	1583	1770	3539	1583	1770	3539	1583	1770	3539	1583
Left Turn Factor (perm)	0.950	1.000	1.000	0.950	1.000	1.000	0.950	1.000	1.000	0.950	1.000	1.000
Right Ped Bike Factor	1.000	1.000	1.000	1.000	1.000	1.000	1.000	1.000	1.000	1.000	1.000	1.000
Left Ped Factor	1.000	1.000	1.000	1.000	1.000	1.000	1.000	1.000	1.000	1.000	1.000	1.000
Saturated Flow Rate (perm)	3433	3539	1583	1770	3539	1583	1770	3539	1583	1770	3539	1583
Right Turn on Red	---	---	Yes	---	---	Yes	---	---	Yes	---	---	Yes
Saturated Flow Rate (RTOR)	0	0	127	0	0	4	0	0	11	0	0	109

Number of lanes and sharing [0 to 8, L, R]　　　　　　13,813　　10,156

Figure 5-1   LANE Settings, Full View

Lanes and Sharing

Select the number of lanes and lane configuration for each lane group by selecting the pull-down list under each movement arrow. See **Rules for Shared Lanes,** below, for information on how to enter lanes that serve more than one movement and how to classify lanes.

Select the **Lanes and Sharing** pull-down list under each traffic movement arrow. You can specify the number of lanes and any shared turning movements from those lanes using the pull-down list. You may also use a short-cut to select the number of lanes using the [0] - [8] keys. You can also quickly vary the shared lane assignment by pressing [L] for a shared left-turn or [R] for a shared right-turn in the lane group.

Rules for Shared Lanes

Use the following rules to determine which lanes belong to a lane group.

- Shared lanes always count as through lanes.
- Only exclusive turning lanes count as turning lanes.

At a 'T' intersection the shared Right-Left lanes count as a left lane.

If there is no turning lane, Synchro will assign turning traffic to the through lane group (or the left turn lane group, if there is no through lane group).

If an approach has a shared turning lane and an exclusive turning lane, the approach can be modeled by Synchro. The exclusive lane is in the turning group, and the shared lane is in the through group. Synchro dynamically assigns traffic between the two lane groups (refer to **Traffic in Shared Lane**, page 6-13).

 To create a new column for U-turns, type [Ctrl] + [U].

 Refer to page 6-2 for details on the **Traffic Volume** setting.

Street Name

Naming a street will cause its name to appear on the map. If a street has several segments, the name will be placed on a segment long enough to fit the name, or on an external link. To change the size of the street name, see **Options→Map-Settings**.

Arterial Route Naming

To create an Arterial Route with multiple street names or that turns corners, include a route number in the street name with the # symbol. For example, the streets Main and 3rd Street are part of the same route. Give these streets the names "Main Street #13" and "3rd Street #13". Synchro will be able to create reports and analysis on the arterial "#13" (see the topic **Viewing and Printing Reports** on page 15-5 for details on how to create a report for a route that turns a corner). You can also see a time-space diagram for route #13 (see the topic **Time-Space Diagram** on page 12-1 for details on how to view a time-space diagram for a named arterial view).

Link Distance

Link distances can be used to adjust the length of the link. Adding a link the exact distance with a mouse can be tricky; this feature allows you to type in the exact distance. If you plan to use this data with CORSIM or SimTraffic, the override distance should be within 20% to the map distance. Otherwise, the simulation software will reject the data because map coordinates are used to simulate runs in CORSIM and SimTraffic.

 Changing the Link Distance in the **LANE** settings changes the internal link length. This setting does not change the coordinates of the underlying intersections. Synchro stores the link length independently from the coordinate distances.

The calculated link distance is shown in blue. Overridden distances appear as red. To revert to the calculated distance, press [F12] when in the cell.

The link distances are the distance from intersection center point to center point. When determining link distances for queuing analysis, Synchro will subtract 80 feet (24m) from the distance to account for the space inside intersections.

Geodetic coordinates accurate within 20 feet are adequate for traffic modeling purposes.

Link Speed

The **Link Speed** should be set to the legal safe speed that you expect along the arterial after the traffic signals along the link are optimized. To set a default speed for newly created intersections or change all of the speeds, use the **Options→Network-Settings** command.

 Enter the free flow speeds and travel times. Do not enter measured speeds from floating car data to account for congestion and delay unless the speed reduction reduction cannot be improved by signal optimization.

Set Arterial Name and Speed

Select a direction button to propagate the name and speed up and down the entire arterial in the selected and opposing direction. For instance, choose the [EB] option will set the street name and speed for the arterial in the eastbound and westbound directions.

Travel Time

Travel Time is recalculated when either the speed or distance fields are changed. The calculated value will appear in blue type. However, you may override this field manually, which will appear in red type. You can force the field to re-calculate based on the speed and distance fields at any time by pressing [F12].

Ideal Saturated Flow

Enter the **Ideal Saturated Flow Rate** for a single lane in this field. The 2000 HCM recommends using 1,900 vehicles per hour per lane. This is the default.

It is not necessary to enter a different Saturated Flow Rate for turning lanes. Synchro will adjust the Saturated Flow Rate automatically with turning movement factors (Refer to **Right Turn Factor**, page 5-10, and **Left Turn Factor**, page 5-10)

It is not necessary to adjust this rate to account for heavy vehicles, bus stops, parking maneuvers, turning traffic, lane widths, grades, or area type. These are automatically adjusted by Synchro.

To set a default for newly created intersections or change all of the Ideal Saturated Flow Rates, use the **Options→Network-Settings** command, Lanes tab.

The Ideal Saturation Flow is a macroscopic model term used by Synchro. To account for changes of this factor for simulation, the Headway Factor is used. For more details, refer to the topic **Headway Factor** on page 9-8).

Lane Width

The default **Lane Width** is 12 feet (3.6 meters). Saturated Flow Rate increases as Lane Width increases. Consult the HCM 2000 for more information on Lane Width.

To set a default for newly created intersections or change all of the lane widths, use the **Options→Network Settings** command, Lanes tab.

The lane width factor is calculated based upon the following formula:

$$Fw = 1 + [(W - 12)/30]$$

Fw = Lane width factor

W = lane width

Grade

The percentage **Grade** is the slope of the roadway approaching the intersection (negative grades are downhill). The default percentage Grade for each approach is zero percent. The Saturated Flow Rate increases when traffic moves downhill (negative Grade).

The factor for grade is based on the following formula:

$$Fg = 1 - \%G/200$$

Fg = Grade adjustment factor

$\%G$ = % grade on a lane group approach

Area Type CBD

Select this checkbox if the lane group is typical of **Central Business District** (or "downtown" area). A CBD is characterized by high parking turnovers, narrow short-block roadways and high pedestrian activity. Selecting Area Type CBD lowers Saturated Flow Rate. See the HCM 2000 for more information about CBD characteristics.

Storage Length

The **Storage Length** is the length of a turning bay in feet (meters). If an intersection has a left turn storage bay of 150 feet (45 meters), enter "150" ("45") in this box. If the left or right turn lane extends to the previous intersection, enter "0".

If two or more storage lanes are present, enter the average length of the lanes, not the sum.

Storage Length data is used for analyzing potential blocking problems, such as through traffic blocking left turn traffic, and left turn traffic blocking through traffic. If "0" is entered, no blocking analysis is performed.

 A storage bay can be coded for through lanes. It is also possible to mix full travel lanes and storage lanes for the turning movement.

To code a flared right or right-turn only lane for unsignalized analysis, code 1 or more right turn lanes and code a turning bay for their lanes.

Storage Lanes

Code the number of **Storage Lanes** in the right and left storage bays. This value only appears when the storage length is greater than 0. By default, the number of storage lanes is equal to the number of turning lanes.

This field can be overridden so that some of the turning lanes are full travel lanes, or so that some of the through lanes can be storage lanes.

A red value indicates an override, while a blue value indicates that the number of storage lanes is calculated.

Right Turn Channelized

This field is active for the rightmost movement. The choices are None, Yield, Free, Stop and Signal. If this value is changed, it will also be updated for unsignalized analysis.

Synchro does not explicitly model a channelized right turn. If you have coded a signal in Synchro, it will be modeled as follows in the **TIMING** settings:

- **None**: No right turn channelization.

- **Yield**: No phases are assigned, the saturation flow is that for the RTOR.

- **Stop**: No phases are assigned, the saturation flow is that for the RTOR. Yield and Stop are handled in the same manner.

- **Free**: The phase assigned is 'Free' (100% green time). The saturation flow used is the permitted saturation flow.

- **Signal**: The movement is controlled by the signal. Set the appropriate turn type and phase in the **TIMING** settings.

For unsignalized 2-way or 4-way stop control, each traffic movement it analyzed using the guidelines in HCM 2000.

Curb Radius

Curb Radius specifies the horizontal curvature of the street intersection and is measured in feet from the back of curb to the center point of the radius.

Add Lanes

Add Lanes controls how a right-turn lane enters the intersection street. Setting Add Lanes to zero (0) creates a yield or merge for drivers completing a right turn. Setting the value to one (1) adds a continuation lane for the right-turn.

Setting a Storage Length greater than zero creates a right-turn "pocket" on the approach side of the intersection. Setting Add Lanes greater than zero extends the right-turn lane on the departure side of the intersection.

 If a channelized right connects to a curved link, the curve points must be placed after any tangents from a right turn Island; otherwise image distortion will occur.

Slip Lanes for Roundabouts

To code a right turn slip lane at a roundabout for SimTraffic, set the Right Turn Channelized to Stop, Yield, or Free. SimTraffic will add additional right turn lane(s) to the roundabout, outside of the **Outside Radius**. The width of the slip lane is determined by the width of the incoming right turn lane group.

The input fields below have the following effect:

- Right Turn Channelized = Yield or Stop: Vehicles in slip lane will yield at end of slip lane if there is a merge.

- Right Turn Channelized = Free: Vehicles in slip lane will merge at end of slip lane if there is a merge.

- Right Turn Channelized = None: No slip lane

- Lanes and Sharing: Controls number of lanes in right turn slip lane, and number of lanes to enter main circle.

- Curb Radius (in the **SIGNING** settings): Has no effect; slip lane controlled by Outside Radius.

- Add Lanes: Slip lane will be add lane(s), provided enough lanes exist downstream.

With a small circle or with tight angles between links, the slip lanes will directly connect to the roundabout. With a larger circle or angle, the slip lanes will be additional lanes on the outside of the roundabout with an additional radius.

Alternate Method

It is also possible to create a slip lane by coding a multilane roundabout with a two lane exit (see page 7-21). To get a direct slip lane it is necessary to code two lane exits at both the entry and the exit links. This method works best for creating a slip lane in all directions.

Combining a slip lane with a two lane Exit may give a three-lane exit or other strange results. It is usually best to use one or the other.

Lane Utilization Factor

The **Lane Utilization Factor** determines how the traffic volumes assigned to a lane group are distributed across each lane. A value of one (1) indicates equal distribution across all lanes. Values less than one lower the saturation flow rate because all lanes are not working at full capacity. The Lane Utilization Factor is selected from the values in **Table 5-1**.

 If there is an exclusive turning lane plus a shared turning lane, then all of the lanes will be placed in the through lane group to calculate this factor.

Table 5-1   Lane Utilization Factors

Lane Group Movements	# of Lanes	Lane Utilization Factor
Thru or shared	1	1.00
Thru or shared	2	0.95
Thru or shared	3	0.91
Thru or shared	4+	0.86
Left	1	1.00
Left	2	0.97
Left	3+	0.94
Right	1	1.00
Right	2	0.88
Right	3	0.76

This field can be overridden. If, for example, there is a busy shopping center entrance just after this intersection on the right side, most of the vehicles will be using the right lane and cause a lower lane utilization factor. If the actual per lane volumes are known, the lane utilization factor can be calculated as follows:

$$f_{LU} = \frac{\text{Total App. Vol.}}{(\text{No. of Lanes}) \times (\text{High Lane Vol.})} = \frac{(100 + 200)}{(2 \times 200)} = 0.75$$

200 vph →
100 vph →

f_{LU} = Lane Utilization Factor

NOTE The f_{LU} is a macroscopic adjustment and will only affect the saturation flow rates. Changes to this value have no impact on the simulated results in SimTraffic. To account for unbalanced flow in SimTraffic, be sure to code in the geometric condition that is causing condition, such as a downstream lane taper.

Right Turn Factors

The **Right Turn Factor** is used to reduce the Saturation Flow Rate based on the proportion of right-turns in the lane group and the type of lane servicing the right-turn. The default calculations from HCM 2000 can be overridden by the user.

Exclusive Lane: $f_{RT} = 0.85$

Shared Lane: $f_{RT} = 1.0 - (0.15) P_{RT}$

Single Lane: $f_{RT} = 1.0 - (0.135) P_{RT}$

P_{RT} = Proportion of right turn traffic in lane group

The permitted right turn factor is used during the through phase for this approach. The protected right-turn factor is used if an exclusive right-turn lane is provided and a Protected Phase is assigned from a concurrent left-turn (right-turn overlap signal).

Left Turn Factors

The **Left Turn Factors** are applied in the HCM Saturated Flow Rate calculation. The default values are calculated from the formulas below, but these may be overridden by the user. The Left Turn Factor for exclusive lanes is:

$f_{LT} = 0.95$

The Left Turn Factor for shared lanes is:

$f_{LT} = 1 / (1.0 + 0.05 P_{LT})$:

P_{LT} = Proportion of left turn traffic in lane group

For permitted left turns, the calculations are quite involved. Synchro has a complete implementation of the 2000 HCM permitted left turn model. The permitted left turn factor is based on actuated green times, the same as the HCM calculation.

The calculation steps are as follows:

- Saturation Flows with maximum greens are used for the Ped Bike (see page 5-12) and Permitted Lefts
- Actuated green times calculated

- Saturation Flows are recalculated with actuated greens used for Ped Bike and Permitted Lefts factors

The permitted left turn factor is used for any permitted left turn phase, including the permitted portion of permitted plus protected left turn phasing. The protected left turn factor is used for protected and split phasing, and for the protected portion of permitted plus protected left turn phasing.

Saturated Flow Rates

The **Saturated Flow Rates** are the actual maximum flow rate for this lane group after adjusting for all of the interference factors. The Saturated Flow Rates represent the number of lanes multiplied by the Ideal Saturated Flow Rate and interference factors due to heavy vehicles, buses, parking maneuvers, lane widths, area type, grade, and turning movements.

 There is a permitted and a protected Saturated Flow Rate. For left and through lane groups the permitted Saturated Flow Rate is used when left turns are permitted and the protected Saturated Flow Rate is used when left turns are protected. For right turn lane groups, the permitted flow rate is used with permitted and free right turn phases. The protected flow rate is used with protected signal indication that overlap with a non-conflicting protected left-turn phase.

The Saturated Flow Rates are used in capacity and delay calculations, and for optimization calculations. The Saturated Flow Rates are not used for simulation modeling in SimTraffic or CORSIM.

These fields are calculated but can be overridden.

The saturation flow rate is based on:

$$S = So * N * Fw * Fn * Fhv * Fg * Fp * Fbb * Fa * Flu * Flt * Frt * FLpb * FRpb$$

where:

S = saturation flow rate for the subject lane group, expressed as a total for all lanes in the lane group, veh/h'

So = base saturation flow rate per lane, pc/h/In,

N = number of lanes in the lane group,

Fw = adjustment factor for the lane width,

Fhv = adjustment factor for heavy vehicles in the traffic stream,

Fg = adjustment factor for approach grade,

Fp = adjustment factor for the existence of a parking lane and parking activity adjacent to the lane group,

Fbb = adjustment factor for the blocking effect of local buses that stop within the intersection area,

Fa = adjustment factor for area type,

Flu = adjustment factor for lane utilization,

Flt = adjustment factor for left turns in the lane group,

Frt = adjustment factor for right turns in the lane group,

FLpb = pedestrian adjustment factor for left-turn movements, and

FRpb = pedestrian/bicycle adjustment factor for right-turn movements.

Right Ped Bike Factor

This factor is calculated based on the number of pedestrians and bicycles that are crossing the right turn movement. The factor takes into account the amount of green time for the pedestrians and the bicycles as well as the number of downstream receiving lanes. For a complete description of the FRpb calculation, see Chapter 16 of the HCM 2000, Appendix D.

The Ped Bike factor used by Synchro has a slight variation from the HCM generated Ped Bike factor for permitted plus protected movements. Synchro does not adjust for the proportion of right turns using the protected phase (Prta) but calculates separate Saturated Flow Rates for permitted and protected movements. The Ped Bike factor shown on the **LANE** settings and on the Intersection reports is for permitted phases only and is only applied to the Permitted Saturation Flow rate.

The Ped Bike factor shown in the HCM Signals report is calculated based on the manual's methods and may vary for permitted plus protected movements. The HCM Ped Bike factor is applied to both permitted and protected saturation flow rates.

For through and left lane groups with right turn traffic, the Ped Bike factor will be applied to all phases. Synchro assumes right turns are always permitted not protected from a left or through lane group. Always code through phases as protected, except at unusually aligned intersections.

Left Ped Factor

This factor is calculated based on the number of pedestrians and bicycles that are crossing the permitted left turn movements. The factor takes into account the amount of green time for the pedestrians and vehicles, the amount of oncoming traffic and the number of downstream receiving lanes. For a complete description of the FLpb calculation, see the HCM 2000, Chapter 16, Appendix D.

The Ped factor used by Synchro has a slight variation from the HCM generated Ped factor for permitted plus protected movements. Synchro does not adjust for the proportion of left turns using the protected phase (Plta), but calculates separate Saturated Flow Rates for permitted and protected movements. The Ped factor shown on the **LANE** settings and on the Intersection reports is for permitted phases only and is only applied to the Permitted Saturation Flow rate.

The Ped factor shown in the HCM Signals report is calculated based on the manual's methods, and may vary for permitted plus protected movements. The HCM Ped factor is applied to both permitted and protected saturation flow rates.

Right Turn on Red (RTOR)

This field is used to specify whether **Right Turns on Red** (RTOR) are allowed. This field can also be used to allow Left Turns on Red from a one-way to a one-way.

Synchro fully models Right Turns on Red. Synchro automatically calculates a Saturated Flow Rate for RTOR and applies this flow rate to movements when they are red. See **Saturated Flow Rate (RTOR)**, page 5-15 for details on its calculation.

This field is also used when modeling in SimTraffic and CORSIM.

The following four options are provided to model right turns on red and free right turns.

1. For exclusive or shared right lanes, set Right Turns on Red to Yes in the **LANE** settings. Synchro will calculate a RTOR Saturated Flow Rate and apply this flow rate during all red times. Each vehicle must stop and wait for a gap, the maximum RTOR saturation flow rate is about 1091 vphpl.

2. For exclusive right lanes (not shared lanes), set the Turn Type to Free in the **TIMING** settings. Synchro will assume that right turns will move unimpeded at all times. Use Free Rights only when the turns move into their own acceleration lane and there are minimal pedestrians.

3. For exclusive right lanes (not shared lanes), set the Turn Type to Permited+Overlap in the **TIMING** settings. Synchro will assume right turns move with a green ball and receive an overlapping arrow during compatible left turn phases. Use Free Rights only when the signal has a right turn arrow. Overlapped right turns can be used together with Right Turn on Red.

4. Reduce the input volumes to account for Right Turns on Red. This is the method prescribed by the HCM for modeling RTOR. Reducing the input volumes will change the results of optimization and will transfer smaller volumes to the simulation models. This can be unreliable because the right turn on red volume is highly influenced by the mix of traffic and the timings used.

Selecting a Right Turn Treatment

Refer to **Table 5-2** for direction on selecting a right turn treatment.

Table 5-2   Selecting a Right Turn Treatment

Right Turn Treatment	Permitted	RTOR	Volume Reduction	Free	Perm +Over
Flow Rate on Ball	1600±	1600±	1600±	1600±	1600±
Flow Rate on Red	0	<1091	0	1600±	0
Flow Rate on Arrow	NA	1600±	0	1600±	1600±
Right turn island, Yield Sign		Yes			
Right turn island plus Acceleration lane				Yes	
Acceleration Lane				Yes	
Overlapped Arrow					Yes
No Right on Red	Yes				
HCM Compatibility	Yes	No	Yes	Yes	Yes

HCM Compatibility

The HCM does not support Right Turn on Red Saturation Flow calculations. Synchro calculations with RTOR enabled will use an equivalent reduction in right turn volume for the HCM Signal Report (see page 15-15).

The RTOR calculations are based on an internally developed model based on the HCM gap acceptance formula for right turns. The RTOR saturation flow rates calculated by Synchro provide similar results to the HCM method of reducing right-turn volumes to account for right turns on red. This approach improves simulation results because traffic volumes are not deducted from the model.

Saturation Flow Rate (RTOR)

Synchro automatically calculates **Saturation Flow rate for Right Turns on Red**. This Saturation Flow Rate is applied to a movement whenever the movement has a red signal. This calculation is also made for Left Turns on Red crossing one-way streets.

The calculation of the RTOR Saturation Flow Rate is quite complex and is based on the signal timing, the volumes of the subject approach, and the volumes of any merging approaches.

It is possible to override the RTOR Saturation Flow Rate to a measured value or hand calculated value. Overriding RTOR Saturation Flow is not recommended because overridden values will not be updated when the volumes or signal timings change. The RTOR Saturation Flow is very sensitive to changes in volumes and timings.

sRTOR = Minimum(sRTOR1, sRTOR2) = RTOR Saturation Flow Rate

sRTOR1 = saturation flow rate based on gaps in merging traffic

sRTOR2 = limit to saturation flow rate based on through traffic blocking access to stop bar

If the RTOR volume is measured in the field, it can be used to calculate the sRTOR for Synchro based on the following:

sRTOR = vRTOR * C/r

r = red time, s

C = Cycle Length

vRTOR = Field Measured RTOR

For example, say 100 vph is the field measure RTOR volume, the movement red time is 80 seconds and the cycle is 120 seconds. Then,

sRTOR = 100 * (120/80) = 150

Gap Acceptance Calculation

The Saturation Flow Rate is calculated for each timing interval while the subject movement is red. Separate interval calculations are provided to account for merging through, merging left turn and intervals with no conflicting movements.

$$sRTORi = \frac{vxi * e^{(-vx*6.2/3600)}}{1 - e^{(-vxi*3.3/3600)}} = \text{saturation flow rate for each timing interval}$$

sRTORi = 1091, when vxi = 0

Ri = length of timing interval i

C = cycle length

vxi = vx * sxi * C / $\sum$(sxi*Ri) = merging volume during timing interval i

sxi = saturation flow rate for movement x during interval i

sRTOR1 = $\sum$(sRTORi * Ri) / Sum(Ri)

The combined RTOR Saturation Flow Rate 1 (sRTOR1) is a time weighted average of each sRTORi calculated for each red interval. The formula for sRTORi is taken from the HCM Unsignalized chapter and assumes a gap time of 6.2 s and a follow-up time of 3.3 seconds. The maximum flow rate with zero conflicting vehicles assumes one vehicle every 3.3 seconds or 1091 vph.

Conflicting pedestrian volumes are added into the merging vehicle volumes, vxi.

The conflicting volume rates (vxi) assume that conflicting flows will be divided proportionately among the conflicting flows green times and saturation flow rates. For example, the conflicting movement is a permitted plus protected left turn with the following values:

vL = left turn volume = 300 vph

R1 = permitted green = 20 s

sL1 = permitted saturation flow = 900 vph

R2 = protected green = 10 s

sL2 = protected saturation flow = 1800 vph

C = cycle length = 60 s

vL1 = permitted volume = 300 * 900 * 60 / (900 * 20 + 1800 * 10) = 450 vph vL2 = protected volume = 300 * 1800 * 60 / (900 * 20 + 1800 * 10) = 900 vph

The conflicting through movement has the following:

vT = through volume = 1000 vph

R3 = permitted green = 20 s

vT3 = 1000 * 1000 * 60 / (1000 * 20) = 3000 vph

The resulting saturated flow calculations are as follows:

vx1 = NA, this is a green interval for subject movement

vx2 = vL2 = 900 vph

sRTORi2 = 900 * exp(-900 * 6.2 /3600) / [1 - exp(-900 * 3.3/3600] = 340

vx3 = vT3 = 3000 vph

sRTORi3 = 3000 * exp(-3000 * 6.2/3600) / [1 - exp(-3000 * 3.3/3600] = 18

sRTOR1 = [340 * 10 + 18 * 20] / (10+20) = 126 vph

Shared Lane Blocking Calculation

The RTOR Saturation Flow Rate is limited because through traffic may block right traffic from reaching the stop bar. sRTOR2 is based on the average maximum number of right lane vehicles served before through traffic is blocked. This calculation is performed for both shared lanes and for exclusive right turn lanes in a storage bay.

sRTOR2 = vR/vTh * (storage +1) * 3600 / R = blocking limit to saturation flow rate

vR = right turn volume

vTh = non-right volume in lane

storage = length of storage bay in vehicles (not multiplied by number of lanes)

R = length of entire red time

Exclusive Right Lane No Storage

For an exclusive right turn lane without storage restriction, the sRTOR2 calculation is not performed.

Exclusive Right Lane with Storage

storage = length / vehicle length

For an exclusive right turn lane with storage, storage is equal to the number of vehicle lengths of the storage bay. If the storage bay is 100 feet and it takes 5 through vehicles to block right turns, storage will be 5.

The non-right volume is equal to the non-right volume in the rightmost through lane.

vTh = vTot / (lanes * laneUtFact) = non-right volume in lane

vTot = total volume in through lane group

lanes = number of lanes in lane group

laneUtFact = lane utilization factor for through lane group

If the through lane group has volume of 1000 vph, 2 lanes, and laneUtFact = 0.95:

vTh = 1000 / (2 *0.95) = 526.

If vR = 200 and R = 60 s, the result sRTOR2 is

sRTOR2 = 200/526 * (5+1) * 3600 / 60 = 137 vph

Shared Through-Right Lane

In a shared lane, the storage is zero. If there is a flared right, or right turns can bypass 2 or 3 cars in parking lane, consider coding a right turn lane with storage of 25 to 75 feet to approximate actual conditions in the field.

vTh = (vTot) / (lanes * laneUtFact) - vR = non-right volume in lane

vTh must be greater then (vTot -vR) * 0.2. This insures that at least some through traffic is in the right lane.

For example:

vTot = 1200

vR = 400

lanes = 2

laneUtFact = 0.95

R = 60 s

vTh = 1200 / (2 * 0.95) - 400 = 231

vTh $\geq$ (1200 - 400) * 0.2 = 160, check OK

sRTOR2 = 400/231 * 1 * 3600 / 60 = 104 vph

sRTOR2 must be less or equal to vR, otherwise non-right traffic will be moving during red.

Chapter 6 – Volume Settings

From the **MAP** view, click on the desired intersection with the Right mouse button and select **VOLUME** Settings.

 From anywhere in the program, press [F8] and select the desired intersection from the list. Then push the *Volume Settings* button or the [**F4**] key.

The **VOLUME** settings display a grid in which you can enter volume information. See Chapter 3 for details on navigating the data entry screens.

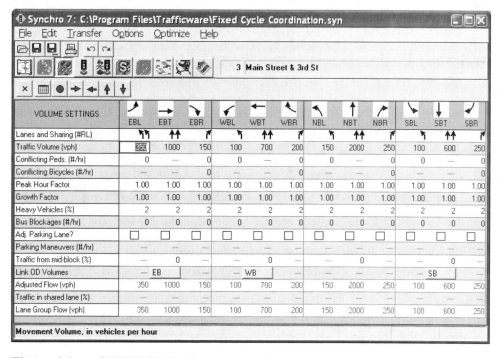

Figure 6-1   VOLUME Settings

 Refer to page 5-2 for details on the **Lanes and Sharing** setting.

Traffic Volumes

In the appropriate **Traffic Volume** cells, enter the traffic volumes for each movement in vehicles per hour.

Synchro models the hourly volumes provided for one design period. However, you may model multiple design periods using the UTDF Volume table.

If you have volume counts in TMC format, it is possible to import them automatically into the UTDF Volume table.

 To create a new column for U-turns, type [Ctrl] + [U].

Conflicting Pedestrians

Enter the number of pedestrians, per hour, that conflict with permitted right turn movements. This number affects the Right Ped Bike Factor (see page 5-12) and the Saturated Flow Rate (see page 5-11) shown in the **LANE** settings for the permitted right turns. If right turns are protected from pedestrians due to an island, or if no pedestrians are allowed during this approach's through phase, then enter zero.

 Do not confuse this field with the Pedestrians Calls setting in the **PHASING** settings. Conflicting Pedestrians are the number of pedestrians that right turning traffic must yield to. Pedestrian Calls are the number of pedestrians activating this phase. These two values will be the same if there is only one pedestrian per ped call.

 It is necessary to enter conflicting pedestrians for permitted left turns. These should be the number of pedestrians crossing the destination link.

Conflicting Pedestrians affect the Ped-Bike Factor in the **LANE** settings. Increasing the number of conflicting pedestrians and bicycles reduces the saturated flow rate of right turns and left turns conflicting with these movements.

To set a default pedestrian value for newly created intersections, or to change all of the pedestrians, use the **Options→Network Settings** command.

Conflicting Bicycles

Enter the number of through bicycles that conflict with right turns. If bicycles cross the right turn traffic ahead of the intersection, enter 0. This input will affect the Right Ped-Bike factor in the **LANE** settings.

Conflicting Bicycles do not need to be entered for left turns. It is assumed that they will clear during the queue clearance time for vehicles.

Peak Hour Factor

The traffic volumes are divided by the **Peak Hour Factor** (PHF) to determine the traffic flow rate during the busiest 15-minute period during the hour. For example:

Hourly Flow Rate: 1000 vph

Peak Hour Factor: 0.9

Adjusted Peak Flow Rate: 1000 / 0.9 = 1111 vph

The HCM 2000 Chapter 10 recommends, "In the absence of field measurements of peak-hour factor (PHF), approximations can be used. For congested conditions, 0.92 is a reasonable approximation for PHF. For conditions in which there is fairly uniform flow throughout the peak hour but a recognizable peak does occur, 0.88 is a reasonable estimate for PHF." If you have 15-minute counts, you can use the highest counts and a PHF of one.

If the Analysis Period is set to a value of greater than 15 minutes, the PHF will be set to 1.0 and cannot be changed. The Analysis Period can be modified using the **Options→Network-Settings** command.

The default PHF is 0.92 following the guidelines of HCM 2000. The user may change the default or reset existing Peak Hour Factors in the current data set under **Options→Network-Settings**. The range of PHF in Synchro is 0.25 to 1.00.

Note that 15-minute traffic volumes read from a UTDF Volume file automatically recalculate PHF for each volume period.

If traffic arrivals fit a Poisson distribution, probability suggests using the values in **Table 6-1** for the PHF. This assumes the highest 15-minute period is the 87.5 percentile based on average 15-minute periods of the hour.

Table 6-1   Suggested Peak Hour Values

Total Approach Volume	PHF
2000 vph	0.95
1000	0.93
500	0.92
200	0.87
100	0.83
50	0.78

If the upstream intersection is at capacity for the entire peak hour, use a PHF of 1.0.

It is important to understand that the variance of traffic increases as the volume decreases. Therefore, lower traffic volumes create greater fluctuations in 15-minute volume levels which tends to increase PHF.

If a large factory or sports arena releases all of its vehicles at once, the traffic may have a large spike and a lower PHF should be used.

Growth Factor

The **Growth Factor** can be used to adjust traffic volumes using a range from 0.5 to 3.0. The raw volume data is multiplied by the Growth Factor when calculating Adjusted Volumes and Lane Group Volumes.

To calculate a Growth Factor (GF) based on a growth rate over several years, use the following formula.

$$GF = (1+r)^Y$$

   r = growth rate

   Y = number of years

For example, the growth factor for 3% growth over 10 years is:

$$GF = (1 + 0.03)^{10} = 1.34$$

Heavy Vehicles

Heavy Vehicles (%) under the **VOLUME** settings represents the percentage of trucks and buses for each traffic movement. Increasing this value decreases the Saturated Flow Rate shown in the **LANE** settings. The default for this field is 2%.

Heavy Vehicle percentages are modeled explicitly in SimTraffic, but do not affect the turning percentages when transferring to CORSIM.

To set a default for newly created intersections or change all of the Heavy Vehicle Factors, use the **Options→Network-Settings** command.

The Heavy Vehicle Factor is:

$$Fhv = 100/[100 + \% \ hv \ (Et - 1)]$$

where:

Fhv = heavy vehicle adjustment factor

$\% \ hv$ = % heavy vehicles for lane group volume

$Et = 2.0 \ pc/hv$

Bus Blockages

Enter the number of buses per hour that stop and actually block traffic. Increasing this factor lowers the Saturated Flow Rate shown in the **LANE** settings. The default for this field is zero buses per hour. Enter **Bus Blockages** for each lane group that is affected by the blockage.

The bus blockages factor is calculated by:

$$Fbb = [N - (14.4Nb/3600)]/N$$

where:

Fbb = bus blockage factor

N = number of lanes in lane group

Nb = number of buses stopping/h

Adjacent Parking Lane, Parking Maneuvers

If there is on street parking for this approach, check the box for **Adjacent Parking Lane** and the number of maneuvers per hour for **Parking Maneuvers**. Increasing the number of parking maneuvers lowers the Saturated Flow Rate shown in the **LANE** settings. The default for this field is "No" adjacent parking lane which does not reduce Saturated Flow Rate. Setting the field to "Yes" reduces Saturated Flow Rate even if the number of parking maneuvers per hour is coded to zero. Therefore, only code a "Yes" value if on-street parking actually impedes traffic flow.

 Each lane group has its own field for parking movements. The general rule is to code the number of movements that affect the lane group. In some cases, a parking movement affects more than one lane group.

Table 6-2 illustrates examples on how to code parking movements.

Table 6-2   Parking Maneuver Coding Examples

Parking	Lanes	Left Parking	Thru Parking	Right Parking
20 right side	1 Th, 1 Rt (no storage)	0	0	20
20 right side	1 Th, 1 Rt (yes storage)	0	20	20
20 right side	2 Th	0	20	0
20 right, 10 left	1 Lt, 1Th, 1 Rt (no storage)	10	0	20
20 right, 10 left	1 Lt, 1 Th, 1 Rt (yes storage)	10	30	20
20 right, 10 left	2 Th	0	30	0

The parking factor is based on the following equation:

$$Fp= [N-0.1-(18Nm/3600)]/N$$

where:

    Fp= parking factor

    N= number of lanes in lane group

    Nm= number of parking maneuvers/h

Traffic from Mid-block

The **Traffic from mid-block** field identifies vehicles originating from mid-block sources between the current intersection and the last upstream intersection modeled in Synchro. A value of 50 indicates that 50% of the traffic is from mid-block sources. A value of zero indicates that 0% of the traffic is from driveways and 100% of the traffic came from the upstream signal. This information is used during optimization and when calculating delays. If volumes for a link originate primarily from mid-block sources, the reduction in delay from signal optimization will not will not be as great if the traffic originated from an upstream signal.

Unbalanced Traffic Between Intersections

Many times the sum of traffic volumes entering a link at an upstream intersection does not equal the sum of traffic volumes at the downstream end of the link. This can occur when the volume data was collected at different times, or due to a mid-block traffic source or sink. Growth Factor and PHF values also affect the net volume balance between adjacent intersections.

To see the volume balance between intersections, click on the [VB] button on the **MAP** view. Refer to page 2-12 for details.

The following procedure is used by SimTraffic to resolve any imbalances between the volumes specified in the LANE settings and the mid-block volumes specified in the VOLUME settings.

VU = sum of flows entering upstream. For an eastbound link, they would be EBT, NBR, plus SBL.

VD = sum of flows exiting downstream. For an eastbound link, they would be EBT, EBR, plus EBL.

MD = percentage of mid-block traffic entered in Volume settings

$VM = max(VD * MD, VD - VU * 1.3)$ = Mid-block traffic entering

$VX = max(0, VU - VD - VM)$ = Mid-block traffic exiting

If upstream traffic is less than non-user-entered mid-block traffic, the upstream traffic flows will be scaled up to a maximum of 30%. Beyond 30% the traffic balance is assumed to come from mid-block sources and the mid-block entries are scaled upwards.

If upstream traffic exceeds downstream plus mid-block traffic, a mid-block sink is assumed. Any extra vehicles will be entering the sink.

For SimTraffic, upstream volumes cannot be scaled upward. Thus, any imbalance is assumed to be mid-block entries.

CORSIM provides one mid-block source per link that either serves as a source or a sink. A source or sink card is created whenever upstream and downstream volumes do not balance.

Here is an example:

$VU = 100$

$VD = 200$

$MD = 10\%$

$MD = \max(200 * 0.1, 200 - 100 * 1.3) = 70$

$VX = 0$

$S = (VD - MD)/VU$ = scaling factor

The flows from upstream are thus scaled upwards by 1.3.

The peak flow at the beginning of green upstream is 4000 vph. This flow would be scaled by 1.3 to 5200 vph downstream and cause a spike in queue and delay. Therefore, it is important that volumes are scaled and mid-block flows are entered correctly. If mid-block traffic is entered as 60%, the upstream volumes would be scaled by 0.8 and the peak flow downstream would be a more reasonable 3200 vph.

In the above example, SimTraffic and CORSIM would assume mid-block source of 100 vehicles per hour.

Link Origin Destination (O-D) Volumes

Purpose

Link Origin-Destination (O-D) Volumes allow detailed control over the origin and destination of two adjacent intersections. Link O-D Volumes can be used to reduce or eliminate certain turn combinations. The most common use is to specify the number of vehicles from an off ramp completing a U-turn at a freeway interchange.

The **LINK ORIGIN-DESTINATION VOLUMES** settings display Movement Weighting Factors that control how volume is allocated between input and output volumes.

To activate the **LINK ORIGIN-DESTINATION VOLUMES** settings, go to the **VOLUME** settings for node that has an adjacent intersection and choose the appropriate button. For external links, the button will not be available.

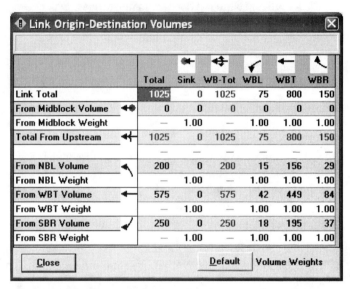

	Total	Sink	WB-Tot	WBL	WBT	WBR
Link Total	1025	0	1025	75	800	150
From Midblock Volume	0	0	0	0	0	0
From Midblock Weight	—	1.00	—	1.00	1.00	1.00
Total From Upstream	1025	0	1025	75	800	150
	—	—	—	—	—	—
From NBL Volume	200	0	200	15	156	29
From NBL Weight	—	1.00	—	1.00	1.00	1.00
From WBT Volume	575	0	575	42	449	84
From WBT Weight	—	1.00	—	1.00	1.00	1.00
From SBR Volume	250	0	250	18	195	37
From SBR Weight	—	1.00	—	1.00	1.00	1.00

Close   Default   Volume Weights

Figure 6-2   LINK ORIGIN-DESTINATION VOLUMES Settings

When to Use

- Use on short links, less than 300 ft (90m) long.

- Multiple intersections controlled by a single controller (Group Control).

- Between intersections of a freeway interchange.

- In the median of a wide arterial.

- Between nodes of a "dog-legged" intersection. (Two closely spaced 'T' intersections.)

- The Link Volume Balancer is also helpful to make sure upstream and downstream volumes match and to make adjustments so that they do match.

When to Skip

- External links.

- Links over 1000 feet (300m) long. Most links over 300 feet (90m) long.

- When origins and destinations have nearly equal "attractions".

 For the majority of links, Link O-D Volumes are not needed. In most cases, Link O-D Volumes make little difference to the timing plan optimization. Collecting Origin Destination traffic data is labor intensive and cannot be automated.

By default, Synchro assumes origin-destination volumes are proportional to the origin and destination volumes for each O-D pair multiplied together. This assumption matches actual traffic in most cases.

To Activate

Link O-D Volumes are available for both directions on links that connect two intersections. The Link O-D Volumes are available from the **VOLUME** settings. All approaches that connect to an intersection have a button available in the **Link O-D Volumes** row. To activate the **LINK ORIGIN-DESTINATION VOLUMES** settings, click on this button ![EB] or press the [space bar] if the *Link O-D Volumes* button is in focus.

The *Link O-D Volumes* buttons appear with a black caption when all Movement Weighting Factors are 1. If one or more Movement Weighting factors have been changed, then *Link O-D Volumes* button appears with a red caption.

Layout

There is one column for each destination turn on the link. There is also a column listing the sink volume, or the traffic that turns off the network on this link.

There are two rows for each origin turning movement at the upstream intersection. There are also two rows listing midblock traffic, or traffic entering the network on this link. The upper row lists the traffic volumes for the origin-destination pair; the lower row lists the Movement Weighting Factor for the origin destination pair; the volumes shown on these settings are adjusted for growth, but not PHF. Volumes shown on the map and volume balance will also show volumes adjusted for growth, but not PHF. This is done so that the volumes match what the user entered unless growth is used, which is not very common.

Cells in the top row can be used to set the actual volumes at the downstream intersection. Cells in the left column can be used to set the actual volumes at the upstream intersection.

The left cell in the From Mid-Block Volume row can be used to set the midblock traffic. This value changes the percent mid-block setting found in the **VOLUME** settings. It is not possible to set this value exactly; the resulting volume will be within 1% of the total link volume.

The sink traffic cannot be entered or overridden. It is calculated based on the upstream, downstream and mid-block traffic volumes. Reading the sink and mid-block traffic volumes can be used to determine if input volumes are balanced between upstream and downstream intersections.

Entering the volume or the weighting factor can set traffic for individual origin-destination movements. The weighting factor is the value stored in the file, the movement volume is calculated. Movement volumes are adjusted to balance volumes between origins and destinations so it may not be possible to get the exact volume desired. It may take multiple entries with movement volumes or weighting factors to get the desired results.

 Differences in traffic volumes under 30 vph will have a negligible effect on optimization results. Do not be overly concerned with getting the exact numbers.

Approximations are usually good enough. It is normally sufficient to set weighting factors to 0.1 for movements to squelch and leave the other weighting factors at 1.

 Do not be overly concerned about collecting origin-destination traffic data. In most cases, common sense about the area's traffic patterns and land use will yield a good guess at the origin-destination patterns. For example, traffic rarely exits a freeway and enters in the opposite direction. Similarly, traffic from a residential collector to a residential collector may be less common than traffic patterns in other areas.

Avoid setting weight factors to zero. It may appear no one makes two left turns in a row under normal circumstances. However, with a road closure, the majority of traffic might be turning around.

Do not set all the factors in a row (or a column) to zero. This will cause zero traffic from an origin (or to a destination) to be generated.

Background

Link O-D volumes provide control over vehicle paths through multiple intersections. An alternate method for specifying this type of data is to have a grid of origins and destinations for all entrances and exits of two or more intersections. An O-D matrix is like the Link Volume Balancer but contains all the entrances and exits for several intersections, rather than for a single link.

O-D matrices are good for controlling traffic through a cluster of 3 or more closely spaced nodes such as for a roundabout. O-D matrices are also good for specifying traffic demand without specifying the actual route for applications involving dynamic traffic assignment. O-D matrices are used extensively in large area planning models.

O-D matrices require the collection of a lot of traffic data. Vehicle paths must be observed through two or more intersections. This type of data is impossible to collect automatically with detectors or other devices.

Synchro uses the Link Volume weighting for individual links. The Weighting Factors allow O-D volumes to be calculated from intersection turning counts. This allows easier data collection and even data collection through automatic detectors. Turning movement data can be collected for many time periods and the O-D volumes are estimated based on the weighting factors.

Link O-D Volume Calculations

All volumes in this discussion are adjusted for growth and PHF. Traffic volume balancing is subject to the following rules:

$Vu = \Sigma(Vi)$ = volume from upstream intersection

Vi = volume from upstream movement i

$Vd = \Sigma(Vd)$ = volume to downstream intersection

Vj = volume to downstream movement j

$Vm = max(Vd - Vu, Vd * \%MB)$ = volume entering mid-block, can be calculated or set with %MB

%MB = percent of traffic entering mid-block, input in **VOLUME** settings

$Vt = Vd + Vm$ = total link volume

$Vx = Vt - Vd$ = sink volume, always calculated

Wij = movement weight factor from origin i to destination j

Vij = volume from origin i to destination j

$Vij = Wij * Vi * Vj / Vt$ = initial calculation, before adjustment to balance volumes

Mid-block Volume is a valid origin I. Sink Volume is a valid destination J.

Movement Volumes (Vij) are adjusted iteratively so that origin and destination volumes are balanced for each IJ movement. Due to volume balancing, Movement Volumes will not usually be proportionate to the Weight Factors. Volume balancing also limits the range of deviation for each IJ movement from its normally weighted value.

By default, all Weight Factors (Wij) are 1 and traffic is allocated in proportion to origin and destination traffic for each movement.

Adjusted Flow

The **Adjusted Flow** (vph) is the entered volume modified by the Peak Hour Factor and Growth Factor.

This field cannot be overridden.

Traffic in Shared Lane

Traffic volumes assigned to exclusive and shared lane are proportioned to each lane as follows.

Vehicles are counted as passenger car equivalents (PCE) as follows

>Throughs: 1

>Rights: 1.18

>Protected Lefts: 1.05

>Permitted Lefts: $1 / [0.95 * (900 - vOp)/900]$, (max 6.67)

>Permitted plus protected Lefts: $2/ [0.95 + 0.95 * (900 - vOp)/900]$, (max 1.82)

>vOp = through volume opposed.

Traffic is assigned so that PCEs are balanced between lanes. The assignment of traffic to the shared lane is between 10% and 90% of the turning traffic.

This simplified left turn factor removes the interdependence of lane assignments from the permitted left turn factor (see page 5-10) calculation. As a practical matter, the need for a permitted left-turn factor is somewhat nullified by this lane assignment procedure.

This value can be overridden to control lane assignment in Synchro. Changes to this setting will not impact the simulation.

Lane Group Flow

The **Lane Group Flow** combines the Adjusted Flow and Traffic in Shared Lane (%) values to assign net volumes to each lane group.

If there are no turning lanes, the turning volume is assigned to the through lane group. The shared lanes are part of the through lane group and the exclusive lanes are part of those movements' lane groups.

If an approach has a shared turning lane *and* an exclusive turning, the Adjusted Flow value in the exclusive turn lane is reduced by the Traffic in Shared Lane (%) value for that lane. The through movement corresponding with the shared lane is increased by this same value. These are calculated fields and cannot be overiden by the user.

Chapter 7 – Timing/Signing Settings

Timing Settings

From the **MAP** view, click on the desired intersection with the Right mouse button and sleclt the Timing Settings.

From anywhere in the program, press [**F8**] and select the desired intersection from the list. Then push the ***Timing Setting*** button or the [**F5**] key.

The **TIMING** settings are displayed with information about the timing and phasing. See Chapter 3 for details on navigating the data entry screens.

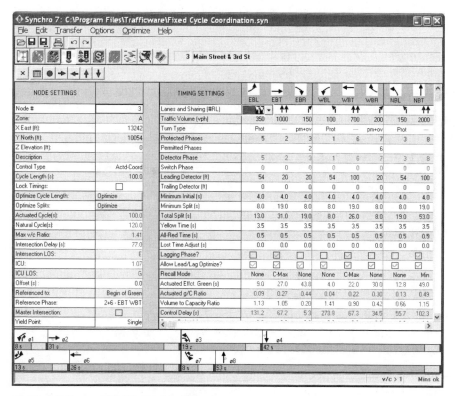

Figure 7-1   TIMING Settings

Layout

The left side of the **TIMING** settings will display the **NODE** settings with alternate rows displayed in yellow. Here you can update data such as the node number, zone name, intersection coordinates, description notes and signal timing data. See Chapter 4 for full details on the **NODE** settings.

On the right side are blue shaded rows and columns. There is a column for every vehicle movement and every vehicle movement can have multiple phases. To enter multiple phases, see the topic on **Protected and Permitted Phases** on page 7-5. There is also a column for a pedestrian only phase and a Hold phase. To make a pedestrian only phase, assign a phase number to this column. Details on the data entry items are found in subsequent sections of this chapter.

Near the bottom of the **TIMING** settings are a Splits and Phasing diagram. This is fully defined on page 7-16.

 Refer to page 5-2 for details on the **Lanes and Sharing** setting and to page 6-2 for details on the **Traffic Volume** setting.

Signing Settings

The **TIMING** settings become the **SIGNING** settings by selecting unsignalized or roundabout from the **Control Type** (refer to page 4-4). The toolbar button becomes a stop sign when an unsignalized intersection is active. [F5] opens the **SIGNING** settings or **TIMING** settings depending on the intersection.

Phase Templates

Phase templates allow phase numbers to be set automatically.

To set phases for an east-west arterial use the menu command **Options→Phase-Templates→Intersection-to-East-West**.

To set phases for a north-south arterial use the menu command **Options→Phase-Templates→Intersection-to-North-South**. Phases 2 and 6 are normally used for the main street. Thus, two templates are provided for each type of arterial.

To edit the phase templates use the menu command **Options→Phase-Templates→Edit-Template-Phases**.

Enter phase numbers for each through and left movement. Local standards may have the phases mirrored from Synchro's defaults. Synchro's defaults are shown in **Figure 7-2**.

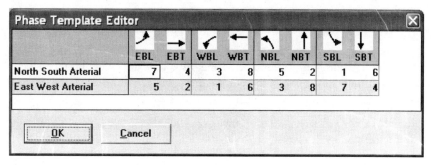

Figure 7-2   PHASE TEMPLATE Settings

 Phase Templates are for dual ring controllers and cannot be used to set up single ring timing or other advanced applications. To set up advanced applications use the Ring-and-Barrier-Designer (see page 8-2).

Use default phase templates to set up phase numbers matching the agency's standard phasing scheme.

The Phase Template is a global setting for all intersections within this file.

Turn Type

The **Turn Type** sets the level of turn protection and assigns default phase and detector numbers to the dedicated turn lane. These defaults can be changed at any time.

Before setting the turn types, set the phase numbers for the through movements using a phase template.

Left Turn Type

The eight types of left turn treatment are:

1. Permitted (Perm): Left turn movements are not protected and vehicles must yield to oncoming traffic and pedestrians in the crosswalk.

2. Protected (Prot): Left turn movements are protected by a dedicated signal and turning traffic can only move during the arrow indication of this signal.

3. Permitted + Protected (pm+pt): Left turn movements are protected during the protected (arrow) signal indication and permitted during the green ball indication. With permitted plus protected phasing, it is common to use four to five signal displays for the turn indications.

4. Split: Left and through traffic share a single protected phase. This type of phasing is commonly used if a lane is shared between left and through traffic. Split phasing insures that shared left-turn lanes are protected and offer a greater level of protection compared with permitted left-turns. If there is no through approach, such as at a T intersection, then the left turn treatment should always be split.

5. Dallas Permitted (D.Pm): A special type of phasing developed in the Dallas, Texas area. The left turn lane has its own signal head. The left signal head is louvered to make it invisible from adjacent lanes. The ball in the left lane displays the same phase displayed to oncoming through traffic. This configuration eliminates the lagging left turn trap problem.

6. Dallas Permitted plus Protected (D.P+P): A special type of phasing developed in the Dallas, Texas area. The left turn lane has its own signal head. The left signal head is louvered to make it invisible from adjacent lanes. The ball in the left lane displays the same phase displayed to oncoming through traffic. This configuration eliminates the lagging left turn trap problem.

7. NA: No phase selected. Left turns are prohibited.

8. Custom: A non-standard left turn phase combination is selected

Right Turn Type

If there is right turn traffic, there is an option for the right turn treatment. There are eight choices.

 Right turn traffic from a through or shared lane will only move during phases for those movements. The right turn phasing only applies to exclusive right lanes.

1. Perm (perm): Permitted right turn movements are not protected and vehicles must yield to pedestrians in the crosswalk.

2. Protected (Prot): Right turn movements are protected by a dedicated signal that provides a right-turn arrow that does not conflict with pedestrian indications.

3. Overlap (Over): This turn type displays a right turn arrow with a protected left-turn movement on the intersecting street.

   Overlap should not be used as a substitute for Right Turn on Red. See **Right Turn on Red** on page 5-13 for guidance on which type to use.

4. Permitted + Protected (pm+ov): This right turn overlap displays a right-turn arrow with a compatible left-turn and a permitted (green ball) indication with the through phase.

5. Protected + Overlap (pt+ov): This right-turn overlap displays a right-turn arrow with the compatible left-turn and the through movement associated with the right-turn.

6. Free: A free right turn movement yields to pedestrians and is not assigned a signal phase. The permitted phase is automatically set to Free by the Free turn type.

   Free should not be used as a substitute for Right Turn on Red. See **Right Turn on Red** on page 5-13 for guidance on which type to use. Free should only be used if the movement has an acceleration lane downstream.

7. NA: A right turn type set to NA (Not Applicable) is prohibited. The volume for the right-turn movement must be coded to zero for this turn type.

8. Custom: Non-standard right turn phases are entered.

Protected and Permitted Phases

The **Phase** rows are used to assign one or more phases for each movement. During protected phases, traffic can move without conflict. During permitted phases, left turning traffic must yield to oncoming traffic and right turn traffic must yield to pedestrians. Conflicting phases have the phase number shown in red. Permitted left turns do not conflict with movements bound for the same link. Permitted through movements do not conflict with left turns bound for the same link.

 In many cases, the phase numbers can be set automatically by using the Phase Templates and the Turn Type controls.

Most signals in North America use dual ring controllers, which service a phase in each ring concurrently.

TIMING WINDOW	EBL	EBT	EBR	WBL	WBT	WBR
Lanes and Sharing (#RL)		↑↑↑	↗	↖↖	↑↑	
Traffic Volume (vph)	0	1800	43	200	1200	0
Turn Type	—	—	Perm	Prot	—	—
Protected Phases	—	2		1	2 1	—
Permitted Phases	—		2			—
Detector Phase	—	2	2	1	2	—
Switch Phase	—	0	0	0	1	—

Figure 7-3   Multiple Phasing (Overlaps)

Multiple phasing is referred to as phase overlaps in controller terminology. Multiple phases can be entered by separating the phase numbers with a space. The Total Split for multiple phases is the sum of all the phases for the movement. In the above diagram, the WBT total split is the sum of the phase 1 split (10 s) and the phase 2 split (30 s) for a total of 40 seconds.

Phase 2 will be assigned as the Detector phase since it is listed first. Phase 1 will be assigned as the Switch Phase since it is listed second.

If a movement is served by two consecutive phases, the clearance intervals (Y+AR) between the phases are not shown and the signal stays green. Synchro automatically takes this into account when calculating effective green times, g/C ratios, and v/c ratios.

Automatic Phase Creation and Removal

A lane group is considered "phase-able" when it has 1 or more lanes. Through, Left, and U-turn lane groups are also "phase-able" when they have traffic volume or a shared lane. Right lane groups are only "phase-able" when they have 1 or more primary lanes.

Table 7-1   What Makes a Lane Group "Phase-able"

	Lane Group					
	U-Turn	Left 2	Left	Through	Right	Right 2
Volume	X	X	X	X		
Primary Lanes	X	X	X	X	X	X
Shared Lanes	X	X	X	X		

Phase-able lane groups must always have at least one phase or be coded Free. Non-phase-able lane groups are coded with zero phases and zero lane group volume. Therefore, all measures (MOE) for a non-phase-able lane group are not applicable.

When a lane group is made phase-able by adding volumes or lanes, a phase is automatically assigned to this lane group. Through lane groups are given a default-protected phase based on the phase templates. Synchro attempts to determine which phase template is in use and assigns a through phase from the appropriate template. Left and right lane groups are given a default permitted phase equal to the through lane group's protected or permitted phases. If the through lane group has no phases or does not exist, the turning lane group is given a permitted phase based on the phase template for through phases.

If a pedestrian or hold phase is added to a lane group by the user or the phase assigner, the phase is no longer a hold or pedestrian phase.

When a lane group is made non-phaseable by removing volumes and lanes, all phases are removed from the lane group. If these phases do not serve other movements, the phases are removed from the timing plan. Care should be used when importing volumes or lanes so as not to lose phase information.

Detector Phase

Detectors in the subject lane group will call and/or extend the **Detector Phases**. The function of the detector is set in the **DETECTORS** settings in the **Detector Type** row (see page 10-1).

Detectors call a protected phase by default or a permitted phase if a protected phase does not exist. Default detector phases are shown in blue font and may be overridden by the user (red font).

Avoid changing the Detector Phase and Switch Phase. To change the phase associated with the lane group, use the Protected Phases or Permitted Phases setting. If you override the Detector Phases, it will not be updated if the phase numbers change later.

If there is no detector for this lane group, code a value of '0' in the setting for Detector Phase and ensure that this is either the coordinated phase, is a pretimed signal, or 'maximum' is coded for the Recall Mode.

Only one phase number can be entered for the Detector Phase.

Switch Phase

The **Switch Phase** is a secondary phase that extends the entered phase when it is green. This setting does not place a call and does not call the primary Detector Phase when the entered switch phase is green.

This setting can be used for the permitted phase of a permitted plus protected left turn. Do not use with a lagging left turn because the protected left will not get called while the permitted phase is green. The default for permitted plus protected is to have the Detector Phase equal to the Protected Phase and Switch Phase set to none.

Leading Detector

This distance in feet (meter) is measured from the stop bar to the leading edge of the detector farthest from the stop bar. Enter this value for each lane group.

This information only needs to be entered if you are using the actuated signal analysis functions of Synchro. This information does not need to be entered for the main street approaches of semi-actuated and coordinated signals.

 Do not set the Leading Detector to zero; the minimum value is 5 feet (1.5 m). If there is no detector for this lane group, code a value of 0 in the setting for Detector Phase and ensure that this is either the coordinated phase, is a pretimed signal, or 'maximum' is coded for the Recall Mode.

Refer to Chapter 10 for full details on entering detector information.

Trailing Detector

This is the distance from the trailing edge of the trailing detector to the stop bar in feet (meters). Enter only extension detectors for each lane group. Do not count calling-only and type-3 detectors in this field. The detector information is used in conjunction with gap-out times and thus only extension detectors are used. A negative value can be entered if the trailing detector extends past the stop bar.

This information only needs to be entered if you are using the actuated signal analysis functions of Synchro. This information does not need to be entered for the main street approaches of semi-actuated and coordinated signals.

 The Leading and Trailing Detector settings are automatically updated if you enter detector information in the **DETECTORS** settings.

Refer to Chapter 10 for full details on entering detector information.

Minimum Initial

The **Minimum Initial** time is the shortest green time that is guaranteed if a phase is serviced. Synchro allows a range from 1 to 840 seconds. This value is called Min Green in actuated controllers and holds the initial green long enough to insure that the phase is extended by detection. The large range will allow for the modeling of unusual timing plans.

 It is not necessary to enter data for values such as added initial and maximum initial. Synchro assumes that the controller and detectors are set so that the signal will not gap-out before the queued vehicles are cleared.

Do not confuse this field with the Minimum Split setting. Minimum Initial is used in determining actuated behavior; Minimum Split is used to optimize splits.

Minimum Split

The **Minimum Split** is the shortest amount of time allowed for a phase.

The Minimum Split must be long enough to accommodate the Minimum Initial interval plus the yellow and all red time (typically 8-12 seconds). The minimum allowed in Synchro is 3 seconds and the maximum value is 840 seconds. When Synchro automatically assigns splits, it will make sure all splits are greater than or equal to their Minimum Splits. (This assumes the cycle length is long enough to accommodate all splits.) See the section **Optimize→ Intersection-Splits** on page 13-4 for information about how splits are calculated.

If the Minimum Split shown is red, it indicates a minimum error. The Minimum Split must be greater or equal to the Minimum Initial plus clearance time (Y + AR). If this phase has a pedestrian phase, the Minimum Split should be greater or equal to the sum of the Walk Time, the Flashing Don't Walk time, the Yellow Time and the All-Red Time. Minimum Splits that violate pedestrian timings can be entered. This will prevent the splits from being reset to the pedestrian timing requirements when optimizing splits or changing pedestrian times.

Enter the minimum split as the number of seconds. If there is a pedestrian movement with this phase, the minimum split should include time for a minimum walk and flashing don't walk time.

To set a default for newly created intersections or change all of the Minimum Splits, use the **Options→Network-Settings** command.

Do not confuse this field with the Minimum Initial setting. Minimum Initial is used to calculate actuated green times. Minimum Split is used to optimize splits.

Split Minimum Rules

Here is a summary of the rules for Minimum and Maximum Splits. If any of the inequalities are false, a minimum error is generated.

MxS = Maximum Split

MnS = Minimum Split

Y = Yellow

AR = All Red

Mi = Minimum Initial Green

W = Walk Time

FDW = Flashing Don't Walk time

$MxS \geq MnS \geq Mi + Y + AR$

$MxS \geq MnS \geq W + FDW + Y + AR$ (if the phase has a pedestrian phase)

If a split is too short for pedestrians, the actuated green time modeled can have strange results. For coordinated and pretimed signals, actuated green times for side streets will be increased and steal time from the coordinated phases. For uncoordinated actuated signals, actuated green times will increase the cycle length.

Pay careful attention to all pedestrian errors.

Many pedestrian errors occur where there is no pedestrian phase. The pedestrian phase can be turned off in the **Pedestrian Phase** setting (see page 8-10).

The Flash Don't Walk (FDW) time is in addition to Yellow Time. This may be the cause of some minimum errors.

Some traffic signal controllers allow a pedestrian actuation to service ped times that violate the Minimum Split time. In this case, the controller leaves coordination for a brief transition period to service an infrequent ped call. The best way to model this condition is to un-check the Pedestrian Phase in Synchro and ignore the walk and ped clearance timing.

Total Split

The **Total Split** time (in seconds) includes the green, yellow and all-red intervals assigned to a phase. The Total Split time may overlap multiple phases and is the sum of the times allocated to each phase. This number is given in seconds. The splits for the intersection can be calculated automatically by selecting the **Optimize→Intersection-Splits**, command from the menu. The range of Split Time is 3 to 900 seconds which is sufficient to model any timing plan encountered.

To adjust a split, type its new value in seconds. This phase will increase or decrease its time and the following phase will decrease or increase by the same amount. The amount a phase can be adjusted is limited by the green time of the following phase(s) and the green time of this phase and any concurrent phase.

To adjust a split with the mouse, move the mouse to the right side of a yellow + all red band on the current Splits and Phasing diagram shown at the bottom of the **TIMING** settings.

 The cursor will change into the shape shown here. Hold down the left mouse button and move the mouse right or left to adjust the split. When the button is released, all of the other colored bands that are affected will automatically adjust their splits, and any changed information will be shown on the numbers above.

It is not recommended that you adjust splits in this manner because Synchro will automatically reassign splits if the cycle length changes, if the phasing changes, or if the intersection layout changes. It is recommended that the Minimum Split reflects the phase times in the controller so that the lowest feasible cycle length can be considered when the signal is optimized.

Refer to the Splits and Phasing diagram at the bottom of the **TIMING** settings for a graphical representation of the current splits.

Synchro will automatically extend a phase to insure that the sum of the phases in each ring equals the cycle length. This extended split is shown in gray on the Splits and Phasing diagram.

The cycle length will be increased if an increase in Total Split causes the sum of the splits in any ring to exceed the cycle length. Adjusting splits graphically on the Splits and Phasing diagram preserves the cycle length.

Yellow Time

Yellow Time is the amount of time for the yellow interval. This value should be set between 3 and 5 seconds, depending on the approach speed, the cross street width, and local standards. The minimum value allowed by Synchro is 2 seconds and the maximum is 10 seconds.

To set a default for newly created intersections or change all of the Yellow Times, use the **Options→Network-Settings** command.

All-Red Time

All-Red Time is the amount of time for the all red interval that follows the yellow interval. The all red time should be of sufficient duration to permit the intersection to clear before cross traffic is released.

CORSIM (pretimed only) does not allow fractional seconds. If you plan to use this data with this model, make sure Yellow Time plus All-Red Time equals a whole number in seconds.

To set a default for newly created intersections or change all of the All-Red Times, use the **Options→Network-Settings** command.

The minimum value allowed is 0 seconds and the maximum is 120 seconds. A large range is used to allow the modeling of unusual timing plans, such as the example for Two Way Traffic Control.

Lost Time Adjustment

The **Lost Time Adjustment** replaces the Total Lost time in the **LANE** settings from previous versions.

Total lost time is calculated as startup lost time plus yellow plus all red, as shown below.

$$tL = Yi + L1 - e = \text{Total Lost Time}$$

$$Yi = \text{Yellow plus All-Red Time}$$

L1 = startup lost time = 2.5 seconds by default

e = Extension of effective green = 2.5 seconds by default

The Lost Time Adjustment is the startup lost time minus extension of effective green. The default for startup lost time and extension of effective green is 2.5 seconds, so the Lost Time Adjustment defaults to zero. The extension of the effective green is time vehicles continue to enter after yellow interval begins.

tLA = L1 – e = Lost Time Adjustment

tL = Yi + tLA

Lagging Phase?

The first two phases within a ring-barrier sequence are considered phase partners. The 3rd and 4th phases within a ring-barrier sequence if used, are also phase partners. Phase Lagging is used to swap the order of phase partners.

Eight phase dual ring operation provides phase partners 1-2 and 3-4 in ring 1 and phase partners 5-6 and 7-8 in ring 2.

If Phase Lagging is set to "on" for a phase, it will follow the phase that it normally proceeds. If Phase Lagging is set to "off" for an even phase, it will precede the odd phase that normally comes before the even phase.

Usually left turns are assigned odd phase numbers and through movements are assigned even phase numbers. If you wish to have a lagging left turn that follows a through movement, then set Lagging Phase to "on" for this phase. The oncoming through phase will have its Lagging Phase automatically set to "off."

Lagging can be used with left turns and their oncoming through approaches. It can also be used to reverse the order of sequential phases. Lead and lag phase partners must be in the same ring and barrier.

With non-standard rings and barriers, lag and lead may not be available.

Lead-lag phasing on the main street occurs when one coordinated phase leads and the other lags. For example, phases 1 and 6 lead, 2 and 5 lag.

Coding **C-Max** recall for a lagging through movement also also forces the lagging left-turn to recall to max. This feature is called lag phase hold.

Coding **C-Min** recall for a lagging through movement allows the lagging through and left-turn movement to gap out. This allows for more flexible lead-lag phasing.

Allow Lead/Lag Optimize?

One of the powerful features of Synchro is that it can optimize the order of phases. When optimizing offsets, Synchro will check all combinations of leading and lagging phasing so as to improve traffic flow. This is accomplished by looking at all combinations of the Lagging Phase setting discussed in the previous section.

If it is okay for the phase to be either leading or lagging, set this field to "on" by checking the box. If the phase must be lagging or must be leading, set this field to "off."

Some jurisdictions require all left turn phases to be leading. If this is the case, set this field to "off" for all left turn movements. This will keep the optimizer from changing these phases to lagging.

When using split or sequential phasing, set this field to "on." This will allow the optimizer to reverse the order of the phases to improve coordination. The exception to this rule is if the phase order is hardwired into your signal controller.

Some jurisdictions are hesitant to use lagging left turn phasing because cars can become "trapped" in the intersection. This phenomenon occurs when one approach allows permitted left turns and the oncoming approach has a lagging left turn signal.

Lagging left turns should not be used if oncoming traffic has any of the following types of left turn treatments:

- Permitted
- Leading Permitted + Protected
- Lagging Permitted + Protected with a different split for the left turn than the oncoming left turn.

However, lagging left turns can be used safely if oncoming traffic has any of the following types of left turn treatments:

- Protected leading

- Protected lagging (if the oncoming left split is less than or equal to this left's split)

- Prohibited (if, for example, this is a "T" intersection, or if a cross street is a one-way street such as freeway ramps.)

- Split Phasing

- Protected - permitted left-turn signals developed by the City of Dallas with louvered green indications

Sequential Phasing

Assign cross street phases to phase 3 and 4 to allow lead/lag optimization with split phasing. Alternatively, open the **Ring-and-Barrier-Designer** (see page 8-2) and change the phase sequence from 3-4-7-8 to 4-8. Lead/Lag optimization is performed on the first two phases in a ring-barrier sequence and on the last two phases in a ring-barrier sequence.

Recall Mode

Each phase can have a recall of None, Minimum, Maximum, Coordinated (maximum or minimum), or Ped.

No Recall: The phase can be skipped.

Minimum Recall: The phase will always service the Minimum Initial and will never skip.

Maximum Recall: The phase will always service the Maximum Split and will never skip.

Pedestrian Recall: The phase will always service a walk and ped clearance interval. The phase can not be skipped or gap out until the walk and "do not walk" intervals have passed.

Coordinated Maximum (C-Max): Used with coordinated signals only. This option is available for phases selected as the reference phase in the Offset settings. The phase services its maximum time, starting at its scheduled start time.

Coordinated Minimum (C-Min): Used with coordinated signals only. This option is available for phases selected as the reference phases in the Offset settings. The phase services its minimum time, starting at its scheduled start time. Coordinated movements must have detection. The Yield Point setting By Phase will not affect phases set with C-Min unless Lagging Phase is set.

For Fully-Actuated signals, the main street through phases will typically be set to Min recall and all other phases will be set to No recall.

For Semi-Actuated signals, the main street phases have maximum recall. Side streets have No recall.

For Actuated-Coordinated signals, the recall for main street phases (usually #2 and #6) is set to Coordinated recall (maximum or minimum). The main street phases will receive all unused time from the side streets, have no detection and always have maximum green. Side street phases usually have No recall.

To change the coordinated phases set the reference phase. To change the signal to Pretimed or non-coordinated, change the Control Type.

Splits and Phasing Diagram

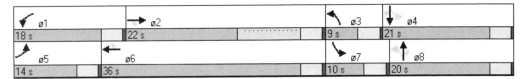

Figure 7-3   Splits and Phasing Diagram Example

The Splits and Phasing diagram is shown at the bottom of the **TIMING** settings. It is a graphical representation of the current splits and phasing and can be used to adjust the splits. To adjust the splits with the mouse, move the mouse to the right side of a yellow + all red band on the current Splits and Phasing diagram.

 The cursor will change into the shape shown here. Hold down the left mouse button and move the mouse right or left to adjust the split. When the button is released, all of the other colored bands that are affected will automatically adjust their splits, and any changed information will be shown on the numbers above.

Permitted movements are shown in gray and protected movements are shown in black. On **Figure 7-3**, the southbound left (phase 7) is first protected and then permitted with phase 4.

Next to the movement diagram is a phase number identified with the phase symbol (ø) and inside the green band is the split time in seconds. For **Figure 7-3**, the southbound left is ø7 and has a 10 s split.

Remember that the split time includes the Yellow Time plus All-Red Time.

Splits for phases within a ring are not required to add up. Synchro will extend a phase to make the rings equal. This extended split is shown in gray on the Splits and Phasing diagram. For **Figure 7-3**, ø2 has 22 s entered on the Total Split row, however, it has extended an additional 10 s to make the rings equal.

ø5 + ø6 = 14 s + 36 s = 50 s

ø1 + ø2 + ø2 extension = 18 s + 22 s + 10 s = 50 s.

Changing one of the values for one phase on the Total Split row will not affect the other phase(s). This however may extend the cycle length. Dragging on the diagram can be used to change a split but preserve the cycle length.

 Holding down the [CTRL] key can be used to swap the phase order. When the [CTRL] key is held down and the mouse cursor is moved over a swappable phase, the cursor changes to indicate the phases can be swapped. Clicking the mouse changes the phase sequence. Locked timing plans cannot be changed. Phases can be manually swapped even if marked 'No' for Allow Lead Lag Optimize.

Group Control (Multiple Intersection Control)

Synchro allows you to model multiple intersections with one controller (group control). This allows for the analysis of complex traffic situations such as a diamond freeway interchange or two closely spaced intersections. To set up a controller to operate with group control, see the **Cluster Editor** and the **Ring-and-Barrier-Designer**, page 8-5.

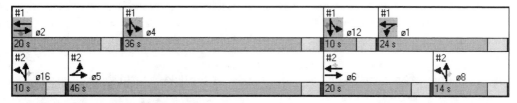

Figure 7-4   Group Control Example

On the Splits and Phasing diagram, each intersection has a color associated with it. In addition, the top number identifies the node number preceded by a # symbol. In **Figure 7-4**, the two intersections modeled are intersection #1 and intersection #2.

Clicking on the movement diagram within the Splits and Phasing diagram will jump to the intersection selected. For instance, if the **TIMING** settings for intersection #1 are active, holding the cursor over any of the movement diagrams for intersection #2 will change the cursor to a hand symbol 👆 . Clicking will now change the **TIMING** settings information to intersection #2.

Pedestrian and Hold Phases

The far right columns allow an entry of pedestrian only or phase hold. Set the PED phase to any phase dedicated solely for pedestrians(often called an exclusive ped phase). This is a phase where all vehicle movements are red and pedestrians can walk anywhere in the intersection. Set the phase number to blank to remove the pedestrian phase.

Sign Control

If Control Type (see page 4-4) is set to Unsig, this intersection becomes unsignalized and the signing settings replace the signal settings.

There are three Sign Control settings in the third row of the signing settings window.

1. Free: Traffic goes through the intersection without stopping.

2. Yield: Traffic has a yield sign and slows down, stopping only if necessary.

3. Stop: All traffic stops, and waits until all conflicting traffic is clear.

Synchro will model unsignalized intersections based on the methods of the Highway Capacity Manual, Chapter 17. When modeling platoons going through unsignalized intersections, traffic on a free approach goes through. Traffic at stop and yield approaches are spread out over the entire cycle.

Use Free at a freeway onramp, even if a yield sign exists in the field. A yield sign will cause vehicles to stay and wait for a gap in the traffic.

Median Width and TWLTL Median

This row appears in the **SIGNING** settings for unsignalized intersections. This field is the same as the **Median Width** in the **SIMULATION OPTIONS** settings (see page 9-4). Changes to this setting will immediately update on the **MAP** view.

The Median Width will be used for two-stage gap acceptance calculations in Synchro. If the Median Width on the main street is larger than the average vehicle length (set in the Network Settings), then two-stage calculations will be performed. The median is assumed to be a raised median unless the two-way left turn lane (**TWLTL**) option is checked.

The number of vehicles that can be stored in the median is equal to the Median Width divided by the Vehicle Length. For a TWLTL median, 2 vehicles can be stored in the median. No partial vehicles are assumed.

If a file created in a past version of Synchro is loaded into version 7, the median for the main street is based on the setting for the side street of the older version. Saving a version 7 file backwards will not set the unsignalized median parameters.

 The Median Width field is used for HCM unsignalized analysis to perform unsignalized analysis with two-stage gap acceptance. SimTraffic will increase the median width visually; however, SimTraffic is not able to model two-stage gap acceptance.

Right Turn Channelized

This row appears in the **SIGNING** settings for unsignalized intersections.

This field is active for the rightmost movement. Enter Yield or Free if this movement has a triangular island and yields or merges with oncoming left turn traffic. One or more right turns must be selected.

For two-way unsignalized analysis, the channelized right turn traffic will not be considered in other movements conflicting volume following the rules for unsignalized analysis.

For all-way stop intersections and roundabouts, the traffic in channelized right turns will not be considered in the analysis. Channelized right turns are not counted in the two lanes per leg per approach limit. This extension is not part of the HCM analysis. To be fully HCM compatible, do not code channelized right turns for all-way stops or roundabouts.

Critical Gap

This row appears in the **SIGNING** settings for unsignalized intersections.

The **Critical Gap**, tC , is defined as the minimum length of time interval in the major street traffic stream that allows intersection entry for one minor street vehicle. The critical gap is defined in Chapter 17 of the year 2000 HCM. The value in Synchro is the value that is defined by equation 17-1 from the HCM. This value is adjusted for heavy vehicles, grades, and geometry.

For two-stage gaps, this is the combined single stage tC. When using two-stage, each stage is 1 second less.

This value can be over-ridden.

Follow Up Time

This row appears in the **SIGNING** settings for unsignalized intersections.

The **Follow Up Time** is the time span between the departure of one vehicle from the minor street and the departure of the next vehicle using the same major street gap, under a condition of continuous queuing on the minor street. The follow up time is defined in Chapter 17 of the year 2000 HCM. The value in Synchro is the value defined by equation 17-2 after adjusting for heavy vehicles.

This value can be over-ridden.

Roundabout Settings

To select a roundabout, set the Control Type (see page 4-4) to Roundabout.

 Synchro provides limited modeling of roundabouts following the HCM 2000 procedures. The only measure of effectiveness is a range of volume to capacity ratios. SimTraffic will model a roundabout based on the settings below. These values are ignored by Synchro.

Roundabout Radius

Inside Radius and **Outside Radius** control the size of the roundabout. 900 feet is the maximum. These settings appear in the **NODE** settings when the Control Type is set to

Roundabout. The maximum radius value is 900 feet. The radius settings are only used by SimTraffic to construct the geometry of the roundabout.

Roundabout Lanes

Roundabout Lanes (#) also appear in the **NODE** settings. This value controls the number of interior lanes within the traffic circle (maximum of 4 lanes). This setting is only used by SimTraffic.

Circle Speed

Circle Speed also appears in the **NODE** settings and controls the speed of vehicles within the roundabout. This setting is only used by SimTraffic.

Two Lane Exit

Two Lane Exit appears in the **SIGNING** settings selected with the "Stop Sign" button. Two Lane Exit controls how many of the interior lanes exit the next downstream departure leg. Your Add Lanes setting should be set to 1 or greater to create at least 2 lanes on the departure leg for the Two Lane Exit feature. This information is only used by SimTraffic. See the sub-topic on **Roundabout Analysis** on page 21-9) for additional details.

If you have a roundabout with a slip ramp, see the topic **Slip Lanes for Roundabouts** (page 5-7).

Measures of Effectiveness

Actuated Effective Green

This value represents the average green time observed while the signal is operating in actuated mode. This value may be less than maximum green time if the phase is skipped or gapped out. The effective green may be higher than maximum green during coordination depending on the Inhibit Max setting and Yield method selected. Effective green for left-turns is also dependent on whether the left-turn is protected, permitted, or both (pm+pt).

The actuated green time is an average of the five percentile green times, subject to the following rules. The actuated effective green time includes yellow plus all-red timewith the total lost time subtracted. The calculation rules for the HCM Report and Control Delay as shown in the **TIMING** settings are slightly different.

$$g' = \sum \left[\frac{gi + YAR}{Ci} \right] * \frac{\sum Ci}{25} - tL \text{ , (Percentile)}$$

g' = Actuated Effective Green Time (s)

(use 0 instead of gi + YAR for skipped scenarios)

$$g' = \sum \left[\frac{gi}{Ci} \right] * \frac{\sum Ci}{25} + YAR - tL \text{ , (Webster)}$$

(g' is zero if less than 0.1 second)

gi = Percentile Green Time

Ci = Percentile Cycle Length

YAR = Yellow + All-Red time (s)

tL = Total Lost Time (s)

Control Delay Notes:

When calculating Ci, dwell time is subtracted from the cycle length for non-recall phases.

gi is equal to the minimum green time for skipped phases.

The sum of actuated splits may exceed the actuated cycle length. Skipped phases are given the minimum initial green time, but other phases will not have this time added to their cycle or deducted from their green time.

Dwelled time is added to the green time of recall phases but not added to the red time or cycle length of non-recall phases.

HCM Report Notes:

The HCM Report calculation differs slightly from the Synchro calculation. The HCM method requires all lost time from other phases to be included in the red time and cycle length. The percentile method discounts part of the lost time for other phases if they sometimes skip.

The green time for coordinated phases is calculated by subtracting actuated splits from non-coordinated splits. The main effect is that yellow time for skipped phases is still subtracted from the split of the coordinated phases.

The sum of HCM actuated phases will always equal the actuated cycle length.

Actuated Green to Cycle Ratio

This is the average actuated green time divided by the actuated cycle length. See **Actuated Effective Green Time** (page 7-21) for notes on actuated green time calculation.

Calculation

$$g/C = \frac{\sum(gi/Ci)}{5}$$

g = Effective Green Time (split minus total lost time)

C = Cycle Length

gi = Percentile Green Time

Ci = Percentile Scenario Cycle Length

HCM Report Calculation

g'/C = g' / C'

g'/C = Actuated Effective Green to Cycle Ratio

C' = Σ (g' + YAR) = Actuated Cycle Length, equals sum of effective green times

g' = Actuated Effective Green Time (split less total lost time)

Ci = Percentile Scenario Cycle Length

For the HCM calculation, C' will always be the sum of the effective splits (taking into account ring and barrier rules). With the Synchro calculation $\Sigma(Ci)/5$ may be less than the sum of the actuated splits. This is because total lost time is not counted for skipped phases when evaluating other phases.

Volume to Capacity Ratio

Timing Settings

The **Volume to Capacity Ratio** (v/c Ratio) uses actuated green times and cycle lengths. The v/c ratio indicates the amount of congestion for each lane group. Any v/c Ratio greater than or equal to 1 indicates that the approach is operating at above capacity. This number is calculated by the formula:

$$X = \frac{v}{s * g / C}$$

    X = Volume to Capacity Ratio

    v = Adjusted Lane Group Volume (see **VOLUME** settings on page 6-1)

    s = Saturated Flow Rate (see **LANE** settings on page 3-1)

    g = Effective Green Time (split minus total lost time)

    C = Cycle Length

If there are separate lane groups for right or left turn traffic, the v/c Ratios for these lane groups are also shown. There is a separate lane group for left traffic, if there are left turn lanes *and* the left turn type is *not* Split. There is a separate lane group for right traffic, if there are right turn lanes. Shared lanes are in the through lane group.

For permitted plus protected movements, each Saturated Flow Rate is multiplied by its respective actuated effective green time and added together.

Defacto Turning Lanes

A dl or dr in the v/c ratio field indicates a Defacto left or right turning lane. If there are two or more through lanes and a heavy turning movement, it is possible to have a defacto turning lane.

Synchro will flag a defacto turning lane if the turning movement using a single lane would have a v/c ratio greater than the group as a whole and its v/c ratio is 0.85 or more.

Defacto lanes should be taken seriously. It is possible that the v/c ratio for the entire group is acceptable, while the turning lane is not acceptable.

To correct a defacto turning lane, change the coding of a through lane into a turning lane. A defacto left or right turn lane usually indicates the need for an additional exclusive turning lane.

Signing Settings

For unsignalized intersections, the volume to capacity ratio is reported for each movement. Unlike signals, the v/c ratio is the maximum for the movement, not the lane group. See the **HCM Unsignalized report** (page 15-19) for more details about the capacity and delays by lane.

For roundabouts, the high capacity v/c ratio is shown for the approach. This is the high capacity range of possible v/c ratios for the method. To see the low capacity ratios, see the **HCM Unsignalized report**.

Control Delay

Timing Settings

See the discussion of **Delay Calculations** (page 13-26) for a complete description of the calculations.

Delays in Synchro are Signal Delay, also called **Control Delay**. These delays are equivalent to the Stopped Delay times a constant of 1.3.

In Synchro, control delays are used for analyzing the effects of coordination, actuation, and congestion. Control delay is the component of delay caused by the downstream control device and does not include Queue Delay.

Signing Settings

For unsignalized intersections, the delay is shown for the movement. Unlike signals, the delay is for the movement, not the lane group. A value of 9999 indicates no capacity is available. See the **HCM Unsignalized report** (15-19) for more details about the capacity and delays by lane.

 For roundabouts, the method does not define a delay, so none is shown.

Queue Delay

Timing Settings

Queue Delay is an analysis of the effects of queues and blocking on short links and short turning bays. This delay includes the analysis of spillback, starvation, and storage blocking. Additional details on queue delay and queue interactions can be found in the topic **Queue Interactions** (page 13-55).

Signing Settings

The unsignalized intersection delay is strictly based on the methods in Chapter 17 of the HCM, which does not include a term for queue delay. Therefore, Queue Delay is not included in the **SIGNING** settings.

Total Delay

Timing Settings

Total Delay is the lane group Control Delay plus the Queue Delay. Additional details on total delay, queue delay and queue interactions can be found in the topic **Queue Interactions** (page 13-55).

Signing Settings

The unsignalized intersection delay is strictly based on the methods in Chapter 17 of the HCM which does not include a term for queue delay. Therefore, Total Delay is not included in the **SIGNING** settings, only Control Delay.

Level of Service

Timing Settings

The **Level of Service** (LOS) for the lane group is calculated by taking the signalized Intersection Delay and converting it to a letter, between A and F, based on the length of the delay. Refer to **Table 4-1** on page 4-10.

The Level of Service is based on the Synchro Control Delay.

Signing Settings

This is based on the movement control delay for an unsignalized intersection. This is based on **Table 4-2** located on page 4-10.

Approach Delay

Timing Settings

This is the delay for the entire approach. The **Approach Delay** is a volume weighted average of the Total Delays for each lane group.

Signing Settings

For unsignalized intersections, the delay is shown for the approach. Unlike signals, the delay is for the movement, not lane group. A value of 9999 indicates no capacity is available. See the **HCM Unsignalized report** for more details about the capacity and delays by lane.

For roundabouts, the method does not define a delay, so none is shown.

The Approach Delay and LOS for main street approaches are not shown because they are not defined for main street approaches. The analyst needs to examine the left turn LOS and delay to rank the vehicles.

Approach Level of Service

Timing Settings

This is the **Approach LOS** based on the Total Delay.

Signing Settings

Based on the approach Control Delay.

Queue Lengths

Timing Settings

The Queue Length rows show the 50th percentile and 95th percentile maximum queue lengths. The 50th percentile maximum queue is the maximum back of queue on a typical cycle and the 95th percentile queue is the maximum back of queue with 95th percentile traffic volumes (also see **Queue Length Calculation**, page 13-71).

 The queue length reported is the one for the lane with the highest queue (feet or meters) in the lane group. The total queue length is divided by the number of lanes and the lane utilization factor.

In many cases, the 95th percentile queue will not be experienced due to upstream metering. If the upstream intersection is at or near capacity, the 50th percentile queue represents the maximum queue experienced.

Similarly, if the upstream intersection has a v/c ratio over 0.8; the maximum queue is approximately equal to the 50th percentile queue divided by the upstream v/c ratio. For example, if the 50th percentile queue is 150ft, and the v/c ratio upstream is 0.90; the maximum possible queue would therefore be 150 / 0.90 = 167ft.

 Due to upstream metering, the 95th queue may be less than the 50th queue. If the upstream intersection is operating with v/c>1, the metered arrival rate will be *less* than the volume for this intersection. Since metering is only performed with the 95th queue, this causes the 95th queue to be less than the 50th queue. This situation may indicate a coding problem. Be sure that the Midblock traffic is coded correctly and that the signal timing and volumes for both intersections are set correctly. This reduced 95th queue does represent a valid queue because vehicles will not be able to clear the upstream intersection to queue at this intersection.

The ~ and # footnote indicate that the volume modeled exceeds capacity. The ~ footnote indicates that the approach is above capacity and the queue length could be much longer. The queue length is theoretically infinite and blocking problems may occur. The value shown for the 50th percentile queue is sufficient to hold one cycle of traffic. This will prevent capacity problems from being compounded by insufficient storage space.

The # footnote indicates that the volume for the 95th percentile cycle exceeds capacity. This traffic was simulated for two complete cycles of 95th percentile traffic to account for the effects of spillover between cycles. If the reported v/c <1 for this movement, the methods used represent a valid method for estimating the 95th percentile queue. In practice, 95th percentile queue shown will rarely be exceeded and the queues shown with the # footnote are acceptable for the design of storage bays.

When the Analysis Period is set to greater than or equal to 30 minutes, the PHFx will be set to 1.0. See the Queue Length Calculation on page 13-72.

The m footnote indicates that volume for the 95th percentile queue is metered by an upstream signal.

Signing Settings

For two-way stops, the 95th percentile queue is shown. The queue is the highest for any lane in the lane group.

A value of 9999 indicates no capacity is available. See the **HCM Unsignalized report** for more details about the capacity and delays by lane.

For circles and all-way stops, the method does not define a queue, so none is shown.

Stops

Stops are calculated with the methods shown in the topic on **Stop Calculations**, page 13-76. Stops are the number of stops per hour.

Fuel Used

The Fuel Consumed is calculated using the methods outlined in the topic on **Fuel and Emissions Calculation**, page 13-77. The fuel is based on the delays, stops, speed, distance traveled, and travel time.

Warning Indicators

The lower right cells (below the Splits and Phasing diagram) of the **TIMING** and **PHASING** settings indicate potential intersection coding errors or timing problems when red.

Timing Settings

Green indicates no errors.

Conflict indicates a phase or coincident phase(s) serve conflicting movements. Look at the Protected Phasing row for red phase numbers. No conflict checking is performed on permitted phases.

v/c > 1 indicates that Volume exceeds capacity for one or more movements. It may also indicate volume was coded without lanes or green time. Look at the v/c row for values greater than 1 or for "No Cap" errors. For congested intersections, a v/c >1 error may be unavoidable.

Min Err indicates that one or more splits violate minimum timing requirements. Look at the Total Split row for values in red. Also, compare the Maximum Split in the **PHASING** settings to the Minimum split. A Min Err may also occur if timings are too short for pedestrian timings.

Signing Settings

Invalid Sign Control for Unsignalized Analysis: Oncoming approaches must both be free or both be signed. The intersection is limited to two free approaches.

Too Many Legs for Unsignalized Analysis: The unsignalized analysis is limited to four leg intersections. It is also possible to get this message if too many legs are on one side of the intersection.

Too Many Lanes for Unsignalized Analysis: Two-way intersections are limited to four lanes per approach. All-way intersections are limited to two lanes per leg; however, channelized right lanes do not count towards this total.

How to Code an Overlap

An overlap signal indication services a movement during two or more phases of the signal cycle. The phases typically follow each other in sequence so the last phase serviced provides the clearance intervals for the overlap. A common application of the use of overlaps is at a diamond interchange using one controller for both ramps. **Figure 7-5** shows the phase assignments for a typical diamond interchange with overlaps.

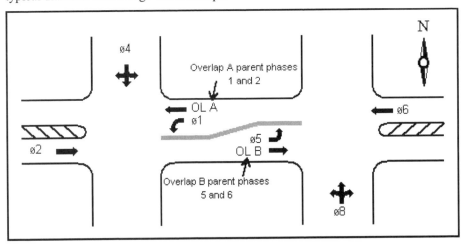

Figure 7-5   Use of Overlaps at a Diamond Interchange

In this illustration, overlap A operates with its parent phases 1 and 2 and overlap B operates with its parent phases 5 and 6.

To code this with Synchro, you do not need to define a new phase number for overlap A and B in the Ring-and-Barrier-Designer. To code this, simply enter 1 and 2, separated with a space, in the Protected Phases row for the WBT movement for the left side intersection. Next, enter a 5 and 6, separated with a space, in the Protected Phases row for the EBT movement for the right side intersection. See **Figure 7-6**.

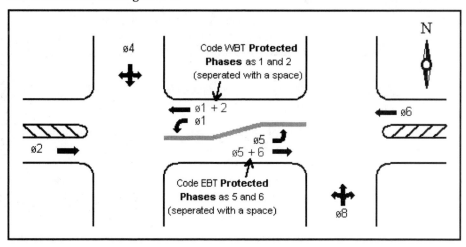

Figure 7-6   Coding Overlaps in Synchro

 If a movement is served by two consecutive phases, the clearance intervals (Y+AR) between the phases are not shown and the signal stays green. Synchro automatically takes this into account when calculating effective green times, g/C ratios, and v/c ratios.

The listed phases will become the Detector Phases. The phase listed first will be used for split optimization.

Pay careful attention to Detector Phases. They are key to controlling split optimization, as well as skipping and gapping behavior with the actuated green times and in SimTraffic.

Normally the first phase in the sequence should be the first Detector Phase listed. With a leading left 1, phase 1 is entered first (1, 2), with a lagging left 1, phase 2 is entered first (2, 1).

Timing Settings Quick Start

There is a lot of information that can be entered into the **TIMING** settings that can be intimidating for new users. The purpose of this section is to give the basic steps that are required to quickly get your data entered into the **TIMING** settings. For a basic intersection, the steps would be as follows:

1. Enter your **LANE** and **VOLUME** settings data for your intersection (refer to Chapter 4 and Chapter 6).

2. Choose the appropriate **Phase Template** (refer to page 7-2) to match your numbering convention. This step is necessary so Synchro can use the appropriate template when setting up Turn Types and phase numbers. To set phases for an east west arterial (the template shown on the left in Figure 7-7), choose **Options→Phase Templates→ Intersection to East-West**. Select **Options→Phase Templates→Intersection to North-South** to use the template on the right in Figure 7-7.

    This step is not necessary if you want to use the Synchro default template (North/South template) or if you are coding an unsignalized intersection.

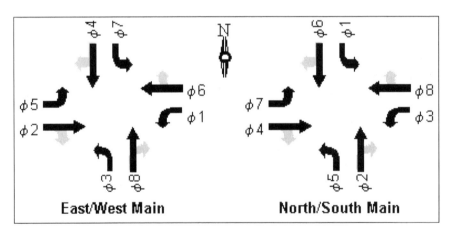

Figure 7-7   Phase Template

3. Choose your Control Type. For signalized intersections, this can be set to a pretimed, semi-actuated uncoordinated, actuated-uncoordinated or actuated-coordinated. For

unsignalized intersections, this can be set to an unsignalized (stop or yield controlled) or roundabout intersection.

4. Select the appropriate Turn Type for your left and right turns. This is the step where you will define how your turning movements are phased (protected, permitted, free, etc.). If you have defined the phase template in step 3, Synchro will automatically assign phase numbers for your turn treatments based on the diagram shown in Figure 7-7.

   If this is an unsignalized intersection, you would select the appropriate sign control (stop, free or yield).

5. Enter the appropriate Cycle Length. If you are not performing an existing conditions intersection analysis, you can determine the cycle length by performing an intersection cycle length optimization or a network cycle length optimization.

6. Enter the **PHASING** settings (see the next chapter).

6. Adjust the phase splits with the Splits and Phasing diagram using your mouse. Move your mouse cursor to the end of the phase split and it will change to the shape shown here (horizontal resize button). Hold down the left mouse button and move the mouse right or left to adjust the split.

Chapter 8 – Phasing Settings

From the **MAP** view, click on the desired intersection with the Right mouse button and select Phasing Settings.

 From anywhere in the program, press **[F8]** and select the desired intersection from the list. Then push the *Phasing Settings* button or the **[F6]** key.

The **PHASING** settings, **Figure 8-1**, are displayed with information about the phase settings. See Chapter 3 for details on navigating the data entry screens.

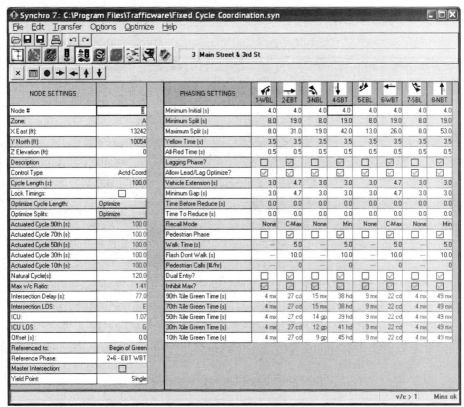

NODE SETTINGS		PHASING SETTINGS	1-WBL	2-EBT	3-NBL	4-SBT	5-EBL	6-WBT	7-SBL	8-NBT
Node #:	3	Minimum Initial (s)	4.0	4.0	4.0	4.0	4.0	4.0	4.0	4.0
Zone:	A	Minimum Split (s)	8.0	19.0	8.0	19.0	8.0	19.0	8.0	19.0
X East (ft):	13242	Maximum Split (s)	8.0	31.0	19.0	42.0	13.0	26.0	8.0	53.0
Y North (ft):	10054	Yellow Time (s)	3.5	3.5	3.5	3.5	3.5	3.5	3.5	3.5
Z Elevation (ft):	0	All-Red Time (s)	0.5	0.5	0.5	0.5	0.5	0.5	0.5	0.5
Description		Lagging Phase?	☐	☑	☐	☑	☐	☑	☐	☑
Control Type	Actd-Coord	Allow Lead/Lag Optimize?	☑	☑	☑	☑	☑	☑	☑	☑
Cycle Length (s):	100.0	Vehicle Extension (s)	3.0	4.7	3.0	3.0	3.0	4.7	3.0	3.0
Lock Timings:	☐	Minimum Gap (s)	3.0	4.7	3.0	3.0	3.0	4.7	3.0	3.0
Optimize Cycle Length:	Optimize	Time Before Reduce (s)	0.0	0.0	0.0	0.0	0.0	0.0	0.0	0.0
Optimize Splits:	Optimize	Time To Reduce (s)	0.0	0.0	0.0	0.0	0.0	0.0	0.0	0.0
Actuated Cycle 90th (s):	100.0	Recall Mode	None	C-Max	None	Min	None	C-Max	None	Min
Actuated Cycle 70th (s):	100.0	Pedestrian Phase	☐	☑	☐	☑	☐	☑	☐	☑
Actuated Cycle 50th (s):	100.0	Walk Time (s)	—	5.0	—	5.0	—	5.0	—	5.0
Actuated Cycle 30th (s):	100.0	Flash Dont Walk (s)	—	10.0	—	10.0	—	10.0	—	10.0
Actuated Cycle 10th (s):	100.0	Pedestrian Calls (#/hr)	—	0	—	0	—	0	—	0
Natural Cycle(s):	120.0	Dual Entry?	☐	☑	☐	☑	☐	☑	☐	☑
Max v/c Ratio:	1.41	Inhibit Max?	☑	☑	☑	☑	☑	☑	☑	☑
Intersection Delay (s):	77.0	90th %ile Green Time (s)	4 mx	27 cd	15 mx	38 hd	9 mx	22 cd	4 mx	49 mx
Intersection LOS:	E	70th %ile Green Time (s)	4 mx	27 cd	15 mx	38 hd	9 mx	22 cd	4 mx	49 mx
ICU:	1.07	50th %ile Green Time (s)	4 mx	27 cd	14 gp	39 hd	9 mx	22 cd	4 mx	49 mx
ICU LOS:	G	30th %ile Green Time (s)	4 mx	27 cd	12 gp	41 hd	9 mx	22 cd	4 mx	49 mx
Offset (s) :	0.0	10th %ile Green Time (s)	4 mx	27 cd	9 gp	45 hd	9 mx	22 cd	4 mx	49 mx
Referenced to:	Begin of Green									
Reference Phase:	2+6 - EBT WBT									
Master Intersection:	☐									
Yield Point:	Single									

Figure 8-1   PHASING Settings

Layout

The left side of the **PHASING** settings will display the **NODE** settings. The rows will be displayed in yellow. Here you can update data such as the node number, zone name, intersection coordinates, description notes and signal timing data. See Chapter 4 for full details on the **NODE** settings.

On the right side are blue shaded rows and columns. There is a column for every phase that has been set in the **TIMING** settings. Details on the data entry items are found in subsequent sections of this chapter.

Percentile Scenarios

The key to modeling actuated signals is to model traffic conditions using multiple traffic scenarios. Synchro uses the Percentile Delay Method for determining delays and green times.

There are five scenarios modeled; they are called the 90th, 70th, 50th, 30th, and 10th percentiles. Traffic volumes for each approach are adjusted up or down to model these percentile scenarios. By adjusting the traffic volumes for different scenarios, the actuated signals can be modeled under a range of traffic conditions.

If traffic is observed for 100 cycles, the 90th percentile would be the 90th busiest, the 10th percentile would be the 10th busiest, and the 50th percentile would represent average traffic.

The percentile scenarios are likely to occur during the hour for which volume data is provided. These scenarios are not intended to represent traffic conditions for other times. To model the signals under other traffic conditions, reanalyze the signals with appropriate traffic volume counts.

Ring and Barrier Designer

The **Ring and Barrier Designer** allows up to 32 phases to be entered in one of 64 fields. This allows for the modeling of complex phasing strategies. Phase numbers are entered into the appropriate barrier, ring and position (BRP) fields in the four rings and four barriers.

When to use the Ring and Barrier Designer:

- Group Control (Multiple intersections on one controller)
- 5 or more legs
- Two intersections on one controller

- Single ring controller, more than 4 phases

- Diamond interchange

- More than 9 phases

Not needed for:

- Split phasing

- Lagging phases

- Standard 8 phase controller

- Single ring controller up to 4 phases

- 8 phase controller + 9

- Many two intersection configurations

To activate, use the menu command **Options→Ring and Barrier Designer**.

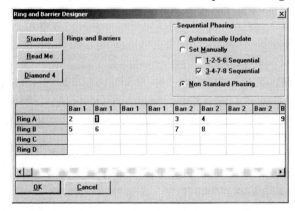

Figure 8-2   RING AND BARRIER DESIGNER

The [Diamond 4] button is used to set the phases for use with a Leading-Alternating diamond interchange. The [Read Me] button will bring up the Help file.

Figure 8-3 displays the default phase assignments within the Ring and Barrier Designer. The values in the table can be modified to meet your particular needs. To revert to the default phasing layout, select the [Standard] button.

	Barrier 1				Barrier 2				Barrier 3				Barrier 4			
Ring 1	Phase 1	Phase 2			Phase 3	Phase 4			Phase 9	Phase 10			Phase 11	Phase 12		
Ring 2	Phase 5	Phase 6			Phase 7	Phase 8			Phase 13	Phase 14			Phase 15	Phase 16		
Ring 3																
Ring 4																

Figure 8-3   Default Phase Assignments in Ring and Barrier Designer

 With group control, it is recommended that each intersection use phases in one ring only. All phases for a node should be in a single ring or possibly two. Normally each ring should contain phases from one node only (see the **Figure 8-4** below).

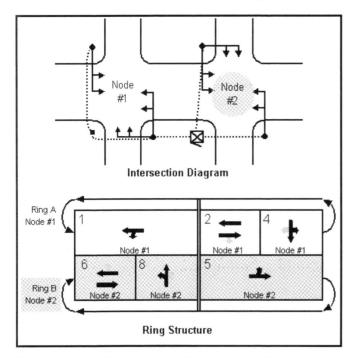

Figure 8-4   Intersection Diagram with Ring Structure

Cluster Editor

The **Cluster Editor** allows multiple intersections to share one controller (Group Control). This is used in conjunction with the Ring and Barrier Designer.

To activate, use the menu command **Options→Cluster Editor**.

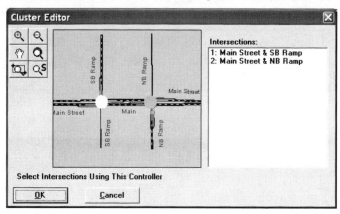

Figure 8-5   CLUSTER EDITOR

Click on an intersection in the Cluster Editor to add or remove intersections from the group (intersection shown on the right).

Each intersection has a color associated with it in the Splits and Phasing diagram. The color can be changed by right clicking on the map.

Group Control

Possible Applications

- Diamond Interchange

- Diamond Interchange with frontage road(s)

- Two or more closely spaced intersections

- Arterial with wide median modeled as two nodes

Use the Cluster Editor to assign group control.

Each intersection has a color associated with it in the Splits and Phasing diagrams.

The controller number used for data exchange is the smallest node number in the cluster. In **Figure 8-5**, the node number 19 is used to identify the two intersection group for data exchange.

The controller number should match the hardware controller number used by Advanced Traffic Management Systems (ATMS).

With group control, it is recommended that each intersection use phases in one ring only. All phases for a node should be in a single ring or possibly two. Normally each ring should contain phases from one node only (see **Figure 8-4**).

Minimum Initial

The **Minimum Initial** is the minimum green time for a phase. This is the shortest time that the phase can show green. A typical value would be 4 seconds. The minimum value allowed in Synchro is 1 second and the maximum value is 840 seconds. The large range will allow for the modeling of unusual timing plans.

This value is also called minimum green by some controllers.

Synchro does not support added initial or maximum initial.

Do not confuse this field with the Minimum Split setting in the **TIMING** settings. Minimum Initial is used in determining actuated behavior; Minimum Split is used to optimize splits.

Minimum Split

The **Minimum Split** is the shortest amount of time allowed for this phase.

The Minimum Split must at least be long enough to accommodate the Minimum Initial interval plus the Yellow and All-Red Time. This will usually be 8 seconds or more. The minimum allowed in Synchro is 3 seconds and the maximum is 840 seconds. When Synchro automatically assigns splits, it will make sure all splits are greater than or equal to their Minimum Splits. (This assumes the cycle length is long enough to accommodate all splits.) See the section on **Optimize-Intersection Splits** for information about how splits are calculated.

For additional details, see the topic on **Minimum Split** in the **TIMING** settings, page 7-9.

Maximum Split

The **Maximum Split** is the current split time, given in seconds. It is the longest amount of split time for actuated movements.

It is the amount of green, yellow, and all-red time assigned for each phase. The splits for the intersection can be calculated automatically by selecting the **Optimize→Intersection-Splits**, command from the menu. The minimum value allowed is 3 seconds and the maximum value is 840 seconds. The large range will allow for the modeling of unusual timing plans.

To adjust a split, type its new value in seconds. This phase will increase or decrease its time and the following phase will decrease or increase by the same amount. The amount a phase can be adjusted is limited by the green time of the following phase(s) and the green time of this phase and any concurrent phase.

For additional details, see the topic on **Total Split** in the **TIMING** settings, page 7-11.

Yellow Time

Yellow Time is the amount of time for the yellow interval. Normally, this value should be set to between 3 and 5 seconds, depending on the approach speed, the cross street width, and local standards. The minimum value allowed by Synchro is 2 seconds and the maximum is 10 seconds.

To set a default for newly created intersections or change all of the Yellow Times, use the **Options→Network-Settings** command.

All-Red Time

All-Red Time is the amount of time for the all red interval that follows the yellow interval. The all red time should be of sufficient duration to permit the intersection to clear before cross traffic is released.

CORSIM (pretimed only) does not allow fractional seconds. If you plan to use this data with this model, make sure Yellow plus All-Red equals a whole number in seconds.

To set a default for newly created intersections or change all of the All-Red Times, use the **Options→Network-Settings** command.

The minimum value allowed is 0 seconds and the maximum is 120 seconds. A large range is used to allow the modeling of unusual timing plans, such as the example for Two Way Traffic Control.

Lagging Phase?

The first two phases within a ring-barrier sequence are considered phase partners. The 3rd and 4th phases within a ring-barrier sequence, if used, are also phase partners. **Phase Lagging** is used to swap the order of phase partners. Normally phase partners are 1 and 2, 3 and 4, 5 and 6, 7 and 8.

For additional details, see the topic on **Lagging Phase** in the **TIMING** settings, page 7-12.

Allow Lead/Lag Optimize?

One of the powerful features of Synchro is that it can optimize the order of Phases. If it is okay for this phase to be either leading or lagging, set this field to "Yes". If this phase must be lagging or must be leading, set this field to "Fixed".

When optimizing Offsets, Synchro will check all combinations of leading and lagging phasing to improve traffic flow. This is done by changing the lagging parameter discussed in the previous section.

For additional details, see the topic on **Allow Lead/Lag Optimize** in the **TIMING** settings, page 7-14.

Vehicle Extension

This is the also the maximum gap. When a vehicle crosses a detector, it will extend the green time by the **Vehicle Extension** time.

 Vehicle Extension must be as long as the travel time from the trailing detector to the stop bar.

Minimum Gap

This is the **Minimum Gap** time that the controller will use with volume-density operation. If volume-density operation is not used, set this value to the same as the Vehicle Extension.

Minimum Gap should be as long as the travel time from the trailing detector to the stop bar.

Time Before Reduce

When using volume-density operation, this is the amount of time before gap reduction begins.

Time To Reduce

When using volume-density operation, this is the amount of time to reduce the gap from Vehicle Extension (or maximum gap) to Minimum Gap.

Recall Mode

Each phase can have a recall of None, Minimum, Maximum, Coordinated (maximum or minimum), or Ped.

No Recall: The phase can be skipped.

Minimum Recall: The phase will always come on to its minimum, the phase cannot be skipped.

Maximum Recall: The phase will always show its maximum and has no detection. The phase cannot skip or gap out, nor can it be extended.

Pedestrian Recall: The phase will always show a walk phase. The phase cannot be skipped or gap out until the walk and do not walk intervals have passed.

Coordinated Maximum (C-Max): Used with coordinated signals only. This option is available for phases selected as the reference phase in the Offset settings. Phase shows for its maximum time starting at its scheduled start time.

Coordinated Minimum (C-Min): Used with coordinated signals only. This option is available for phases selected as the reference phase in the Offset settings. Phase shows for its minimum time starting at its scheduled start time. Coordinated movements must have detectors. No affect with By Phase yield points except with lead-lag phasing.

For Fully-Actuated signals, all phases will have No recall or Minimum recall.

For Semi-Actuated signals, the main street phases have Maximum recall. Side streets have No recall.

For Actuated-Coordinated signals, the recall for main street phases (usually #2 and #6) is set to Coordinated recall (maximum or minimum). The main street phases will receive all unused time from the side streets, have no detection and always have maximum green. Side street phases usually have No recall.

To change the coordinated phases set the Reference Phase (refer to page 4-13). To change the signal to pretimed or non-coordinated, change the Control Type (refer to page 4-4).

Pedestrian Phase

Set this field to yes (check the box) if there is a pedestrian phase for this movement.

Setting **Pedestrian Phase** to no (unchecked box) will disable the pedestrian phase and the input fields for walk, do not walk, and pedestrian calls.

Walk Time

This is the amount of time for a pedestrian walk phase.

Pedestrian phases only come on when the phase has pedestrian calls, or if the phase has pedestrian recall.

This value can be ignored if the phase is in maximum recall and the split is long enough to accommodate pedestrians.

Flashing Don't Walk Time

This is the amount of time for a pedestrian **Flash Don't Walk** phase.

This value can be ignored if the phase is in maximum recall and the split is long enough to accommodate pedestrians.

When checking and optimizing splits, Synchro requires that the green time be greater or equal to the walk plus flashing don't walk times. The clearance time is NOT part of the flashing don't walk interval.

Some agencies may allow using the yellow interval as part of the pedestrian clearance time. If this is the case, subtract the yellow time from the required pedestrian clearance time for use with the Flash Don't Walk field. For example, the required pedestrian clearance time is 15 s and the yellow time is 4 s. If the yellow time can be used for pedestrian clearance, the required flashing don't walk is then 11 s. This can give shorter side street phases and more efficient operation.

Pedestrian Calls

This is the number of pedestrian push button calls for this phase. This value is only needed if this phase has a pedestrian push button.

Do not confuse this field with the Conflicting Pedestrians setting in the **VOLUME** settings. Conflicting Pedestrians is the number of pedestrians that right turning traffic must yield to. **Pedestrian Calls** are the number of pedestrians activating this phase. Normally the two values will be the same.

When counting pedestrians, people traveling in groups can be counted as a single pedestrian call. This value is used to determine how many cycles per hour will need to have a pedestrian phase.

Collecting data about the numbers of pedestrians can be quite time consuming. The following paragraphs give some guidance on when pedestrian numbers can be estimated.

If you know there are 100 or more pedestrian calls per hour, the walk phase will almost always be called and exact pedestrian counts are not needed. Set the pedestrian calls setting to 100.

If there are between 1 and 15 pedestrians per hour, the walk phase may only be called for the 90th percentile. If you know there are some pedestrians, but less than 15 per hour, enter 5 in place of better data. If there are less than 10 pedestrians per day, set pedestrian calls to 0.

If the phase has pedestrian recall, this field can be ignored.

Dual Entry

Dual Entry can be set to "On" or "Off" for the given phase.

Select "On" (check) to have this phase appear when a phase is showing in another ring and no calls or recalls are present within this ring and barrier.

Normally, even phases are set to "On" and odd phases are set to "Off." Recall has priority over dual entry. Below are examples for a typical eight-phase, dual ring controller.

Examples:

Phases	1	2
Dual Entry	No	Yes
Recall	None	None

If there are no calls on phases 1 or 2, phase 2 will show when phases 5 or 6 are showing.

Phases	1	2
Dual Entry	No	Yes
Recall	Min	None

If there are no calls on phases 1 or 2, phase 1 will show when phases 5 or 6 are showing.

Phases	1	2
Dual Entry	No	No
Recall	None	None

If there are no calls on phases 1 or 2, no phase from this ring will show when phases 5 or 6 are showing.

Inhibit Max

Used for Actuated-Coordinated signals only. When "On" (check the box), a non coordinated phase can show more than its maximum time when it starts early.

In **Figure 8-6**, phase 4 can start early due to phase 3 being skipped. With **Inhibit Max** set to "On," phase 4 can use all of phase 3's unused time. Otherwise this time would revert to the main street phases

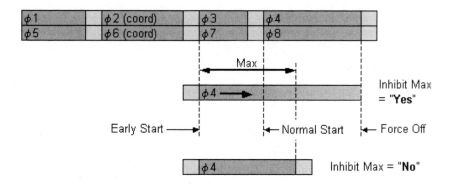

Figure 8-6   Example of Inhibit Max

Set Inhibit Max to "On" to give more time to side streets, set Inhibit Max to "Off" to give all extra time back to the main street.

The amount of time available for side street phases and their starts can also be manipulated by the Yield Point and using Actuation for the Coordinated phases.

Percentile Green Times

There are five scenarios modeled. They are called the 90th, 70th, 50th, 30th, and 10th percentiles. Traffic volumes for each approach are adjusted up or down to model these percentile scenarios. By adjusting the traffic for different scenarios, the actuated signals can be modeled under a range of traffic conditions.

If traffic is observed for 100 cycles, the 90th percentile would be the 90th busiest, the 10th percentile would be the 10th busiest, and the 50th percentile would represent average traffic.

For each percentile scenario and phase, a green time is given. The range of green times for each phase gives an indication of how often the phase will max-out, gap-out, or be skipped.

Next to each green time is a code indicating how the phase terminates. Here is a list of codes.

Table 8-1   Phase Termination Codes

Code	Phase Termination
sk	Phase is skipped
mn	Phase shows for minimum time
gp	Phase gaps-out
hd	Phase held for other ring to cross barrier
mx	Phase maxes out
pd	Phase held for pedestrian button or recall
mr	Phase has max-recall
dw	Main street phases dwells or green
cd	Coordinated phase

Modeling Occasional Pedestrians with Actuated Signals

A common problem with modeling actuated signals is how to deal with a phase with occasional pedestrians. For example, consider an actuated signal with medium side street volumes and about 10 pedestrians per hour. With normal traffic, a split of maybe 15 seconds is required, but the occasional pedestrian requires a split of 25 seconds. The predicted delay and capacity of the main street will be strongly influenced by which split is modeled for the side street. Should the signal be modeled with a split of 15 s, 25 s or something in between? The choice can change the predicted delay on the main street by 30% or more in many cases.

Synchro's solution to this problem is to model multiple percentile scenarios. With this example the 90th percentile scenario will use a 25 s split and the others will use 15 s splits. The resulting delay and actuated capacity in this case is a combination of 80% calculated without the pedestrian phase and 20% calculated with the pedestrian phase. If you are using the Percentile Delays of Synchro, no special treatment is required for modeling occasional pedestrians.

Occasional Pedestrians with Other Models

Modeling the occasional pedestrian is more of a challenge with the traditional traffic models. The HCM 2000 allows the user to enter actuated phase times. The manual does not state how to handle pedestrian actuations, but a reasonable interpretation would be to average greens with and without pedestrian times based on pedestrian frequency. The actuated green times calculated by Synchro for use with HCM Signals Report and HCM input files are an average of the five percentile green times. Some of these percentiles will include time for pedestrians and some will not, depending on the number of Pedestrian Calls.

Some engineers recommend using short phases in conjunction with coordination only in areas where there are less than 10 pedestrians per day.

Chapter 9 – Simulation Settings

From the **MAP** view, click on the desired intersection with the Right mouse button and select Simulation Options.

 From anywhere in the program, press [**F8**] and select the desired intersection from the list. Then push the *Simulatin Options Settings* button or the [**F10**] key.

The **SIMULATION OPTIONS** setting displays a grid in which you can enter SimTraffic simulation specific information. See Chapter 3 for details on navigating the data entry screens.

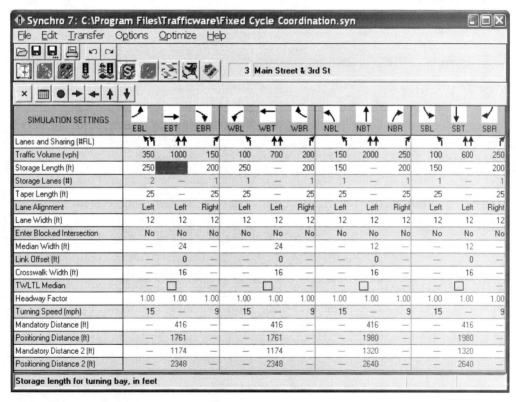

SIMULATION SETTINGS	EBL	EBT	EBR	WBL	WBT	WBR	NBL	NBT	NBR	SBL	SBT	SBR
Lanes and Sharing (#RL)	↟↟	↟↟	↗	↟	↟↟	↗	↟	↟↟	↗	↟	↟↟	↗
Traffic Volume (vph)	350	1000	150	100	700	200	150	2000	250	100	600	250
Storage Length (ft)	250		200	250	—	200	150	—	200	150	—	200
Storage Lanes (#)	2	—	1	1	—	1	1	—	1	1	—	1
Taper Length (ft)	25	—	25	25	—	25	25	—	25	25	—	25
Lane Alignment	Left	Left	Right	Left	Left	Right	Left	Left	Right	Left	Left	Right
Lane Width (ft)	12	12	12	12	12	12	12	12	12	12	12	12
Enter Blocked Intersection	No	No	No	No	No	No	No	No	No	No	No	No
Median Width (ft)	—	24	—	—	24	—	—	12	—	—	12	—
Link Offset (ft)	—	0	—	—	0	—	—	0	—	—	0	—
Crosswalk Width (ft)	—	16	—	—	16	—	—	16	—	—	16	—
TWLTL Median	—	☐	—	—	☐	—	—	☐	—	—	☐	—
Headway Factor	1.00	1.00	1.00	1.00	1.00	1.00	1.00	1.00	1.00	1.00	1.00	1.00
Turning Speed (mph)	15	—	9	15	—	9	15	—	9	15	—	9
Mandatory Distance (ft)	—	416	—	—	416	—	—	416	—	—	416	—
Positioning Distance (ft)	—	1761	—	—	1761	—	—	1980	—	—	1980	—
Mandatory Distance 2 (ft)	—	1174	—	—	1174	—	—	1320	—	—	1320	—
Positioning Distance 2 (ft)	—	2348	—	—	2348	—	—	2640	—	—	2640	—

Storage length for turning bay, in feet

Figure 9-1   SIMULATION OPTIONS Settings

Refer to page 5-2 for details on the **Lanes and Sharing** setting and to page 6-2 for details on the **Traffic Volume** setting.

 The **Lanes and Sharing** and **Traffic Volume** settings are the only two rows that apply to Synchro. All other rows are only used by SimTraffic. If a simulation is not going to be performed, these settings do not need to be entered.

Storage Length

The **Storage Length** is the length of a turning bay in feet (meters) and is the same value found in the **LANE** settings. If an intersection has a left turn storage bay of 150 feet (45 meters), enter "150" ("45") in this box. If the left or right turn extends back to the previous intersection, enter "0". For additional information, see the topic in the **LANE** settings, page 5-6.

Storage Lanes

Code the number of lanes in the right or left storage bay. This value only appears when the Storage Length is greater than 0. By default, the number of **Storage Lanes** is equal to the number of turning lanes. This is the same value found in the **LANE** settings. For additional details, refer to page 5-6.

Taper length

The **Taper Length** affects the visual **MAP** view drawing. In SimTraffic, the Taper Length impacts when vehicles can start entering the storage. The default is 25 ft (7.5 m).

Lane Alignment

When adding a lane, lanes are added on the right or left. The setting will allow the user to specify how lanes align through an intersection. **Figure 9-2** illustrates the options. The choices are as follows:

    A. Left

    B. Right

    C. L-NA (left, no add)

    D. R-NA (right, no add)

The default is Right for right turns, Left for left turns and through, and Right-NA for U-turns.

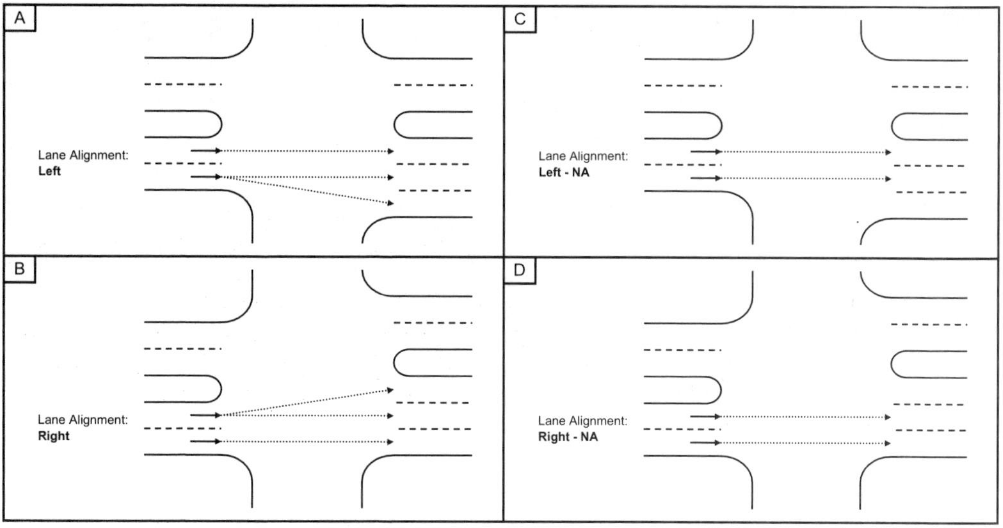

Figure 9-2 Lane Alignment Options

Consider the examples in **Figure 9-3**. Part A shows an example where the EBT and NER are green at the same time. There are four upstream lanes (two EBT and two NER) flowing into four downstream lanes. In order to prevent a conflict, the EBT is forced to use the left lanes downstream by setting the Lane Alignment to L-NA. The NER is forced into the downstream right lanes by setting the Lane Alignment to R-NA.

Part B of **Figure 9-3** shows a T intersection with continuous flow in the eastbound direction. In this case, the EBT and SBL are allowed to operate without conflict. To do this, set the EBT Lane Alignment to R-NA and the SBL to L-NA.

NOTE: Some adjustment in median width and/or link offset may be necessary to align the approach lanes with the departure lanes. You can check Intersection Paths under **Options→Map Settings** to graphically show the path of the vehicles crossing the intersection and verify lane alignment.

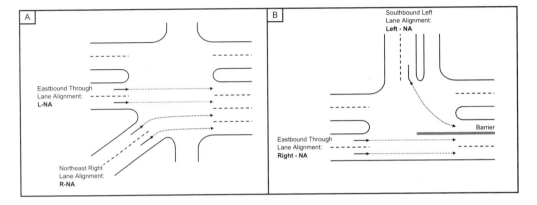

Figure 9-3   Lane Alignment Examples

Lane Width

Lane Width is the width of a single lane in feet (meters). The default is 12 feet (3.7 meters). Also see the topic on **Lane Widths** on page 5-5.

Enter Blocked Intersection

The **Enter Blocked Intersection** setting controls simulation modeling gridlock avoidance. The four options for modeling blocked intersections are "Yes", "No", "1" and "2". The default value is "No", for intersections and "Yes", for bends and ramp junctions. We suggest that you set Enter Blocked Intersection to "No", for high speed approaches and movements.

A vehicle will slow for an intersection, if there are 4 other vehicles ahead of it, but behind the stop bar.

A side street of an unsignalized intersection can be set to 1 or 2. This will allow 1 or 2 vehicles to enter a blocked intersection from the side. This can help the capacity of driveways.

Median Width

The **Median Width** is used to set the width of the median. Left turn lanes are considered to be positioned in the median even if they are not defined as storage lanes.

This setting can be overridden. The default is calculated as follows:

Formula for a link:

1) sum of (width of left turn lanes + width of left storage lanes for reverse departing link)

2) reduced by minimum of (left storage, left storage for reverse departing link)

3) widen to match wider median on through approach

Median Width must be set for each direction independently. Each setting affects the median width at each end.

Figure 9-4 illustrates some examples of median width. In A and C, the median width has been set automatically. Parts B and D show a manual over-ride of the Median Width setting.

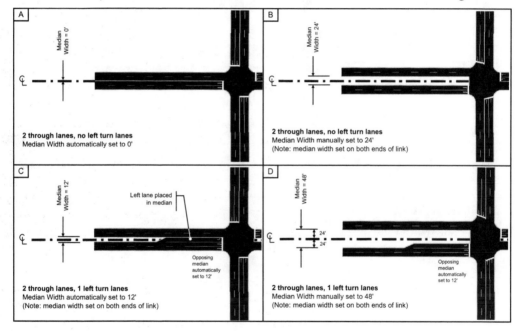

Figure 9-4   Median Width Examples

Link Offset

The **Link Offset** setting is used to offset the roadway alignment to the right or left of the centerline. This can be used to create a dog-leg intersection, if there are no internal stop bars (see **Figure 9-5 A**).

For an onramp or other acute intersection, use a positive link offset value for onramp, and a negative link offset value for an offramp (see **Figure 9-5 B**). In the figure below, w is the width of the mainline lanes used as the link offset for each ramp.

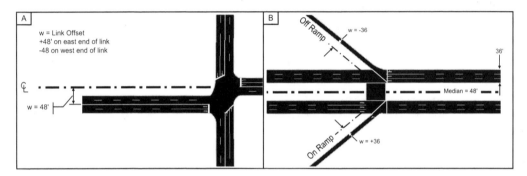

Figure 9-5   Link Offset Examples

Crosswalk Width

The **Crosswalk Width** is used to control the width of the crosswalk and the location of the stop bar. **Figure 9-6** illustrates the crosswalk in SimTraffic. The stop bar is located on the upstream end of the crosswalk.

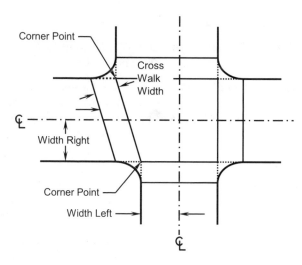

Figure 9-6   Cross Walk Width

TWLTL Median

 The TWLTL Median is visual only. Vehicles will not use the TWLTL.

The two-way left turn lane **(TWLTL) Median** setting draws a TWLTL in the median. The median will be colored with the pavement color and dashed yellow lines will be added. Storage taper lengths still apply. Setting the TWLTL "on" (check) will also set the TWLTL for the reverse link.

Notes about driveways:

Avoid placing too many driveways along your link. Some driveways with short storage and taper lengths can be used. To reduce space of driveway intersections, set crosswalk width on the main street to 4ft. and draw the driveways at 90 degree angles.

Vehicles will not initiate or complete lane changes within an intersection. Too many driveways reduce opportunities for lane changes.

The TWLTL Median setting on one end of a link sets the TWLTL Median on the reverse end of the link.

Headway Factor

SimTraffic applies the **Headway Factor** to model Saturated Flow Rates for individual lane groups. Headway Factor is not used in any of the capacity calculations in Synchro.

The Headway Factor is based on the Ideal Saturation Flow, lane width factor, the grade factor, the parking factor, the bus stops factor, and the area factor. The headway factor is magnified by 30% because at cruise speeds, about 30% of the time per vehicle is taken by vehicle passage and 70% by the headways.

$$HWF = \frac{1.3 * 1900}{fw * fg * fp * fbs * fa * Ideal} - 0.3 = \text{Headway Factor}$$

The Headway Factor is calculated but can be overridden.

Turning Speed

This is the **Turning Speed** for vehicles in miles/hour (km/h) while inside the intersection.

Synchro does not use this information. It is only used when modeling in SimTraffic.

The **NETWORK** settings have a network wide turning speed option. This setting affects the turn speed in CORSIM.

For large intersections or intersections with large turning radii, increase the Turning Speeds. This will give improved capacity in SimTraffic.

The Turning Speed should be adjusted if you are using SimTraffic to model a freeway section.

Turning speed is adjusted by driver speed factor.

Lane Change Distances

The **Lane Change Distances** are used for calibration of SimTraffic lane changing logic. Editing these values will not affect Synchro or CORSIM.

There are four parameters as shown below.

- Mandatory Distance is the distance back from the stop bar where a lane change must commence.

- Positioning Distance is the distance back from the Mandatory point where a vehicle first attempts to change lanes.

- Mandatory 2 Lane Distance is added to Mandatory Distance if a second lane change is required during the simulation.

- Positioning 2 Lane Distance is added to both Mandatory 2 Lane Distance and Mandatory Distance to determine the beginning of the positioning zone for the first of two lane changes.

All distances are measured from the stop bar. See the discussion on **Lane Choice and Lane Changes** on page 24-8.

Chapter 10 – Detector Settings

From the **MAP** view, click on the desired intersection with the Right mouse button and select Detector Options.

From anywhere in the program, press **[F8]** and select the desired intersection from the list. Then push the *Detectors Settings* button or the **[F11]** key. Clicking on a map detector also activates. The **DETECTOR** settings display a grid in which you can enter detector information. See Chapter 3 for details on navigating the data entry screens.

DETECTOR SETTINGS	EBL	EBT	EBR	WBL	WBT	WBR	NBL	NBT	NBR	SBL	SBT	SBR
Lanes and Sharing (#RL)	↟↟	↑↑	↗	↟	↑↑	↗	↟	↑↑	↗	↟	↑↑	↗
Traffic Volume (vph)	350	1000	150	100	700	200	150	2000	250	100	600	250
Number of Detectors (#)	4	1	1	4	2	1	4	2	1	4	2	1
Detector Phase	5	2	3	1	6	7	3	8	1	7	4	5
Switch Phase	0	0	0	0	0	0	0	0	0	0	0	0
Leading Detector (ft)	54	20	20	54	100	20	54	100	20	54	100	20
Trailing Detector (ft)	0	0	0	0	0	0	0	0	0	0	0	0
Detector Template	Lefta	Left	Right	Lefta	Thru	Right	Lefta	Thru	Right	Lefta	Thru	Right
Add/Update Template												
Detector 1 Position (ft)	0	0	0	0	0	0	0	0	0	0	0	0
Detector 1 Size (ft)	6	20	20	6	6	20	6	6	20	6	6	20
Detector 1 Type	Cl+Ex	Cl+Ex	Cl+Ex	Cl+Ex	Cl+Ex	Cl+Ex	Cl+Ex	Cl+Ex	Cl+Ex	Cl+Ex	Cl+Ex	Cl+Ex
Detector 1 Channels												
Detector 1 Extend	0.0	0.0	0.0	0.0	0.0	0.0	0.0	0.0	0.0	0.0	0.0	0.0
Detector 1 Queue	0.0	0.0	0.0	0.0	0.0	0.0	0.0	0.0	0.0	0.0	0.0	0.0
Detector 1 Delay	0.0	0.0	0.0	0.0	0.0	0.0	0.0	0.0	0.0	0.0	0.0	0.0
Detector 2 Position (ft)	16	----	----	16	94	----	16	94	----	16	94	----
Detector 2 Size (ft)	6	----	----	6	6	----	6	6	----	6	6	----
Detector 2 Type	Cl+Ex	---	---	Cl+Ex	Cl+Ex	---	Cl+Ex	Cl+Ex	---	Cl+Ex	Cl+Ex	---
Detector 2 Channels		---	---			---			---			---
Detector 2 Extend	0.0			0.0	0.0		0.0	0.0		0.0	0.0	
Detector 3 Position (ft)	32	---	---	32	---	---	32	---	---	32	---	---
Detector 3 Size (ft)	6	---	---	6	---	---	6	---	---	6	---	---
Detector 3 Type	Cl+Ex	---	---	Cl+Ex	---	---	Cl+Ex	---	---	Cl+Ex	---	---
Detector 3 Channels		----	----		----			----			----	

Figure 10-1   DETECTOR Settings

Refer to page 5-2 for details on the **Lanes and Sharing** setting and to page 6-2 for details on the **Traffic Volume** setting.

Number of Detectors

This is the number of longitudinal detector sets, not the number across the lanes. Detectors are numbered from the stop bar back, detector 1 is at the stop bar. You can enter up to 5 detectors.

Detector Phase

The Detector Phase is primary phase for a detector. This is the same as the Detector Phase setting in the **TIMING** settings.

New in Version 7: There is only one detector phase and one switch phase per lane group.

Switch Phase

The **Switch Phase** is a secondary phase that extends the entered phase when it is green. This setting does not place a call and does not call the primary Detector Phase when the entered switch phase is green (per NTCIP specifications).

This setting can be used for the permitted phase of a permitted plus protected left turn. Do not use with a lagging left turn because the protected left will not get called while the permitted phase is green. The default for permitted plus protected is to have the Detector Phase equal to the Protected Phase and Switch Phase set to none.

Leading Detector, Trailing Detector

Leading and **Trailing Detector** settings maintain backward compatibility with earlier versions of Synchro. The Detector Template method in Version 7 allows the user to specify the position, size, and call/extend value of each detector rather than accept the assumed geometry in the Leading/Trailing Detector method. The Detector Template automatically updates the Leading/Trailing Detector fields.

Leading/Trailing Detectors are also found in the **TIMING** settings (page 7-8). Note that Call detectors at the stop bar and Queue (type 3) detectors are not included in the Leading/Trailing zone.

Detector Template

Detector Templates allow the user to define the number, position, type and size of each detector. Default templates named **Left, Thru,** and **Right** are used to setup detectors for new approaches. You can modify these templates, but you cannot remove them. It is recommended that you setup templates for all of the standard detector layouts your agency uses. Give them names such as "Thru 300" for through detectors located 300 feet in advance of the stop bar.

Add Template

Activate the Detector Template Editor (**Figure 10-2**) by selecting **Options→Detector Templates**, or by double clicking on the left column of the DETECTOR settings. The Detector Template Editor allows the user to define additional templates in separate columns. Data fields are identical with the DETECTOR settings.

The inputs on the Template are the same as those in the DETECTOR settings, except for the detector phase and detector channel.

Select the [New] button to create an empty template and specify the template name.

Select the [Copy] button to duplicate the active column. The copied column will be inserted to the right. Data can be edited and template renamed.

The [Delete] button will remove the active column. The default Left, Thru and Right columns cannot be removed.

Use the Update Lane Detectors to Template [This Template] button to update all lane groups with that detector template name.

Use the Update Lane Detectors to Template [All Templates] button to update all lane groups with any detector template name.

Detectors associated with a template are not automatically updated when the template is modified. Therefore, apply the Update Lane Detectors to Template button after modifying a template.

There is no cancel button. Use the undo command to rollback to the previous settings.

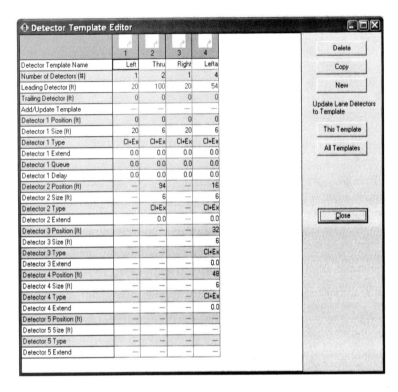

	1	2	3	4
Detector Template Name	Left	Thru	Right	Lefta
Number of Detectors (#)	1	2	1	4
Leading Detector (ft)	20	100	20	54
Trailing Detector (ft)	0	0	0	0
Add/Update Template	—	—	—	—
Detector 1 Position (ft)	0	0	0	0
Detector 1 Size (ft)	20	6	20	6
Detector 1 Type	Cl+Ex	Cl+Ex	Cl+Ex	Cl+Ex
Detector 1 Extend	0.0	0.0	0.0	0.0
Detector 1 Queue	0.0	0.0	0.0	0.0
Detector 1 Delay	0.0	0.0	0.0	0.0
Detector 2 Position (ft)	—	94	—	16
Detector 2 Size (ft)	—	6	—	6
Detector 2 Type	—	Cl+Ex	—	Cl+Ex
Detector 2 Extend	—	0.0	—	0.0
Detector 3 Position (ft)	—	—	—	32
Detector 3 Size (ft)	—	—	—	6
Detector 3 Type	—	—	—	Cl+Ex
Detector 3 Extend	—	—	—	0.0
Detector 4 Position (ft)	—	—	—	48
Detector 4 Size (ft)	—	—	—	6
Detector 4 Type	—	—	—	Cl+Ex
Detector 4 Extend	—	—	—	0.0
Detector 5 Position (ft)	—	—	—	—
Detector 5 Size (ft)	—	—	—	—
Detector 5 Type	—	—	—	—
Detector 5 Extend	—	—	—	—

Buttons: Delete, Copy, New, Update Lane Detectors to Template, This Template, All Templates, Close

Figure 10-2   DETECTOR TEMPLATE Settings

Detector *n* Position

This is the distance from stop bar to the trailing edge (closet to stop bar) of detector *n*. This setting is for all lanes in the lane group.

Refer to the example in **Figure 10-3**. In this example, detector 1 (D1) has a position of zero feet, detector 2 (D2) has a position of d2, detector 3 (D3) has a position of d2 plus d3, and detector 4 (D4) has a position of d2 plus d3 plus d4.

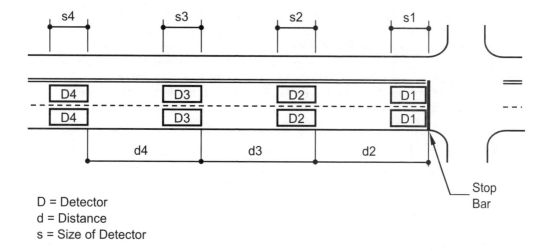

D = Detector
d = Distance
s = Size of Detector

Figure 10-3   Detector Position

Detector *n* Size

This is the size of the detector in the traveled direction. The default for detectors made from Leading Distance is 6 ft (1.8m). This setting is for all lanes in the lane group.

Refer to **Figure 10-3** for an example. In this example, detector 1 (D1) has a size of s1, detector 2 (D2) has a size of s2, detector 3 (D3) has a size of s3 and detector 4 (D4) has a size of s4.

Detector *n* Type

The options are Calling, Extend, Cl+Ex; Calling places a call when the phase is yellow or red. Extend places a call when the phase is green. Options for delay, queue, and extend detectors are set by using a non-zero time for these options.

All detectors modeled in Synchro are presence detectors, not passage (or pulse) detectors.

Detector *n* Channel

Enter the detector number used by the controller. If there is a different detector channel for each lane, enter each value separated by columns. Traditionally the detector number is the same as the phase number, and one channel is used for all the detectors for a phase. Newer installations may have a separate detector input for each lane to allow volume counts. If the detector channels across three lanes (left to right) are 11,12, and 13; enter "11,12,13".

 The Detector Channel is not currently used by Synchro or SimTraffic, but can be imported and exported in UTDF data access. In the future there may be a conversion program to convert counts by detector number into counts by turning movement for use by Synchro.

Detector *n* Extend

Detector Extend, or "carry over" is specified in tenths of a second. This value extends the call for the specified value after the call drops.

One application is to have 3 seconds extend time on advance detectors, and 0 extend time at the stop bar, in conjunction with a gap time of 0.5 seconds. This will allow the advance detectors to hold the phase green, while the stop bar detectors will not.

Detector 1 Queue

Enter the Queue time here to have the stop bar detector act as a queue detector, the old name is "Type 3 detector". A queue detector will extend the phase during the first q seconds, then be silent. Queue detection is useful for extending the phase during the queue clearance time, then later allowing the advance detectors to extend the phase.

If the stop bar detector extends the phase for 3 seconds, this will create 3 seconds of green after the last vehicle enters the intersection. This vehicle will be well beyond the intersection during the clearance interval. This will create extra delay for the opposing movements.

Detector 1 Delay

Enter the Delay time here to have the stop bar detector act as a Delay detector. A delay detector will not place a call on red or yellow, until the vehicle has been there for at least d seconds. A delay detector will extend normally on green. Delay detectors are useful for right turn lanes with right turn on red allowed; If a vehicle is able to turn on red within, for example, 10 seconds, it is not necessary to bring up this phase.

Chapter 11 – Network Settings

Network Settings

The **NETWORK SETTINGS** allow you to make changes that impact the entire network. These settings affect the default values for entries in the **LANE, VOLUME, TIMING, PHASING** and **SIMULATION OPTIONS** settings.

To access the **NETWORK** settings, select the **Options → Network Settings** command from the menu.

 To quickly access the **NETWORK SETTINGS** window, double click with the mouse on the related row in any of the data entry settings.

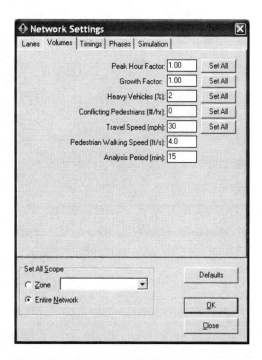

Figure 11-1   NETWORK Settings

Because these settings will influence newly created intersections, it is strongly recommended that these settings be entered first.

Most values have a button next to it marked [**Set All**]. Pushing this button will set all of the intersections in the network to that value. **Use these buttons with extreme caution.** Pressing [**Set All**] for Cycle Lengths, for instance, will cause all of the intersections in the network or zone to take on the new Cycle Length. Any custom Split, Offset, or Cycle Length information will be lost. One or more zones can also be changed by choosing the Scope prior to selecting [**Set All**] which will only change the cycle length within the selected zone.

The **Set All Scope** can be used to apply the settings to the Entire Network or a particular Zone.

All of these values, except Vehicle Length, Maximum Cycle Length, Pedestrian Walking Speed, Analysis Period, and ICU Reference Cycle Length are defaults can be changed locally at the intersection.

To switch between sections press [**Ctrl**]+[**Tab**] or [**Ctrl**]+[**Shift**]+[**Tab**].

The [Default] button restores default values for all items in the **NETWORK SETTINGS**. The undo command can be used after selecting the [Default] button to switch back to the previous settings (after closing the **NETWORK SETTINGS**).

Lane Settings
Lane Width

Lane Width is the width of a single lane in feet (meters). The default is 12 feet (3.7 meters). Also see the topic on **Lane Widths** on page 5-5.

Flow Rate

Flow Rate is the ideal Saturated Flow Rate per lane in the absence of any interference. The 2000 HCM recommends using 1,900 vphpl as the default. Also see the topic on **Ideal Saturated Flow Rate** on page Ideal Saturated Flow.

Vehicle Length

Vehicle Length is the average length of vehicles, in ft (m), including the space between them when stopped. This value is used to calculate queue lengths and for detecting blocking problems. The default value is 25 ft (8 m).

The Vehicle Length is used in conjunction with the Storage Length and the length of links to determine if there is adequate storage space for vehicles.

Allow Right Turn on Red

This field is used to specify whether Right Turns on Red (RTOR) are allowed by default.

Right Turn on Red is used to specify whether RTORs are allowed. Synchro automatically calculates a **Saturated Flow Rate (RTOR)** if this option is selected. This field is also used for modeling RTOR in SimTraffic and CORSIM.

Volume Settings

Peak Hour Factor

The PHF is the ratio of the flow rate for the entire hour, to the flow rate for the peak 15 minutes. The default is 0.92. See the topic on Peak Hour Factor (page 6-3) for more information.

Growth Factor

The Growth Factor can be used to adjust all volumes by a set amount. This is commonly used to convert current traffic counts into future projections. See the topic on Growth Factor (page 6-4) for more information.

Heavy Vehicles

Heavy Vehicles is the percentage of trucks and heavy vehicles in the traffic stream. The default is 2%. If you are analyzing an area with many trucks, consider using a higher value. See the topic on Heavy Vehicles (page 6-5) for more information.

Conflicting Pedestrians

Conflicting Pedestrians is the number of pedestrians per hour crossing a given approach. The default is zero. If you are analyzing an area with many pedestrians, consider assigning a default value. See the topic on Conflicting Pedestrians (page 6-2) for more information.

Do not confuse this value with pedestrian calls. Conflicting pedestrians is the number of pedestrians that right turns must yield to. Pedestrian Calls is the number of pedestrians activating the pedestrian push button. Normally they will be the same.

Travel Speed

Travel Speed is the speed limit or predominant speed given all green lights. The default is 30 mph (50 km/h). To set the speed for an individual link, go to the map and double-click on the link.

Pedestrian Walking Speed

This setting is used for unsignalized intersection analysis. This setting also controls the pedestrian speed in SimTraffic.

Analysis Period

This setting is used to modify the Analysis Period T that is used for delay calculations. Additional information on the Analysis Period can be found in Chapter 1, Optimizations and Calculations.

Timings Settings

Cycle Length

This is the cycle length, in seconds. See the topic on **Cycle Length** (page 7-8) for more information.

Maximum Cycle Length

The Maximum Cycle Length is the longest cycle length, in seconds, that is evaluated when optimizing the cycle length. When optimizing intersection and network cycle lengths, Synchro will try a range of cycle lengths up to the Maximum Cycle length. The Cycle Length chosen will have the lowest combination of stops, delays, and queue penalty.

Cycle lengths above 120s may offer incrementally more capacity, but they also have long queues, and may increase frustration of motorists. It is difficult to maintain the saturation flow rate with long green times.

Allow Lead/Lag Optimize?

This is the default value for the **Allow Lead/Lag Optimize?** field in the **TIMING SETTINGS** window. Check this box to allow lead-lag optimization by default.

Yellow Time

This is the amount of time for the Yellow Interval in seconds. See the topic on Yellow Time (page 7-12) for more information.

All Red Time

This is the amount of time for the all-red interval following the yellow interval. See the topic on All-Red Time (page 7-12) for more information.

Lost Time Adjustment

The Lost Time Adjustment is the adjustment to the Total Lost time. The Total Lost Time used in calculations is the Y+AR plus the Lost Time Adjustment. The default for both startup lost time and extension of effective green is 2.5 seconds, so the Lost Time Adjustment defaults to zero. See the topic on **Lost Time Adjustment** on page 7-12 for more information.

Reference Phase

This is the coordinated phase(s) to which offsets are referenced. Normally phases 2 and 6 are the coordinated phase.

Offset Reference Style

Offset Reference Phase is the part of the phase to which offsets are referenced. Beginning of Green is the default for new intersections and when using [Set All].

The options for Offset Reference Style are:

Begin of Green: Offsets are referenced to the beginning of the last reference phase to turn green. This is traditional NEMA referencing.

Begin of Yellow: Offsets are referenced to the beginning of the first reference phase to turn yellow. This is 170 style referencing.

Begin of Red: Offsets are referenced to the beginning of the first reference phase to turn red.

TS2 -1st Green: Offsets are referenced to the beginning of the first reference phase to turn green. This is the referencing used with some NEMA TS2 controllers.

170 Style: Referenced to start of FDW or start of yellow.

Minimum Splits, Left and Through

The Minimum Splits are the shortest allowable split, in seconds. Newly created intersections will have these values for their minimum splits. Minimum Splits are used when optimizing the splits for an intersection.

 Through phases will normally have a pedestrian phase associated with them, while left turn phases will not. Therefore, the minimum required splits for through phases are typically longer than for left turn phases.

See the topic on Minimum Splits (page 8-6) for more information.

Control Type

This is the type of controller used. The options are Pretimed, Actuated-Uncoordinated, Semi Actuated-Coordinated, Actuated-Coordinated, Unsignalized and Roundabout. Refer to the topic on Control Type (page 4-4) for more information.

ICU Reference Cycle Length

This is the reference cycle length used by the ICU calculations (see page 13-41 for additional details).

Phases Settings

Minimum Initial

This is the minimum green time. This value is used for computing actuated green times (see page 8-613-6 for additional details).

Vehicle Extension

This is the maximum gap time (see page 8-8 for additional details).

Minimum Gap

This is the minimum gap time, used with volume-density operation (see page 8-8 for additional details).

Time Before Reduce

Time Before Reduce is used with volume-density operation (see page 8-9 for additional details).

Time To Reduce

Time To Reduce is used with volume-density operation (see page 8-9 for additional details).

Pedestrian Phase

This field controls whether through phases will have a pedestrian phase by default or after [**Set All**].

Left phases do not normally have a pedestrian phase associated with them. Refer to page 8-10 for additional details.

Walk Time

Time for pedestrian walk interval in seconds (see page 8-10 for additional details).

Flash Don't Walk Time

Time for pedestrian clearance interval in seconds (see page 8-10 for additional details).

Pedestrian Calls

The number of pedestrian calls per hour at a push button (see page 8-11 for additional details).

Inhibit Max

This option will control the Inhibit Max setting. Refer to page 8-12 for additional details.

Yield Point

This setting allows the Yield Point to be set for the network or zone. Refer to page 4-15 for additional details.

Simulation Settings

Taper Length

This setting controls the taper length for storage lanes. See page 9-2 for full details.

Enter Blocked Intersection

The Enter Blocked Intersection setting controls simulation modeling gridlock avoidance. Checking the box will set this value to Yes. An unchecked box is No. See the topic on page 9-4 for full details.

Crosswalk Width

This setting controls the width of the crosswalk. See page 9-6 for full details.

Simulation Turning Speed

This is the default turning speed for vehicles in miles/hour (km/h) while inside the intersection. Synchro does not use this information. It is only used when modeling in SimTraffic or CORSIM. Turning speed is adjusted by driver speed factor. See page 9-8 for full details.

Chapter 12 – Time-Space Diagram

Time-Space Diagrams can be used to graphically see how traffic flows between intersections. To view a Time-Space Diagram (TSD), first click on the desired intersection or the desired link to select it, then press the *Time-Space Diagram* button or the [**F7**] key.

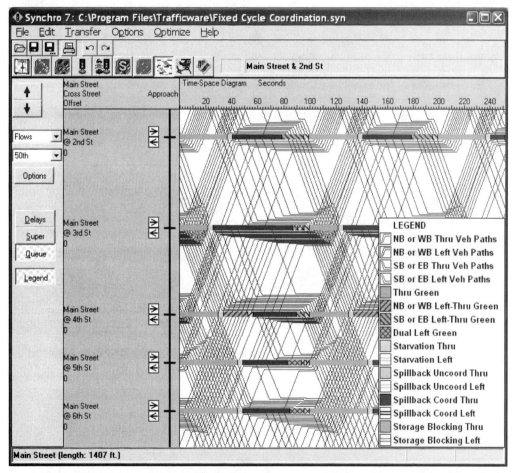

Figure 12-1   TIME-SPACE DIAGRAM

Arterial view: Invoking a time-space diagram with a link selected will bring up a time-space diagram showing that link's arterial TSD from one end to the other.

Intersection view: Invoking a time-space diagram with an intersection selected will bring up a time-space diagram showing all the links connecting to that intersection and one intersection in each direction.

Named Arterial view: Invoking a time-space diagram with a named arterial from the SELECT INTERSECTION window (press the **Select-Intersection** button or the [**F8**] key) will bring up a time-space diagram showing a named arterial. The Named Arterial view can show part of an arterial based on its name, zone, or route #. The Named Arterial view can also show an arterial that turns corners. See the section on Interacting with the Time-Space Diagram on page 12-9 for details on creating a route number.

Parts of a Time-Space Diagram

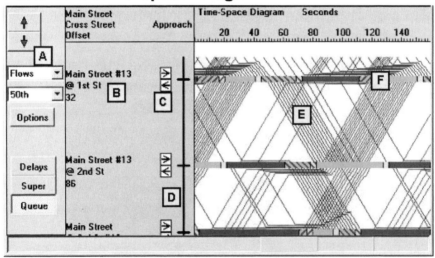

Figure 12-2   Parts of a TIME-SPACE DIAGRAM

Synchro's time-space diagrams display time along the horizontal axis and distance along the vertical axis.

The following information summarizes each part of the time-space diagram in **Figure 12-2**.

A Toolbar- These buttons change the views of the **TIME-SPACE DIAGRAM**. They are explained in detail below.

B Street Names and Offsets- These are the street names of the intersection shown. The top name is the name of the street with the time-space diagram being shown. The bottom name is the name of the cross street. Underneath the street names is the intersection offset. The offset is referenced to the reference phase even if it is not one of the approaches in the diagram.

C Direction Icon- These icons indicate the direction of the street in question. The top icon shows the direction of traffic moving downward in the diagram, usually Southbound or Westbound. The bottom icon shows the direction of traffic moving in the upward direction in the diagram, usually Northbound or Eastbound. These directions also match the direction of the average delays showed in delays options and the colored timing bands (F).

D Street and Intersection Diagram- The vertical line represents the street with the time-space diagrams. The horizontal lines are crossing streets. These lines identify which links connect two intersections and which are external links. These lines also show where the diagrams stop, when two or more streets are shown in **Intersection View**. Clicking on or near a vertical line will display an Arterial View centered on that link. Clicking on or near a horizontal line will display an Intersection View for that intersection.

E Traffic flow lines or Traffic Density Diagram- The diagonal and horizontal lines show traffic flow. (See the Traffic Flow Diagram in this topic for a complete description.)

F Timing Bands. The red, green, and yellow bands indicate the phase of the signal for each part of the cycle. The different colors and hatching are as follows:

- **Green** represents a green phase for through traffic in both the upwards and downwards direction.
- **Red** represents a red phase for both directions through and left movements.
- **Teal** represents an unsignalized intersection or a bend.
- **Downward Hatching** (\\\\\\) represents a green phase for downward through and left traffic. Left turns, if any, are protected.
- **Upward Hatching** (/////) represents a green phase for upward through and left traffic. Left turns, if any, are protected.
- **Cross Hatching** (XXXX) represents a green phase for left turns in both

directions. Through traffic has a red phase.

- **Solid Yellow** or **Hatched Yellow** represents a yellow phase for one or more phases in the movement.

The green bands for an actuated signal may start or end early. The times shown are actuated times and this represents the phases gapping out early. Select [**Max**] to show maximum green times.

A scale on the top of the timing bands shows the time scale. The scale can be changed with the **Options → Time-Space Diagram** command. Refer to the icons in (C) to see which direction the cycle bands represent.

 If your time-space diagrams only show 2 or 3 intersections, it may be because you are displaying an intersection view. See the Switching Views section below for information about arterial views.

Time-Space Diagram Features

Scrolling

To scroll or move the time space diagram vertically, use the arrow buttons, the arrow keys, or by clicking and dragging on the diagram (away from the timing bands).

Show Bands

The show bands (bandwidth option) shows arterial bandwidths. Bandwidth is the part of the cycle that allows the vehicles to go through all intersections without stopping (in theory). Synchro shows both arterial bands and link bands.

Arterial bands are green bands that carry a vehicle along the entire corridor without stopping. Link bands are green bands that carry a vehicle between two intersections without stopping.

The following default colors are used in bandwidth displays.

- NB and WB Arterial Through Bands Red
- SB and EB Arterial Through Bands Blue
- NB and WB Link Bands and NB and WB Left Turn Bands Purple

- SB and EB Link Bands and SB and EB Left Turn Bands Teal

Legend

The default colors can be changed with the time-space options. Clicking the [Legend] button will display a legend of the colors.

| Legend |

Vehicle Flow Option

This diagram also shows the speed and position of the vehicles. Each line represents one or more vehicles (see the table below). The slope of the line is proportional to the vehicles' speed. Horizontal lines represent stopped cars. The best timing plans are the ones with the fewest and shortest horizontal lines.

The triangles of horizontal lines represent stopped vehicles queued at a red light. The width of the triangle is the longest waiting time. The height of the triangle represents the maximum queue. A tall, skinny triangle represents a long queue making a short stop. A short, wide trapezoid represents a few vehicles making a long stop.

The following default colors are used in flow displays.

- NB and WB Through Traffic Red

- SB and EB Through Traffic Blue

- NB and WB Through Traffic and NB and WB Left Traffic Purple

- SB and EB Through Traffic and SB and EB Left Traffic Teal

Normally each line represents one vehicle. On high volume lane groups, a line could represent two or more vehicles. **Table 12-1** indicates how many vehicles each line represents.

Table 12-1   Time-Space Vehicles per Line

Adj Lane Group Volume	Vehicles per line
0 to 899 vph	1
900 to 1899	2
1800 to 2699	3
2700 to 3599	4

Percentile Options

Traffic flow is not constant but varies, even over the course of an hour. Synchro models traffic flow, actuated green times, and traffic flows with five different traffic scenarios. These scenarios represent 90th, 70th, 50th, 30th, and 10th percentile cycles for the hour for which volume data is given. If you looked at 100 cycles, the 90th percentile would have 90 cycles with less volume (10 with the same or more). The 50th percentile represents average traffic conditions.

The time-space diagrams allow you to see traffic flow for these scenarios. To see the varied flow options, select the appropriate drop-down from the toolbar on the left.

Maximum Option

With Maximum, green bands show maximum green times, even for actuated signals.

 Max can only be used with the **Bandwidth** option. This is because Synchro calculates departures internally using actuated green times. Synchro does not calculate departure patterns for actuated signals with maximum green settings. The **Flow** option can only be used with the Percentile scenarios.

90th, 70th, 50th, 30th, and 10th Percentile views

With one of these options selected, the green bands show the actuated green times and actuated start times.

Traffic flows represent the flows from the percentile scenario.

The 90th percentile scenario will have heavier traffic; the 10th percentile traffic will have lighter traffic.

50th ▼
Max
90th
70th
50th
30th
10th

Bandwidths in percentile scenarios are based on actuated green times. This feature can actually allow greater bandwidths around intersections that have light side-street traffic.

Early Return to Green

Viewing actuated signals in percentile view can highlight several potential problems with coordination. If some phases are skipped or gap out, the main street green will start earlier than predicted with pretimed coordination. These vehicles will arrive at the next intersection early and may have to stop a second time.

When coordinating side streets or left turn phases, it is possible for the signal to skip or gap-out before the platoon arrives. This view can highlight these problems. This is especially a problem with leading left turns.

 When showing a Percentile flow, splits cannot be adjusted. Maximum splits must be shown in order to adjust splits.

Show Delays

Delays | To show the **total delay** for each movement and the intersections overall, push in the *Show Delays* button. Showing delays gives you feedback about how well a timing plan works. Turning off the delays makes more space available for the diagrams, and speeds up diagram generation.

Push [**Delays**] a second time to turn delay display off.

Total Delays - These values are the estimated total delay for all traffic moving in the given direction. Total delay includes control delay and queue delay. The first three columns are the total delay for traffic in the left, through, and right turn lane groups. The fourth column is the total delay for the intersection, including traffic in all directions.

Show Super Saturated

Super | Push the *Show Super Saturated* button to show lane groups operating above capacity. They are shown with their queues filled at the beginning of green. When this option is off, the time-space diagram assumes that all queues are cleared at the end of green. If you want to hand create a timing plan for super saturated conditions, turn on this option. If you want a timing plan that works for unsaturated conditions, turn off this option. This option only affects lane groups whose volume-to-capacity ratio is greater than 1.0 and who have compatible cycle lengths.

If the intersections have incompatible cycle lengths, the diagram does not repeat and a queue builds with each successive cycle.

Show Queue Interaction Problems

Queue | Push the *Show Queue Interactions* button to show queue interaction problems. Queue interaction problems will be shown as colored rectangles in the time-space diagram at the stop bar. The color coding is as follows:

- Red indicates blocking delay. A red rectangle at a stop bar indicates that the upstream intersection queues are spilling back and blocking.

- Yellow indicates starvation delay. Starvation delay is congestion caused by a short upstream link in conjunction with poor/no coordination .

- Brown shows storage delay.

Blocking for left turns is shown with two strips as red or brown. If the cycles are uncoordinated, blocking time is shown as pink across the entire width. More details can be found in the topic on **Queue Interactions** page 13-55.

Show Legend

Legend

Select the *Legend* button to display a color-coded legend. The legend shows the color for the flow lines and the through and left timing bands. If the [Queue] button is selected, the legend will include queue interaction color-coding.

Time-Space Diagram Options

Select the [**Options**] button to:

- change the scale of the diagrams

- change the flow line colors

- turn on or off some of the flow directions or flows to left turns

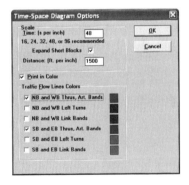

Figure 12-3   TIME-SPACE DIAGRAM Options

Normally time-space diagrams print the green portion of the timing bands as white. This makes the diagrams clearer on a black and white printer.

To print the timing bands as red and green on a color printer, check the following setting:

1. Choose [Options].

2. Check the box, Print in color.

 The Time Space diagrams have an option "Expand Short Blocks". This allows space for text or users can keep them small. The option is on the Time Space diagram options settings and the Print Settings options.

Time and Distance Scale

For the time scale, enter a number between 16 and 96. The higher the number, the smaller each cycle is. Since there are 96 dots per inch on the screen, it is recommended that the time scale be an even divisor of 96. Good numbers for the time scale are 16, 24, 32, 48, and 96. For the distance scale enter a number between 100 and 3,000 feet per inch (30 to 1,000 meters per inch). As the scale increases, the distance between intersections decreases.

Enabling Flow Lines and Changing Colors

Viewing traffic flows for four movements simultaneously can be a bit overwhelming. There are options to limit the movements shown simultaneously.

For each movement, the color can be changed by clicking the color box to the right of the text.

The flow lines can be added/removed by checking/unchecking the appropriate box.

Interacting with the Time-Space Diagram
Switching views

To switch to a different **Intersection View** you can do any of the following,

- Click on the Street and Intersection Diagram (D in **Figure 12-1**), on a horizontal line.

- Go to the **MAP** view (press [F2]), click on a different intersection, then return to the **TIME-SPACE DIAGRAM** (press [F7]).

- Press [F8] to get the intersection list and select an intersection.

To switch to a different **Basic Arterial View** you can do one of the following:

- Click on the Street and Intersection Diagram, (D in **Figure 12-1**) on a vertical line (do not click near any horizontal line).

- Go to the **MAP** view (press [F2]), click on a different link, then return to the **TIME-SPACE DIAGRAM** (press [F7]).

The Basic Arterial view shows an entire corridor of through streets regardless of name or zone. When in basic arterial mode, the Intersection Name panel in the upper tool bar is blank.

 To switch to a **Named Arterial view**, select the Helicopter button or press [F8] to activate the **SELECT INTERSECTION** settings. 1) Select an arterial by name or number. 2) To select part of an arterial by zone, choose the By Zone option.

The Named Arterial view can show an arterial with bends or for a specific zone. When in named mode, the arterial name appears in the Intersection Name panel on the upper toolbar.

To set up a route with multiple street names or that turns corners, enter a route number as part of the street name with a # sign. For example, a street name of "Ashby Ave, SR #13" can be referred to as route #13.

To make an arterial bend from North to East for example, make sure that '#13' is in the north and east links and NOT in the south or west links.

To display an arterial that splits into a one way pair, include the route numbers "5th Street #101N" and "4th Street #101S" in the name of the one way sections. Include both route numbers in the name of the two way section separated by a space such as "Broadway #101N #101S".

Adjusting Splits and Offsets

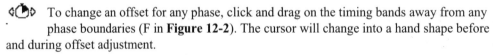 To change an offset for any phase, click and drag on the timing bands away from any phase boundaries (F in **Figure 12-2**). The cursor will change into a hand shape before and during offset adjustment.

 Offsets cannot be changed for actuated and semi-actuated signals because they are not coordinated and thus do not use offsets.

 To change a split for a phase, click and drag on the timing bands at a phase boundary. The cursor will change into a splitter shape before and during split adjustment. This feature changes the maximum splits.

 Splits can only be changed when in MAX mode. When in a percentile mode, the splits shown are actuated splits; this feature only works with maximum splits.

When adjusting splits and offsets, you should attempt to make the right end of traffic flow lines hit the timing bands in the green section, or to the left of the green section. This represents traffic arriving at the intersection when the signal is green or just before the signal turns green.

When manually adjusting the timing, be sure to look at the average delay values. When you reduce the delay for one direction, you may be increasing it for another direction. Make sure you consider the delay for all movements. It is probably easier to let Synchro determine the best timing plans for you.

Swap Phases

Holding down the [**CTRL**] key can be used to swap the phase order. When the [**CTRL**] key is held down and the mouse cursor is moved over a swappable phase, the cursor changes to indicate that the phases can be swapped. Clicking the mouse changes the phase sequence. If the cursor is over two phases, the phase with the closest center point is chosen. Locked timing plans cannot be changed. Phases can be manually swapped even if marked 'No' for **Lead/Lag Optimize**.

Printing the time space diagram

The time-space diagram can be printed using the **File→Print Window** command.

The red and green bands will print as gray and white with a black and white printer. The color option can be changed with the **Options→Time Space Diagram** command.

Notes on Timing Bands
Actuated Splits

When a percentile option is shown, the displayed green times are actuated green times. The green times may be more or less than the inputted Maximum Green times. It is possible that some bands show 100% red or 100% green; this indicates that a phase has been skipped. Phase skips are common with volumes less than 100 vph, and for the 10th and 30th scenarios.

It is also quite possible for the main street green to start early. This is caused when side street phases gap-out or skip. This behavior is called **"early return to green"**, and the Time-Space diagram shows this when a percentile option is selected.

Splits cannot be adjusted when a percentile option is shown. This is because the timings shown are the calculated actuated splits and not the maximum input splits. To edit splits in the Time-Space diagram, choose the [Max] option.

Maximum Splits

When the [Max] option is selected, flow lines cannot be displayed. The vehicle flows are calculated using an iterative process based on coordination and actuated green times. It would make no sense to show vehicle flows with maximum green times because the flows do not exist without actuated green times.

Uncoordinated Intersections

Uncoordinated Intersections do not have an Offset or a fixed cycle length. With uncoordinated intersections, the first phase always starts at time 0, and offsets cannot be adjusted.

Relating the Time-Space Display to Delays and Queues

Delays

The width of the horizontal lines in the Flow diagrams represents the signal delay incurred by each vehicle. The sum of the line widths divided by the vehicles per cycle is equal to the uniform delay for the percentile scenario shown.

The control delay shown with the Delay option is same stopped delay shown in the **TIMING window** and in the Intersection reports. The Percentile delays are volume weighted average of the five percentile scenario delays with the incremental delay added.

To convert from the delays represented by the flow lines to Percentile Delays the following steps are applied:

1. Uniform Delay for each percentile scenario is the sum of horizontal widths divided by vehicles per cycle.

2. Take Volume weighted average of five scenarios

3. Add Incremental delay for congestion

One might ask why the delay option does not show the delay associated with the percentile shown. The percentile scenario is an unstable event that does not exist for more than one cycle. In real life, traffic will vary between the maximum and minimum scenario volumes each cycle. One cycle could be 90th percentile traffic followed by a 30th, a 50th, a 10th, and a 78th. To show delays for a single scenario has no meaning because the scenarios all exist together in a 15 or 60 minute analysis period.

A follow-up question might be why the time space diagram does not show a mix of percentile scenarios. This type of display would be too difficult to present in a clear and informative method.

Queues

Each horizontal line represents one (or more) vehicles in queue. The height of the queue stack is equivalent to the length of the queue. The height with the 50th Percentile Flows is roughly equivalent to the **50th Percentile Maximum Queue**. Each vehicle takes up the space of the average vehicle length, which is 25ft (7.5m) by default. With 2 or more lanes, the space per vehicle is divided by the number of lanes. A delay of 6 seconds or less represents a vehicle slowing but not stopping. The maximum queue will thus be at the top vehicle with a delay of 6 s or more.

The **95th Percentile Maximum Queue** is normally 10 to 20 percent longer than the height of the 90th Percentile Flows' Queue Stack. A delay of 6 seconds or less represents a vehicle slowing but not stopping. The maximum queue will thus be at the top vehicle with a delay of 6 s or more.

In a coordinated system, it is possible to change the queue length and delay by changing the offsets. Remember that the widths of the horizontal lines represent delay and the height of the queue stack represents the maximum queue.

Chapter 13 – Optimization and Calculations

Introduction

This chapter will provide details on the optimization and calculations performed by Synchro. The section on optimization will define how to perform the various optimization commands, along with the objectives of these optimizations. The calculations section will provide in-depth details regarding the underlying calculations found within Synchro.

Optimizations

Overview of Optimizations

Synchro contains a number of optimization functions. It is important to understand what each function does and use the optimizations in the correct order.

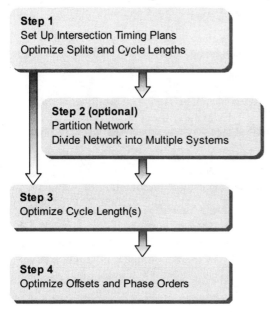

Figure 13-1   Optimization Steps

Step 1: Set Up Intersection Timing Plans

The first step is to make timing plans for each individual intersection. This step includes:

- Enter volume data (refer to Chapter 6)

- Enter lane data (refer to Chapter 5)

- Set up phase numbers for each movement along with phase parameters (refer to Chapter 7 and Chapter 8)

- Optimize cycle lengths and splits

- Check capacity

- Check for coding errors (see the topic on Coding Error Messages on page 17-1)

Step 2: Partition Network

The next step is to divide the network into subsystems. This step is optional.

The Partition Network command will divide the network into multiple zones. This function assigns a zone name to each intersection. Each zone can be optimized as a separate system in the cycle length optimization.

Step 3: Optimize Network Cycle Length

The next step is to determine a system cycle length. It is possible to create multiple zones and assign a different cycle length to each zone.

The **Optimize → Network Cycle Length** command will set up a timing plan for each cycle length, and select the cycle length with the best performance based on Measures of Effectiveness (MOE).

When optimizing cycle lengths, it is necessary to optimize offsets to see how well the cycle length performs. In this step, a quick offset optimization is usually sufficient to determine how the cycle length will perform. Once the cycle length is selected, a thorough offset optimization can take place.

Step 4: Optimize Offsets, Lead/lag Phasing

After determining a system cycle length (or several cycle lengths), the last step is to optimize offsets. Use the Synchro command **Optimize → Network Offsets**.

If you have set **Allow Lead/Lag Optimize?** to "yes", this step will also optimize phase orders.

SimTraffic and CORSIM can be used afterwards to simulate the timing plans.

Table 13-1 shows the six types of optimizations and which parameters they optimize.

Table 13-1   Optimization Commands

Optimization Type	Scope	Values Optimized	Values Needed for Input
Intersection Cycle Length	Current Intersection	Cycle Length, Splits	Volumes, Lanes, Fixed Timings
Intersection Splits	Current Intersection	Splits	Volumes, Lanes, Left Turn Type, Cycle Length, Fixed Timings
Partition Network	Network	Zone	Volumes, Lanes, Fixed Timings
Network Cycle Lengths	Network or Zone	Cycle Lengths, Splits, Offsets, Lead/Lag Order	Volumes, Lanes, Fixed Timings
Intersection Offsets	Current Intersection	Offsets, Lead/Lag Order	Volumes, Lanes, Fixed Timings, Cycle Lengths, Splits
Network Offsets	Network or Zone	Offsets, Lead/Lag Order	Volumes, Lanes, Fixed Timings, Cycle Lengths, Splits

Tips to Improve Optimizations

Be sure to set the *Maximum Cycle Length* using the **Options→Network-Settings** command. Congested intersections will be set to the Maximum Cycle Length in many situations.

If there are permitted left turn movements with a v/c of greater than 1, consider making a protected left turn phase or prohibiting left turns at this intersection.

If you find that there are blocking problems between closely spaced intersections, consider using alternative phase orders, such as lagging lefts, lead-lag phasing, or split phasing. If you set the **Allow Lead/Lag Optimize?** field in the **PHASING** settings to "Yes" then Synchro will try both leading and lagging for that phase. Synchro measures queue interaction delay, which will be accounted for during the optimization process (see the section on Queue Interactions, page 13-55).

When optimizing Offsets, optimizing the lead-lag phasing slows down the optimization process. If you want a faster optimization, turn off Allow Lead/Lag Optimize?.

The Cycle Length Optimization can take quite a while. Consider limiting the number of cycles evaluated and using the Quick offset option.

Optimize-Intersection Splits

The **Optimize→Intersection-Splits** command will automatically set the splits for all the phases. Time is divided based on each lane group's traffic volume divided by its adjusted Saturated Flow Rate. The Split Optimizer will respect **Minimum Split** settings for each phase whenever possible.

Optimizing Splits by Percentile

When optimizing splits, Synchro first attempts to provide enough green time to serve the 90th percentile lane group flow. If there is not enough cycle time to meet this objective, Synchro attempts to serve the 70th percentile traffic and then the 50th percentile traffic. Any extra time is given to the main street phases.

By attempting to serve the 90th percentile, Synchro gives splits that will clear the queue 90% of all cycles. Because low volume approaches have more variability in traffic than high volume approaches, this method will tend to give lower v/c ratios for low lane group flow approaches. Consider the following examples

Phase #1, Lane Group Flow = 120 vph, Cycle Length = 60, capacity is 1800 vph

50th percentile Lane Group Flow per cycle is 2.

90th percentile Lane Group Flow per cycle is 3.8.

Green time assigned is 8 seconds

v/c is 0.44

Phase #2, Lane Group Flow = 1000 vph, Cycle Length = 60, capacity is 1800 vph

50th percentile Lane Group Flow per cycle is 17.

90th percentile Lane Group Flow per cycle is 22.

Green time assigned is 44 seconds

v/c is 0.74

In practice, percentile optimization gives short phases a few extra seconds to process an occasional extra vehicle. Longer phases also get extra time, but their extra time is less as a proportion of the total time.

If the volume exceeds capacity, Synchro will attempt to balance v/c ratios for each phase, while still respecting all minimums.

Other Rules

If **two or more lane groups** move concurrently, the maximum volume to saturation flow rate is used to set the split. For example, if there is a right turn lane and a through lane, the one with the highest volume to saturation flow rate is used.

If two rings are used, the maximum sum of ratios is used for this barrier. For example, the time requirement for NBT + SBL is compared to the time requirement for NBL + SBT. The maximum is used for these phase pairs.

All phases are assigned a split greater than or equal to their Minimum Split. The Optimize Splits algorithm calculates splits repeatedly to ensure all minimums are met. If the minimums exceed the cycle length, then all splits are reduced proportionately and there is a Min Error at the bottom of the **TIMING** settings. To use a split less than the ped timings, set the Minimum Split less than Walk + FDW + Yellow + All Red.

If there are **permitted left turns**, the entire process above is done repeatedly; the first time using protected left turn factors. Permitted left turn factors are then calculated based on these splits. Next, splits are recalculated using the permitted left turn factors. Finally, the left turn factors are recalculated using the new splits.

If a lane group is served by two or more phases, its volume will be divided among the phases that serve it. However, the lane group's volume will only be used to request time for the first Detector Phase. Make sure that the first Detector Phase is set correctly for each movement.

If there is a **shared turning lane plus an exclusive turning lane**, the calculations are repeated even further. The traffic is assigned among the various lane groups based on volume-to-capacity ratios. Lane group assignment affects permitted left turn factors and volume-to-saturation flow ratios. These, in turn, change the optimum splits, which means that the traffic may need to be reassigned further.

At low volume intersections, there may be extra time available even after accommodating the 90th percentile traffic. In these cases, extra time is divided evenly among phases at all intersections.

New in Version 7

There was a problem with using the saturated flow rates of pass n-1 for use in calculating splits for pass n. The permitted left turn factors (f_{lt}) in some cases can be quite volatile and cause the resulting splits to oscillate between two values without converging. As an example,

> NBL, volume = 300
>
> Cycle = 120
>
> Saturated Flow Rate Protected = 1800
>
> f_{lt} Permitted with a green of 45 seconds is 0.47
>
> f_{lt} Permitted with a green of 40 seconds is 0.42
>
> Longer splits can have a higher f_{lt} due do a longer unsaturated period with oncoming traffic
>
> Required green with $f_{lt} = 0.47$; $= v * C / (s * f_{lt}) = 300 * 120/ (1800 * 0.47) = 40$
>
> Required green with $f_{lt} = 0.42$; $= v * C / (s * f_{lt}) = 300 * 120/ (1800 * 0.47) = 45$

With this example the green time for successive passes alternates between 40 and 45 seconds without converging. A similar problem can also occur with permitted plus protected movements. Each pass of traffic is alternating between the permitted phase and the protected phase. Version 7 implements a smoothing process to insure that splits converge, and improves the split optimization.

Notes on Permitted Left Turn Factors

On pass 1, the permitted left turn factor used is an estimate independent of a timing plan. This is the same estimate used for calculating the percent traffic in a shared lane.

> f_{lt} Est = (900 - volOp)/900 * 0.95; (minimum of 0.15),
>
> volOp = opposing volume

On subsequent passes f_{lt} is based on the previous passes timings. Pretimed maximum timings are used for the calculation of F_{lt} in split optimization. After split optimization, the final calculated F_{lt} is based on actuated green times.

For version 7, split optimization does consider RTOR saturation flow during red times. In previous version, RTOR saturation flow was not considered.

Optimize-Intersection Cycle Length

The Natural Cycle length is the lowest acceptable cycle length for an intersection operating independently. The natural cycle length appears on the **TIMING** settings.

The **Optimize→Intersection Cycle Length** command will set the intersection to the Natural Cycle Length.

The Natural Cycle Length will be one of three possibilities.

1. Shortest Cycle Length that clears the critical percentile traffic.

2. Cycle Length with the lowest Performance Index, provided lowest PI cycle length is shorter than cycle length found in (1). This option is used to give reasonable cycles for intersections over capacity.

3. If no cycle is able to clear the critical percentile traffic, but a shorter cycle is able to give satisfactory v/c ratios, the shorter cycle length will be used. This is a special case to handle near capacity intersections with permitted left turns.

 In some cases, a longer cycle length will give lower delays or other performance benefits. The Cycle Length Optimization attempts to determine the shortest cycle length with acceptable performance.

Synchro starts with a short cycle length and optimizes the splits for that cycle length. If the splits for each phase are not able to clear the critical percentile traffic, Synchro will try a higher cycle length until the critical percentile traffic is cleared. For cycle lengths above 90, the v/c ratios simply need to be less than 1. If no acceptable cycle length is found, the cycle length is set to the cycle length with the lowest PI. To set the Maximum Cycle Length, use the **Options→Network Settings** command. **Table 13-2** shows the acceptable Critical Percentile Traffic for each range of cycle lengths.

Table 13-2   Acceptable Critical Percentile Traffic for Cycle Length

Cycle Length	Critical Percentile Traffic
40 - 60	90th
61 - 90	70th
91+	50th (v/c ≥ 1)

Over-Capacity Cycle Length Optimization

With one or more movements at or over capacity, the standard optimization procedure is to try successively longer and longer cycle lengths. Longer cycle lengths add additional capacity because a lower proportion of the cycle is used by yellow and total lost time.

When cycle lengths exceed 120 seconds, however, further increases to cycle length start to have less impact on intersection capacity, while incremental delay continues to increase. In one example, changing the cycle length from 150 seconds to 160 seconds increases the capacity for the intersection by 80 vehicles per hour, but adds 3 seconds of delay to all 5000 vehicles using the intersection. At some point, the cost of the extra delay does not outweigh the extra capacity due to increasing the cycle length.

The cycle length optimization will choose the cycle length with the lowest performance index. The PI is calculated as follows.

$$PI = [(D * 1) + (St * 10)] / 3600$$

> PI = Performance Index
>
> D = Total Delay (s)
>
> St = Vehicle Stops

The Percentile Signal Delay adds 450 seconds of delay for each unserved vehicle. This causes the cycle length to stop increasing when adding capacity for one vehicle will increase delay to other vehicles by 450s (7.5 minutes). In general, shorter cycle lengths have a shorter uniform delay, and will be favored when comparing delays of various cycle lengths. The Signal Delay calculation helps to favor longer cycle lengths in congested situations.

In previous versions of Synchro, over capacity intersections were always set to the Network Maximum cycle length. In many cases, these intersections can have a significantly shorter cycle length with much less delay and only a slight drop in capacity.

Shorter cycle lengths may also have other operational benefits. Queue lengths are generally shorter and storage bays can operate more efficiently.

Special Case for Permitted Left Turns

In some cases with permitted left turns, it is possible that capacity decreases as cycle length increases. In some cases, a short cycle length will give acceptable capacity while longer cycle lengths fail. In this case, Synchro may recommend a short cycle length that does not meet the percentile criteria.

Why Optimize for Critical Percentile Traffic?

By optimizing to accommodate percentile flows, Synchro will not recommend short cycle lengths unless there is extra capacity to accommodate traffic fluctuations. In previous versions of Synchro, the cycle length optimization only attempted to find acceptable v/c ratios. In some cases, Synchro 2 recommended cycle lengths that were considered too short. At a low volume approach, the traffic can be quite variable and a low v/c ratio is needed. If 2 vehicles per cycle are expected, it is quite likely to have 4 vehicles in some cycles. To accommodate these extra vehicles, 8 seconds of green is needed rather than 4 and a v/c ratio of 0.50. By looking at percentile flows, Synchro can be more confident that all vehicles will be handled on busy cycles when short cycle lengths are used.

Partition Network

This allows a network with multiple systems and cycle lengths, allowing timing plans to be tailored to local conditions. Choose **Optimize→Partition Network** to divide a network into multiple systems. Each intersection is assigned a zone. Existing Zone assignments will be changed. This command does not actually change timings, but it sets up the network to have multiple cycle lengths when Optimizing Network Cycle Lengths.

Reasons to use multiple systems:

- Large distances separate various parts of the network.

- Various parts of the network have different traffic characteristics. For example, the CBD may contain two phase signals with short cycle lengths, while the suburban areas may contain eight phase signals with long cycle lengths.

- It is possible to use shorter cycle lengths in some areas and longer cycle lengths in the more congested areas.

Reasons to use all one system:

- Controller hardware will not support multiple systems.

- All intersections are close together (less than 500 ft apart).

Even if all of the intersections are in the same zone, the Cycle Length Optimization may still recommend individual intersections to be operated independently. This means that candidates for independent operation can be included in the same zone.

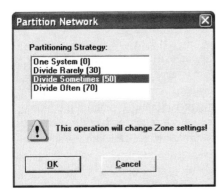

Figure 13-2 PARTITION NETWORK Settings

The partition network optimization calculates Coordinatability Factors (CFs) for each pair of adjacent intersections. Any intersections with a CF above the threshold value are put into the same zone. See the description of the CF calculation later in this section (page 13-22).

The CF value will range between 0 and 100. When choosing a Partitioning strategy the number in parenthesis is the threshold CF. If *One System* is selected all connected intersections will be placed in the same zone.

After partitioning the network, the zones can be observed on the map by pressing the *Show Intersection Zones* button. You may wish to change the zone recommendations based on personal experience with the network or to match the current network partitioning.

Even though there are multiple zones, the intersections can still be in the same system by assigning them the same cycle length.

Optimize-Network Cycle Lengths

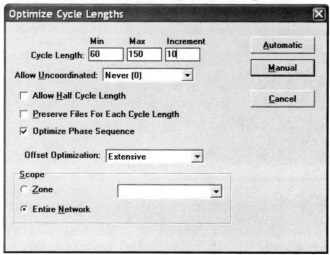

Figure 13-3   OPTIMIZE CYCLE LENGTHS Settings

Choose the **Optimize→Network Cycle Lengths** command to optimize cycle lengths for the network.

Optimize Network Cycle Lengths Options

Minimum, **Maximum**, and **Increment Cycle Length**: Enter the minimum and maximum cycle lengths to evaluate. The optimizer will evaluate every cycle length between the minimum and maximum at increment intervals. If the values are set to 60, 100, and 10; the optimizer will evaluate cycle lengths of 60, 70, 80, 90, and 100 seconds.

If Allow Half Cycles is selected, only even numbered cycle lengths will be evaluated. If min, max, and incr are set to 80, 120, and 5, and half cycles are allowed, the optimizer will evaluate 80, 86, 90, 96, 100, 106, 110, 116, and 120.

Allow Uncoordinated: This option may recommend that some intersections be left uncoordinated. The number in parentheses is the threshold Coordinatability Factor (CF). Intersections will be made independent and uncoordinated when either one of the following apply:

1. CF with all neighbors is less than threshold CF and space required for one cycle of traffic is less than 80% of the storage space.

2. The sum of Minimum Splits exceeds the Evaluation Cycle, the intersection will be set to uncoordinated.

Allow Half Cycle Length: This option will test some intersections at half cycle length. This option can give snappier operation and less delay at less congested intersections. Half Cycle Intersections will be given a cycle length of 1/2 the evaluated cycle. Intersections will be half cycled when they meet both of the following criteria:

1. Natural Cycle $\leq$ Evaluation Cycle / 2

2. Space required for one cycle of traffic is less than 120% of the link storage space.

Preserve Files: With this option a file is saved for each cycle length. These files can be loaded afterwards for evaluation or used for a multi-file comparison report. The files are given the name "filename-050.syn" where filename is the name of the file and 50 is the cycle length evaluated.

Optimize Phase Sequence: If this box is checked, leading and lagging left turn combinations will be tested. However, lead/lag combinations will not be checked if the **Allow Lead/Lag Optimize?** setting in the Phasing window is unchecked (see page 8-8).

Offset Optimization: Choose Quick to evaluate many cycle lengths quickly. Choose Medium or Extensive to analyze several cycle lengths in detail.

Table 13-3   Offset Optimization Options

Offset Option	Optimizations Performed
Quick	Incremental Offsets and Phase Orders, step 4
Medium	Incremental Offsets and Phase Orders, step 8
	Cluster Offset Optimization, step 2
	Incremental Offsets, step 2
Extensive	Incremental Offsets and Phase Orders, step 2
	Cluster Offset Optimization, step 2
	Incremental Offsets, step 1

Automatic: The automatic option will automatically select the best cycle length based on the cycle with the lowest Performance Index (PI). It is possible to have each zone assigned a different cycle length.

Manual: The manual option will create a table of cycle lengths with MOEs listed. The user can choose the best cycle length. Each zone can be assigned its own cycle length or all zones can be assigned a single cycle length.

Printing Cycle Length Optimization Results

The network cycle length optimization creates a table of Measures of Effectiveness (MOEs) for each cycle length evaluated. This table is not printable (other than a screen capture).

To view the cycle length comparison table, choose the [Manual] option. The [Automatic] option bypasses this settings.

To print a report similar to this comparison:

1. Choose the option Preserve Files for Each Cycle Length.

2. After performing the optimization, select **File→Create Reports** from the main settings.

3. Choose the report Summary Multifile Comparison.

4. Select all the files created by the cycle length optimization. These files have the name filename-50 where 50 is the cycle length.

Performance Index

The best cycle length is found by calculating a performance index. Previous versions of Synchro included a queuing penalty component within the PI. This is now directly accounted for with the Total Delay, which includes Queue Delay.

The PI is calculated as follows.

$$PI = [D * 1 + St * 10] / 3600$$

Where:

PI = Performance Index

D = Total Delay (s)

St = Vehicle Stops (vph)

The Total Delay above includes the Control Delay plus the Queue Delay. When multiple zones are optimized, the MOEs assume that intersections in adjacent zones are not coordinated.

Using a longer analysis period tends to favor longer cycle lengths in the network cycle length optimization. Unserved vehicles will be delayed on average for 1/2 of the analysis period. (Individual vehicles are not delayed this long, but is the cumulative affect of added delays). With a longer analysis period, serving as many vehicles as possible tends to dominate more than reducing uniform delays by having shorter cycle lengths.

Congestion lasting for 1 hour or longer tends to favor longer cycle lengths than spot congestion for 15 minutes. Changing to a longer analysis period (refer to page 11-4) may cause the cycle length optimization to recommend longer cycle lengths.

Faster Optimizations

It can take several minutes to evaluate each cycle length depending on the number of intersections and the speed of your computer. To get the best solutions quickly, a two-step optimization is recommended.

Pass 1: Evaluate a wide range of cycle lengths with a large increment (e.g., 60 to 150 at increment 15). Use quick offset optimization and manual optimization.

Pass 2: From the first pass, it will become clear which range of cycle lengths work best. At this point, focus the optimization on this range of cycle lengths (e.g., 80 to 100 at increment 5). Use Medium or Extensive offset optimization.

Manually Selecting a Cycle

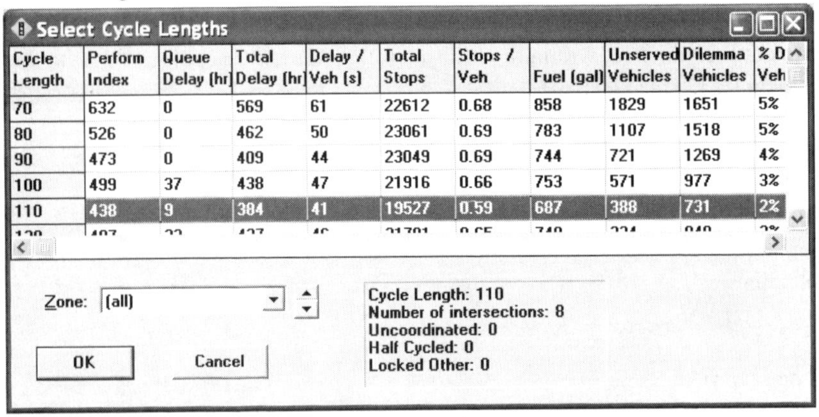

Cycle Length	Perform Index	Queue Delay [hr]	Total Delay [hr]	Delay / Veh [s]	Total Stops	Stops / Veh	Fuel [gal]	Unserved Vehicles	Dilemma Vehicles	% D Veh
70	632	0	569	61	22612	0.68	858	1829	1651	5%
80	526	0	462	50	23061	0.69	783	1107	1518	5%
90	473	0	409	44	23049	0.69	744	721	1269	4%
100	499	37	438	47	21916	0.66	753	571	977	3%
110	438	9	384	41	19527	0.59	687	388	731	2%
1̃2̃0̃	4̃9̃7̃	2̃2̃	4̃2̃7̃	4̃6̃	2̃1̃7̃8̃1̃	0̃.6̃5̃	7̃4̃8̃	3̃2̃4̃	8̃4̃8̃	3̃%

Zone: (all)

Cycle Length: 110
Number of intersections: 8
Uncoordinated: 0
Half Cycled: 0
Locked Other: 0

OK   Cancel

Figure 13-4   SELECT CYCLE LENGTHS Settings

After performing a manual cycle length optimization, the **SELECT CYCLE LENGTHS** settings will appear. Each cycle has MOEs listed for Performance Index, Queue Delay, Total Delay, Delay/Vehicle, Total Stops, Stops/Vehicle, Fuel Consumption, Unserved Vehicles, Dilemma Vehicles, Percent Dilemma Vehicles, Speed, and Average Speed.

These MOEs can be used to choose the optimal cycle length.

When the Select Cycle lengths settings appears, each zone is set to the cycle length with the lowest Performance Index (PI).

One cycle length can be used for the entire network or each zone can have its own cycle length.

The box in the lower right displays the number of intersections in the zone. For the selected zone and cycle length, the number of half, double and uncoordinated intersections is also listed.

The performance indexes shown for zones in the **SELECT CYCLE LENGTHS** settings are for the zone independent of neighboring zones and without coordination across zones. The performance indexes in the **SELECT CYCLE LENGTHS** settings are for the entire network and do consider coordination across zones. The network PI for a cycle may be less or more than the sum of the zone PIs.

The **SELECT CYCLE LENGTHS** settings cannot be used to determine the benefits of coordination across zones. The zone MOEs in the **SELECT CYCLE LENGTHS** settings assume no coordination with neighboring zones. Improved solutions may exist which provide coordination across zones. The automatic method and the initially recommended manual solution do consider coordination across zones.

Locked Intersections

Using the cycle length optimization with locked intersections presents a number of problems. If the locked intersection is pretimed or actuated-coordinated, its timings will not change for cycle lengths other than its original. There will thus be no coordination from locked intersections. Caution should be exercised in using cycle length optimization with locked intersections. If the intersection's original cycle length is chosen, it will keep the same timing and neighboring intersections will be optimized with it.

If the locked intersection is actuated-uncoordinated, it will remain uncoordinated with the same timings. No attempt will be made to optimize the timings.

Isolated Intersections

With some options, isolated and uncoordinated intersections are set to their natural cycle length for all evaluated cycle lengths. To view the performance of a single intersection at each cycle length, do one of the following:

- Assign the intersection to its own zone.
- Select "Never" for Allow Uncoordinated.

Multiple Zones

Network Cycle Length Optimization calculates a separate set of MOEs for each cycle length in each zone.

Initially each zone is assigned a cycle length with the best set of MOEs for that zone.

Next, each set of adjacent zones is evaluated for a combined cycle length. If the zones have lower MOEs due to inter-zone coordination, both zones are assigned the cycle length with the lowest combined PI.

The automatic cycle length optimization attempts to combine zones at the same cycle length for inter-zone coordination. This feature allows the user to set up many zones without fear of losing coordination across zones, but will still allow for multiple cycle lengths when appropriate.

Example:

	Performance Indexes	
	80 s	90 s
Zone 1	100	112
Zone 2	310	300
Zone 1+2 (independent)	410	412
Zone 1+2 (coordinated), less than sum due to coordination across zone	390	395

Best Independent Solution: Zone 1 @ 80 s + Zone 2 @ 90 s = 400

Best Coordinated Solution: Zone 1 +Zone 2 @ 80 s = 390

The performance indexes can be calculated assuming random and coordinated arrivals across zones. In the above example, the best solution for independent zones uses different cycle lengths. However, when the benefits of coordination across zones is considered, the best solution is to use one cycle length.

Master Intersection

In Synchro, there is one or zero master intersections for each cycle length. Half cycled intersections share the master. When changing offsets it is possible to combine two masters into the same cycle length and only one intersection will remain a master.

A common misconception is that there is one master per zone. This is not true, there is one master per cycle length. Two zones with one cycle length can have only one master, even if they are not physically connected.

Optimize - Intersection Offsets

To change a single intersection's timing plan so that it works best with its neighbors, click on an intersection to select it, then choose the **Optimize→Intersection Offsets** command. This command tests all possible offsets and lead-lag combinations. This command chooses the timing plan for this intersection that minimizes delays on links between this intersection and its immediate neighbors.

Network Minimum delay score is a relative measure of delay, so that you can see how the optimization is progressing. These scores are not convertible into an actual delay measure and will vary by cycle length.

The scoring used for offset optimization uses the 50th and 90th percentile scenarios only, with the 50th percentile being double weighted.

This command only changes the selected intersection. It does not make any changes to surrounding intersections. There may be better timing plans available by changing the timings of surrounding intersections, but **Optimize→Intersection Offsets** and Phasing will not find them. To find the best timing plans overall, use the **Optimize→Network-Offsets** command discussed in the next section.

For each offset and lead-lag combination Synchro will re-evaluate the departure patterns at this and surrounding intersections and recalculate delays. Synchro will also recalculate skipping and gap-out behavior at actuated-coordinated intersections.

When optimizing offsets, Synchro will look at offsets every 16 seconds around the cycle. Synchro will take those with the lowest delay score and look at offsets nearby every 4 seconds. Synchro will then take those with the lowest delays and look at offsets nearly every 1 second.

Optimize - Network Offsets

The final step in network optimization is to optimize offsets. This step should be performed after the cycle length has been determined.

Choose the **Optimize→Network Offsets** command.

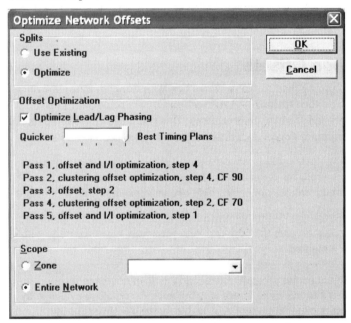

Figure 13-5   OPTIMIZE NETWORK OFFSETS Settings

The offset optimization function is used to evaluate the delays by varying the offset for every 8 seconds around the cycle. The optimizer then varies the offset by step size increments (1 or 4 seconds) around the 8 second choices with the lowest delays or close to the lowest delays. This finds the offset with the lowest delays, even if there are multiple "valleys" with low delay. The cluster optimization will vary groups of intersections so that local clusters can be synchronized with other local clusters rather than with just each other.

Scope

Choose **Zone** and enter a zone to perform optimizations on a group of intersections. To select multiple zones, separate the zones with a comma.

Choose **Entire Network** to optimize the entire network.

Optimizations

Optimize Splits will perform a Split Optimization for all intersections in the current scope. Cycle lengths and offsets are not affected. Perform this step if volumes or geometry has changed since the cycle length was last changed.

Offset Optimization Speed controls how many optimization passes are performed and the step size of each pass.

The **Step Size** controls how many offsets are looked at with incremental offset optimization. Using a value of 1 will check offsets in 1 second intervals. Using a value of 2 will check offsets in 2 second intervals and will take less time. It is recommended that offsets be optimized with a step size of 4 first and followed with a step size of 1.

[OK] starts the optimization process. All of the checked optimizations will be performed in order.

To fine-tune a network after minor changes, only use the incremental offset options.

Do not select **Optimize Splits** if splits have been set manually. These values will be optimized and any custom splits will be lost.

Allow Lead/Lag Optimize? is enabled for some passes. This feature will try reversing phase orders to improve coordination. This optimization is only performed for phases with **Allow Lead/Lag Optimize?** set to **Yes**.

Cluster vs. Individual Optimization

During passes 1, 3, and 5, Synchro performs **individual** intersection offset optimization. With individual optimization, each intersection's offset is set to a representative sample of every possible value between 0 and the cycle length -1. With each offset value traffic flow bands, actuated green times, and delays are recalculated. The offset resulting in the lowest delays is selected. The delays for the subject intersection and its neighbors are considered. In some cases the timing of the subject intersection can affect delays at an intersection two or more links away.

During passes 2 and 4, Synchro performs **cluster** optimization. With cluster optimization, Synchro finds groups of intersections that are connected and treats them as a single group. Synchro will adjust the offsets of the entire group together.

Consider an arterial of 4 intersections. With cluster optimization, the left two intersections will have their offsets adjusted together while the right two intersections are held constant. Whenever a group of two or more intersections is connected to the remainder of the network via a single link, they will be treated as a **dangling** cluster. **Dangling** cluster optimization works well with linear arterial(s).

Another type of cluster is a CF cluster. If two or more intersections have Coordinatability Factors between them of 90 (or 70) or more, they are considered a cluster and have their offsets optimized together. CF Cluster optimization helps with situations when two or more intersections that are very close have a lot of traffic between them. Without CF cluster optimization, these intersections would tend to be optimized for the benefit of each other only and not for the surrounding intersections.

Platoon Dispersion

Some traffic models such as TRANSYT-7F implement platoon dispersion. With platoon dispersion it is assumed that some vehicles will go faster or slower than the defined speed and platoons spread out over greater distances. One result of platoon dispersion is that coordination has less beneficial impact on longer links.

Synchro does not implement platoon dispersion. Synchro offers two other features that reduce the weightings of far-apart intersections.

Entering mid-block traffic can be used to "soften" the platoons and provide an effect similar to platoon dispersion.

Synchro calculates a Coordinatability Factor that takes the travel time between intersections into account. In many cases Synchro's optimizations will recommend not coordinating intersections when the travel time between the intersections exceeds 30 seconds. Therefore, in places where platoon dispersion might reduce the benefits of coordination, Synchro may recommend no coordination at all.

To reduce the weighting of coordination on longer links, enter mid-block traffic (see page 6-7). Also consider not coordinating intersections that are more than 30 s apart.

Check Phase Orders

In many cases, using alternate phase orders, such as lead-lag phasing, can significantly reduce delays, stops, and queues. Many parts of North America only use leading left turns and never consider alternate phase orders. When performing Network Offset Optimization and Automatic Network Cycle Length Optimization, Synchro performs a check to see if using alternate phase orders can reduce delays. The Check Phase Orders optimization does not change phase orders in the final timing plan, it merely recommends changes that could reduce delays.

A phase pair is the 1st and 2nd phases or the 3rd and 4th phases of a ring-barrier sequence. During Lead/Lag optimization, the optimizer will test timing plans by reversing the order of the phase pairs. During improvement optimization, the optimizer will test all combinations of phase reversals, including those marked "Fixed" for Allow Lead/Lag optimization. This may result in some suggestions that the engineer had not previously considered.

When an improvement is found that reduces delay by at least 1800 vehicle seconds per hour, the improvement is listed, like this example:

```
Consider changing the phase order at Node 3: E Pine ST & Freeman RD
Node #3 Phase:1 WBL, Change to a lagging phase.
Node #3 Phase:5 EBL, Change to a leading phase.
Total Delay is reduced by 10295 vehicle seconds per hour!
Node #3 Intersection delay is reduced by 8395 veh-s/hr!
Node #3 NBR Delay is reduced from 28.2 to 20.3 seconds per vehicle!
Node #3 WBT Delay is reduced from 9.7 to 4.0 seconds per vehicle!
Node #15 EBL Delay is reduced from 28.1 to 25.7 seconds per vehicle!


To optimize phase orders:
Check the "Optimize Lead/Lag Phasing" option AND
Set "Allow Lead/Lag Optimize" to YES in the Phasing settings.
Performing a complete Lead/Lag optimize may find even greater timing
improvements.
Combining these suggestions may reduce total delay more or less than
the sum of the improvements.
WARNING, Permitted left turns should not be used with lagging left
turns.
All delays listed above are uniform delays only. The incremental
portion of delay is not affected by offset optimization.
```

In this example, changing some of the phase orders at node #3 would reduce network delay by over 10,000 seconds per hour. This reduction may occur at node #3 and its neighboring intersections. Intersection delay reductions are listed that exceed 1800 veh-s/hr and individual movement reductions are listed that exceed 900 veh-s/hr or 50%.

To implement one or more of these suggestions, go to the **PHASING** settings and change the Lead/Lag field of the recommended phases. When using lagging left turns, the oncoming left turn treatment should be changed from Permitted-plus-Protected to Protected (see topic on Left Turn Trapping, page 7-14).

Check Phase Orders cannot be disabled. The ratio of time saved by motorists to the time spent analyzing these alternatives can exceed 10,000 to 1. Check Phase Orders is not performed if at least 66% of phase pairs have Allow-Lead/Lag-Optimize set to "Yes". Check Phase Orders is not performed on any intersection that has Allow-Lead/Lag-Optimize set to "Yes" for all phase pairs and the preceding optimization allowed for Lead/Lag optimize.

Coordinatability Factor

The Coordinatability Factor (CF) is a measure of the desirability of coordinating the intersections. Several criteria are used in an attempt to determine whether coordination is warranted. These criteria are used to determine a CF on a scale from 0 to 100 or more. Any score above 80 indicates that the intersections must be coordinated to avoid blocking problems; any score below 20 indicates the intersections are too far apart, or coordination is otherwise not desirable.

The CF is used with the Partition Network optimization. Intersections with CF values above the threshold CF are placed in the same zone or signal system.

The CF is also used with cycle length optimization when uncoordinated intersections are allowed. Intersections with CF values below the threshold CF are allowed to be independent and uncoordinated.

 The calculation of Coordinatability Factors is highly empirical. The application of these factors should be used with caution. They are primarily meant to call attention to the different criteria that make coordination desirable or undesirable.

The following criteria are used to determine the Coordinatability factor and are discussed here.

$$CF = Max(CF1, CF2) + Ap + Av + Ac$$

Where:

CF = Coordinatability Factor

CF1 = Initial Coordinatability Factor from Travel Time

CF2 = Initial Coordinatability Factor from Volume per Distance

Ap = Platoon Adjustment

Av = Volume Adjustment

Ac = Cycle Length Adjustment

Travel Time Between Intersections: This is the single most important element. The travel time affects the CF in the following ways. For links greater than 80 seconds apart, (5,300 ft. at 45 mph or 3,500 ft. at 30 mph), the intersections are assigned an initial CF of 0 because they are too far apart. For links less then 4 seconds apart, the intersections are assigned an initial CF of 100. These intersections are so close together, they could cause blocking problems. For links between 4 and 80 seconds, the initial CF is assigned using the formula CF1 = 100 - (time - 4) * 100 / 76.

Many agencies use the distance between intersections as the sole criteria for determining coordinatability. Using travel time instead of distance takes into account the speed of the links. High-speed expressways require coordination over longer distances than low-speed city streets.

Average Traffic Per Cycle Exceeds Link Distance: This criteria is similar to the previous criteria in that it uses the distance between intersections. This test also considers the traffic volume on the link and the cycle length of the intersection to see if the average traffic per cycle length will exceed the storage space between the intersections. If the average volume per cycle for either direction between the two intersections exceeds the available storage space, there is a potential blocking problem. Synchro assumes there is a blocking problem when AverageTraffic > 0.80 x StorageSpace.

$vc = v * C / 3600 =$ volume per cycle

StorageSpace $= n * LinkDist / VL$

Where:

v = volume in lane group

C = Cycle Length of destination intersection (s)

n = lanes in through lane group

LinkDist = link distance minus 150 feet (45 m) for the space in intersection and extra space.

VL = average vehicle length, entered in **NETWORK** settings

Similar checks are also made for the right and left turn lane groups as well. CF2 is the maximum factor of the internal lane groups.

CF2 = 100 * AverageTraffic / StorageSpace

Platooning of Traffic During the Cycle: This criteria looks at how much of the traffic arriving is compressed into the busiest 30% and 60% part of the cycle. If vehicle arrivals are spread out over the entire cycle, due to traffic coming from the side streets or from mid-block, coordinating this link will have less effect on reducing delays overall. If there is a short red time upstream, the traffic will be spread out over most of the cycle and coordination will have less effect. A pulse factor of 45 indicates that vehicles arrive uniformly across the cycle, coordination will provide no benefit. A pulse factor of 100 indicates that all of the traffic arrives in the busiest 30% of the cycle and coordination is a good idea.

PulseFactor = (v30 + v60) / (2 * vc) * 100%

Where:

PulseFactor = proportion of upstream traffic in busiest part of cycle

v30 = volume of traffic arriving during the busiest 30% of the cycle

v60 = volume of traffic arriving during the busiest 60% of the cycle

vc = volume per cycle

The adjustment to the CF for platoons is calculated by the following formula:

Ap = Platoon Adjustment = 10 - (100 - PulseFactor) * 30 / 55

A Pulse Factor of 45 reduces the CF by 20 points. A Pulse Factor of 100 increases the CF by 10 points. For a two way link, the maximum Pulse Factor for the two directions is used.

Main Street Volume: This criteria looks at the volume of the main streets. The assumption is that high volume arterials are more suitable for coordination than low volume streets. The arterial volume is the total hourly volume on the link in both directions including turning movements. The Volume Adjustment, Av is adjusted according to the following formula.

Av = (v2 - 700) / 50, when v2 < 1200

Av = (v2 - 200) / 100, when v2 < 2200

$Av = 20$, when $v2 \geq 2200$

Where:

Av = Volume Adjustment

$v2$ = sum of two way volume on link (vph)

The following summarizes how volumes affect Av.

v2	Av
200	-10
700	0
1200	10
1700	15
2200	20

Incompatible Cycle Lengths: This criteria looks at the natural cycle lengths of the adjacent intersections, or groups of intersections, to see if they are compatible. The Natural Cycle Length is the cycle length the intersections would have if they were operating as independent intersections, and it is the shortest cycle length that gives an acceptable level of service. If the two intersections have close to the same cycle length, they can be coordinated together without increasing delays to uncoordinated movements. Conversely, if one intersection only needs a short cycle length and the other needs a longer cycle length, both intersections would have to operate at the longer cycle length. This increases delays at the intersection with the shorter natural cycle length. The following test attempts to calculate, empirically, how much delay is increased when the intersection(s) with the shorter cycle length is increased to the longer cycle length:

Ac = Cycle Length Adjustment = $- (\Sigma \; IncreaseInCycle) / 2$

Where:

$-30 \leq Ac \leq 0$

IncreaseInCycle = amount to increase cycle length for coordination

If the shorter cycle of the two adjacent intersections can be half cycled, then IncreaseInCycle = LongerCycle / 2 - ShorterCycle. For example Intersection 1 has a natural cycle length 100 and intersection 2 has a natural cycle length of 40. Intersection 2 can be half cycled so its cycle length is increased from 40 to 50 and IncreaseInCycle is 10.

If one or both intersections are operating actuated or semi-actuated with a floating cycle length, the increase in cycle length is the difference between the longer natural cycle length and the average actuated cycle length without dwell time. If both intersections are actuated, the IncreaseInCycle for both intersections is used. For example, intersection 1 has a natural cycle of 70 seconds and an actuated cycle without dwell of 46 seconds. Intersection 2 has a natural cycle of 100 and actuated cycle without dwell of 78. To coordinate these intersections, intersection 1 increases from 46 to 100 and intersection 2 increases from 78 to 100. The IncreaseInCycle is thus (100-46) + (100-78) or 76.

This factor will avoid coordination when it significantly increases the cycle length of intersections. This factor also avoids coordinating actuated signals when they can shorten their cycle with skipped and gapped-out phases.

Summary of Coordinatability Factor

To see CFs select the **Show Natural Coordinatability Factors** button or the **Show Current Coordinatability Factors** button. The CF for each link will appear on the map. To see a detailed listing of the factors of the CF select the **File→Create Report** command and include a report for Coordinatabilities, or double-click on any link while the CFs are displayed.

Current versus Natural Coordinatability Factor

The Current Coordinatability Factor uses the current cycle length and timings to calculate the CF. The Natural Coordinatability Factor uses the intersection's natural cycle lengths. The Natural CF is used to initially determine which intersections should be coordinated. The Current CF is used to analyze the current timing plan and justify whether or not to coordinate additional intersections.

To answer the question, 'why were these two intersections coordinated together?', look at their natural CF. To answer the question, 'why are these two intersections not coordinated together?', look at their current CF.

Delay Calculations

Synchro's core delay calculation is called The Percentile Delay Method. The percentile delay calculation looks at five levels of traffic arrivals so that actuated signals can be evaluated under varying traffic loads. This allows the percentile delay method to capture and rationally model the non-linear behavior of actuated signals.

The Percentile Delay calculations in Synchro are also interval based. Vehicle arrivals from adjacent intersections are evaluated in intervals to determine the influence of coordination.

The calculations for The Percentile Delay Method can be quite complex, multiple intervals to be evaluated with detailed information about arrival patterns from adjacent signals. The HCM Delay equation (Webster's Formula), can be calculated by hand.

Choosing a Delay Formula

Synchro allows you to choose which delay method is used, the Synchro control delay or an HCM Signals Report delay. The delay shown in the **TIMING** settings is the Synchro control delay.

Use the HCM Signals Report When:

- Compatibility with Highway Capacity Manual is desired

Use Synchro Delay When:

- Evaluating actuated signal parameters
- Optimizing offsets
- Detailed modeling of coordination is needed
- Detailed modeling of actuated signals is needed

The following sections explain the differences between the two methods' calculations in detail.

Webster's Formula (HCM Signals Report)

The current Webster's formula as it appears in the Transportation Research Board's, 2000 HCM formula is defined as:

$D = D_1 * PF + D_2 + D_3 = $ Webster's Delay (s)

$$D_1 = 0.5 * C * \frac{[1 - (g/C)]^2}{[1 - (g/C) * \min(X,1)]} = \text{Uniform Delay}$$

PF = Progression Factor to account for coordination or controller type

$$D_2 = 900 * T * \left[(x-1) + \sqrt{(x-1)^2 + \frac{8 * k * I * X}{c * T}} \right] = \text{Incremental Delay}$$

D_3 = Residual Demand Delay, caused by existing queue at beginning of analysis, not used in Synchro

C = Cycle Length (s)

T = duration of analysis in hours, default 0.25 (see Network Settings)

g = Effective green time (s)

X = Volume to Capacity Ratio (v/c)

c = Capacity (vph)

k = incremental delay factor, dependent on controller settings (0.5 for pretimed or near saturation)

I = upstream filtering factor (1.0 for isolated intersections)

Webster's Formula is used when compatibility with the HCM is required. Webster's Formula and the HCM methods are a nationally recognized standard for measuring intersection performance. The formula provides a uniform set of rules for all design reports and planning studies. For these types of applications, Webster's formula should still be used.

The Progression Factor (PF) is used by the HCM to account for the effects of coordination. Synchro has already explicitly calculated the delay with coordination effects, so Synchro actually can determine the true PF by the following formula:

PF = DelayCoord / DelayUnCoord

PF = Progression Factor

DelayCoord = uniform delay calculated by Synchro with coordination

DelayUnCoord = uniform delay calculated by Synchro assuming random arrivals

The Uniform Delay shown in the Delays Report assumes random arrivals, to get the total delay, multiply the Uniform Delay by the PF and add the Incremental Delay.

Analysis Period

The analysis period, T, in Synchro can be modified. To change this, go to the **NETWORK** settings, Volume Settings tab.

The typical (and default) analysis period is 15 minutes (T = 0.25 hours). As the v/c ratios begin to increase to about 0.90, the control delay is significantly effected by the length of the analysis period. When the flows for each 15 minute interval remains relatively constant, consideration should be taken to increase the analysis period. If v/c exceeds 1.0 during the analysis period, then the length of the analysis period should be extended to cover the period of oversaturation in the same fashion, as long as the average flow during that period is relatively constant.

If the Analysis Period is changed to 30 minutes or greater, the PHF is automatically set to 1.0 and is not editable. The PHF is only used in conjunction with a 15 minute analysis. The delay equations (both Percentile and HCM) have provisions to accommodate traffic fluctuations that would occur for the peak 15 minute period during a 60 minute analysis.

How Analysis Period Affects Delay

The length of the analysis period will affect the control delay. Adjusted volumes and v/c ratios will be lower due to not using a PHF adjust. Uniform delays will be lower at 60 minutes due to lower volumes. Incremental delays will be lower at 60 minutes due to lower volumes, but higher due to longer analysis period. Movements under and near capacity may see a reduction in delay. Movements over capacity will likely see a big increase in delay. This reflects over capacity movements having standing queues for 60 minutes rather than 15 minutes.

Use a 15 minute period when:

- Most of the intersections in the study area are operating at less than capacity.

- If the agency has a goal of LOS D or better for all intersections.

- The study area has a short term spike in traffic, such as a shift change at a major employer.

- Traffic counts are available in 15 minute intervals

Use a 60 minute analysis period when:

- Most of the intersections in the study area are operating near or over capacity for 30 minutes to 2 hours.

- The agency is forced to accept intersections over capacity and is looking at incremental improvements.

- Traffic counts are not available in 15 minute intervals.

Use a 120 minute analysis period when:

- Most of the intersections in the study area are over capacity for 2 hours or longer.

- The agency is forced to accept intersections over capacity and is looking at incremental improvements.

The Percentile Delay Method

Basic Delay Calculation

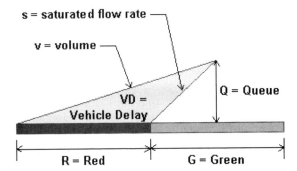

Figure 13-6   Vehicles Queued at Red light

The average delay for a lane group at a pretimed signal is represented by the area in the triangle in **Figure 13-6**. The width of the triangle's base is equal to the effective red time of the phase. The slope of the left side is the arrival rate of vehicles in vehicles per second. The slope of the right side is the departure rate or Saturated Flow Rate in vehicles per second. The height of the triangle is the maximum queue in vehicles. The maximum queue can thus be found with the following formula.

$$Q = \frac{v}{(1 - v/s) * 3600} * R = \text{Maximum Back of Queue (vehicles)}$$

     v = Volume (vph)

     s = Saturated Flow rate (vph)

     R = Red Time (s)

The vehicle delay per cycle is the area of the triangle; the delay per vehicle is the area of the triangle divided by the vehicles served per cycle.

$$VD = \frac{v}{(1 - v/s) * 3600} * \frac{R^2}{2} = \text{Vehicle Delay}$$

$$Dp = \frac{VD}{C * 3600} = \text{Uniform Delay per vehicle, for scenario p (s)}$$

C = Cycle Length (s)

Thus this gives...

$$Dp = \frac{0.5}{(1 - v/s)} * R * \frac{R}{C}$$

Given that...

$$X = \frac{v}{s * g / C}$$

R / C = 1 - G / C

$$Dp = 0.5 * C * \frac{[1 - (g/C)]^2}{[1 - X * g/C]}$$

This formula is identical to the definition for Webster's formula for D_1. The primary differences between the Percentile and Webster calculations lie in the determination of green time, and the handling of nearly- and over-saturated conditions.

Percentile Scenarios

Over the course on an hour or 15 minute period, traffic will not arrive at an intersection uniformly. Some cycles will have more traffic and some cycles will have less. A Poisson distribution can be used to predict how traffic arrives.

To account for variations in traffic, Synchro models traffic flow under five percentile scenarios, the 90th, 70th, 50th, 30th, and 10th percentile scenarios. If 100 cycles are observed, the 90th percentile cycle will be the 90th busiest cycle. Each of these scenarios will represent 20% of the cycles actually occurring.

The traffic volumes for each scenario are adjusted up or down according to the following formulas.

The expected number of vehicles, λ, is the hourly flow rate divided by the number of cycles per hour.

$$\lambda = v * \frac{C}{3600}$$

v = Volume (vph)

C = Cycle Length (s)

The variance, or standard deviation, in traffic is the square root of the expected number of vehicles for a Poisson arrival.

ρ = Sqrt(λ) = standard deviation in expected arrivals per cycle

The expected number of vehicles for a given percentile can be calculated using a Poisson distribution. A Normal Distribution can be used if the expected number of vehicles is greater than 6. This gives the formula:

$$vP = (\lambda + z\rho) * \frac{3600}{C} = \text{volume for percentile P}$$

C = Cycle Length (s)

z is the number of standard deviations needed to reach a percentile from the mean. It can be determined from this table.

Percentile	z
10	-1.28
30	-0.52
50	0
70	0.52
90	1.28

The simplified formula to determine adjusted volumes is thus:

$$vP = v + \left[z * \sqrt{v * C / 3600} \right] * \frac{3600}{C}$$

with vP ≥ 0

Using five scenarios instead of one has several advantages. Even though an approach is below capacity, it may be above capacity for the 90th percentile traffic. By modeling the 90th percentile traffic, it is possible to better model nearly saturated intersections.

Using multiple scenarios allows actuated signals to be modeled under multiple loadings. The complex operation of actuated signals will vary under the five scenarios and give a range of expected green times over the course of an hour.

For example a phase serving a low volume movement may skip 40% of the time. With percentile modeling this phase is skipped in two of five scenarios. The alternative used by HCM is to assume a split or green time of 60% of the non skipped time. Similar non-linear behavior occurs with pedestrian activated phases.

To get basic delays for pretimed, unsaturated signals with uniform arrivals, the formulas are:

$$D_1 = \frac{VD10 + VD30 + VD50 + VD70 + VD90}{(v10 + v30 + v50 + v70 + v90) * C / 3600}$$

D_1 = average percentile delay

$VD10$ = 10th percentile Vehicle-Delay per hour

$$VD10 = 0.5 * \frac{v10}{(1 - v10/s)} * \frac{R^2}{C} * 3600$$

$v10$ = 10th percentile volume rate (vph), volume rate is adjusted using methods described earlier

Vehicle-Delay values and Arrival rates for other percentiles are calculated similarly.

If volume exceeds capacity for a percentile scenario, the capacity, rather than the volume is used in the uniform delay calculation. For congested percentile conditions the following apply:

$$VD10 = 0.5 * s / 3600 * \frac{R^2}{C} = \text{uniform delays calculation for congested links}$$

Actuated Signal Considerations

To estimate the delay for actuated signals, it is necessary to determine how skipping and gapping behavior will change their timings. These actuated timings are then used with the Percentile Delay formulas. This section describes how actuated signals are modeled.

The key to determining actuated behavior is to predict if each phase will be skipped and when each phase will gap out. Once these behaviors are determined, the green and red times from the actuated signals can be used to model delays.

Determining Skip Probability

To determine the probability of a phase being skipped it is necessary to determine the expected number of vehicles that arrive during red. Synchro assumes the phase will be skipped if there is a greater than 50% chance that zero vehicles arrive during the red time. If the expected number of vehicles is less than 0.69, there is a 50% chance that zero vehicles arrived.

The red time can be a tricky number to determine. The red time occurs at the beginning of the unusable yellow time or about 2 to 3 seconds into the yellow time. The red time extends to the end of the permissive period for this phase. The permissive period ends at the yield point of the previous phase. If there are advanced detectors, this will allow more vehicles to be detected and extend the detection time for avoiding a gap.

$$R' = R + L2 + Tlead - Ymain = \text{Red time for calculating skips (s)}$$

   R = Actual Red Time (s)

   $L2$ = Clearance Lost Time (s) = 1 to 2 s.

   $Tlead$ = Travel time from first advanced detector to stop bar. (s)

   $Ymain$ = Yellow time for main street. Only subtract if main street has not yielded to another phase. (s)

When determining the probability of a skip, traffic from all lane groups calling the phases are added and pedestrian calls are added as well.

Any phases with recall will not be skipped.

If this signal is not in coordination, the actual cycle length may be less than the maximum cycle length and the skipping and gapping calculations must be done iteratively with shorter cycle lengths.

If this signal is in coordination, the arrival flow will reflect the departures from the upstream intersection. It is possible for a phase to be skipped if the platoon arrives after the permissive period, this occurs most often with leading left turn phases. In this case, Synchro will calculate delays by modeling two cycles. In the first cycle, the phase is skipped. In the second cycle, all vehicles are served. Synchro will not skip phases if the v/c ratio is 0.9 or greater.

Synchro assumes that any phase with traffic of at least 1 vph will not be skipped during the 90th percentile cycle. This insures that every phase gets at least some green time.

Determining Queue Clear Time

The queue clearance time is equal to the startup lost time plus the service time for any vehicles that arrived during red plus vehicles arriving during the clearance time. Synchro has the startup lost time set for 2.5 seconds. The service time is 3600 divided by the Saturated Flow Rate and the number of lanes.

$$Tq = L1 + \frac{v}{s-v} * (L2 + R + L1) = \text{queue clearance time (s)}$$

$L1 = 2.5 \text{ s} = \text{startup lost time (s)}$

$v = \text{arrival rate (vph)}$

$s = \text{Saturated Flow Rate (vph)}$

$R = \text{Actual Red Time (s)}$

$L2 = \text{Clearance Lost Time (s)}$

If the signal is in coordination, the arrival rate will not be constant.

If this phase serves two or more lane groups, the lane group with the highest Volume to Saturation ratio is used.

If the lane group for this phase is also served by another phase such as a permitted + protected left turn phase or a right turn phase with an overlap, the vehicles arriving on red will be reduced by the vehicles served by the other phase.

Synchro does not actually model stop bar detectors or initial intervals. Synchro assumes that the detectors and initial interval settings are set up in such a way that the phase will not gap out before the queue is cleared.

An "overflow queue" calculation is used to prevent gap-out at lower percentiles for movements near or over capacity. The unserved vehicles from the 90th percentile cycle are assumed to be in the initial queue for the lower percentile cycles. The overflow queues are assigned as follows:

$uI = (vI - cI)*C/3600 = \text{unserved vehicles for percentile I.}$

$vI = \text{percentile volume for percentile I}$

$cI = \text{capacity for percentile I, based on maximum green times}$

o70 = u90/4 = 70th percentile initial overflow queue (vehicles / cycle)

o50 = u90/4 + u70/3 = 50th percentile initial overflow queue (vehicles /cycle)

o30 = u90/4 + u70/3 + u50/2 = 30th percentile initial overflow queue

o10 = u90/4 + u70/3 + u50/2 + u30 = 10th percentile initial overflow queue

C = cycle length, using maximum green times

The overflow queue calculations are based on maximum green times.

Determining Time to Gap-Out

The time-to-gap-out is the time from when the queue clears until there is a 50% chance of gap out.

The effective gap time, GapEff, is the time required between two vehicles for the signal to gap out. A single vehicle can extend the phase from the time it hits the first detector until the time it leaves the last extension detector plus the gap time. GapEff is thus equal to the controller's actual gap time plus the travel time between the first and last extension detectors. Only extension detectors are counted when determining the effective gap time.

GapEff = Gap + Tlead - Ttrail = Effective gap time (s)

Gap = Vehicle Extension time. (s)

Tlead = Travel time from leading detector to stop bar. (s)

Ttrail = Travel time from trailing extension detector to stop bar. (s)

The probability of an immediate gap-out is the probability of 0 vehicles in the first GapEff seconds. If the expected vehicles are less than 0.69 in this time, there is more than 50% chance of an immediate gap-out.

The probability of a gap-out in any subsequent second is the probability of no vehicles in the new second and the probability of no vehicles in the trailing GapEff -1 seconds. The expected number of vehicles in the trailing time is arrivals + 1 since we know there was at least one vehicle in the trailing GapEff seconds.

Coordination

One of the best ways to reduce delays at signalized intersections is through coordination. When a signal is in coordination its arrival flows from adjacent intersections will vary over the course of a cycle. Under perfect coordination all traffic arrives on green, there are no stops or delays.

Synchro models coordination by varying the arrival rate at intersections based on the departures at upstream intersections. This causes the arrival rate to vary across the cycle.

Determining Arrival Patterns

Synchro takes all traffic from upstream intersections moving toward the subject intersection, both through and turning traffic. If the upstream green interval is not saturated, the traffic flow leaving the upstream intersection will vary across the green band.

Normally traffic from the upstream intersection will be heavy during the upstream intersection's queue clearance period and then the flow will decrease to the upstream intersection's arrival rate. If a platoon arrives at the middle or end of the upstream intersection's green time, the platoon will carry through to this intersection.

For a graphical representation of how vehicles leave the upstream intersection, look at the flows in the time-space diagram (page 12-5).

If the upstream intersection is actuated-uncoordinated or if it has an incompatible cycle length, the traffic is assumed to arrive uniformly. A compatible cycle length is the same cycle length, double the cycle length, or half the cycle length.

If the upstream intersection has half the cycle length, traffic will be modeled over two of its cycles. If the upstream intersection has double the cycle length, this intersection will be modeled with two cycles.

Actuated-coordinated intersections always see traffic arriving uniformly.

If the upstream intersection is unsignalized or a bend, Synchro will look beyond the unsignalized intersection for any signalized intersections. Any vehicles arriving at a free approach to an unsignalized intersection are assumed to depart immediately.

Vehicles arriving at a stop or yield approach to an unsignalized intersection are assumed to depart uniformly across the cycle. If mid-block traffic is coded, this traffic is represented as arriving uniformly.

Traffic volumes from upstream traffic are adjusted up or down to match the required traffic at the subject intersection. Traffic adjusted downward can be used as an automatic traffic sink. Traffic flows from upstream intersections will be adjusted upward by as much as 30%. Any additional traffic is assumed to arrive uniformly.

The vehicle flows from upstream are time adjusted based on the travel time between the intersections. Synchro has no option for platoon dispersion.

It is possible that the departures of a distant intersection can affect the arrival pattern at this intersection. For this reason, departure patterns are recalculated iteratively and this causes Synchro to take a while to recalulate.

Modeling Over Capacity and Cycle Failures
Saturated Links

At links near or above capacity, the delay will have two parts:

$D = D_1 + D_2$ = total percentile delay

D_1 = Uniform delay, weighted average of percentile scenarios (sec)

D_2 = Incremental Delay (sec)

As volume approaches capacity, some or all vehicles will not be accommodated on the first cycle. Both the Synchro Delay and HCM Signals Report include an incremental delay term (D_2) to account for delays from vehicles waiting for extra cycles. The D_2 in both models accounts for delays due to near saturation and over saturation.

Incremental delay is now calculated using the HCM formula. Earlier versions of Synchro performed a 100 cycle simulation to determine the incremental delay. Trafficware conducted research that showed the HCM formula gives essentially the same results for a wide range of v/c ratios, cycle lengths, and green times, provided the same definition of delay is used. Synchro 6 switched to using the HCM formula to give consistency with the other method, and to facilitate fast D_2 calculations to model queue interactions during optimization.

$$D_2 = 900 * T * \left[(x-1) + \sqrt{(x-1)^2 + \frac{8 * k * I * X}{c * T}} \right] = \text{Incremental Delay}$$

Synchro allows for analysis periods other than 15 minutes. D_2 will be higher when using longer analysis periods. However, with a 60 minute analysis period, there is no adjustment for PHF, this will normally reduce the adjusted volume. The resulting delay could be higher in some cases and lower in others than using a 15 minute analysis period.

Upstream Metering

The I term is determined by Exhibit 15-9 in the HCM 2000. If this is an isolated intersection or there is no upstream intersection, I = 1.0 for random arrivals. Exhibit 15-9 of the HCM is as follows:

EXHIBIT 15-9. RECOMMENDED I-VALUES FOR LANE GROUPS WITH UPSTREAM SIGNALS							
	Degree of Saturation at Upstream Intersection, Xu						
	0.40	0.50	0.60	0.70	0.80	0.90	≥ 1.0
I	0.922	0.858	0.769	0.650	0.500	0.314	0.090

Note: $I = 1.0 - 0.91 \, X_u^{2.68}$ and $X_u \leq 1.0$

Source: Year 2000 Highway Capacity Manual, Chapter 15

Percentile Delay Summary

The basic premise of the Percentile Delay Method is that traffic arrivals will vary according to a Poisson distribution. The Percentile Delay Method calculates the vehicle delays for five different scenarios and takes a volume weighted average of the scenarios. The five scenarios are the 10th, 30th, 50th, 70th, and 90th percentiles. It is assumed that each of these scenarios will be representative of 20% of the possible cycles. For each scenario, traffic for each movement is adjusted to that percentile.

If the signal is actuated or semi-actuated, the skipping and gap-out behavior for these traffic conditions are used to determine the green times for each scenario. If the signal is in coordination, an arrivals flow pattern is calculated to account for the affects of coordination. Delays are calculated using the adjusted volumes and calculated green times.

Estimating actuated operation or coordination arrivals may require that the calculations be performed iteratively. A D_2 term is calculated to account for signals near or above saturation.

Percentile Delay and Webster's Formula Compared

In most situations, the delays calculated by the Synchro Percentile and HCM Signals Report method are similar and will be within a few seconds of each other. The HCM 2000 has added capabilities for calculating delays of actuated signals and for congested movements; these improvements allow the two delay methods to be similar in most cases.

Actuated Signals

Webster's formula calculates delay using a single set of green times. These green times are an average of the actual green times encountered by the signal operating in actuated mode. The percentile method uses five sets of green times, by using five levels of traffic. Delays are calculated using each scenario and a weighted average is taken.

In most cases, the difference between using one and five scenarios will be less than a few seconds. The biggest differences occur with the non-linear behavior associated with pedestrian phases and skipped phases. If an intersection has pedestrian actuated phases with 1 to 50 pedestrians per hour or skipped phases and traffic under 100 vph; the delay to other phases will be calculated more accurately using the Percentile method.

Coordination

Webster's formula calculates the affects of coordination by using a Progression Factor (PF). The PF is calculated by estimating the percentage of vehicles arriving on green. The formula does not discriminate between vehicles arriving at the beginning or end of red so the entire process is an approximation.

The Percentile Method calculates the affects of coordination by looking at actual arrivals from adjacent intersections. The queue length and delays are calculated by integrating the expected arrival rate across the cycle length. The delays calculated this way explicitly account for coordination and give the detail necessary for offset optimization.

Summary

	Percentile	Webster
Models Actuation	Yes	Yes
Models Skips	Yes	Approximate
Models Pedestrian Actuation	Yes	Approximate
Models Traffic Variance	Yes	Yes
Models Congestion	Yes	Yes
Models Coordination	Yes	Approximate

Delay Calculations for Approaches with Left Turn Phasing, but no Left Turn Lane

Delay calculations for approaches with left turn phasing, but no left turn lane are modeled as follows. Traffic is assumed to flow freely (both left and through) during the protected left turn phase. During the through phase, traffic is somewhat or fully constrained. For **Permitted+Protected** operation, the flow rate during the permitted part of the cycle is reduced by the left turn factor calculated using the methods shown in the 2000 Highway Capacity Manual. For **Protected** operation, it is assumed that the left lane will be blocked by a left turning vehicle. The capacity is thus reduced by one lane, or the capacity is zero for a one lane approach.

Intersection Capacity (ICU) Calculations

The Intersection Capacity Utilization (ICU) method is a simple yet powerful tool for measuring an intersection's capacity. The ICU can be calculated using a single page worksheet, that is both easy to generate and easy to review. The ICU is the perfect tool for planning applications such as roadway design and traffic impact studies.

The method sums the amount of time required to serve all movements at saturation for a given cycle length and divides by that reference cycle length. This method is similar to taking a sum of critical volume to saturation flow ratios (v/s), yet allows minimum timings to be considered. The ICU can tell how much reserve capacity is available or how much the intersection is overcapacity. The ICU does not predict delay, but it can be used to predict how often an intersection will experience congestion.

The ICU is timing plan independent, yet has rules to insure that minimum timing constraints are taken into account. This removes the choice of timing plan from the capacity results. The ICU can also be used on unsignalized intersections to determine the capacity utilization if the intersection were to be signalized.

 Additional Details can be found in the *Intersection Capacity Utilization 2003* book. A copy of this can be found in Adobe PDF format in your Trafficware installation directory.

ICU 2003 includes new procedures for analyzing Diamond Interchanges and Single Point Urban Interchanges. The Diamond method includes procedures recognizing the special timing needs of a diamond interchange to prevent spillback.

Level of Service

The ICU is the sum of time required to serve all movements at saturation given a reference cycle length, divided by the reference cycle length.

$$ICU = sum (max (tMin, v/si) * CL + tLi) / CL = \text{Intersection Capacity Utilization}$$

CL = Reference Cycle Length

tLi = Lost time for critical movement i

v/si = volume to saturation flow rate, critical movement i

tMin = minimum green time, critical movement i

The ICU Level of Service should not be confused with delay-based levels of service such as the HCM. Both are providing information about the performance of an intersection while measuring a different objective function. The ICU LOS reports on the amount of reserve capacity or capacity deficit. The delay based LOS reports on the average delay experienced by motorists.

The ICU 2003 uses one-hour volume counts with no adjustment for Peak Hour Factor. Older versions of the ICU used one-hour volume counts with a peak hour adjustment factor (with a default of 0.90). The scale has been adjusted to reflect this change while still providing the same LOS.

Old ICU	New ICU	Level of Service
0 to 60%	0 to 55%	A
>60% to 70%	>55% to 64%	B
>70% to 80%	>64% to 73%	C
>80% to 90%	>73% to 82%	D
>90% to 100%	>82% to 91%	E
>100% to 110%	>91% to 100%	F
>110% to 120%	>100% to 109%	G
>120%	>109%	H

A brief description of the conditions expected for each ICU level of service follows:

LOS A, ICU ≤ 0.55: The intersection has no congestion. A cycle length of 80 seconds or less will move traffic efficiently. All traffic should be served on the first cycle. Traffic fluctuations, accidents, and lane closures can be handled with minimal congestion. This intersection can accommodate up to 40% more traffic on all movements.

LOS B, 0.55 < ICU ≤ 0.64: The intersection has very little congestion. Almost all traffic will be served on the first cycle. A cycle length of 90 seconds or less will move traffic efficiently. Traffic fluctuations, accidents, and lane closures can be handled with minimal congestion. This intersection can accommodate up to 30% more traffic on all movements

LOS C, 0.64 < ICU ≤ 0.73: The intersection has no major congestion. Most traffic should be served on the first cycle. A cycle length of 100 seconds or less will move traffic efficiently.

Traffic fluctuations, accidents, and lane closures may cause some congestion. This intersection can accommodate up to 20% more traffic on all movements.

LOS D, 0.73 < ICU ≤ 0.82: The intersection normally has no congestion. The majority of traffic should be served on the first cycle. A cycle length of 110 seconds or less will move traffic efficiently. Traffic fluctuations, accidents, and lane closures can cause significant congestion. Sub optimal signal timings cause congestion. This intersection can accommodate up to 10% more traffic on all movements.

LOS E, 0.82 < ICU ≤ 0.91: The intersection is right on the verge of congested conditions. Many vehicles are not served on the first cycle. A cycle length of 120 seconds is required to move all traffic. Minor traffic fluctuations, accidents, and lane closures can cause significant congestion. Sub optimal signal timings can cause significant congestion. This intersection has less than 10% reserve capacity available.

LOS F, 0.91 < ICU ≤ 1.00: The intersection is over capacity and likely experiences congestion periods of 15 to 60 minutes per day. Residual queues at the end of green are common. A cycle length over 120 seconds is required to move all traffic. Minor traffic fluctuations, accidents, and lane closures can cause increased congestion. Sub optimal signal timings can cause increased congestion.

LOS G, 1.00 < ICU ≤ 1.09: The intersection is 10% to 20% over capacity and likely experiences congestion periods of 60 to 120 minutes per day. Long queues are common. A cycle length over 120 seconds is required to move all traffic. Motorists may be choosing alternate routes, if they exist, or making fewer trips during the peak hour. Signal timings can be used to "ration" capacity to the priority movements.

LOS H, 1.09 < ICU: The intersection is 20% over capacity and could experience congestion periods of over 120 minutes per day. Long queues are common. A cycle length over 120 seconds is required to move all traffic. Motorists may be choosing alternate routes, if they exist, or make fewer trips during the peak hour. Signal timings can be used to "ration" capacity to the priority movements.

The length of the congested period is heavily dependent on the source of traffic and the availability of alternate routes. If traffic is generated by a single factory shift change, the congested period may be shorter. However, a shopping mall could generate congested traffic for several hours. If alternate routes exist, motorists may know to avoid the congested intersections during the peak hour and this reduces congestion.

If intersections have LOS E to LOS G, queues between intersections can lead to blocking problems. Signal timing plans should be analyzed with microscopic simulation to insure that spillback is not causing additional problems.

ICU LOS and HCM Level of Service

The ICU 2003 is designed to be compatible with the HCM. The default Saturated Flow Rates and volume adjustments are the same as those recommended by the HCM. The two methods are closely interrelated. If the intersection has an ICU LOS of E or better, a timing plan exists that will give LOS E or better with the HCM. With an ICU of F, the intersection will be over capacity for the peak 15 minutes. It may possible to get an acceptable HCM LOS when the intersection is over capacity by using a timing plan favoring the highest volume movements.

Overview of Calculations

The primary calculation for ICU 2003 is to calculate an Adjusted Reference Time for each movement. The Reference Time is the amount of time required for each movement at 100% capacity. The reference time is volume times Reference Cycle Length divided by Saturated Flow Rate.

$tRef = vC/s * CL$ = reference time

vC = adjusted volume combined for lane group

s = saturation flow rate for lane group

CL = reference cycle length

The Reference Time must be greater than the Minimum Green time and is added to the Lost Time to give the Adjusted Reference Time. The ICU is the sum of the critical Adjusted Reference Times divided by the Reference Cycle Length. The Reference Cycle Length is a fixed input value; the default is 120 seconds.

$tAdj = max(tRef, tMin) + tL$ = adjusted reference time

$tMin$ = minimum green time

tL = lost time

There are further adjustments to account for pedestrian time and pedestrian interference.

The reference times for the critical movements are added together to get the combined time required.

Additional Details can be found in the *Intersection Capacity Utilization 2003* book. A copy of this can be found in Adobe PDF format in your Trafficware installation directory.

Permitted Lefts and Shared Lanes

The modeling of permitted left turns, particularly for shared lanes is problematic in the ICU methodology. This is especially a problem for single lane approaches.

The ICU method requires a movement to be protected to determine its timing requirements based of the v/s ratio (volume to saturated flow ratio). If there is no left turn lane, protected phasing cannot be used. The two options available are to use Split phasing or to assume a de-facto left turn lane. For modest left turn volumes, neither of these solutions is satisfactory because a large proportion of the time there will be no left turn vehicles and the lanes will function as though they were normal through lanes.

Permitted left turns will be able to go under three conditions:

1. A gap in oncoming traffic due to low oncoming traffic volumes

2. Sneakers at the end of green

3. A gap in oncoming traffic caused by a left turn from a single lane approach.

Trafficware conducted research using simulation to determine the average amount of green time a left turner spends at the stop bar. The simulations were performed for a complete range of left turn proportions for the subject approach and a complete range of left turn proportions for the oncoming approach. If the oncoming approach has multiple lanes then the behavior is assumed to be equivalent to zero oncoming left turns.

Comparison of ICU and HCM Delay Based Methods

Currently the most popular method for analyzing capacity is the HCM. The HCM method is based on estimating delay for the intersection.

The ICU 2003 is designed to be compatible with the HCM and can be used in conjunction with the HCM and other methods. The default Saturated Flow Rates and volume adjustments are the same as those recommended by the HCM. In most circumstances, the volume to Saturated Flow Rates in ICU 2003 (v/s), will be the same as those in the HCM. When an agency requires an acceptable HCM Level of Service, an acceptable ICU Level of Service will insure that the HCM Level of Service is met.

An acceptable ICU Level of Service guarantees that a timing plan exists that will meet all of the following:

- Acceptable HCM level of service
- All minimum timing requirements are met
- All movements have acceptable v/c ratios
- All movement volumes can have their volume increased by the reciprocal of the ICU and be at or below saturation.

With an acceptable HCM level of service, the following is guaranteed:

- Average delays are less than the amount for that Level of Service
- The majority of traffic has acceptable v/c ratios or short red time

The ICU is inherently more precise because the delay equation is unstable near capacity. The calculation of delay requires an estimate for the affects of coordination, which adds greatly to the resulting uncertainty.

One consequence of the high range of uncertainties is that it makes the method easy to manipulate. In some cases, it is possible to get a 20% reduction in delay or two Levels of Service by increasing capacity 5% and reducing volume 5%.

If a real estate developer is attempting to get project approval with a minimum of mitigation measures, it is not too difficult to adjust the input factors, platoon factors, and so forth to get a significant reduction in delay. Some communities have regulations requiring developers to maintain a certain LOS. There is unfairness to this method of regulation because all developers up to the critical LOS pay nothing and the first developer to go over is saddled with high mitigation costs. A more equitable approach is to assess all developers equally based on the number of trips generated. Because of this unfairness, there is a huge incentive to manipulate the numbers to get the desired LOS.

Diamond Interchanges

The ICU 2003 includes a special procedure for evaluating diamond interchanges. This method considers the special timing requirements for a diamond interchange due to the limited storage space and susceptibility for spillback. Refer to the *Intersection Capacity Utilization 2003* book for a complete description of the ICU for Diamond Interchanges.

Single Point Urban Interchanges

The ICU 2003 includes a special procedure for evaluating Single Point Urban Interchanges. This method considers the special timing requirements for an Urban Interchange including the long clearance times necessary due to the long turning paths. Refer to the ICU 2003 book for a complete description of the ICU for Urban Interchanges.

Stopped Delay vs. Signal Delay

Previous versions of Synchro and the HCM used stopped delay. Stopped delay includes the time vehicles are stopped while signal delay also includes the time lost due to slowing.

The delay used by Synchro (version 4 and later) and the 2000 HCM Chapter 16 is Signal Delay. TRANSYT 7F also uses signal delay. When looking at delays calculated by Synchro Version 3.2 and the 1994 HCM, you may need to multiply those delays by 1.3 to be equivalent to the Signal Delays used in Synchro version 5.

Comparison of Analysis Methods

Synchro offers three independent methods to analyze signalized intersections: Synchro Percentile Delays, HCM Signalized Method, and Intersection Capacity Utilization (ICU). The table below summarizes some of the features of each method.

Table 13-4   Comparison Analysis Method Summary

	Synchro Delay	HCM Method	ICU
Measures of Effectiveness	Delay	Delay and v/c	v/c
Target Applications	Operations, Signal Timing	Operations and Planning	Planning, Impact Studies, Roadway Design
Expected Precision	10% to 27%	10% to 29%	3% to 10%
Other Sources For Calculation	No	HCM compatible software	Spreadsheet and Worksheet
Pedestrian Timing Requirements	Yes	No	Yes
Detailed Modeling of Coordination	Yes	No*	No
Detailed Actuated Signal Modeling	Yes	No*	No

* The HCM Delay calculation within Synchro explicitly models coordination and actuated signal timings.

For a complete discussion about accuracy, see the topic **Precision in Traffic Analysis** on page 13-50.

Choosing an Analysis Method

Table 13-5 helps to choose the appropriate analysis method for your project needs.

Table 13-5   Data Requirement by Analysis Method

Data Requirement	Analysis Method
High Accuracy is required	ICU or HCM v/c
True Measure of Capacity is required	ICU
Client Requires HCM report	HCM
Planning Applications, site impact studies, and roadway design	ICU
Operations, signal timing optimization	Synchro Delay
Optimization of actuated signal parameters	Synchro Delay
Offset Optimization	Synchro Delay
Independent Validation Required	ICU

Intersection Capacity Utilization

The ICU method is designed to be used for planning applications; its primary benefits are higher accuracy, ease of use, and reproducibility. The theory of ICU is to add up the times required for a phase to serve each movement at 100% saturation with a cycle length of 120 seconds. The sum of critical phases is divided by the reference cycle length of 120 seconds. The result is similar to adding the critical volume to saturation (v/s) ratios, but the sum of required phase times takes into account lost times and minimum timing requirements.

The ICU method is completely documented with step-by-step instructions. The method is also available as a Microsoft® Excel spreadsheet and a single page worksheet that can be calculated by hand. Because the method is less complex and well-defined, it is possible for results to be reproduced by an independent analyst.

The ICU method is designed for high accuracy. Volume capacity ratios are inherently more accurate than delay calculations. The ICU assumes that all left turns are protected so there is no uncertainty from permitted left turn factors. Coordination is not considered so there are no inaccuracies introduced by coordination.

The ICU is designed to be a true measure of capacity. Unlike the HCM v/c calculation, conflicting movements are not allowed to use the intersection at the same time so that capacity is not double counted.

Highway Capacity Method

This method is based on HCM Manual. The manual is authored by a committee of the Transportation Research Board which is a division of the National Academy of Sciences, a nonprofit organization based in Washington DC. The HCM is designed to be used for both operations and planning. It is based on research projects sponsored by the FHWA, the NAS, and other agencies. The HCM methods are widely used throughout North America and many agencies specify that analysis will be performed based on these methods.

The signalized sections of the HCM total over 170 pages. This presents a lot of detail but in some cases the details are interpreted differently by different analysts or software packages. An operations analysis can require up to 8 worksheets and many complex calculations. Because of the complexity, most users rely on software to implement the methods.

Delay based methods such as the HCM are less accurate than capacity based methods. See the section **Precision in Traffic Analysis** for a complete analysis. The HCM method requires the analyst to estimate of the affects of coordination and actuated signals. These estimates lead to a further loss of accuracy.

The Synchro HCM delay calculation explicitly calculates actuated green times and progression factors, so it will be more accurate for these situations.

Synchro Delay Method

The Synchro delay calculations are designed for operations and signal timing optimization. Synchro's method is called The Percentile Delay Method. The Percentile Delay Method is designed to model coordination and actuated signals in detail.

Delay based methods including Synchro's are inherently less accurate than capacity based methods. However, Synchro's delay method does explicitly account for actuation and coordination thereby reducing those sources of inaccuracy.

The calculations are too complicated to be performed by hand or described completely on paper. The Synchro results are therefore not reproducible by other software or by hand methods.

For optimizing signal timing for coordination, Synchro's delay method is the best choice because it is explicitly calculating the affects or coordination. Similarly, for analyzing actuated signal parameters, Synchro's delay method is also the best choice.

Precision in Traffic Analysis

This section contains a short discussion about accuracy and precision. The uncertainties of the inputs are analyzed along with their affects on the resulting values. A simplified method is presented to show how uncertainties in input values propagate to uncertainties in results.

Table 13-6 below lists the primary inputs for an ICU calculation, and an intersection delay calculation along with typical uncertainties.

The general volume to capacity ratios can be calculated with more accuracy than delay. The following illustrates how inaccuracies can compound in an ICU or delay analysis; the numbers in parenthesis are the typical level of certainty.

Table 13-6   Compounding Inaccuracies in Analysis

Value	Typical	Uncertainty	Percent
Volume	500	50	10%
Saturated Flow	2000	100	5%
Lane Utilization	0.9	0.05	6%
Lost Time	4	0.5	13%
Permitted Left Factor	0.3	0.03	10%
Green Time	40	2	5%
Platoon Factor	1	0.3	30%

The Table below shows how these certainties combine to affect the overall uncertainty in the resulting ICU. The ICU affect was calculated using a spreadsheet. The relevant input variable was increased 1% and the resulting ICU for a typical intersection was compared to the baseline ICU. A value of 0.88 indicates that a 1% increase in volume increases the ICU by 0.88%. Each input value's percent uncertainty is multiplied by the affect factor and squared. The root of the sum of the squares is the combined uncertainty for all input uncertainties. For this example, the ICU has an uncertainty of 10.6%.

If the ICU had been calculated without permitted left turns, the resulting ICU uncertainty would be 9%. Most ICU calculations do not use permitted left turns.

Table 13-7   Uncertainties Affect on ICU

Value	u_i	m_i (ICU)	$(u_i * m_i)^2$
Volume	7%	0.88	0.0036
Saturated Flow	5%	-0.87	0.0019
Lane Utilization	6%	-0.87	0.0023
Lost Time	13%	0.12	0.0002
Permitted Left Factor	10%	-0.57	0.0032
Green Time	5%	na	
Platoon Factor	30%	na	
Sum			0.0113
Combined Uncertainty (CU)			10.6%

Table 13-8 examines the same uncertainties affect on delay. Two cases are considered, the first has a v/c of 0.75 and the second has a v/c of 1.0. Note that uncertainty to volume and capacity has a multiplying affect of over 3 at capacity, but only about 1 at lower v/c ratios.

If the intersection is assumed to be uncoordinated and uses protected lefts, the platoon factor and permitted left turn factor contributions are removed and the resulting uncertainties are **13%** and **41%** for the 0.75 and 1.0 cases.

Table 13-8   Uncertainties Affect on Delay

Value	u_i	m_i (HCM 0.75)	$(u_i * m_i)^2$	m_i (HCM 1.00)	$(u_i * m_i)^2$
Volume	7%	0.92	0.0039	3.33	0.0517
Saturated Flow	5%	-1.04	0.0027	-3.60	0.0325
Lane Utilization	6%	-1.04	0.0033	-3.60	0.0401
Lost Time	13%	-0.16	0.0004	-0.40	0.0025
Permitted Left Factor	10%	-1.04	0.0108	-3.60	0.1299
Green Time	5%	-1.59	0.0063	-3.87	0.0375
Platoon Factor	30%	0.82	0.0611	0.53	0.0257
Sum			0.0886		0.3199
Combined Uncertainty (Sum of Squares)			30%		57%

The following table summarizes the amount of uncertainty that can be expected from ICU and HCM methods for various scenarios. The uncertainty for ICU is relatively low and constant for all options. The uncertainty for HCM is acceptably low when v/c is under capacity, left turns are protected, and the approach in uncoordinated. The HCM and delay based calculations become very uncertain when v/c approaches 1 because small changes to input values have a 3x affect on the resulting delay. The HCM relies on estimates of platoon factor to account for the affects of coordination. This adds greatly to the affects of uncertainty in the HCM delay values.

Table 13-9   Uncertainties Summary

	ICU	HCM
Protected Lefts, Uncoordinated, v/c = 0.75	9%	11%
Protected Lefts, Uncoordinated, v/c = 1	9%	41%
Protected Lefts, Coordinated, v/c = 0.75	9%	28%
Protected Lefts, Coordinated, v/c = 1	9%	44%
Permitted Lefts, Uncoordinated, v/c = 0.75	11%	17%
Permitted Lefts, Uncoordinated, v/c = 1	11%	54%
Permitted Lefts, Coordinated, v/c = 0.75	11%	30%
Permitted Lefts, Coordinated, v/c = 1	11%	57%

The ICU is inherently more precise because the delay equation is unstable near capacity. The calculation of delay requires an estimate for the affects of coordination, which adds greatly to the resulting uncertainty.

One consequence of the high range of uncertainties is that it makes the method easy to manipulate. In some cases, it is possible to get a 20% reduction in delay or two Levels of Service by increasing capacity 5% and reducing volume 5%.

If a real estate developer is attempting to get project approval with a minimum of mitigation measures, it is not too difficult to adjust the input factors, platoon factors, and so forth to get a significant reduction in delay. Some communities have regulations requiring developers to maintain a certain LOS. There is unfairness to this method of regulation because all developers up to the critical LOS pay nothing and the first developer to go over is saddled with high mitigation costs. A more equitable approach is to assess all developers equally based on the number of trips generated. Because of this unfairness, there is a huge incentive to manipulate the numbers to get the desired LOS.

Figure 13-7 illustrates how delay is related to volume. Note that delay increases significantly once capacity is reached. This steepness of the graph illustrates how small changes to volume or capacity can make a huge difference in delay. The v/c ratio increases linearly and also provides information about when the delay slope will start to increase.

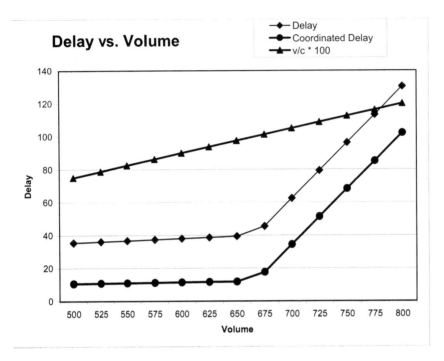

Figure 13-7   Delay vs. Volume

Traffic volumes fluctuate as discussed in Chapter 4 of the ICU 2003 book. Volume will change by day of week, hour of the day, by time of year, and even within the peak hour. Volume will also change due to special events, accidents, and bad weather.

Some days can experience 10% or higher volumes in the peak hour than the design volumes. The delay for these days can be 30% higher and the LOS 2 levels worse. The ICU for these days will only be 10% higher and 1 level worse. The ICU does a better job of predicting reserve capacity.

Queue Interactions

Synchro 6 introduced a new series of traffic analysis called Queue Interactions. Queue Interactions looks at how queues can reduce capacity through spillback, starvation, and storage blocking between lane groups.

Spillback

Spillback is caused when a queue from a downstream intersection uses up all the space on a link and prevents vehicles from entering the upstream intersection on green. (See **Figure 13-8**)

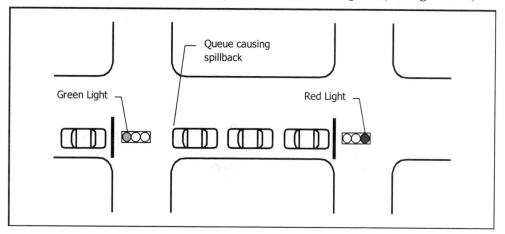

Figure 13-8   Spillback

Starvation

Starvation occurs when a downstream signal is green, but the signal cannot service at full capacity efficiency because the upstream signals is red, see **Figure 13-9**.

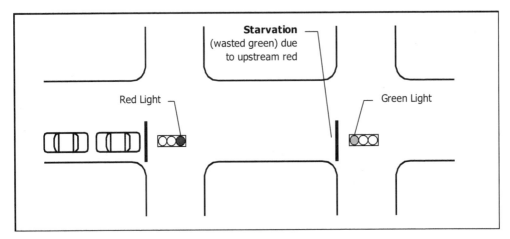

Figure 13-9   Starvation

Queue Interactions

Queue Interactions have the potential to not just increase delay, but also reduce capacity, even on movements that normally are under capacity. With movements at or above capacity, queue interactions become even more critical because they have the potential to reduce capacity even further.

Historically Synchro has modeled how good coordination can reduce delay. With Queue Interaction modeling, Synchro is modeling how bad coordination or no coordination can exponentially increase delays and reduce capacity.

Queue Interactions look at queues on short links and short turning bays. Less storage space than one full cycle of traffic causes higher delays along with a reduction in capacity. It is not just a bad problem, it is a terrible problem. In addition to the problems previously noted, it is also a safety problem. Vehicles holding at a green light can get rear-ended. Vehicles stuck within an intersection can get into a right angle collision.

Spillback and starvation are tightly interrelated. It is possible to initially have one and not the other depending on which intersection is more capacity constrained. The reduction in capacity due to starvation will eventually lead to spillback upstream. Spillback and starvation are caused by no coordination or bad coordination in conjunction with short block spacing.

To reduce spillback and starvation; all major movements for a direction need to be green at the same time. Using shorter cycle lengths and/or longer block distances can also reduce queue interaction problems.

Changes to Synchro 6 and later

The Queue Interaction calculations are used throughout Synchro 6 and later, including the following areas.

A new queue delay term is introduced. All displays and reports that show a percentile delay now have an additional term called Queue Delay. This delay measures the additional delay incurred by the capacity reduction of queues on short links.

Queue delay is part of the objective function used for optimizations. Optimized timing plans will now take into account the affects of queue interactions. This will tend to favor timing plans that hold all movements green simultaneously on short links and shorter cycle lengths.

The Time-Space Diagrams can now show times where queue interactions occur. Starvation, spillback, and storage blocking times are shown at the stop bar with colored rectangles.

The Coding Error Check feature now looks for queue interaction problems. Any significant problems are reported in detail as a warning.

The Queue report now contains detailed information about the three types of queue interactions. The Queuing penalty is removed.

Calculations

The queue interactions calculations generally have 3 steps:

1. Determine if the volume per cycle to distance ratio is critical.

2. Determine the capacity reduction, due to the amount of time per cycle that the movement is starved or blocked.

3. Determine the additional delay incurred by this capacity reduction.

Compare Volume to Distance

The first step is to determine if the ratio of volume per cycle to distance is critical. Queue Interactions only cause a reduction in capacity when the storage space is less than one cycles worth of traffic.

If a movement is over capacity, it will cause spillback at any distance; but system capacity will not be reduced because there is enough storage space to accommodate an entire cycle of traffic.

A link is subject to spillback and starvation whenever:

Min(capDist, volDist) > Dist

capDist = L * [2 + C * c / (n * 3600)] = distance per lane used by one cycle of capacity

volDist = L * [2 + v90 * C / (n * 3600)] = distance per lane used by one cycle of 90th percentile volume

Dist = Internal Link Distance

c = lane group capacity

n = number of lanes

v90 = 90th percentile volume

C = cycle length

L = average vehicle length

The addition of 2 vehicles is to accommodate a possible truck.

A storage bay is subject to storage blocking whenever:

Min(capDist, volDist) > Store

Store = Storage Bay Distance

This test must be true for both the blocking and the blocked movement. Both movements need to have a queue extending past the storage bay opening for an interaction to occur.

These tests do not actually determine if queue interactions are occurring, only if they have the potential to occur.

Determine Capacity Reduction

The next step is to determine the time that the movement is blocked or starved. For storage blocking and spillback, the capacity during this time will be zero. For starvation, the capacity during this time will be reduced to the upstream saturation flow rate active at the time.

Starvation Capacity Reduction

The time-space diagram in **Figure 13-10** illustrates a case of starvation.

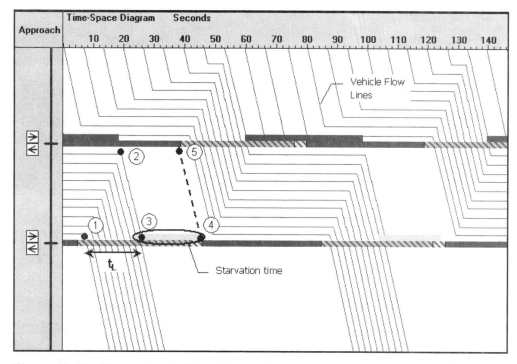

Figure 13-10 Starvation in Time Space view

Note that at the beginning of green vehicles begin to clear the queue at point (1), the queue is drained at time (2) and the last queued vehicle clears the stop bar at time (3). From time (3) to time (4), the only vehicles that can be serviced are those that enter the intersection from times (2) to time (5). The storage space cannot be used after time (3).

If the upstream signal is red between times (2) and (5), only vehicles using the intersection will be vehicles turning from side streets upstream or entering mid-block. The capacity of the downstream intersection is limited by the Saturated Flow Rate of allowed movements upstream during this time.

For starvation analysis, the green time is divided into two portions. The beginning of green for queue clearance time Tq is able to clear vehicles stored on the link. After Tq, the capacity is limited to the upstream Saturated Flow Rates of traffic given a green during that time.

Tq = queue clearance time = $D/L/[s/(n*3600)]$

D = link distance

L = average vehicle length

s = Saturated Flow Rate

n = number of lanes

Refer to **Figure 13-11** for an example.

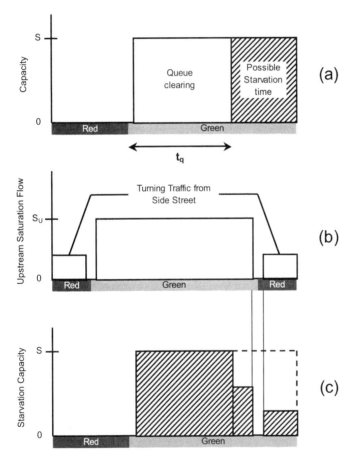

Figure 13-11   Starvation Capacity Reduction

Figure 13-11(a) shows the basic capacity for the downstream intersection versus time for one cycle. **Figure 13-11**(b) shows the upstream Saturated Flow Rates for vehicles bound to the downstream intersection. The Saturated Flow Rates are adjusted to account for the proportion of vehicles in that stream bound for this movement. Note that there is a big flow for the upstream through movement, and smaller flow on red for vehicles turning from side streets upstream. **Figure 13-11**(b) is time adjusted to account for the travel time between intersections.

Figure 13-11(c) shows the combination of the two flow profiles. The shaded area is the reduced starvation capacity. The difference between **Figure 13-11**(a) and **Figure 13-11**(c) is the reduction in capacity due to starvation.

In the case where the upstream intersection has a different cycle length, the average volume is used for the capacity during the Starvation time.

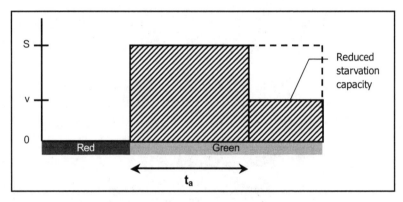

Figure 13-12   Reduced Starvation Capacity

Note that at some cycles, the starvation time will be fully utilized and other cycles will be starved.

The link clearance time for a 300 ft link with saturation flow rate of 2000 vphpl is:

$tQ = 300ft / 25ft / (2000/3600) = 21.6$ s

If the two intersections operate at different cycle lengths, starvation may occur on some cycles but not others. Over time the flow rate serviced after time tQ will be equal to the volume. During some cycles it will be greater and some cycles it will be less.

The capacity at the downstream intersection is reduced depending on the amount of vehicles that can be serviced after tQ.

If starvation is a potential problem, it is essential to use good signal coordination and/or shorter cycle lengths.

Spillback Capacity Reduction

For spillback analysis, the upstream capacity will be zero whenever the queue extends to the upstream link.

Refer to **Figure 13-13**. The first step is to simulate the traffic flow of the downstream movement. This will determine the queue time upstream. In **Figure 13-13** this is from time (2) to (4). The capacity of the upstream movement(s) are reduced to zero during this time.

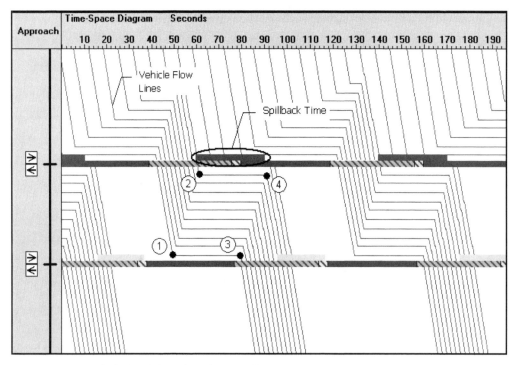

Figure 13-13   Spillback in Time Space view

Note that side street movements may also have their capacity reduced during the spillback time. If a side street lane group has two lanes of Thru and Thru-Right, its capacity will be reduced by ½ during the time the right movement is blocked.

In the case where the two intersections have different or variable cycle lengths, the calculations are performed multiple times. The upstream intersection's departure and capacity profiles are rotated at 5 second increments over their entire cycle. At each 5 second increment, the profiles are truncated or extended to match the downstream cycle length and the spillback analysis is performed. The capacity reduction is averaged for all the 5 second offset rotations. This allows all offset combinations to be evaluated and considered. It is likely the spillback affects will vary greatly among offset rotations. It is necessary to test all offset rotations in order to determine whether there are damaging spillbacks with incompatible cycle lengths.

For half cycling or double cycling, offset rotation is not used; the analysis is performed using a double cycle.

For queue delay calculations, the capacity reduction is calculated using both 50th percentile traffic and 90th percentile traffic with the 50th percentile traffic counting for 2/3 of the total.

crSB = (crSB50 * 2 + crSB90)/3 = capacity reduction due to spillback

crSB50 = capacity reduction due to spillback using 50th percentile traffic

crSB90 = capacity reduction due to spillback using 90th percentile traffic

Storage Blocking Capacity Reduction

Storage blocking combines a spillback and a starvation analysis. The first step is to determine the time that the entrance to the storage bay is blocked by the blocking movement.

Refer to **Figure 13-14**. In this example through traffic is simulated for a cycle to determine the queue time at the top of the storage bay. In **Figure 13-14** this is from time (1) to (2).

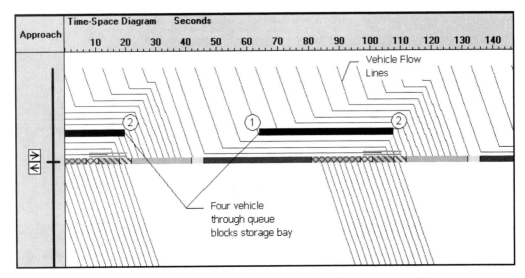

Figure 13-14   Storage Blocking in Time Space view (Through Traffic)

Refer to **Figure 13-15** , this shows left traffic on the same link.

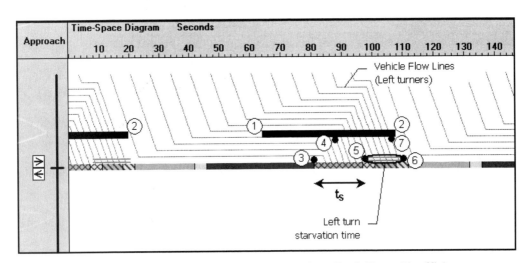

Figure 13-15   Storage Blocking in Time Space view (Left Turn Traffic)

Next the storage clearance time is determined:

$tS = St/L/[s/(n*3600)]$ = storage clearance time

St = storage distance

L = average vehicle length

s = Saturated Flow Rate

n = number of lanes

The time from (3) to (5) is the storage clearance time. From time (5) to (6), the capacity will be zero if the storage entrance is blocked.

Figure 13-16(a) shows the basic capacity for the blocked movement versus time for one cycle. **Figure 13-16**(b) shows the time the entrance to the storage bay is blocked. **Figure 13-16**(b) is time adjusted to account for travel time.

Figure 13-16(c) shows the combination of the two flow profiles. The capacity is reduced after t_s whenever the storage bay is blocked. The shaded area is the reduced storage blocking capacity. The difference between **Figure 13-16**(a) and **Figure 13-16**(c) is the reduction in capacity due to storage blocking.

Storage blocking is not considered with queue delay. Initial versions of Synchro 6 included this feature, but it was found that this behavior is too complex to model macroscopically.

Some examples: For a two lane through movement, through vehicles can move around queued left vehicles in the right lane. In many cases the capacity was not reduced as much as predicted. Blocking through traffic prevented left traffic from entering and queueing, and vice versa. The best way to model the interactions of queued traffic with storage bays is with simulation.

The storage blocking is still shown on the time space diagrams, but the queue delay is not affected.

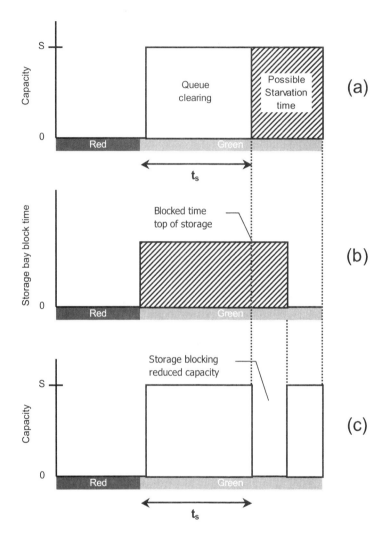

Figure 13-16   Storage Blocking Capacity Reduction

Determine Queue Delay

Queue delay is the additional delay associated with the capacity reduction of queue interactions. It is calculated using the incremental delay formula with and without the capacity reduction.

The purpose is to penalize queue interactions that increase v/c above 1, but not penalize queue interactions that keep v/c < 1. This delay also penalizes interactions in proportion to the amount they increase delay by reducing capacity on the critical links.

$$D_2 = 900 * T * \left[(x-1) + \sqrt{(x-1)^2 + \frac{8 * k * I * X}{c * T}} \right] = \text{Incremental Delay}$$

T = duration of analysis period (hours)

X = v/c = volume to capacity ratio

c = capacity

k = incremental delay factor, 0.50 is used here because these movements are at capacity

I = upstream filtering, 0.3 is used here, because these movements are metered

qd = queue delay = d2' – d2

d2' = incremental delay using c – cr instead of c

cr = capacity reduction due to queue interactions = max(crSB, crS)

crSB = capacity reduction due to spillback

crS = capacity reduction due to starvation.

Here are some examples of how capacity reduction affects queue delay:

v	c	cr	X	X'	qd
800	1000	100	0.80	0.89	2.3
900	1000	100	0.90	1.00	12.0
1000	1000	100	1.00	1.11	39.8
500	1000	300	0.50	0.71	1.4
1200	1000	50	1.20	1.26	28.0

Note that qd is much larger when v/c is pushed over 1. In the 4th example, a 30% reduction in capacity has minimal affect because excess capacity is available. In the last example, a 5% reduction in capacity has a large affect because the movement is already over capacity.

The Uniform Delay is not part of the Queue Delay calculation. Synchro already calculates the affect of coordination (good or bad) on Uniform Delay.

Implications

Queue Interactions can have very negative impacts on traffic flow. In addition to increasing delays, they also can reduce available capacity and even create safety problems. The calculation of queue interactions is very complex and prior to Synchro 6 was only available through microscopic simulation.

The queue delay quantifies the impact of queue interactions. Queue delay is used during optimizations to find offsets, phase sequences and cycle lengths with minimal impact from queue interactions. Queue Interactions can be seen visually on the time space diagram, and listed in the Coding Error Check.

The best way to minimize queue interactions is to use good coordination. With short links, all movements for a given direction need to be green at the same time. Using shorter cycle lengths can also reduce the impacts.

If Storage Blocking is a problem, there are several options available. The simplest is to use lead-lag or split phasing. Using longer storage bays, shorter cycle lengths, or better coordination can also help reduce Storage blocking.

Sometimes bandwidth style timing plans can have bad queue interactions, especially on the link where timing plans alternate. **Figure 13-17** shows a bandwidth timing plan for a two way arterial. **Figure 13-18** shows the flow lines for the same timing plan.

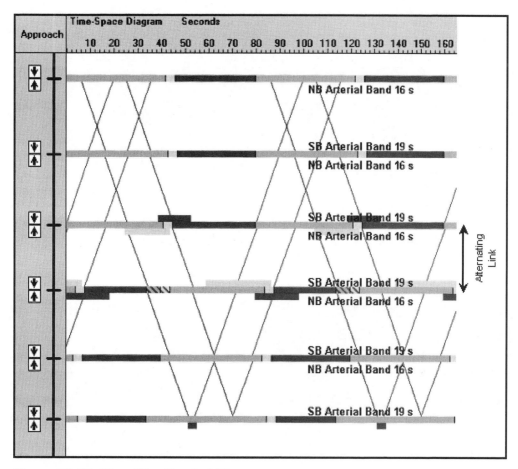

Figure 13-17   Two-Way Bandwidth

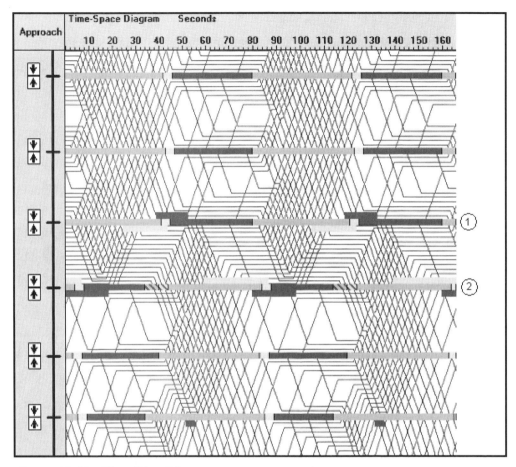

Figure 13-18   Flow Line Diagram

Note that on the link between (1) and (2), all traffic is stopped nearly for the entire red period. Note that these queues are causing spillback SB at (1) and NB at (2). The short block spacing is also causing starvation SB at (2) and NB at(1). The conclusion is to watch out for queue interactions (and excessive delays) when the timing plans alternate on a bandwidth style timing plan.

 It is of vital importance to coordinate closely spaced intersections, especially when there is not enough space on the link to store a full cycle of traffic.

Uncoordinated intersections can cause spillback and starvation. Even when the signals are controlled by different agencies; it is imperative to use coordination to keep the intersections operating safely and at full capacity.

Queue Length Calculation

This section explains how queue lengths are calculated.

The queue reports show the 50th percentile and 95th percentile queue. This queue represents maximum back distance where vehicles stop during a cycle.

 NOTE The queue lengths shown are the queue for each lane. The total queue length is divided by the number of lanes and the lane utilization factor.

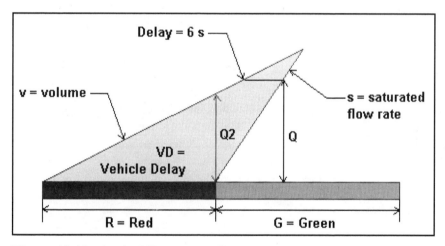

Figure 13-19   Arrival Departure Graph

Consider the arrival departure diagram in **Figure 13-19**. The base of the triangle is the effective red time, R.

The slope of the left side is the arrival rate in vehicles per hour, v. In a coordinated system, the arrival rate may vary across the cycle.

The slope of the right side is the Saturated Flow Rate in vehicles per hour, s.

The height of the triangle is the maximum back of queue in vehicles, Q. Vehicles delayed a short time will only slow but not stop. For this reason, Synchro does not consider vehicles delayed by less than 6 seconds to be part of the queue. The Queue is actually the height to the point where the triangle is 6 seconds wide.

The value Q2 is the number of vehicles arriving on red. After the signal turns green, additional vehicles may queue up in back while the front of the queue dissipates. Other queuing methods such as the ITE and SIGNAL 94 queuing methods are based on the lower Q2 value.

 Synchro's delay, capacity, and LOS outputs now take into account delays and reduced capacity from queuing and blocking problems. Details on this can be found in the topic Queue Interactions. In addition, you could use microscopic simulation, such as SimTraffic, to determine the affects of queuing on traffic flow.

Calculation of Queues

Based on **Figure 13-19**, the formula for the queue is.

$$Q = \frac{v}{3600} * (R - 6) * \left[1 + \frac{1}{s/v - 1} \right] * \frac{L}{n * fLU} = \text{Queue Length (ft)}$$

R = Red time (s)

s = Saturation Flow Rate (vph)

v = Arrival Rate (vph)

L = Length of vehicles including space between (ft)

n = Number of Lanes

fLU = Lane Utilization Factor

If the volume to capacity ratio (v/c) exceeds 1, the queue length is theoretically infinite. Synchro calculates the queue length as the maximum queue after two cycles. This will equal

Q' = (v * (C - 6) + (v - s*g/C)* C / 3600 = Queue Length for Saturated Links (ft)

95th Percentile Queue

The 95th percentile queue is calculated by increasing the arrival rate to account for fluctuations in traffic. The volume is unadjusted by the Peak Hour Factor because the 95th volume adjustment accounts for traffic fluctuations.

$$v95 = v * PHFx * \left[1 + 1.64 * \frac{\sqrt{vc}}{vc} \right] = 95^{\text{th}} \text{ Percentile Arrival Rate (vph)}$$

vc = Vehicles per cycle = v * C / 3600

PHFx = minimum of PHF or 0.9

 If the Analysis Period is set to 30 minutes or greater, PHFx is set to 1.0.

The 95th percentile queue will be calculated using v95 rather than v.

In many cases, the 95th percentile queue will not be experienced due to upstream metering. If the upstream intersection is at or near capacity, the 50th percentile queue represents the maximum queue experienced.

Similarly, if the upstream intersection has a v/c ratio over 0.8; the maximum queue is approximately equal to the 50th percentile queue divided by the upstream v/c ratio. For example, if the 50th percentile queue is 150ft, and the v/c ratio upstream is 0.90; the maximum possible queue would therefore be 150 / 0.90 = 167ft.

Queue Length Sample Calculation

Here is a complete step-by-step calculation of queue lengths. Note that the formulas presented here are simplifications of the flow rate integration used internally by Synchro. These formulas will not work with platooned arrivals or with complex phasing such as permitted plus protected left turns.

Input Data

Adjusted Volume (v): 351 vph

Saturated Flow Rate (s): 1770 vph

Lanes (n): 1

Cycle Length (C): 90 s

Effective Green Time (G): 23 s

Average Vehicle Length (L) : 25 ft

Peak Hour Factor : 0.9

Lane Utilization Factor (F_u): 1.0

Solution

Part 1, 50th Percentile Queue

50th percentile queue is average traffic, so no volume adjustment is needed.

First check v/c ratio:

$$v/c = v / (s * g/C) = 351 / (1770 * 23/90) = 0.78$$

v/c ratio is less than 1, proceed with normal method.

$$Q = v / 3600 * (R - 6) * (1 + 1 / (s/v-1)) * L / (n * F_u) =$$

$$= 351 \text{ vph} / (3600 \text{ s/hr}) * (90s - 23s - 6s) * (1 + 1 / (1770 \text{ vph} /351 \text{ vph} - 1)) * 25 \text{ ft} / (1 * 1.0) = 185 \text{ ft}$$

Part 2, 95th Percentile Queue

First convert volume to 95th percentile volume

$$VC = \text{Vehicles per cycle} = v * C / 3600$$

$$VC = 351 * 90 / 3600 = 8.8$$

$$v95 = v * \text{PHFx} * (1 + 1.64 * \text{SquareRoot}(VC) / VC) = 351 * 0.9 * (1 + 1.64 * \text{SquareRoot}(8.8) / 8.8) = 491 \text{ vph}$$

Next check v/c ratio:

$$v/c = v / (s * g/C) = 491 / (1770 * 23/90) = 1.08$$

95th percentile v/c ratio exceeds 1, use alternate queue method.

Queue is unserved vehicles from first cycle, plus all arrivals on second cycle.

$$Q = [(v95 - s * g/C) * C / 3600 + v95 * C / 3600] * L / n$$

$$= [(491 \text{ vph} - 1770 \text{ vph} * 23 \text{ s} / 90 \text{ s}) * 90 \text{ s} / (3600 \text{ s/hr}) + 491 \text{ vph} * 90 \text{ s} / (3600 \text{ s/hr})] * 25 \text{ ft} / 1$$

$$= [1.0 \text{ veh} + 12.2 \text{ veh}] * 25 \text{ ft} / 1$$

$$= 331 \text{ ft}$$

Upstream Metering

The arrival volume for the 95th queue, but not the 50th queue, is adjusted to account for metering at the upstream intersection.

If the upstream intersection has volume equal to capacity, v/c=1, the 95th queue will equal the 50th queue. If the upstream intersection has v/c=0.95, the volume for the 95th queue will be limited to 105% of the 50th percentile traffic and the 95th queue will only be about 5% longer than the 50th queue. The above cases assume no mid-block sources of traffic.

Upstream metering is not performed if the upstream intersection has a incompatible cycle length, or if either intersection is actuated with different controllers. Upstream metering is not performed at stop controlled unsignalized intersections, but is performed for signals beyond if traffic flows freely through the unsignalized intersection.

Upstream metering is used to determine the rate only. The arrival profile is calculated without metering and may be overly weighted towards metered movements. Metering is not used in the calculation of arrival profiles and uniform delay calculations.

 Synchro's delay, capacity, and LOS outputs now take into account delays and reduced capacity from queuing and due to upstream metering, The 95th queue may be less than the 50th Percentile queue. If the upstream intersection is operating with v/c>1, the metered arrival rate will be **less** than the volume for this intersection. Since metering is only performed with the 95th queue, this causes the 95th queue to be less than the 50th queue. This situation may indicate a coding problem. Be sure that the Midblock traffic is coded correctly and that the signal timing and volumes for both intersections are set correctly. This reduced 95th queue does represent a valid queue because vehicles will not be able to clear the upstream intersection to queue at this intersection.

Example Calculation

Adjusted Volume: 1000 vph

PHFx = 0.90

C = 90s

Volume from Midblock: 100 vph or 10%

Volume from upstream through: 700 vph or 70%

Upstream Through v/c: 0.95

Volume from upstream left: 200 vph or 20%

Upstream Left v/c: 0.8

VC = Vehicles per cycle = v * C / 3600

VC = 1000 * 90 / 3600 = 25

v95 unmetered = v * PHFx * (1 + 1.64 * SquareRoot(VC) / VC) = 1000 * 0.9 * (1 + 1.64 * SquareRoot(25) / 25)

$\qquad$ = 1195 vph

v95 metered = v * sum(PropI * min(1/(vi/ci), v95/v))

$\qquad$ = 1000 * [0.1 * 1195/1000 + 0.70 * min(1/0.95, 1195/1000) + 0.2 * min(1/0.80, 1195/1000)]

$\qquad$ = 1095 vph

In this example traffic from upstream through is not able to increase by more than 5% due to the high v/c ratio. Traffic from midblock and from upstream left is able to fluctuate. The resulting metered v95 is less than the unmetered v95 but is more than the 5% increase allowed from upstream through.

Stop Calculations

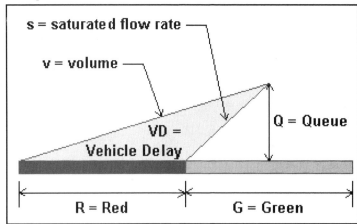

Figure 13-20   Arrival Departure Graph

Stops are calculated similarly to the calculation of delays. Consider the arrival departure graph above. The total number of vehicles being delayed is equal to the number of vehicles queued or Q in the diagram above. However, vehicles being delayed for less than 10 seconds do not make a full stop. Synchro calculates the number of stopped vehicles by counting the number of delayed vehicles for each delay time and adjusting these vehicles by the following table.

Table 13-10   Stop Adjustment

Vehicle Delay(s)	Percent of Stop
0	0%
1	20%
2	58%
3	67%
4	77%
5	84%
6	91%
7	94%
8	97%
9	99%

This table is taken from the TRANSYT 7-F Users Manual and is the same adjustment made for partial stops used by TRANSYT.

These stops are calculated for each percentile scenario and averaged for cycle failures and over capacity vehicles. The stop calculations model 100 cycles similar to the delay calculations, to calculate stops for congestion.

Fuel and Emissions Calculation

 At the time of publication, Trafficware was investigating new fuel and emission models. These models were not available for publication in the User Guide. Check the on-line (**Help**→**Contents**) on this topic for the most up to date information.

Fuel Consumption is calculated using the following formulas:

$$F = TotalTravel * k1 + TotalDelay * k2 + Stops * k3$$

$k1 = .075283 - .0015892 * Speed + .000015066 * Speed \wedge 2$

$k2 = .7329$

$k3 = .0000061411 * speed \wedge 2$

F = fuel consumed in gallons

Speed = cruise speed in mph.

TotalTravel = vehicle miles traveled

TotalDelay = total signal delay in hours

Stops = total stops in vehicles per hour

For metric users, the values are converted.

These are the same as the default formulas for fuel consumption used by TRANSYT 7-F.

It may be useful to create this report with a before and after scenario to access the amount of improvement gained by adding coordination.

Emissions Calculations

The emissions calculations are based only on fuel consumption. The somewhat simplified calculation multiplies fuel consumption by the following factors to determine emission rates.

CO = F * 69.9 g/gal = Carbon Monoxide Emissions (g)

NOx = F * 13.6 g/gal = Nitrogen Oxides Emissions (g)

VOC = F * 16.2 g / gal = Volatile Oxygen Compounds Emissions (g)

F = Fuel Consumption (gal)

These simplified rates are based on an unpublished letter to the Federal Highway Administration from Oak Ridge National Labs.

Unserved Vehicles Calculation

The Unserved Vehicles calculation is simply the volume minus the capacity. The capacity is the Saturated Flow Rates multiplied by the effective green time. For an actuated signal, the capacity will be based on an average of the actuated green times from the five percentile scenarios.

u = v - c = Unserved Vehicles per hour

v = Adjusted Lane Group Volume

c = Actuated Capacity

The unserved vehicles are shown in the MOE reports and the Optimize Cycle Length table to quickly show where and by how much capacity is exceeded.

When optimizing, it is desirable to minimize and keep at zero the number of Unserved Vehicles. In some cases, it may be acceptable to accept some unserved vehicles. Many times a long cycle length exceeding 100 seconds will be recommended to accommodate an extra 10% capacity. Long cycle lengths can have negative operation aspects including long queues, inefficient use of turning lanes, and blocking. Lower cycle lengths may be better because the reduced queues will generally increase capacity and provide smoother operation.

If alternate routes exist, some unserved vehicles are acceptable because drivers will select alternate routes when faced with congestion.

Dilemma Zone Vehicles and Safety
Discussion

Traditionally traffic engineers have used MOEs such as delays, stops, and bandwidth when timing signals in order to move vehicles as efficiently as possible. However today many engineers are being called on to implement traffic calming and improve safety. The traditional MOEs do not provide a measure of safety, so new MOEs are needed. The Dilemma Zone MOE is a new measurement that considers safety.

The **Dilemma Zone Vehicles** measures the number of vehicles arriving while the signal is turning yellow. Vehicles in the Dilemma Zone are more likely to have accidents because they must either:

- Stop quickly and risk being hit from behind.

- Continue through the intersection after the signal turns red and risk a pedestrian or right angle accident.

- Regular users of a coordinated system are likely to know that the signal will change and thus exceed the speed limit to avoid the upcoming yellow signal. Sometimes speeders will ignore pedestrian right-of-way and exhibit other dangerous behaviors in order to keep up with the coordination platoon.

It is therefore desired to have timing plans with minimal numbers of vehicles in the dilemma zone. A timing plan that delays the platoon by 5 or 10 seconds will be safer than a timing plan that "cuts off" the last 5 or 10 seconds of the platoon.

The original design goal of Synchro was to encourage the use of lead-lag phasing to improve coordination. Many engineers are hesitant to use lead-lag phasing because they perceive it to be a safety problem due to driver confusion and false starts. It is hoped that the Dilemma Vehicles MOE can show that lead-lag phasing is actually safer in many cases because fewer vehicles are in the Dilemma Zone. Vehicles in the Dilemma Zone are a much bigger safety issue because they are moving at full speed while false starts are starting from a stop.

Many times agencies have money available for safety improvements but not for signal coordination. The Dilemma Zone MOE can be used to show that coordination is a safety improvement and qualify signal timing for additional sources of funding.

 Only lane groups with a speed ≥ 35mi/h (≥ 55 km/hr) are counted as dilemma vehicles. Turning groups with turning speed less than 35 (55) are not counted as dilemma.

Calculation

The dilemma zone is a summation of the vehicles expected in the dilemma zone. The zone starts at

$DS = RS - L2 - 2 =$ Dilemma Start Time

$DE = RS - L2 + 3 =$ Dilemma End Time

$RS =$ Red start time (end of yellow)

$L2 =$ Clearance Lost Time (Total Lost time less 2.5 s)

As an example:

$Y + AR =$ Clearance Time $= 4$ s

$tL =$ Total Lost time $= 4$ s

$L2 = tL - 2.5 = 1.5$ s

$DS = RS - 1.5 - 2 = RS - 3.5$

$DE = RE - 1.5 + 3 = RS + 1.5$

In this example the dilemma time starts 3.5 seconds before the end of red or 0.5 seconds after the start of yellow; and the dilemma time ends 1.5 seconds after the beginning of red.

For an uncoordinated phase, the Dilemma Vehicles will equal to:

dv = 5 * v / C = Dilemma Vehicles for uncoordinated movements

v = Adjusted volume

C = Cycle Length

For actuated signals, the dilemma zone vehicles may be reduced for phases that gap-out. If the gap times and detectors locations are set up so that gap-out occurs when no vehicles are expected to be in the dilemma zone.

If the phase gaps out for a given percentile scenario, the arrival profile will remove vehicles in the "gap-out shadow".

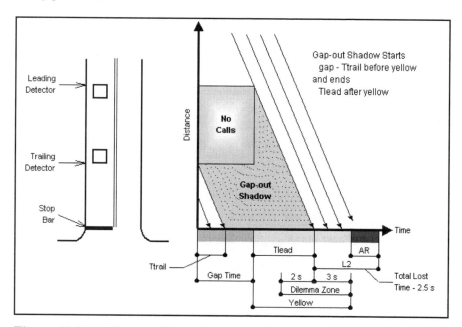

Figure 13-21   Dilemma Zone Gap-out Shadow

To reduce vehicles in the dilemma zone, use a long distance from the leading detector. Using a gap time longer than the time between detectors will not remove vehicles from the dilemma zone. Using a long gap time, without leading detectors will not remove vehicles from the dilemma zone, because the signal will not detect late arriving vehicles until after the signal turns yellow. If the phase has max recall, or maxes out; there will be no dilemma reduction for the gap-out shadow.

Synchro does not consider Dilemma Vehicles when optimizing offsets. There is a loose relationship between delay and Dilemma Vehicles, so Synchro optimized timing plans should be safer than bandwidth style timing plans in most cases.

Chapter 14 – File and Project Management

File and Project Management Overview

Synchro has a variety of tools for use in file and project management. This includes the ability to merge two files into one larger file and saving parts of larger files into a smaller file. In addition, this chapter will discuss the Scenario Manager, transferring and using Synchro with other software, and the purpose for the files that are created and used by Synchro and SimTraffic.

Save As

Use the **File** → **Save As** command to save a file with a new name or to save a Synchro 7 file to a version 6 or comma separated (CSV) format. The CSV format can be used with Synchro's UTDF format (see page 16-1).

Merge Files

Use the **File** → **Merge** or the **Transfer** → **Data Access** → **Merge Data** command to combine or merge two files (both commands get to the same place).

The Merge command can combine some data, such as volumes, from one file with other data, such as lane geometry and timings, from another file.

New in Synchro Version 7: File Merge now works with data files in the CSV format (Combined, Lanes, Phasings). File Merge will not add links or nodes, nor change geometry.

To Merge files, perform the following:

1. Open the file to be overwritten. If some intersections exist in both files, start with the file that will be overwritten.

2. Select the **File→Merge** command.

3. Locate and select the filename of the second file to merge (Synchro 6, 7 or CSV formats).

4. Select [**Open**].

5. The **MERGE OPTIONS** settings will appear (Synchro file only). Select options and press [**OK**].

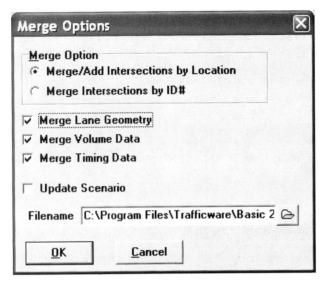

Figure 14-1   MERGE OPTIONS Settings

The **MERGE OPTIONS** settings control how to combine data from intersections that exist in both files.

Merge Options only appears for Synchro files. Data files are always merge by ID. To merge selective data from a data file, edit the data file in Excel or Word and remove the sections you don't want to merge,

Selecting **Merge/Add Intersections by Location** will cause intersections from the merged file to be merged if they are at the same location as intersections in the overlaid file. Other intersections in the merged file will be added to the merged file. Select this option when both files have the same coordinate system and when combining different intersections.

Selecting **Merge Intersections by ID#** will cause intersections from the merged file to be merged when their node numbers match a node number in the overlaid file. Intersections in the merged file without matching ID numbers will be ignored. Select this option to combine data from files with different coordinate systems or when transferring partial intersection data between two files.

Select **Merge Lane Geometry**, **Merge Volume Data**, and **Merge Timing Data** to control how intersections are merged. When the box is checked, the data is taken from the merged file; otherwise, the data in the overlaid file is preserved. Lane Geometry includes all the data in the

LANE settings. Volume Data include all the data in the **VOLUME** settings. Timing data includes all the data in the **TIMING** and **PHASING** settings.

The **Update Scenario** option can be used to combine the **Scenario Manager** information between the two files. The Date and Time information will be taken from the merged file if the Merge Volume option is selected. The Alternative will be taken from the merged file if the Merge Lane Geometry option is selected. The Timing Plan ID will be taken from the merged file if the Merge Timing option is selected.

Merge a Small File into a Bigger File

Open the large file first. **Select File→Merge** and choose the smaller file. Check all of the merge options on, and merge by ID.

The data from the smaller file will be merged into the larger file. Only the data from matching IDs will be merged in. Non-matching IDs will be ignored.

Merge Two Files from Separate Areas

Open one file first. Use the *Transform-Map* button if necessary to adjust coordinates. Select **File→Merge** and choose the other file. Check all of the merge options on, and merge by location. This must be performed with two Synchro files, not CSV data files.

The two files will now be merged into one file. Links between the two separate areas may need to be created to connect to them.

Change Coordinates of a File

This option allows you to correct the coordinates of a file to a file with correct coordinates.

Open the file with correct coordinates first. Select **File→Merge** and choose the Synchro or data file with incorrect coordinates. Check all of the merge options on, and merge by ID. Use the **File→Save As** to save the file with a new name.

Save Part of a File

The **File→Save Part** command can be used to split a file into sections or to save a part of a file into a separate file.

To use this command:

1. Select one or more intersections to include. See Selecting Multiple intersections, page 4-2, for more information.

2. Select the **File→Save Part** command. Enter a filename for the new section. If you choose an existing filename, its data will be overwritten.

Team Management

The **File→Save Part** command can be useful for allowing multiple people to work on the same file. Parts of a large network can be saved as separate files (see Save Part of File above). Each team person can work on each piece of the network. The pieces can be combined later using the **File→Merge** command.

Scenario Manager

The Scenario Manager (**Options → Scenario Manager**) allows detailed descriptions of the network to be recorded. These descriptions can appear on the top and bottom of report pages and are also used in conjunction with data management.

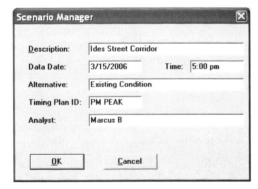

Figure 14-2   SCENARIO MANAGER

In a typical traffic study, it is common to create multiple scenarios of the same network. It is possible to have two or more current traffic counts. Each of these counts may be scaled into 10 and 20 year projected traffic volumes. There may also be multiple time-of-day timing plans and alternate lane geometry for different alternatives. With a large project, it can be difficult to track all of the scenarios. The scenario manager provides a convenient method to track each alternate.

When working with multiple scenarios, it is suggested that each scenario have its own file. Selected data can be transferred between files using the Merge File feature and the database access feature. The Merge File can help to keep the Scenario information synchronized.

Data from multiple timing plans and volume counts can be stored in data files with the Data Access feature (refer to Chapter 1). The Scenario Manager works with the Data Access to track the Data date and time as well as the Timing Plan IDs.

The **Description** should be used to describe the location of the network. The description might include the city name and the section of the city for a large city. Normally the description will be the same for all time periods and alternates.

The **Data Date** and **Data Time** are the date and time of the data collection. For a future projection they are the date and time of the traffic projection. If performing an AM and PM peak study, the Time could be set to 7:00 AM and 5:00 PM for each scenario to indicate which time is analyzed. The Analysis Date is the date the data was collected, not the date the study is performed.

The Data Date and Time track the volume data. The Data Date and Time should be updated when reading and writing Volume data with the UTDF feature (see page 16-1). When Merging data with Merge Volume data and Update Scenario selected, the Data Date and Time will be taken from the merged file.

The **Alternative** is used to describe the alternative being studied. This could describe "Before Improvements" and "After Improvements" or could be used for "Baseline Traffic" or "Traffic with Mondo Mall".

The **Alternative** tracks the lane and geometry data. When Merging data with Merge Lane Geometry and Update Scenario selected, the Alternative will be taken from the merged file.

The **Timing Plan ID** is the name of the timing plan used. The timing plan ID might be AMPeak and PMPeak to indicate which time-of-day plan is used. The Timing Plan ID tracks the lane and geometry data. The Timing Plan ID is used and updated when reading and writing Timing data with the Data Access feature. When Merging data with Merge Timing Data and Update Scenario selected, the Timing Plan ID will be taken from the merged file.

The **Analyst** is the name of the person or company performing the traffic analysis.

Using Synchro with HCS, SimTraffic and CORSIM

Synchro can build input files for CORSIM and the Highway Capacity Software (HCS). Enter data once with Synchro, and then perform optimizations using Synchro. The timing plans can be simulated using SimTraffic or CORSIM for analysis that is more detailed. You can also use the reports generated by the HCS, SimTraffic and CORSIM.

The following table lists the features of each program and suggests how the programs can be used to complement each other.

Table 14-1   Features of the Major Traffic Models

Program	Primary Strengths
Synchro	Easy Data Entry Complete, Flexible Optimizations Graphical Reports and Time-Space Diagrams
HCS	HCM Capacity Analysis Official HCS Reports
SimTraffic	Microscopic Simulation Animation Simulate Roundabouts
CORSIM	Microscopic Simulation Animation

See the topics on CORSIM Analysis in Chapter 18 for more information on how to use Synchro with this program. For instructions on how to use CORSIM (or for background information on this programs), please refer to the respective manuals.

Save to HCS

Use the command **Transfer→Save-to-HCS** to create input files for the Highway Capacity Software, Signal and Unsignalized modules.

1. Select one or more intersections. Multiple intersections can be selected by dragging a box around them.

2. Choose **Transfer→Save-to-HCS**.

3. Select a filename to save the files as. The default filename is "filename #.hcs" where filename is the Synchro filename and # is the node number.

The green times transferred to the HCS are Actuated green times. The actuated green times are calculated by Synchro by averaging the Green times used by the five percentile scenarios. The Actuated Effective Green times shown in the **TIMING** settings are the same Actuated timings after adjusting for clearance and total lost time.

 Synchro calculates delay based on actuated green times, not the maximum green times. Files exported to the HCS will have the actuated green times not the maximum green times. Entering maximum green times in Synchro to match HCS green times will not give the same answer for actuated signals because Synchro will calculate the actuated green times internally. In addition, if the Analysis Period is set to 30 minutes or greater, the PHF transferred will be 1.0.

RTOR Volume Reduction

Synchro will export a RTOR reduction for the HCS export. The RTOR reduction is calculated as follows:

vRTOR = minimum (sRTOR,v) * r/C

vRTOR = RTOR reduction to volume

sRTOR = RTOR saturation flow as calculated by Synchro

r = effective red time

v = adjusted lane group volume (before RTOR reduction)

C = cycle length

Percent Turns Using Shared Lanes

Synchro calculates the percentage of traffic in a shared lane when there is both an exclusive and turning lane and transfers this information to the HCS file. The exclusive lane is in the turning group, and the shared lane is in the through group. Details on how Synchro balances traffic in a shared lane can be found in the topic **Traffic in Shared Lane** on page 6-13.

HCS Release Notes

Synchro saves to the HCS2000 version 4.1c file format. This format will be read by HCS 2000 with some limitations.

Signals

Average Queue Spacing is not supported and must be input manually.

Available Queue Storage Length is not supported and must be input manually.

Receiving Lanes, Travel Distance, Cross walk width is not supported and must be input manually for minimum green calculation.

Unsignalized, two way

Upstream Signals: There have been some recent changes to the method. Be sure you are using the latest release of the HCS.

Right turn channelized is not supported and must be input manually.

Roundabouts

HCS roundabout export not currently supported.

File Extensions

The following are the file extensions used by Synchro and SimTraffic:

Filename.SY6   Synchro data, version 4 and 5

Filename.ST6   SimTraffic configuration data v 4 and 5

Filename.SY7   Synchro data, version 6

Filename.ST7   SimTraffic configuration data version 6

Filename.SYN   Synchro data, version 7

Filename.SIM   SimTraffic configuration data version 7

Filename.HST   SimTraffic history file, all versions

Filename.S3D   SimTraffic history files for 3D graphics, all versions

Version 7 will save to v7 format (syn) or v6 format (sy7).

When saving to version 6, data for all new features are lost, including map backgrounds, detector information, detector templates, and new simulation parameters.

Version 7 will read sy6, sy7, and syn (versions 4, 5, 6, 7) files.

If you open an older version Synchro file with version 7 and simulate the old HST file will be overwritten.

The S3D file can be viewed with **3D Viewer**. Refer to Chapter 25 for details on operation.

Synchro 7 can create a comma delimited (csv) file format. Refer to Chapter 1 for details.

Chapter 15 – Reports and Printing

Printing Views

To print the current Synchro view, type [Ctrl] + [P]. This will print the currently active **MAP** view, or the **TIME-SPACE DIAGRAM** to the default printer. When you select the **File→Print-Window** command from the **VOLUME, LANE, TIMING, SIGNING, PHASING, DETECTORS** or **SIMULATION OPTIONS** settings, a report is created containing information for those settings.

Printing the **MAP** and **TIME-SPACE DIAGRAM** (**File→Print-Window** command) has an options settings dialog. The user can set up headers and footers and select the font. The scale is also adjustable and there are a number of options including fixed scale or print to fit.

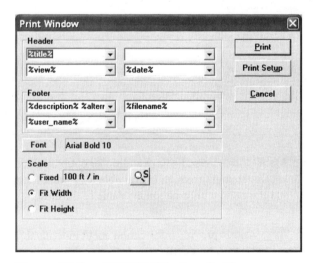

Figure 15-1   PRINT Window Settings

When printing the **MAP view** with fixed scale, it will use the scale specified by Zoom-Scale. The printout will be centered on the center point of the current **MAP view**.

To change the current printer, select the **File→Printer-Setup** command.

Select Reports Dialog

When choosing the **File→Create-Report** command, the **SELECT REPORTS** dialog appears (**Figure 15-2**). From here, you can select the reports to include and the options for each report.

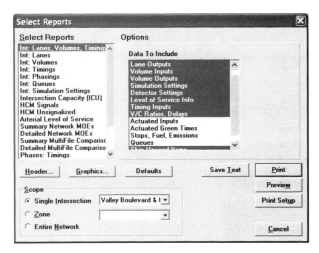

Figure 15-2   SELECT REPORTS Dialog

Select Reports

There are twenty-one (21) reports available. Many of these reports have additional options to select. A brief summary of each report follows. Detailed information is available for some of the reports below. The undocumented reports contain the same information available in the **data entry** setting chapters.

There are seven (7) **Intersection Reports.** These reports provide information about individual intersections. Refer to **Intersection Reports** on page 15-6 for details.

The **ICU Report** gives the Intersection Capacity Utilization report. Details can be found on page 15-11.

The **HCM Signals** and **HCM Unsignalized Reports** will give HCM style reports. These reports are described on page 15-15 and page 15-19, respectively.

Arterial Level of Service is an arterial travel time report. This report is very similar to the HCM Chapter 15 reports for Arterials.

The **Network Measures of Effectiveness** reports show the performance of intersections, arterials and the entire zone or network. These reports can be customized with the panel on the right.

The **Multi-file Comparison Reports** list Measures of Effectiveness (MOEs) from multiple files side by side so that various alternatives can be compared. To use these reports it is necessary to have multiple versions of the same network stored as different files.

The **Phases: Timings Report** contains all of the timing information sorted by phase number. This report is useful for programming controllers.

The **Actuated Green Bars Report** shows the range of actuated green times for each phase in an actuated signal. The **Actuated Greens and Starts Report** also shows the start times and is useful for actuated-coordinated signals. The **Actuated Details Report** shows the green times as well as the time to clear the queue and the time to gap out. The Details report is useful for examining actuated signal behavior in detail.

The **Permitted Left Turn Factors Report** contains detailed information about the calculation of F_{lt}. This report is used for capacity analysis.

The **Coordinatability Factors Report** displays information about the calculation of CFs for each pair of adjacent intersections. The CF is a measure of the need to coordinate a pair of adjacent intersections.

Header and Footer Options

In the **Select Reports** Window, press the [**Header**] button to set the header, footer, report, and page numbering options.

The report header and footer can have two lines each with information on the right and left sides. The eight input boxes control which information appears in each line and each side. The header and footer include macros to display dynamic information, these macros are as follows.

Table 15-1   Header/Footer Options

Macro	Description	Notes
%report_title%	Title of Report	Name of the report type being printed
%report_title2%	Title of Report2	Secondary name of report, if applicable
%filename%	Filename	Filename and path of file analyzed or "Multiple"
%page%	Page Number	Starting page number can be changed
%date%	Current Date	Date report was created, not analysis date
%description%	Description	Set in **Options→Scenario Manager**, location of analysis
%alternative%	Alternative	Set in **Options→Scenario Manager**, alternative being analyzed
%analyst%	Name of Analyst	Set in **Options→Scenario Manager**, person or firm performing study
%data_date%	Date of Data	Set in **Options→Scenario Manager**, date of volume counts or projection
%data_time%	Time of Data	Set in **Options→Scenario Manager** time of volume counts or projection
%planid%	Timing Plan ID	Set in **Options→Scenario Manager**, name of timing plan

Part of the program key code prints under the footer. The key code identifies the name to which Synchro is registered. The key code will not appear if the analyst is shown and the registered name appears within the analyst field of the **Scenario Manager**.

Graphic Options

Press the [**Graphics**] button to set the line colors, fonts and picture options.

Shade Rows, **Horizontal Lines**, **Section Color**, and **Back Color** control the look of the printed report.

The **Font** buttons allow for editing of the fonts used in the reports. The default font is Arial Narrow 10 for data and Arial 12 for titles. The narrow font of the data is better for separation of the twelve data columns.

Set **Pictures to Color** for color pictures, **B/W** for pictures to print on a black and white printer, or **None** to exclude the picture from the report.

Defaults

Press the [**Defaults**] button to change the settings back to the user defaults. Refer to page 2-27 for additional details.

Scope

At the bottom of the **Select Reports** window, the **Scope** determines which intersections are included in the report.

Choose **Single Intersection** and select an intersection to create reports for a single intersection.

Choose **Zone** and enter a zone to create reports for a group of intersections. To select multiple zones, separate the zones with a comma (i.e., "A, B, C" to print reports for zone A, B and C).

Choose **Entire Network** to report the entire network.

Viewing and Printing Reports

After selecting the desired report options, select [**Preview**] to view the report, or [**Print**] to print the report.

Viewing Reports

Select [Preview] from the Report Options settings to view reports. To change pages use the buttons [|<], [<<], [>>], and [>|]. You can also change pages using the [Page Up], [Page Down], mouse scroll wheel, [Home], and [End] keys. To move around the current page, click on it and drag with the mouse. You can also move the page with the arrow keys. To return to the **SELECT REPORTS** settings, use the [Back] button.

Printing Reports

To print the report, select the [Print] button from the Report Options or **REPORT PREVIEW** settings. To change the printer, select **File→Print-Setup** command or the [Print Setup] button.

Intersection Reports

There are seven (7) **Intersection Reports** ("A" in **Figure 15-3**). These reports provide information about individual intersections. Each of these reports can be customized with the Options panel on the right side of the **SELECT REPORTS** settings ("B" in **Figure 15-3**). The **Lanes, Volumes, Timings, Phasing** and **Simulation Options** Reports contain the same information found in the **data entry** settings. The **Queue** Report contains information about queues and blocking.

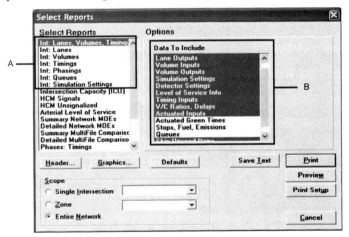

Figure 15-3   Intersection Reports

Intersection Report Options

When an Intersection Report is selected in the left panel ("A" in **Figure 15-3**), its options are included in the right panel ("B" in **Figure 15-3**). It is possible to select any or all options for each report. In some cases the same data appears in more than one option; the report generator will only include this data once in a logical order.

Intersection reports have an option to skip unused rows. With this feature, rows for items such as pedestrians, busses, growth factor, will not be included if they contain default or blank data. This can be used to shorten the report if desired.

Lane Inputs, **Lane Outputs**, **Volume Outputs**, **Simulation Settings**, **Detector Settings**, **Timing Inputs**, **Actuated Inputs** and **Actuated Green Times** mirror the data contained in the input settings.

The reports with the **Lane Inputs** option will include link speed and distance, plus travel time.

Level of Service Info contains a summary of information needed in a capacity analysis report for the control delay calculation. **v/c Ratios** contain the output information in the **TIMING** settings for each delay type.

The delay measures include the **Control Delay**, the **Queue Delay** and the **Total Delay**. The Control Delay is uniform delay plus the impacts of coordination and incremental delays. Queue Delays are the additional delay caused by reduction in capacity due to spillback and starvation. Total Delay is the combination of the Control Delay and the Queue Delay.

Stops, **Fuel**, **Emissions** contain these **MOEs** in the report. The **Queues** option includes information about maximum queue lengths and blocking times in the reports.

Most of the information contained in Intersection Reports mirrors the data shown on input screens. Some notes about special cases are listed below.

The **Stops**, **Fuel Consumption**, and **Emissions** are calculated based on the methods shown in the topic on **Fuel and Emissions Calculation** (see page 13-77).

Footnotes

There are number of footnotes possible on intersection reports. Below are the definitions of the possible footnotes:

*   **User Entered Value**: Indicates that the calculated value was changed with a user entered value. This applies to adjusted volumes, lane utilization factors, Saturated Flow Rates, turning factors, and delay factors.

~   **Volume exceeds capacity, queue is theoretically infinite**: This is used with Intersection Queue Reports, see page 15-8.

\# **95th percentile volume exceeds capacity**: This is used with Intersection Queue Reports, see page 15-8.

m **Upstream metering is in effect**: This is used with Intersection Queue Reports, see page 15-8.

dl **Defacto Left Lane**: Indicates the shared left lane has congestion exceeding the level of other through lanes. Synchro does not model this situation correctly. Convert a shared-through lane into an exclusive left lane to model correctly.

dr **Defacto Right Lane**: Indicates the shared right lane has congestion exceeding the level of other through lanes. Synchro does not model this situation correctly. Convert a shared-through lane into an exclusive right lane to model correctly.

! **Phase conflict between lane groups**: Indicates that two or more conflicting movements may have concurrent phases.

@ **Some critical lane groups may be at other intersections sharing controller**: Used in volume to capacity report. Not all lane groups are listed in this report. The controller at this intersection serves other intersection and some of the critical lane groups may be at the other intersection.

Intersection Queue Report

The **Intersection Queue Report** contains information about Maximum Queue Lengths and Blocking Information (also see, **Queue Length Calculation**, page 13-71). In addition, the Queue report contains information on the Control Delay, Queue Delay, v/c ratio, capacity reductions and more.

 The queue length shown for a lane group is the queue for each lane. The total queue length is divided by the number of lanes and the lane utilization factor. For instance, if the lane group has 2 lanes, do not divide the queue reported by Synchro by 2 since this has already been done by Synchro.

The **Lane Group Flow** is the adjusted lane group flow.

The Queue report shows the 50th Percentile and 95th Percentile Maximum Queue lengths. The 50th percentile maximum queue is the maximum back of queue on a typical cycle. The 95th percentile queue is the maximum back of queue with 95th percentile traffic volumes. Synchro's queues may be longer than those in other queue methods, because Synchro's queues include traffic that arrives during the queue clearance stage. Vehicles delayed for less than 6 seconds are not counted because these vehicles slow but do not stop.

The 95th percentile queue accounts for upstream metering. The 95th percentile volume is unadjusted for peak hour factor.

The ~ and # footnote indicate that the volume modeled exceeds capacity.

The ~ footnote indicates that the approach is above capacity for the 50th percentile traffic and the queue length could be much longer. The queue length is theoretically infinite and blocking problems may occur. See the topic on Queue Length Calculations for more information (page 13-71).

The # footnote indicates that the volume for the 95th percentile cycle exceeds capacity. This traffic was simulated for two complete cycles of 95th percentile traffic to account for the affects of spillover between cycles. If the reported v/c < 1 for this movement, the methods used represent a valid method for estimating the 95th percentile queue. In practice, 95th percentile queue shown will rarely be exceeded and the queues shown with the # footnote are acceptable for the design of storage bays.

The m footnote indicates that volume for the 95th percentile queue is metered by an upstream signal.

 Due to upstream metering, the 95th queue may be less than the 50th queue. If the upstream intersection is operating with v/c > 1, the metered arrival rate will be **less** than the volume for this intersection. Since metering is only performed with the 95th queue, this causes the 95th queue to be less than the 50th queue. This situation may indicate a coding problem. Be sure that the Midblock traffic is coded correctly and that the signal timing and volumes for both intersections are set correctly. This reduced 95th queue does represent a valid queue because vehicles will not be able to clear the upstream intersection to queue at this intersection.

When designing the size of storage bays, it is normally sufficient to store a single cycle of queues. The idea being that through and left traffic will move at different times during the cycle and enough storage should be provided so the two movements do not block each other from using their green time effectively.

The **Link Length** is the link distance minus 80ft (24m) to account for the space inside the intersections. The link distance is entered center-point to center-point.

The Queue report lists "Internal Link Dist" to distinguish from Total Link Distance.

```
Queues                                                                    1/23/2006
1: Main Street & 1st St
```

	↗	→	↙	←	↖	↑	↘	↓	↙

Lane Group									
Lane Group Flow (vph)									
v/c Ratio	0.82	0.76	0.77	0.65	0.30	0.85	0.93	0.34	0.51
Control Delay	57.1	30.2	52.1	8.0	24.4	45.3	24.4	26.9	5.1
Queue Delay	0.0	0.0	0.0	0.0	0.0	0.0	0.0	0.0	0.0
Total Delay	57.1	30.2	52.1	8.0	24.4	45.3	24.4	26.9	5.1
Queue Length 50th (ft)	181	325	137	54	46	279	60	93	0
Queue Length 95th (ft)	#306	412	m184	77	90	#444	#164	153	63
Internal Link Dist (ft)		420		1755		608		603	
Turn Bay Length (ft)	250		150		100		100		100
Base Capacity (vph)	389	1449	283	1237	354	630	114	639	806
Starvation Cap Reductn	0	0	0	0	0	0	0	0	0
Spillback Cap Reductn	0	0	0	0	0	0	0	0	0
Storage Cap Reductn	0	0	0	0	0	0	0	0	0
Reduced v/c Ratio	0.77	0.76	0.71	0.65	0.28	0.79	0.88	0.31	0.50

Intersection Summary									

\# 95th percentile volume exceeds capacity, queue may be longer.

   Queue shown is maximum after two cycles.

m Volume for 95th percentile queue is metered by upstream signal.

Figure 15-4   Queues

Queue Report Additional Measures of Effectiveness

The **v/c Ratio** is the volume to capacity ratio for the lane group.

The **Control Delay** is the delay caused by the downstream traffic control device for the lane group.

Queue Delay is an analysis of the affects of queues and blocking on short links and short turning bays.

Total Delay is the combination of the Control Delay and the Queue Delay.

Base Capacity is the capacity of the lane group if unimpeded. Capacity is the lane group saturation flow multiplied by the lane group green to cycle ratio.

The **Starvation Capacity Reduction** is the reduction to the base capacity due to starvation. Starvation is congestion caused by a short upstream link in conjunction with poor/no coordination.

Spillback Capacity Reduction is a reduction to the base capacity caused by a short downstream link becoming filled up.

Storage Capacity Reduction is a reduction to the base capacity caused when turn pockets cannot accommodate queue lengths.

Reduced v/c Ratio is the modified volume to capacity ratio with the adjustments to the base capacity.

Intersection Capacity (ICU) Report

The Intersection Capacity Utilization report provides a straightforward method to calculate an intersection's level of service. The method simply takes a sum of the critical movement's volume to saturation flow rates.

Line by Line Explanation

This section contains line by line description of the ICU report. Lines not described are self-explanatory.

For a complete reference on the calculations, see the topic on **Intersection Capacity (ICU) Calculations**, page 13-49.

 Additional Details can be found in the *Intersection Capacity Utilization 2003* book. A copy of this book can be obtained from Trafficware.

Pedestrian Timing Required: This is the walk plus Do not Walk time from the primary phase associated with this direction. If no pedestrian timing is provided and pedestrians are present, this value is 16 seconds.

Ideal Flow: This is the Ideal Saturated Flow and 1900 vphpl by default. If the intersection has Area Type of CBD, the Ideal Flow is multiplied by 0.90.

Lost Time: This is the Total Lost time for the movement. By default it is 4 seconds.

Reference Cycle Length: This is set to 120 seconds.

Adjusted Volume: Volume adjusted for peak hour factor.

Volume Combined: This is the volume assigned to lane groups.

Volume Separate Left: The volume assigned to lane groups, assuming no shared left-through lane. A shared lane is considered exclusive left or exclusive through for each lane group's analysis.

Lane Utilization Factor: This factor adjusts the Saturated Flow Rate when there are 2 or more lanes. This adjustment accounts for the unequal use of lanes.

Turning Factor Adjustment: This factor adjusts for the number of right or left turners in the lane group.

Saturated Flow Rate Combined: This is the adjusted Saturated Flow Rate adjusting for turning factors, number of lanes, and lane utilization.

Saturated Flow Rate Separate: This is used with a shared left-through lane. This value will be used for some capacity checks in the permitted and split options.

Minimum Green Time: This is the minimum time a signal can show green. This is the Minimum Initial value for the phase or 4 seconds for unsignalized intersections.

Pedestrian Interference Time: This is the estimated time per cycle that right turn traffic will be blocked by pedestrians.

Pedestrian Frequency (freq): This is the probability of a pedestrian activating the pedestrian timings on any cycle. If there are no pedestrians it is 0. If there are no push buttons and there are pedestrians, it is 1.

Protected Option

Protected Option Allowed: The protected option is allowed only when both opposing directions do not have a shared left-through lane. Otherwise, the intersection is only analyzed with split or permitted phasing. In some cases, a shared left-through lane can be recoded as a left only lane to give better performance with the protected option.

Reference Time: This is the time required to serve the adjusted volume at 100% saturation. It is equal to the Adjusted Volume divided by the Saturation Flow Rate Combined multiplied by the Reference Cycle Length and added to the Pedestrian Interference time.

Adjusted Reference Time: This is the reference time adjusted for minimums, pedestrians, and lost time.

Permitted Option

This option calculates the ICU using a permitted left turn option. Traditionally the ICU method did not allow for permitted left turns because it is taking a sum of conflicting movements. However using the protected option requires a dedicated left lane. Many intersections in urban areas have shared left-through lanes that are analyzed too harshly with the protected or split options.

The ICU 2003 contains two options for treating permitted left turns. Option "A" assumes that there are relatively few left turners. These left turners will be accommodated as sneakers at the end of a green or when there is a left turn on an oncoming single lane approach. Option "A" should only be used when the left turn volume is less than 60 vph or the oncoming approach is single lane with some left turn traffic.

Option "B" assumes that the oncoming traffic is relatively light and that oncoming traffic will only block the left turns for the first 8 seconds of green. Option "B" is only available when the oncoming traffic is less than 120 vph.

If the volume exceeds the requirements for both Options "A" and "B", it is considered that the intersection would operate as efficiently using protected or split phasing. It may be necessary to reclassify a left-through lane as a left only lane for the analysis.

Permitted Option Allowed: The permitted option is allowed for opposing approaches, when either left traffic is less than 60 vph or the oncoming through traffic is less than 120 vph. This condition must be met for both sets of conflicting movements for the opposing approaches for permitted analysis to be allowed.

Adjusted Saturation A: This is the saturation flow rate of the through and shared lanes adjusted for blocking by left turn traffic.

Reference Time A: This is the reference time for the through movement, when the shared lane is blocked by less than 60 vph of left traffic. If vL is greater than 60, enter "NA".

Adjusted Saturation B: This is the Saturated Flow Rate of the through lanes without the shared lane.

Reference Time B: This is the reference time assuming the lanes will be blocked for 8 seconds by oncoming through traffic. If oncoming through traffic is greater than 120 vph, the B option is not allowed.

Reference Time: The minimum of Reference Time A and Reference Time B is allowed.

Adjusted Reference Time: This is the reference time adjusted for minimums, pedestrians, and lost time.

Split Option: The split option is always allowed, in some cases the split option is the only option allowed. The split option analyzes the lanes combined and also checks the left and through traffic independently.

Reference Time Combined: This value is for the combined lanes and volumes. This is the time required to serve the adjusted volume at 100% saturation. It is equal to the Adjusted Volume divided by the Saturation Flow Rate Combined multiplied by the Reference Cycle Length and added to the Pedestrian Interference time.

Reference Time By Movement: This Reference Time calculates lefts and throughs and rights separately. This adds an additional check against uneven lane distribution.

Reference Time: The maximum of Reference Time Combined and the Reference Times by Movement.

Adjusted Reference Time: This is the reference time adjusted for minimums, pedestrians, and lost time.

Summary

This section summarizes and combines the required times for left and through traffic by approach pairs. The best solution is found for each approach pair and combined.

Protected Option: Maximum of the Sums of the opposing Adjusted Reference times.

Permitted Option: Maximum of the Permitted Adjusted Reference Times is allowed.

Split Option: Sum of the opposing Adjusted Reference times.

Minimum: For each approach pair, take the minimum combined adjusted reference time.

Combined: The sum for all approaches.

Right Turns

Right turns from exclusive lanes are calculated by a separate calculation. This accounts for free rights, overlapping right turn phases, and right turns on red.

Adjusted Reference Time: The Adjusted Reference Times for right turns. For approaches with 0 exclusive right lanes, this value will be 0.

Cross Through Adjusted Reference Time: The minimum Adjusted Reference Times for the cross through movement.

Oncoming Adjusted Left Reference Time: The minimum Adjusted Reference Times for the cross left movement. This does not include the permitted time for oncoming left. The split reference time for left movements should be the same as for through movements.

Combined: The sum of the above lines. If this movement is a free right, it is simply the right turn's Adjusted Reference time. For intersections with 5 or more legs, the cross through times and oncoming left times may include multiple movements. There may be additional time added if there are "interlocking" right times that are both critical.

Final Calculations

Intersection Capacity Utilization: The maximum of the Combined times for through and right turn sections, divided by the Reference Cycle Length. This is the Intersection Capacity Utilization. It is similar to, but not exactly the same as the intersection volume to capacity ratio. A value less than 100% indicates that the intersection has extra capacity. A value greater than 100% indicates the intersection is over capacity.

Level of Service: A letter A to H based on the table and the Intersection Capacity Utilization. Note that the ICU 2003 includes additional levels past F to further differentiate congested operation.

HCM Signals Report

This report provides a full implementation of the HCM 2000 Signalized Operations method. This report will match other HCM 2000 (Chapter 16) implementations except for the items listed below.

Report Items Line by Line

Unless noted here, the report line items are self-explanatory or match the same fields found on the Synchro input settings.

Total Lost Time: This is the sum of the Startup lost time and the Clearance lost time. Do not confuse this value with the Startup Lost time. Refer to page 7-12 for details on the Lost Time adjustment.

Frpb, Flpb: Bike and Ped factors, these may vary slightly from the bike and ped factors shown in other Synchro reports because these are calculated based on actuated green times for HCM compatibility. These factors are applied to both the permitted and protected phases. The bike/pedestrian factors in other Synchro reports are calculated based on maximum green times for calculation efficiency and only apply to the permitted phases.

F$_{lt}$ Permitted: The permitted left turn factor may vary slightly from the left turn factor shown in other Synchro reports because these are calculated based on actuated green times for HCM compatibility. The permitted left turn factors in other Synchro reports are calculated based on maximum green times for calculation efficiency.

RTOR Reduction: The HCM Signal Report now includes a RTOR reduction calculation. The Lane Group Flow is now equal to the Adjusted Lane Group flow minus the RTOR reduction. The RTOR reduction is calculated as follows:

vRTOR = minimum (sRTOR,v) * r/C = RTOR reduction to volume

sRTOR = RTOR saturation flow as calculated by Synchro

r = effective red time

v = adjusted lane group volume (before RTOR reduction)

C = cycle length

The vRTOR value cannot be over-ridden. However, the sRTOR can be changed in the **LANE** settings. The sRTOR can be calculated with observed vRTOR using the formula sRTOR = vRTOR * C/r.

Actuated Green: The green times used for the HCM signals report are actuated green times which may be less than the maximum green times for actuated signals. When comparing to other HCM compatible software, be sure to compare the same green times.

v/s Ratios: The volume to Saturated Flow Rate ratios for permitted and protected movements. A "c" indicates that this is a critical movement. The HCM volume to capacity ratio is based on a sum of the critical v/s ratios.

Progression Factor: The progression factor is calculated by dividing Synchro's control delay with coordination by the control delay without coordination. This may vary from the progression factor used in other HCM implementations.

The HCM Signals Reports will skip unused or default rows. With this feature, rows for items such as pedestrians, busses, growth factor, will not be included if they contain default data.

Multiple options can be selected when printing reports. For example, the HCM Signal Report can be printed with the Queue report. In the **SELECT REPORT** settings, choose the HCM Signal Report, hold the [Ctrl] key and select Int: Queues.

Discussion

In some cases, Synchro will give results different than the HCM and the HCS. Some of these deviations are necessary to accommodate modeling of coordination and actuation. Other differences can be attributed to varying input methods and rounding errors. The following section outlines the known deviations of Synchro from the HCM and recommended work arounds.

The following table lists the reasons why the Synchro HCM report may deviate from the HCM and HCS reports. Synchro version 5 and later have eliminated many of the differences found in earlier versions of Synchro by using the HCM delay formulas instead of time-slice analysis. The remaining differences are mostly due to limitations in the other software and Synchro's explicit calculation of coordination.

Table 15-2   Synchro HCM vs. HCM & HCS Differences

Issue	Reason	Work Around	Capacity Difference	Delay Difference
Queue Delay is not included in the HCM and HCS	New in Synchro 6 is an added measure for queue interaction delays. This measure is not included in the HCM Signal Report or the HCS.	Accept Synchro's delay	No	Yes
PF (Platoon Factor) Does not match HCM	Affects of coordination are calculated explicitly.	Synchro's PF is based on calculations versus a ±25% estimate in the HCM method.	No	Yes
Input Data different	User has entered data differently for each model.	Export data from Synchro or check data carefully	Yes	Yes
Different Green Times	Any reasonable actuated green time is allowed in HCM 2000. For actuated signals, the timings in HCS are equivalent to Synchro's actuated green times. Do not attempt to compare Synchro's maximum splits and green times to the HCS green times.	Export data from Synchro	Yes	Yes

Issue	Reason	Work Around	Capacity Difference	Delay Difference
Dual Ring Controller	The HCS and other HCM software do not support dual ring controllers. The HCS cannot model overlapping clearance intervals (yellow times) for the two rings overlap. It is possible to have actuated green times overlap even if the maximum green times are not overlapping. About 15% of all actuated signal timing plans have overlapping clearances.	HCS values are less accurate because the timing plan is modified.	Yes	Yes
Rounding Differences	Programs round numbers to different precision.		Minor	Minor
Effective Green Times with Permitted + Protected Left Turns	When both directions have a leading Permitted plus Protected left turn of the same length, the HCS assumes (incorrectly in our opinion) that the interval between the green arrow and the green ball is part of the permitted green time. This causes the HCS to give higher effective green times, lower v/c ratios and F_{lt} and lower delays.	Accept Synchro's truer numbers or use HCS	Yes (Synchro has lower capacity)	Yes (Synchro has higher delay)
Effective Green Times with lagging Permitted + Protected Left Turns	With lagging Permitted plus Protected left turn phasing, the HCS assumes (incorrectly in our opinion) that the interval between the green ball and the green ball counts towards the protected green time. This causes the HCS to give higher effective green times, lower v/c ratios and lower delays.	Accept Synchro's Truer numbers or use HCS	Yes (Synchro has lower capacity)	Yes (Synchro has higher delay)

Changes in the 2000 HCM

In 2000, the Transportation Research Board released a update to the HCM including changes to Chapter 16 (previously Chapter 9). Many of the procedures in the HCM have been changed since the 1994 and 1997 versions.

The 1997 and 2000 HCM use Signal Delay or Control Delay. Signal delay is 30% higher than stopped delay. Earlier versions of Synchro, the HCS, and the HCM used stopped delay. The current versions of all programs now use signal delay for easy comparison. The scale for LOS values has been adjusted to reflect signal delays rather than stopped delay.

The 1997 and 2000 HCM includes changes to model actuation. The model requires the analyst to determine "actuated" green times for input. There is an Appendix to the HCM with recommendations for calculating actuated green times. This appendix is similar to the methods used by Synchro for calculating actuated green times. Synchro uses an average of the five percentile green times for calculating the actuated green times used with the HCS and the HCM Signal Delay report. The actuated green times will be similar to green times calculated by using the HCM Chapter 16, Appendix 2.

The 1997 and 2000 HCM recommends using a Total Lost Time equal to the Yellow + All-Red time. The HCM 1994 and Synchro 3.2 recommended using a Total Lost Time of 3 seconds. This causes a reduction in capacity of 2 to 10%. The Total Lost Time is now divided into Startup Lost time and Change Interval Lost time. The Change Interval lost time is calculated based on the Yellow Time, All-Red time, and Extension of Effective Green. The new methods increase the lost time and then hide the changes by adding new input fields that indirectly affect the lost time.

HCM Unsignalized Report

The HCM Unsignalized Report is based on the HCM 2000 Chapter 17. More information about the calculations and the variables in the report are found in the HCM.

Two Way Report

Hourly Flow Rate: Movement volume divided by PHF.

tC, single: The critical gap time for single stage crossing.

tC, 2 stage: The critical gap time for each stage of a two stage crossing.

tF: The follow up time.

p0: The probability of a queue free state for this movement.

cM: The capacity for the movement. This value considers the impacts of two stage gap acceptance and plattooned flows. However, this capacity does not consider the influence of shared lanes or flared right turns.

Lane Section

The lower part of the unsignalized report has information on a per lane basis. One column appears for each lane.

cSH: The capacity for each lane considering the affects of sharing and flared right turns. The capacity of free movements is assumed to be 1700 vphpl.

Queue Length: This is the 50th percentile queue for each lane in feet or meters.

Synchro's unsignalized analysis does implement the upstream signals methodology for two-way stops. In 2000, Trafficware discovered errors in the HCM methodology and has determined that results calculated with the upstream signals methodology should not used. In June 2002 and again in July of 2003, an errata to the HCM was released that addresses most of these errors.

 Intersection wide delay and level of service is not defined by the HCM for two-way stop controlled intersections, therefore, it is not shown in the report. The analyst needs to look at the delay and LOS for the individual movements.

The LOS for main street approaches is not shown because it is not defined for main street approaches. The analyst needs to examine the left turn LOS and delay to rank the vehicles.

All Way Report

If a right turn lane is marked channelized, it is not included in the headway calculations and its volume does not affect the intersection calculations.

Hourly Flow Rate: Movement volume divided by PHF.

Hadj: Headway adjustments based on turning percentages and proportion of heavy vehicles.

Departure Headway: This is the value Hd, computed by multiple iterations of Worksheets 4a and 4b from the Highway Capacity Manual, Chapter 17. It is the average time each vehicle requires at each lane. Hd takes into account the number of lanes, and occupancy of conflicting lanes.

Degree Utilization, x: This is the volume divided by the departure headway. Note that x is not the v/c ratio because increases to the volume on this approach will increase the headways and occupancies for conflicting approaches and in turn increase the headways for this approach.

Capacity: This is the capacity for the lane. The method iteratively increases the volume for each lane until x is 1. The volume to capacity ratio is based on the Capacity.

Roundabout Report

Hourly Flow Rate: Movement volume divided by PHF.

Approach Volume: Sum of movement volumes for approach.

Crossing Volume: Sum of movement volumes crossing this movement in front of the roundabout. The method is only applicable for crossing volumes up to 1200 vph. If the crossing volume exceeds 1200, the results are not valid.

High Capacity: High range of capacity. The method has a high and low range of possible capacities. It is the analyst's responsibility to decide which is more applicable.

High v/c: The high capacity volume to capacity ratio.

Low Capacity: High range of capacity. The method has a high and low range of possible capacities. It is the analyst's responsibility to decide which is more applicable.

Low v/c: The low capacity volume to capacity ratio.

The roundabout's method has not been very well developed. There are no delay or queue outputs. The method is only applicable to single lane roundabouts with up to 1200 vph crossing volume. The output is a range of v/c values; it is the analyst's responsibility to decide which v/c ratio is most applicable.

Arterial Level of Service Report

The Arterial Level of Service report contains information about the speed and travel time for an arterial. This report mirrors the reports used in the Arterials section of the HCM, Chapter 15. The Arterial report can also be compared with field travel time studies.

When creating an Arterial LOS report, select one or more arterials in the right panel of the **SELECT REPORTS** settings. To create an arterial with multiple street names or that turns corners, include a route number with the # symbol in the street names, such as "Ashby Ave #13".

A report is created for each direction of the arterial.

The **Arterial Class** is calculated automatically based on the distances between intersections and the link speeds. The Speed is the total distance divided by the total travel time. The segment distance is the total distance divided by the number of segments.

Table 15-3   Arterial Class

Speed (mph)	Segment Distance	Class
1 to 29	any	IV
30 to 35	<2000 ft	IV
30 to 35	≥2000 ft	III
36 to 45	any	II
above 45	any	I

The **Flow Speed** is the free flow speed or link speed input for each link.

For segments over 0.5 miles, the **Running Time** is the link distance divided by the flow speed. For shorter links, the running time is based on the running times in the HCM 2000, Table 15-3. This table is based on FHWA research that shows longer running times on networks with short segments. This will cause longer travel times and lower LOS than using the free flow speeds.

The **Signal Delay** is the Synchro Control delay for the through lane group. This will match the Control Delay as shown in the **TIMING** view.

The **Travel Time** is equal to Running time plus Signal Delay. **Arterial Speed** is thus Distance divided by Travel Time.

The **Arterial LOS** is based on the speed and the Arterial Class.

Arterial Level of Service

1/23/2006

Arterial Level of Service: EB Main Street

Cross Street	Arterial Class	Flow Speed	Running Time	Signal Delay	Travel Time (s)	Dist (mi)	Arterial Speed	Arterial LOS
1st St	II	40	10.9	30.2	41.1	0.09	8.3	F
2nd St	II	40	34.4	11.2	45.6	0.35	27.4	C
3rd St	II	40	29.3	75.2	104.5	0.27	9.2	F
4th St	II	40	28.0	16.0	44.0	0.25	20.8	D
5th St	II	40	16.2	8.9	25.1	0.14	20.2	D
6th St	II	40	16.2	21.2	37.4	0.14	13.6	E
Total	II		135.0	162.7	297.7	1.25	15.1	E

Arterial Level of Service: WB Main Street

Cross Street	Arterial Class	Flow Speed	Running Time	Signal Delay	Travel Time (s)	Dist (mi)	Arterial Speed	Arterial LOS
6th St	II	40	17.5	23.2	40.7	0.15	13.4	E
5th St	II	40	16.2	6.0	22.2	0.14	22.9	C
4th St	II	40	16.2	10.7	26.9	0.14	18.9	D
3rd St	II	40	28.0	46.6	74.6	0.25	12.3	F
2nd St	II	40	29.3	12.6	41.9	0.27	22.9	C
1st St	II	40	34.4	8.0	42.4	0.35	29.5	B
Total	II		141.6	107.1	248.7	1.30	18.9	D

Figure 15-5   Sample Arterial Level of Service Report

Network Measures of Effectiveness Reports

The Summary Network MOEs and Detailed Network MOEs reports display quantitative information about the performance of intersections and the network.

The MOEs can include delays, stops, fuel consumption, queuing penalty, dilemma vehicles and emissions.

The network reports can display information about each approach, each intersection, for an arterial, and for the entire zone or network selected.

Measure Of Effectiveness (MOE) Report Options

The MOE Report options are available for the Network reports and the Multi-file reports ("A" in **Figure 15-6**).

Select the MOEs to include in the report. Detailed information about each MOE is listed later in this topic.

Select the Level of Detail to include in each report ("B" in **Figure 15-6**). It is possible to list MOEs for each approach, for each intersection, for selected arterials, and for the entire network or zone.

Select one of more Arterials to include in the report ("C" in **Figure 15-6**). The report will summarize the MOEs along the arterial for arterial approaches only. Through and turning lane groups are included.

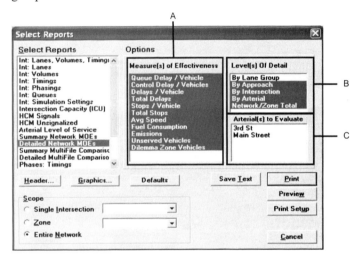

Figure 15-6   Network Report Options

MOE Notes

The delays shown are Synchro's Control delay.

The volumes are not adjusted for PHF or Lane Utilization. Volumes are adjusted for growth factors.

Delays per vehicle are the Synchro Control Delay, Queue Delay and Total Delay. The Total Delay per vehicle would be the Control Delay per vehicle plus the Queue Delay per vehicle. The **Total Delay** is the Total Delay per vehicle multiplied by the number of vehicles in the network/zone in one hour.

Stops are calculated with the methods shown in the topic, **Optimizations and Calculations** (see page 13-76). Stops are the number of stops per hour.

The **Average Speed** is the link distance divided by the travel time including delays. Average Speed includes the speed of vehicles in turning lanes and will not match the Average Speeds in the Arterial Travel time report.

The **Total Travel Time** is an hourly summary of delays and travel time.

The **Distance Traveled** is the volume times the link distance. Bend distances are included at the downstream intersection. Travel on exit links is not counted.

The **Fuel Consumed** is calculated using the methods outlined in the topic **Fuel and Emissions Calculation** (see page 13-77). The fuel is based on the delays, stops, speed, distance traveled, and travel time.

The **Emissions** are calculated based on the fuel consumption. The conversion rates are shown in the topic **Fuel and Emissions Calculation** (see page 13-77).

The **Unserved Vehicles** is the Adjusted Volume less Actuated Capacity. A value of 10 indicates that the volume exceeds capacity by 10 vehicles per hour.

The **Vehicles in Dilemma Zone** is a count of the vehicles arriving while the signal turns yellow and soon thereafter. This is rough measure of the safety of the movement. It is undesirable to create timing plans that turn yellow when a platoon is approaching the intersection.

The **Performance Index** is a combination of the delays and stops. When optimizing, Synchro selects the cycle length with the lowest PI. See the topic on **Optimize→Network-Cycle-Lengths** on page 13-11 for more details.

A sample Network MOE report is shown in **Figure 15-7**.

```
Detailed Measures of Effectiveness
                                                          1/23/2006

Network Totals

Number of Intersections              8
Control Delay / Veh (s/v)           40
Queue Delay / Veh (s/v)              5
Total Delay / Veh (s/v)             45
Total Delay (hr)                   419
Stops / Veh                       0.63
Stops (#)                        21092
Average Speed (mph)                 11
Total Travel Time (hr)             574
Distance Traveled (mi)            6057
Fuel Consumed (gal)                729
Fuel Economy (mpg)                 8.3
CO Emissions (kg)                50.98
NOx Emissions (kg)                9.92
VOC Emissions (kg)               11.82
Unserved Vehicles (#)              793
Vehicles in dilemma zone (#)       907
Performance Index                477.4
```

Figure 15-7 Detailed MOE Report Example

Arterial Summaries

Select a street name or route number to generate an Arterial Summary ("C" in **Figure 15-6**). The Arterial Summary summates the MOEs for approaches on the arterial including turning lane groups. Side street approaches are not counted. The MOEs are summarized by direction and totaled.

To create an **Arterial Route** with multiple street names or that turns corners, include a route number in the street name with the # symbol. For example, the streets Ashby Avenue and Tunnel Road are part of the same route. Give these streets the names "Ashby Ave SR #13" and "Tunnel Road SR #13". Synchro will be able to create reports and analysis on the arterial "#13".

The values summarized by arterial are volume weighted and include turning lane groups. The values will not match the average speeds and total travel times listed in the Arterial Report.

Multi-File Comparison Report

The Multi-file Comparison Report is used to compare multiple alternatives side-by-side.

The report could be used to compare a before-and-after condition, or the report can be used to compare MOEs for two or more different timing plans.

When performing a cycle length optimization, select the **Preserve File for Each Cycle Length** option. These files can be used to create a Comparison Report.

The files used should contain mostly the same intersections with the same arterial names. Be sure to correctly enter the **Scenario Manager** information so that each alternative can be identified.

To create a Multi-File Comparison Report, use the following steps (files to compare must be in the same directory):

- From the **SELECT REPORTS** dialog, choose Detailed or Summary Multi-File Comparison
- Select the options you would like to include
- Select the [Print], [Save-Text] or [Preview] button to create your report
- A dialog to select your files to compare will appear
- Navigate to the directory with the files
- To show all Synchro files in the directory, enter *.syn in the File Name and press [Enter]
- Choose the files you want to compare by holding the [Ctrl] key and clicking on the files you want
- Select [Open]

 If your computer is configured to open files on a single click, hold the **[Ctrl]** key down when selecting the first file. Then hold the **[Shift]** key to select the last file. Clicking a file with the **[Ctrl]** key down can select or deselect a file. Multiple files can also be selected by dragging a rectangle around their names. Start the rectangle to the right of any filenames.

The first page of the comparison report lists each alternative with its scenario information and basic statistics (**Figure 15-8**).

Detailed Alternative Comparisons

1/23/2006

Scenario Information

Scenario #1
Filename: C:\Program Files\Trafficware\Fixed Cycle Coordination-100.syn
Location: Fixed Cycle Problem
Data Date: 8/16/1999
Timing Plan ID: PM PEAK
Alternative: Baseline
Number of Signalized Intersections: 8
Most Popular Cycle Length: 100

Scenario #2
Filename: C:\Program Files\Trafficware\Fixed Cycle Coordination-110.syn
Location: Fixed Cycle Problem
Data Date: 8/16/1999
Timing Plan ID: PM PEAK
Alternative: Baseline
Number of Signalized Intersections: 8
Most Popular Cycle Length: 110

Figure 15-8   Detailed Alternative Comparisons

Succeeding pages list the MOEs with one column for each alternative. The MOE information follows all of the rules for the Network report listed above (**Figure 15-9**).

Detailed Alternative Comparisons

1/23/2006

Network Totals

Scenario #	1	2
Number of Intersections	8	8
Most Popular Cycle (s)	100	110
Alternative	Baseline	Baseline
Timing Plan ID	PM PEAK	PM PEAK
Data Time		
Control Delay / Veh (s/v)	41	38
Queue Delay / Veh (s/v)	5	1
Total Delay / Veh (s/v)	46	39
Total Delay (hr)	424	363
Stops / Veh	0.63	0.56
Stops (#)	20907	18611
Average Speed (mph)	10	12
Total Travel Time (hr)	579	518
Distance Traveled (mi)	6057	6057
Fuel Consumed (gal)	731	660
Fuel Economy (mpg)	8.3	9.2
CO Emissions (kg)	51.09	46.12
NOx Emissions (kg)	9.94	8.97
VOC Emissions (kg)	11.84	10.69
Unserved Vehicles (#)	649	469
Vehicles in dilemma zone (#)	870	761
Performance Index	482.1	414.4

Figure 15-9   Detailed Alternative Comparisons Example

Timing Report - Sorted by Phase Number

Timing Report, Sorted by Phase Number option (Phases: Timings) provides information about the signal timing parameters determined by Synchro. For each phase that is in use, the following information is given:

Movement	Time To Reduce (s)
Lead/Lag	Walk Time (s)
Lead-Lag Optimize	Flash Don't Walk (s)
Recall Mode	Dual Entry
Maximum Split (s)	Inhibit Max
Maximum Split (%)	Start Time (s)
Minimum Split (s)	End Time (s)
Yellow Time (s)	Yield/Force Off (s)
All-Red Time (s)	Yield/Force Off 170 (s)
Minimum Initial (s)	Local Start Time (s)
Vehicle Extension (s)	Local Yield (s)
Minimum Gap (s)	Local Yield 170 (s)
Time Before Reduce (s)	

Most of these values are the same values shown in the **TIMING** settings or **PHASING** settings.

Movement is the lane group(s) served by this phase. For through movements, for example NBT or EBT, the movement ends in T. For left turn phases the movement ends in L. For split phasing, for example NBTL, the movement ends with TL, because the phase serves through and left traffic. For a single phase serving two directions, the movement is NB-SB for northbound and southbound.

The report includes a start time, an end time, a yield/force off and yield/force off 170. These times are phase references to the beginning of the system clock. The 170 yield (to the coordinated phase) is referenced to the beginning of the flashing don't walk.

The report also contains the Cycle Length, Natural Cycle Length, Control Type and Offset Information at the top, and a **Splits and Phasing Diagram** at the bottom.

A sample **Timing Report, Sorted By Phase** is shown in **Figure 15-10**.

Timing Report, Sorted By Phase
3: Main Street & 3rd St   1/23/2006

Phase Number	1	2	3	4	5	6	7	8
Movement	WBL	EBT	NBL	SBT	EBL	WBT	SBL	NBT
Lead/Lag	Lead	Lag	Lead	Lag	Lead	Lag	Lead	Lag
Lead-Lag Optimize	Yes	Yes	Yes	Yes	Yes	Yes	Yes	Yes
Recall Mode	None	C-Max	None	Min	None	C-Max	None	Min
Maximum Split (s)	8	31	19	42	13	26	8	53
Maximum Split (%)	8.0%	31.0%	19.0%	42.0%	13.0%	26.0%	8.0%	53.0%
Minimum Split (s)	8	19	8	19	8	19	8	19
Yellow Time (s)	3.5	3.5	3.5	3.5	3.5	3.5	3.5	3.5
All-Red Time (s)	0.5	0.5	0.5	0.5	0.5	0.5	0.5	0.5
Minimum Initial (s)	4	4	4	4	4	4	4	4
Vehicle Extension (s)	3	4.7	3	3	3	4.7	3	3
Minimum Gap (s)	3	4.7	3	3	3	4.7	3	3
Time Before Reduce (s)	0	0	0	0	0	0	0	0
Time To Reduce (s)	0	0	0	0	0	0	0	0
Walk Time (s)		5		5		5		5
Flash Dont Walk (s)		10		10		10		10
Dual Entry	No	Yes	No	Yes	No	Yes	No	Yes
Inhibit Max	Yes	Yes	Yes	Yes	Yes	Yes	Yes	Yes
Start Time (s)	87	95	26	45	87	0	26	34
End Time (s)	95	26	45	87	0	26	34	87
Yield/Force Off (s)	91	22	41	83	96	22	30	83
Yield/Force Off 170(s)	91	12	41	83	96	12	30	83
Local Start Time (s)	87	95	26	45	87	0	26	34
Local Yield (s)	91	22	41	83	96	22	30	83
Local Yield 170(s)	91	12	41	83	96	12	30	83

Intersection Summary

Cycle Length   100
Control Type   Actuated-Coordinated
Natural Cycle   130
Offset: 0 (0%), Referenced to phase 2:EBT and 6:WBT, Start of Green

Splits and Phases: 3: Main Street & 3rd St

ø1	ø2	ø3	ø4
ø5	ø6	ø7	ø8

Figure 15-10   Sample Timing Report, Sorted By Phase

Actuated Green Times Summary

The Actuated Phase Start and Green summary report shows the green time for each phase. This information is provided for each of the five percentile scenarios. This report is helpful for looking at actuated signals to see the range of green times.

For each phase and percentile scenario, the following information is listed:

Phase

Percentile

Green

Termination

Detail Bar Graph

Phase: Each phase has its number and lane group listed here.

Percentile: This is the percentile scenario for this row. Synchro models traffic under five percentile scenarios (see the topic on the **Percentile Delay Method**, page 13-30).

Green: This is the actual green time for this scenario. This value is normally equal to the sum of the Queue and the Gap-out times. Many times the green time is constrained by the minimum or maximum times or the phase is skipped altogether.

Termination: This code explains how the phase was terminated. The available options are as follows:

Skip: Phase is skipped, no calls.

Min: Phase shows for minimum time.

GapOut: Phase gaps out

Hold: Phase held for phase in other ring. Lagging main street phases are also held.

Max Out: Phase shows for maximum time.

Ped: Phase extended for pedestrian phase due to ped button or ped recall.

Max Recall: Max Recall, phase is set for maximum recall.

Dwell: Signal rests or dwells on this phase, conflicting volume is very light.

Coordinated: This phase is the main street phase in coordination. Any extra time reverts to this phase.

Detail Bar Graph: The bar graphs to the right show the green times graphically. Each graph shows the green and yellow time as green and yellow.

For non-coordinated actuated signals, the cycle length and the rest-in-red time are shown at the bottom. If all phases have no recall, the signal may rest with all phases red. The blue bars represent the cycle length and the red bars represent rest-in-red time.

For pretimed and fixed-cycle signals, the cycle length is listed at the bottom.

A sample Actuated Green Times Report is shown in **Figure 15-11**.

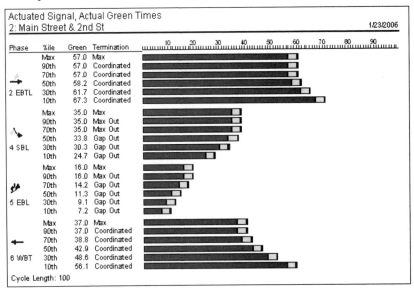

Figure 15-11   Sample Actuated Green Times Report

Actuated Start and Green Times Summary

The Actuated Phase Start and Green summary report shows the green time for each phase along with the phases' start time. This information is provided for each of the five percentile scenarios. This report is helpful for looking at actuated signals in coordination, to see if phases may be starting early.

For each phase and percentile scenario, the following information is listed:

Phase

Percentile

Green

Start

Termination

Detail Bar Graph

Phase: Each phase has its number and lane group listed here.

Percentile: This is the percentile scenario for this row. Synchro models traffic under five percentile scenarios. Also see **Percentile Scenarios** (page 13-31) for more information.

Green: This is the actual green time for this scenario. This value is normally equal to the sum of the Queue and the Gap-out times. Many times the green time is constrained by the minimum or maximum times or the phase is skipped altogether.

Start: This is the start time for each phase. The start times are referenced to the system cycle clock. These start times are the same as appear on the time space diagram. If this signal has offset 0, referenced to the yield point of phase 2, phase 2 will yield at time 0.

Termination: This code explains how the phase was terminated. The available options are as follows:

Skip: Phase is skipped, no calls.

Min: Phase shows for minimum time

GapOut: Phase gaps out

Hold: Phase held for phase in other ring. Lagging main street phases are also held

Max: Out Phase shows for maximum time.

Ped: Phase extended for pedestrian phase due to ped button or ped recall.

Max Recall: Max Recall, phase is set for maximum recall.

Dwell: Signal rests or dwells on this phase, conflicting volume is very light.

Coordinated: This phase is the main street phase in coordination. Any extra time reverts to this phase.

Detail Bar Graph: The bar graphs to the right show the start and green times graphically. Each graph shows the green and yellow time as green and yellow.

For non-coordinated actuated signals, the cycle length and the rest-in-red time are shown at the bottom. If all phases have no recall, the signal may rest with all phases red. The blue bars represent the cycle length and the red bars represent rest-in-red time.

For pretimed and fixed-cycle signals, the cycle length is listed at the bottom.

A sample Actuated Start and Green Times Report is shown in **Figure 15-12**.

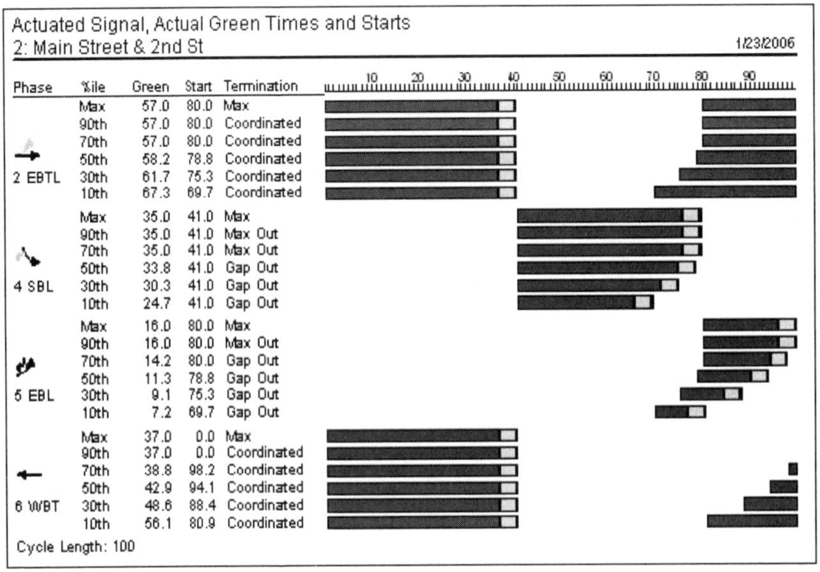

Actuated Signal, Actual Green Times and Starts
2: Main Street & 2nd St 1/23/2006

Phase	%ile	Green	Start	Termination
	Max	57.0	80.0	Max
	90th	57.0	80.0	Coordinated
	70th	57.0	80.0	Coordinated
	50th	58.2	78.8	Coordinated
2 EBTL	30th	61.7	75.3	Coordinated
	10th	67.3	69.7	Coordinated
	Max	35.0	41.0	Max
	90th	35.0	41.0	Max Out
	70th	35.0	41.0	Max Out
	50th	33.8	41.0	Gap Out
4 SBL	30th	30.3	41.0	Gap Out
	10th	24.7	41.0	Gap Out
	Max	16.0	80.0	Max
	90th	16.0	80.0	Max Out
	70th	14.2	80.0	Gap Out
	50th	11.3	78.8	Gap Out
5 EBL	30th	9.1	75.3	Gap Out
	10th	7.2	69.7	Gap Out
	Max	37.0	0.0	Max
	90th	37.0	0.0	Coordinated
	70th	38.8	98.2	Coordinated
	50th	42.9	94.1	Coordinated
6 WBT	30th	48.6	88.4	Coordinated
	10th	56.1	80.9	Coordinated

Cycle Length: 100

Figure 15-12 Sample Actuated Start and Green Times Report

Actuated Phase Details

The Actuated Phase Details report shows the green and yellow time for each phase alongside the time to clear the queue and the time to gap out. This information is provided for each of the five percentile scenarios. This report is helpful to observe in detail the operation of actuated phases.

For each phase and percentile scenario, the following information is listed:

Phase

Percentile

Queue Clearance Time

Gap-Out Time

Green

Termination

Detail Bar Graph

Phase: Each phase has its number and lane group listed here.

Percentile: This is the percentile scenario for this row. Synchro models traffic under five percentile scenarios. Also see **Percentile Scenarios** (page 13-31)for more information.

Queue Clearance Time: This is the time to clear the queue. This time includes the startup-lost time which is 2.5 seconds. This time includes the time for the vehicles arriving on red to clear as well as any new vehicles arriving during the clearance time. A value of 50+ in the queue time or gap-out field indicates 50 or more seconds.

Gap-Out Time: This is the time for the phase to gap-out. It is calculated as the time till there is a 50% chance of a gapout. This value also includes the unused green time.

Green: This is the actual green time for this scenario. This value is normally equal to the sum of the Queue and the Gap-Out times. Many times the green time is constrained by the minimum or maximum times or the phase is skipped altogether.

Termination: This code explains how the phase was terminated. The available options are as follows:

Skip: Phase is skipped, no calls.

Min: Phase shows for minimum time

GapOut: Phase gaps out

Hold: Phase held for phase in other ring. Lagging main street phases are also held

Max: Out Phase shows for maximum time.

Ped: Phase extended for pedestrian phase due to ped button or ped recall.

Max Recall: Max Recall, phase is set for maximum recall.

Dwell: Signal rests or dwells on this phase, conflicting volume is very light.

Coordinated: This phase is the main street phase in coordination. Any extra time reverts to this phase.

Detail Bar Graph: The bar graphs to the right show these times graphically. The top half of each graph shows the queue time and gap-out time as brown and cyan respectively. The lower half of each graph shows the green and yellow time as green and yellow.

For non-coordinated actuated signals, the cycle length and the rest-in-red time are shown at the bottom. If all phases have no recall, the signal may rest with all phases red. The blue bars represent the cycle length and the red bars represent rest-in-red time.

If a value is too big to fit in the bar graph, it has broken bars at the right of the scale.

For pretimed and fixed-cycle signals, the cycle length is listed at the bottom.

A sample Actuated Phase Details Report is shown in **Figure 15-13**.

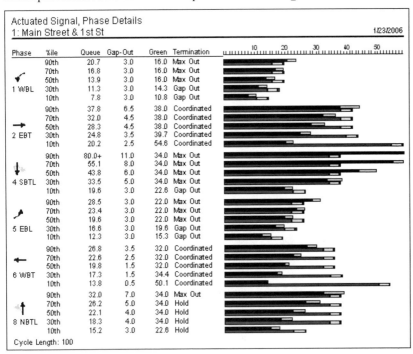

Figure 15-13   Sample Actuated Phase Details Report

Permitted Left Turn Factors Report

The Permitted Left Turn Factors report provides information about the lanes and saturation flow rates. It is roughly equivalent to the HCM's Supplemental Worksheet for Permitted Left Turns.

For details on all of these values, refer to the 2000 HCM, Chapter 16. The value f_{lt} is the permitted left turn factor that is seen in the **LANE** settings.

 F_{LT} is calculated based on maximum green times rather than actuated green times. This may cause the Synchro F_{LT} to vary slightly from the HCM calculations.

If there is an exclusive left turn lane plus a shared left turn lane, a separate F_{lt} is calculated for each lane. This is a feature not found in the HCM or the Highway Capacity Software. If an approach is opposed by an exclusive turning lane and a shared lane, only the opposing shared lane and through lanes are considered to be opposing.

This report is used both for approaches that are opposed by single lane and multilane approaches. The values *Prop LT Opp.*, *n*, P_{THo}, E_{L2} and *Gdiff* only apply to approaches that are opposed by a single lane approach. *Fm* only applies for multiple shared lane approaches.

The value f_{min} is the left turn factor assuming that the only left turns are "sneakers" (turners who complete their turns during or after the yellow phase). If f_{min} is greater than f_m, f_{min} is used.

If either the subject or opposing approach has a protected phase, then the appropriate adjustments are made to the g_u, g_f, and g_q.

A sample of a **Supplemental Worksheet for Permitted Left Turns Report** is shown in **Figure 15-14**.

Lane Group	NBL	SBL
Cycle Length (s)	100	100
Actual Green	34	34
Eff. Green	34	34
Opp. Eff. Green	34	34
Lanes	1	1
Opp. Lanes	1	1
Adj. LT Flow	100	100
Prop LeftTurns	1.00	1.00
Prop LT Opp.	0.00	0.00
Adj. Opp. Flow	200	500
Total Lost Time	4.0	4.0
LTC	2.78	2.78
Volc	5.56	13.89
Rpo	1.00	1.00
qf	0.00	0.00
qro	0.66	0.66
qq	4.25	21.38
gu	29.75	12.62
n		
PTHo		
EL1	1.58	2.08
PL	1.00	1.00
fmin	0.12	0.12
fm		
EL2		
Gdiff		
fLT	0.55	0.18

Figure 15-14   Sample Supplemental Worksheet For Permitted Left Turns Report

Coordinatability Analysis Report

The Coordinatability Analysis report gives information about Coordinatability factors and elements used to calculate them. (See **Coordinatability Factors** for more information about CFs and their calculation, page 13-22.)

Each element that affects the Coordinatability Factor (CF) is shown, along with the affect it has on the CF. A CF ranges from 0 to 100 or more. Any value above 50 means that coordination is recommended. The higher the CF, the more likely that this link will benefit from coordination.

The six factors used to determine Coordinatability are as follows:

Travel Time

Traffic to Storage Space

Proportion of Traffic in Platoon

Main Street Volume

Increase in Cycle Lengths needed for coordination

In the report, each of these values is listed along with how it affects the CF. There may be a comment next to the factor explaining its effect on the CF.

A sample Coordinatability Factors report is shown in **Figure 15-15**.

To quickly view a CF Report for a single link:

1. In the **MAP** view, press the Show Coordinatability Factors button ⬚ or the Show Natural Coordinatability Factors button ⬚.

2. Double click on a link with the CF value shown.

Coordinatability Analysis Using Current Cycle Lengths:
8: Mall Ent. & 3rd St   1/23/2006

Link: Main Street, 1st St to 2nd St

Variable	Value	Comments
Travel Time (s)	31	Travel Time okay For Coordination
CF1	64	
Traffic / Storage Space	0.21	Storage Space is adequate
CF2	21	
Proportion of Traffic In Platoon	0.86	Traffic heavily platooned, coordination is appropriate
Ap, platoon adjustment	2	
Main Street Volume (vph)	2200	High Volumes, coordination is high priority
Av, volume adjustment	20	
Cycle Length	100	at 1st St
Cycle Length	100	at 2nd St
Combined Cycle Length	100	
Cycle Length Increase	0	
Ac, Cycle Adjustment	0	
CF, Coordinatability Factor	86	Coordination definitely recommended

Figure 15-15 Coordinatability Factors Report – Sample

Chapter 16 – UTDF 2006 Edition

Universal Traffic Data Format (UTDF) is a standard specification for transferring data between various software packages. UTDF can also be used to share data between software and traffic signal controller hardware. UTDF is also useful for storing multiple volume counts and multiple timing plans for the same intersection.

In past version of UTDF, data was stored in separate files for volumes, lanes, timings, phasing and layouts. In 2006, UTDF was reformatted to contain all the data in one combined file. The data is divided by sections in the comma delimited (CSV) format. The UTDF Combined file can be accessed through the **File→Open**, **File→Save-As**, **File→Merge** and **File→Save-Part** commands.

Below are some of the applications for UTDF.

Hardware Related:

- Existing detectors can be refitted to provide traffic counts and can be stored in UTDF.

- A library of timing plans can be stored in UTDF and uploaded to the controller on demand.

- A generation 1.5 traffic control system can be developed that automatically performs the above steps in conjunction with the analysis software in real time.

Software Related:

- UTDF allows data to be shared between otherwise incompatible software packages. There are several traffic oriented developers vendors supporting UTDF. This allows data to be easily shared among software from different vendors.

- For planning purposes, it is possible for planning departments to store traffic counts for various scenarios and use them for capacity analysis as well as other purposes. With UTDF compatible software, it could be possible for planners to completely automate traffic impact studies for future development and roadway improvements.

UTDF uses text files to store and share data in comma delimited (CSV) format. The comma-delimited text files (CSV) can be easily viewed and edited by spreadsheets such or Microsoft® Excel.

Text files are easy for end users to edit with any text editor such as Microsoft® Notepad. The column-aligned TMC format is provided for compatibility with Turning Movement Count (TMC) files and for easy editing with text editors. The TMC format is the only column aligned format supported by Synchro 7.

New in Synchro Version 7

Combined file format: a new format contains multiple sections so that a single file can completely define a network. The combined format includes the data previously found in the LAYOUT, LANES, and PHASING files. These individual file formats will be phased out in the future. The combined file includes sections for Network, Nodes, Links, and Timing Plan allowing a better mapping of data.

More items in Lanes section: The lanes section includes data for UP ID and DEST NODE. This allows lane groups to be easily mapped to OD nodes for use with transfers to/from planning software

All data items included: The combined file and its respective sections now include all data available in Synchro.

Data Format Support

The following table shows the file formats available, and the evolution of UTDF. Starting with Synchro version 7, only CSV and TMC formats are supported.

Table 16-1   UTDF Supported Formats

File Format	Version 6	Version 7	Future
Volumes.csv	Yes	Yes	Yes
Volumes.dat	Yes	No	No
Vdate.csv (all counts for one date)	Yes	Yes	Yes
Vdate.dat (all counts for one date)	Yes	No	No
TMC####.vol	Yes	Yes	Yes
TMC####.csv (TMC in comma delimited)	Yes	No	No
Layout.dat	Yes	No	No
Layout.csv	Yes	Yes	No
Lanes.dat	Yes	No	No
Lanes.csv	Yes	Yes	No
Timing.csv	Yes	Yes	Yes
Timing.dat	Yes	No	No
Phasing.csv	Yes	Yes	No
Phasing.dat	Yes	No	No

In the future, the LAYOUT, LANES, and PHASING formats will be discontinued in favor of the combined format.

Volumes and Timings data tables will remain to provide a repository for multiple counts and multiple timing plans in addition to use with SimTraffic data access.

Some Synchro Version 6 UTDF formats are supported by Version 7. The supported formats are listed in **Table 16-1**. To access Version 6 UTDF, use the command **Transfer→Data-Access→Version 6 Data Access**. Documentation on Version 6 UTDF is included in a separate document available from Trafficware.

Planning a Network for UTDF

Before setting up a UTDF it is necessary to do some planning. The following data items must be agreed upon and set up before using UTDF:

- Intersection Node Numbers

- Approach and Lane Group Designation: Especially at intersections where 5 or more legs and diagonal legs exist, make sure lane group data in the UDTF file is consistent with Synchro's view of the approaches. For instance, eastbound (EB) is defined for the same movement(s) in Synchro and the UTDF file.

- Phase Numbers: Make sure the phase numbers in Synchro match the phase numbers in controllers and in the data files.

Node Numbers

Before starting, it is essential to carefully assign node numbers to each intersection.

If possible, these node numbers should match the controller's intersection numbers in any centralized control system.

If multiple intersections have the same controller (Group Control), the Timing and Phasing data will use the smallest node number of the intersections.

If there are multiple systems in your agency, it may be desirable to assign a range of node numbers for each system. For example, the central system could use node numbers 1 to 99 and the north system could use node numbers 100 to 199. This will allow systems to be combined into one data file and will prevent mixing up data from different systems.

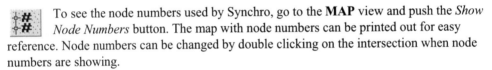 To see the node numbers used by Synchro, go to the **MAP** view and push the *Show Node Numbers* button. The map with node numbers can be printed out for easy reference. Node numbers can be changed by double clicking on the intersection when node numbers are showing.

 Synchro node numbers can range from 1 to 9999.

Approaches and Lane Group Designations

Normally lane groups will have designations from the four cardinal directions, (north, south, east, and west) and the six turn movements (U-turn, left-2, left, through, and right, right-2).

At intersections with diagonal approaches or with more than four legs, the designations may be ambiguous. Diagonal directions will be designated NE, NW, SE, or SW if the cardinal directions are already taken.

If there are any questions, write data from Synchro to a UTDF file to see which approaches are assigned by looking at the Name records. Also be sure to look at which lane groups are actually assigned; these will match the rules used by Synchro.

Data saved to a Volume or Lane section of the UTDF file will always include the basic 12 lane groups, even if they are not used. This applies to T intersections and to intersections with diagonal legs. This facilitates the development of external utilities for accessing Synchro data. The first 12 columns for the basic lane groups will always be present. Additional columns will be present when U-turns or diagonal legs are used.

Phase Numbers

Be sure that the phase numbers in Synchro match the phase numbers in the Phase and Timing tables. Failure to use the same phase number could have disastrous results. These phase numbers should also match the phase numbers in the hardware controllers.

It is probably best to make a list matching phase numbers to lane groups for each intersection. The Phase records of the Lanes table can help with this, and can even be used to reassign Synchro's phase numbers.

Reading and Writing UTDF Data

Data for UTDF 2006 is stored in one combined file. Data is separated into sections as detailed in the following topics in the chapter. Often, users want a sample UTDF compatible format. The best way to see this is to open an existing Synchro file and create (write) the data to UTDF.

To **write** out a UTDF file, do the following:

1. Open the Synchro file for which you want to write data out.

2. Select the menu command **File→Save-As**.

3. Choose **Comma Delimited** from the '**Save as Type**' dropdown

4. Enter a 'File name' and press **[Save]**.

5. The data from this Synchro file will now be in CSV file.

Synchro CSV data can be modified with a text editor or a spreadsheet. See the topic on **Editing UTDF Data with Other Software** on page 16-6.

To **read** CSV data into an **existing** Synchro file, do the following:

1. Backup your Synchro file.

2. Select the menu command **File→Merge**.

3. Choose a CSV file from the list and press **[Open]**.

The data from the selected CSV file will now be in the Synchro file. This process does not create new links or nodes, and does not move or renumber nodes. It will merge in data from the Data Settings screens for matching node numbers.

 If there is data in the CSV file that you do not want to merge, delete from the CSV file prior to merging.

To **read** CSV data into a **new** Synchro file, do the following:

1. Select the menu command **File→Open**.

2. Choose **Comma Delimited** from the '**Files of type**' dropdown

3. Choose a CSV file from the list and press **[Open]**.

The data from the selected CSV file will now be in the Synchro file. This process imports all of the CSV data into the Synchro file, including nodes and links. For the minimum data needed in the CSV file, refer to page 16-20.

Editing UTDF Data with Other Software

The UTDF 2006 file is a comma delimited (CSV) file. To edit the CSV files simply open the files with a spreadsheet such as Microsoft® Excel. Be sure to save the file as comma-aligned and not as Excel format. If you have created any formulas in your spreadsheet, be sure to first save the file in spreadsheet format. Then, save the file to UTDF CSV format.

Using TMC Files

TMC files are text files that store timing data from a single intersection from multiple time periods. The data is stored in a fixed length format with each line representing a single time period. Some sample data from a TMC file is shown here:

```
┌──────────────────────────────────────────────────────────────────────────┐
│                     15 Minute Turning Movement Count                       │
│   Reference #07 - 1st St at Main St: 05/14/03                               │
│                                                                            │
│   ================================================================         │
│   TIME   NBL   NBT   NBR   SBL   SBT   SBR   EBL   EBT   EBR   WBL   WBT   WBR│
│   ================================================================         │
│   0700    32   130    11     6   168    13     4     4     8     6     4     1│
│   0715    38   174    31    11   204    10     5     3    10    12     4     6│
│   0730    32   226    31    10   265    12    12     7    24    16     1     1│
│   0745    47   261    36    19   347    29    21     8    14    21     1     8│
│   0800    79   304    44    21   282    33    24    21    14    14     3     6│
│   0815    34   226    36    14   226    19     9     5    22    21     2    13│
└──────────────────────────────────────────────────────────────────────────┘
```

The first line must say 15 MINUTE TURNING MOVEMENT COUNT. The second line lists the column names. Subsequent lines list the start time and turning movement counts for each direction.

Converting TMC Data to and from UTDF Data

Synchro can read and write TMC files directly. Use the command **Transfer→Data-Access→Version 6 Data Access** and choose the Read Volume tab. Be sure to set the file style to "By Int, TMC Style (TMC###.VOL)".

The TMC files must have the filenames of TMC#.VOL where # is the node number. A TMC file for node # 31 would have the name TMC31.VOL for example.

UTDF Specifications

Each section is started by a line with the section title in square brackets. Between each section is a blank line. The sections in the UTDF file are discussed below.

[Network]

Data common to the network goes in this section.

[Nodes]

Data for a node goes here, including data common to the network. This includes node type, coordinates, etc.

[Links]

This section includes data for a link, name, speed, distance, curve points, etc.

[Lanes]

Data for a lane group or movement, includes volumes, lanes, and most data from these screens. Phase numbers, detector data,

[Timeplans]

Data specific to a timing plan

[Phases]

Data specific to a phase

Network Section

The data found in the Network section includes some of the network wide settings as follows:

```
[Network]
Network Settings
RECORDNAME,DATA
Metric,0
yellowTime,5.0
allRedTime,0.0
Walk,5.0
DontWalk,15.0
HV,0.02
PHF,0.90
DefWidth,12
DefFlow,1900
vehLength,25
growth,1.00
PedSpeed,4.0
LostTimeAdjust,0.0
```

Metric: 0 for feet, and 1 for meters. It is very important to include this value first so that the file is setup with the correct units. All distances after will be feet (+-1 ft) or meters (+- 0.1m). Speeds are mi/hr or km/hr unless noted.

The other values are default settings defined in the Network settings. Times are (+-0.1s).

vehLength: Network wide setting for the calculation of queue lengths

PedSpeed: Network wide setting for SimTraffic (ft/s or m/s).

Nodes Section

Node and Link sections replaces the Layout table of past version of UTDF. The settings are as follows:

```
[Nodes]
Node Data
INTID, Type, X, Y, Z, Description, CBD
1, 0, 1000, 1000, 0, "", 0
```

Type: 0 for signalized intersection, 1 for external node, 2 for bend, 3 for unsignalized, 4 for roundabout

X, Y, Z: Coordinates of node, Z is elevation.

Description: Textual description, enclosed in quotes. Replace new line/CR with "ÿ" (ANSI character 255).

When reading a nodes section, existing nodes with the same number will be moved to this location. Existing nodes at this location will not be renumbered. Do not attempt to use this data to renumber nodes.

Links Section

Links records contain data to create a link and also information specific to a link.

Unlike the Lanes records, Link records are used for external nodes and bend nodes.

```
[Links]
Link Data
RECORDNAME,INTID,NB,SB,EB,WB,NW,SE
Up ID,241,4971,290,289,243,,
Lanes,241,3,1,2,4,,
Name,241,Washington,Washington,Broad,Broad,,
```

```
Distance,241,248,304,854,391,,
Speed,241,30,30,30,30,,
Time,241,5.6,6.9,19.4,8.9,,
Grade,241,0,0,0,0,,
Median,241,0,0,24,24,,
Offset,241,0,0,0,0,,
TWLTL,241,0,0,0,0,,
Crosswalk Width,241,16,16,16,16,,
Mandatory Distance,451,,,200,200,200,
Mandatory Distance2,451,,,1320,1320,1320,
Positioning Distance,451,,,880,880,880,
Positioning Distance2,451,,,1760,1760,1760,
Curve Pt X,241,,,820,,,
Curve Pt Y,241,,,-22,,,
Curve Pt Z,241,,,767112,,,
```

Links are by direction, two links are needed to connect two nodes.

Link records are used for every node including externals and bends.

Link "Up ID" record is used to connect nodes upon reading; and also for setting the direction of these nodes.

UPID: Upstream node number

Lanes: Number of lanes, for bend or external; calculated by Synchro unless marked with *

Distance: travel distance, calculated by Synchro unless marked with *

Time: Travel time; calculated by Synchro unless marked with *

Speed: Travel speed, mph or km/h

Grade: Grade in percent

Median: Median width, calculated by Synchro unless marked with *

Offset: Offset of link to right of center line, normally zero.

TWLTL: 1 indicates a TWLTL for link (Visual Only).

Crosswalk Width: Width of crosswalk at end of link. Also affects the radius of the curb and right turns.

Mandatory and Positioning Distances: For lane change start points. See SIMULATION settings topic for full details.

Curve Pt X, Curve Pt Y, Curve Pt Z: If not blank, used to define a curve point. The other curve point is defined in the reverse link. Blank indicates a straight link.

Lanes Section

Information in this section is specific to the lanes approaching an intersection. The data included is as follows.

```
[Lanes]
Lane Group Data
RECORDNAME,INTID,NBU,NBL2,NBL,NBT,NBR,SBL,SBT,SBR,EBL,EBT,EBR,WBL,WBT,W
BR,NWL,NWR,SEL,SER,SER2
Up ID,241,4971,,4971,4971,4971,290,290,290,289,289,89,243,243,243,,,,,
Dest
Node,241,4971,,289,290,243,243,4971,289,290,243,4971,4971,289,290,,,,,
Lanes,241,0,,0,2,1,0,1,0,0,2,0,2,2,0,,,,,
Shared,241,,,0,1,,0,3,,0,3,,0,2,,,,,,
Width,241,12,,12,12,12,12,12,12,12,12,12,12,12,12,,,,,
Storage,241,,,,,,,,,,,,100,,,,,,,
Taper,241,,,,,,,,,,,,25,,,,,,,
StLanes,241,,,,,,,,,,,,2,,,,,,,
Grade,241,,,,,,,,,,,,,,,,,,,
Speed,241,,,,30,,,30,,,30,,,30,,,,,,
Phase1,241,,,,2,,,6,,,8,,,4,,,,,,
PermPhase1,241,,,2,,2,6,,,8,,,4,,,,,,,
LostTime,241,3,,3,3,3,3,3,3,3,3,3,3,3,3,,,,,
Lost Time Adjust,241,-1,,-3,-3,-3,-3,-3,-1,-2,-2,-1,-2,-2,-1,,,,,
IdealFlow,241,1900,,1900,1900,1900,1900,1900,1900,1900,1900,1900,1900,1
900,1900,,,,,
SatFlow,241,0,,0,3412,1583,0,1775,0,0,3487,0,3433,3510,0,,,,,
SatFlowPerm,241,0,,0,2874,1559,0,1309,0,0,3273,0,1855,3510,0,,,,,
Allow RTOR,241,1,,1,1,1,1,1,1,1,1,1,1,1,1,,,,,
SatFlowRTOR,241,0,,0,0,89,0,7,0,0,7,0,0,7,0,,,,,
Volume,241,0,,266,90,75,31,13,6,7,178,9,22,370,18,,,,,
Peds,241,0,,3,0,3,3,0,3,11,0,83,83,0,11,,,,,
Bicycles,241,0,,0,0,0,0,0,0,0,0,0,0,0,0,,,,,
PHF,241,0.90,,0.84,0.84,0.84,0.83,0.83,0.83,0.82,0.82,0.82,0.79,0.79,0.
79,,,,,
Growth,241,100,,100,100,100,100,100,100,100,100,100,100,100,100,,,,,
HeavyVehicles,241,2,,2,2,2,2,2,2,2,2,2,2,2,2,,,,,
BusStops,241,0,,0,0,0,0,0,0,0,0,0,0,0,0,,,,,
```

```
Midblock,241,,,,0,,,0,,,0,,,0,,,,,,
Distance,241,,,,248,,,304,,,854,,,391,,,,,,
TravelTime,241,,,,5.6,,,6.9,,,19.4,,,8.9,,,,,,
Right Channeled,241,,,,,4,,,0,,,0,,,0,,,,,
Right Radius,241,,,,,50,,,,,,,,,,,,,,
Add Lanes,241,,,,,0,,,,,,,,,,,,,,,
Alignment,241,3,,0,0,1,0,0,1,0,0,1,0,0,1,,,,,
Enter Blocked,241,0,,0,0,0,0,0,0,0,0,0,0,0,0,,,,,
HeadwayFact,241,1.00,,1.00,1.00,1.00,1.00,1.00,1.00,1.00,1.00,1.00,1.00
,1.00,1.00,,,,,
Turning Speed,241,9,,15,35,9,15,35,9,15,35,9,15,35,9,,,,,
FirstDetect,241,,,50,100,20,50,100,,50,70,,20,100,,,,,,
LastDetect,241,,,0,0,0,0,0,,0,0,,0,0,,,,,,
DetectPhase1,241,,,2,2,2,6,6,,8,8,,4,4,,,,,,
DetectPhase2,241,,,0,0,0,0,0,,0,0,,0,0,,,,,,
ExtendPhase,241,,,2,2,2,6,6,,8,8,,4,4,,,,,,
SwitchPhase,241,,,0,0,0,0,0,,0,0,,0,0,,,,,,
numDetects,241,,,1,2,1,1,2,,1,2,,1,2,,,,,,
DetectPos1,241,,,0,0,0,0,0,,0,0,,0,0,,,,,,
DetectSize1,241,,,50,6,20,50,6,,50,6,,20,6,,,,,,
DetectType1,241,,,3,3,3,3,3,,3,3,,3,3,,,,,,
DetectExtend1,241,,,0,0,0,0,0,,0,0,,0,0,,,,,,
DetectQueue1,241,,,0,0,0,0,0,,0,0,,0,0,,,,,,
DetectDelay1,241,,,0,0,0,0,0,,0,0,,0,0,,,,,,
DetectPos2,241,,,,94,,,94,,,64,,,94,,,,,,
DetectSize2,241,,,,6,,,6,,,6,,,6,,,,,,
DetectType2,241,,,,3,,,3,,,3,,,3,,,,,,
DetectExtend2,241,,,,0,,,0,,,0,,,0,,,,,,
```

The Lanes section is similar to Lanes table in UTDF 2 (Synchro version 6 format). These notes apply to both the table and the section of UTDF 2006.

Up ID: Upstream node number, write only. Used for assistance in converting data for use with planning software. Planning software sees a lane group as an origin and destination node, rather than NBL.

Dest Node: Destination node number for this movement, write only. For assistance in converting data for use with planning software.

Lanes: For each lane group, enter the number of lanes. Shared lanes count as through lanes, unless there is no through movement, in which case LR lanes count as left lanes,

Shared: Enter code for sharing of this lane with adjacent movements. This field specifies which movements the through lanes are shared with. Enter 0, 1, 2, 3 for No-sharing, Shared-with-Left, Shared-with-right, Shared-with-both. This field is normally 0 for turning lane groups. If a left lane shares with left2 or u-turns, the sharing is coded as a '1'.

Width: Enter the average lane width for the group in feet or meters. Decimal meters permitted.

Storage: Enter the length of a turning bay if applicable. Leave this field blank for through lane groups or if the turning lane goes all the way back to the previous intersection.

Taper: The value of the storage taper length.

StLanes: Enter the number of lanes in the storage bay. This can be more or less than the number of turning lanes, but must be at least 1.

Grade: Write only, use the new Links section.

Speed: Write only, use the new Links section.

Phase1, Phase2, Phase3, Phase4: Each lane group can have four primary phases associated with them. Enter phases that give a green to this movement in these fields. Enter -1 for an uncontrolled movement.

PermPhase1, PermPhase2, PermPhase3, PermPhase4: Each lane group can have four permitted phases associated with them. With permitted phases, left turns must yield to oncoming traffic, right turns must yield to pedestrians.

LostTime: Write only, use Lost Time Adjust.

Lost Time Adjust: Combination of Startup Lost time minus Extension of Effective Green. Total Lost Time = Yellow + All Red + Lost Time Adjust

IdealFlow: Ideal Saturated Flow Rate per lane. 1900 by default.

SatFlow: Saturated flow rate for protected movements. Normally calculated, * indicates overridden value.

SatFlowPerm: Saturated flow rate for permitted movements. Normally calculated, * indicates overridden value.

SatFlowRTOR: Saturated flow rate for RTOR movements. Normally calculated, * indicates overridden value.

Allow RTOR: 1 = RTOR allowed, 0 = no

Volume: The volume table is the preferred method for storing volumes. This entry is provided to allow convenient transferring of all data.

Peds: Number of pedestrians conflicting with the right turn movement

Bicycles: Number of bicycles conflicting with the right turn movement

PHF: The volume table is the preferred method for storing volumes. Synchro automatically calculates the PHF when reading 15 minute count data from volume tables. This entry is provided to allow convenient transferring of all data.

Growth: The percent growth rate applied to volumes. 100 by default.

HeavyVehicles: The percent of trucks, busses, and RVs for each movement.

BusStops: The number of bus stops per hour blocking traffic.

Midblock: Percent of traffic originating from mid-block driveways.

Distance: Write only, use the new Links section.

TravelTime: Write only, use the new Links section.

Right Channeled: If R and R2 movements exist; listed for R2 movement. Values are

> 0 no
>
> 1 yield
>
> 2 free
>
> 3 stop
>
> 4 signal;

Right Radius: If right turn channeled, curb radius of right turn

Add Lanes: Number of add lanes after right turn channel

Alignment: Controls how add lanes align thru an intersection;

> 0 align left, 1 align to right, 2 align left no adds, 3 align right no adds

Enter Blocked: 0 vehicles wait if no space in node, 1 vehicles do not make check

HeadwayFact: Headway factor. Adjusts headways in simulation

Turning Speed: The simulation turning speed.

FirstDetect: Distance from the leading extension detector to stop bar in feet or meters. Leave blank if no detectors for lane group. Supplemented by actual detector information.

LastDetect: Same definition as ver 6, supplemented by actual detector information

DetectPhase1, 2, 3, 4: is being discontinued in favor of Extend Phase and Switch Phase

DetectPhase1: Write only for compatibility, use extend phase

DetectPhase2: Write only for compatibility, use switch phase

ExtendPhase: Detector calls go to this phase

SwitchPhase: Will set switch phase. Be very careful with switch phase, because extend phase will not get called when switch phase is green, per NTCIP specs.

numDetects: Number of detector rows

DetectPos1... DetectPos5: Distance from detector to stop bar. Detector 1 is closest to stop bar

DetectSize1... DetectSize5: Size of detector longitudinally

DetectType1... DetectType5: Detector type, sum of these flags, only 1 and 2 are currently implemented in Synchro.

> 1 = call
>
> 2 = extend
>
> 4 = queue detector (set non-zero value for queue time)
>
> 8= count volume
>
> 16 = count occupancy
>
> 32 = yellow lock
>
> 64 = red lock
>
> 128 = passage detector, Synchro currently assumes all detectors are presence
>
> 256 = added initial

DetectExtend1... DetectExtend5: Extend time for detector

DetectQueue1: Queue time for detector, detector 1 only

DetectDelay1: Delay time, detector 1 only

Any input data item appearing in the following screens is included:

Settings	Notes
Lanes	all inputs expect: name, distance, travel time, speed, grade
Volumes	all inputs, including link OD volumes
Timings	phase mappings, others in Phase section
Signing	sign control, median to be redone, right turn channelized
Phasings	none, in phase section
Simulate	all except those appearing in Link section
Detectors	all

Also included, origin node and destination node, WRITE ONLY, for assistance when transferring to and from planning models.

Time Plan Section

This section contains data common to a timing plan, but not for a phase. The combined file uses Timeplan data in conjunction with Phases data.

```
[Timeplan]
Timing Plan Settings
RECORDNAME,INTID,DATA
Control Type,241,3
Cycle Length,241,100.0
Lock Timings,241,0
Referenced To,241,0
Reference Phase,241,206
Offset,241,16.0
Master,241,0
Yield,241,0
Node 0,241,241
Node 1,241,0
```

Control Type: 0 pretimed, 1 actd uncoord, 2 semiact uncoord, 3 actd coordinated

Cycle Length: Cycle length; write only; cycle length on read is sum of phase split times

Lock Timings: 0 unlocked, 1 locked; timings will still be read from Time Plan and Phasings section when locked

Referenced To: The part of phase to which offsets are referenced.

   0: refGreen, the last of the phases to turn green (TS1 style)

1: refYellow, the first phase to turn yellow (170 style without rest in walk)

2: refRed, the first phase to turn red (not used often)

3: refFirstGreen, the first referenced phase to turn green (TS2 style)

4: ref170, the beginning of flashing don't walk (170 style with rest in walk)

Reference Phase: phase number(s) offsets are referenced to. If two phases are referenced, the phase for ring A is multiplied by 100, phases 2 and 6 are written 206.

Offset: offset in seconds; Offset is referenced as specified by Referenced to and Referenced Phase. On reading, the **Start Times** in Phasings section read after will override the offsets here. To read offsets, include a second TimePlan section with offset records only, after the Phasings section.

Some NEMA TS-2 controllers reference offsets to the **first** coordinated phase to turn green. Use TS2 referencing by adding a '+' character, a refphase of 26+ indicates that offsets are referenced to the first of phase 2 or 6 to turn green.

With negative refPhase, the offset is referenced to the controllers yield point. A value of 26- indicates that offsets are referenced to the first of phases 2 or 6 to turn yellow. A value of 0 indicates that offsets are referenced to the beginning of the first phase.

Master: 0 normal; 1 master controller, master controller will keep offset at zero, only one master allowed per cycle length

Yield: 0 single, 1 flexible, 2 by phase. Defines yield points for non-coordinated phases.

Node 0, Node 1, ..., Node 7: Used to assign multiple nodes to one controller. If nodes 101 and 102 use the same controller; the timing plan and phasing data will only be included for INTID 101. The node records for INTID 101 will be:

```
Node 0,101,101
Node 1,101,102
Node 2,101,0
```

A zero value indicates no more nodes. There will be no time plan and phasing records for node 102, they are defined by node 101.

Phasing Section

This section contains phasing data. The combined file uses Phases data in conjunction with Timeplan data.

```
[Phases]
Phasing Data
RECORDNAME,INTID,D1,D2,D3,D4,D5,D6,D7,D8
BRP,241,111,112,211,212,121,122,221,222
MinGreen,241,,6,,7,,6,,7
MaxGreen,241,,44,,45,,44,,45
VehExt,241,,2,,2,,2,,2
TimeBeforeReduce,241,,0,,0,,0,,0
TimeToReduce,241,,0,,0,,0,,0
MinGap,241,,2,,2,,2,,2
Yellow,241,,5,,4,,5,,4
AllRed,241,,1,,1,,1,,1
Recall,241,,0,,3,,0,,3
Walk,241,,7,,7,,7,,7
DontWalk,241,,18,,15,,18,,15
PedCalls,241,,0,,0,,0,,0
MinSplit,241,,32,,27,,32,,27
DualEntry,241,,1,,0,,1,,0
InhibitMax,241,,1,,1,,1,,1
Start,241,,16,,66,,16,,66
End,241,,66,,16,,66,,16
Yield,241,,60,,11,,60,,11
Yield170,241,,42,,96,,42,,96
LocalStart,241,,0,,50,,0,,50
LocalYield,241,,44,,95,,44,,95
LocalYield170,241,,26,,80,,26,,80
ActGreen,32.1
```

Used for data specific to a phase. One entry for each input row on the phasings settings.

BRP:Eentry is for rings and barriers.

MinGreen: Minimum green time (tenths of seconds)

MaxGreen: This is the maximum time the phase is green.

VehExt: This is the time the signal is held green by each actuation. It is also the maximum gap when using a volume density controller (hundredths of seconds).

TimeBeforeReduce: This is the time before gap reduction starts on volume density controllers (seconds).

TimeToReduce: This is the amount of time to reduce the gap from VehExt to MinGap.

MinGap: This is the minimum gap to achieve (hundredths of seconds).

Yellow: This is the time each phase displays yellow (tenths of seconds). AllRed + Yellow must equal a whole number of seconds.

AllRed: This is the time each phase displays all-red clearance before the next phase (tenths of seconds). AllRed + Yellow no longer need to equal a whole number of seconds for Synchro.

Recall: This field can have the following values, 0 = no recall, 1 = minimum recall, 2 = pedestrian recall, 3 = maximum recall, 4 = rest in walk. If recall is not zero, the phase will be serviced on every cycle for the miminum green time, walk+don' walk time, or maximum green time respectively.

If only one (or two simultaneous phases) are set to recall, the signal will rest on those phases. If these phases are set to RestInWalk, the signal will rest on walk in these phases. Note that with some 170 controllers, if Rest in walk is used, the offsets are referenced to the beginning of Dont Walk.

Walk: This is the time for the Walk indication or 0 for no pedestrian phase (seconds).

DontWalk: This is the time for the Flashing Don't Walk interval (seconds). Note that Flashing dont walk ends at the start of yellow time.

PedCalls: This is the number of pedestrian calls per hour received by this phase. Set this field to blank for no pedestrian phase. Set this field to zero or other number to activate a pedestrian phase. If PedCalls is not used, a 0 or blank in DontWalk can be used to turn off the pedestrian phase.

MinSplit: Minimum Split is used by Synchro during split optimization. This value does map to a value found in traffic signal controllers.

DualEntry: Can be set to Yes or No (1=Yes, 0=No). Select Yes to have this phase appear when a phase is showing in another ring and no calls or recalls are present within this ring and barrier.

InhibitMax: Can be set to Yes or No (1=Yes, 0=No). Inhibit maximum termination is used to disable the maximum termination functions of all phases in the selected timing ring.

Start: Is the begin time referenced to the system clock

End: Is the end time of the phase referenced to the system clock.

Yield170: Is the phase yield or force-off time, referenced to the system clock, beginning of yellow. It is referenced to the beginning of FDW if recall is set to CoordMax.

LocalStart, LocalYield, LocalYield170: These are the same values as above except they are referenced to the local offset point.

Start Time is read and used to set offsets.

ActGreen is the actuated green time and is the average of the five percentiles used for HCM analysis. To get the Actuated Split, add the Yellow and All Red time (from this section). This record is write only, Synchro will not read it.

Minimum Data Necessary to build a Synchro file

If you want to build a Synchro file from scratch, these data items are needed.

[Network]

First record is Metric. Always include Metric record first so that speeds and distances are interpreted correctly. Use "0" for feet and mph and "1" for m and km/h

The other records can be blank for defaults

[Node]

Coordinate and node number information is needed, along with node type.

You need to build external nodes for links that do not connect to another signal.

[Link]

Build two links for all connected nodes.

Up and down node numbers for all links.

Street Name and speed.

Distance and travel time can be calculated by Synchro and left blank.

Other fields can be left blank.

[Lane]

Required Records:

```
Lanes
Shared
StLanes
Storage
Phase1
PermPhase1
Volume
Peds
DetectPhase1
```

The remaining records can be skipped to use defaults.

[Timeplan]

Required Records:

```
Control Type
Cycle Length
Referenced To
Reference Phase
Offset
```

The remaining records can be skipped to use defaults.

[Phasing]

Required Records:

```
MinGreen
MaxGreen
VehExt
Yellow
AllRed
Recall
Walk
DontWalk
```

The remaining records can be skipped to use defaults.

Chapter 17 – Errors and Warnings

Coding Error Messages

Synchro and SimTraffic includes a feature that will check data files for coding errors. This topic lists the possible errors along with suggestions for correcting them.

General Coding Errors

To check for general coding errors in Synchro, simply choose the **Options→Coding Error Check**. To check for errors in SimTraffic, launch SimTraffic from Synchro.

Synchro Errors and Warnings

Warnings indicate likely problems, but they may be acceptable in certain circumstances. Errors indicate serious problems that require fixing.

Next to each error number, letters appear indicating to which checks the error applies.

Code	Applies To
S	General Synchro Error
C	CORSIM related error
H	HCS related error

Table 17-1   Synchro Warnings

Error #	Code	Cause & Resolution
100	SC	Volume received at intersection, less than 70% sent. This is a problem with balancing volumes. Less volume is put onto a link upstream than volume exists downstream. This problem may occur due to volume counts collected at different times. It is possible to have a mid-block traffic source. In this case, specify mid-block traffic or add an unsignalized intersection and route traffic onto the link.
101	SC	Volume received at intersection, more than 200% sent. This is a problem with balancing volumes. More volume is put onto a link upstream than volume exists downstream. This problem may occur due to volume counts collected at different times. It is possible to have a mid-block traffic sink. In this case, add an unsignalized intersection and route traffic off the link.

Error #	Code	Cause & Resolution
102	SCH	Turning Volume entered with no turning or shared lane. A turning lane was not explicitly coded. Synchro will assume that a through lane is shared. This warning may indicate a problem with volume inputs at a one-way street.
108	S	Volume exceeds capacity. The lane group listed has volume exceeding capacity. This could be a fatal error or everyday operation depending on the area studied. Check the data to make sure this intersection was coded correctly.
109	SCH	Defacto Left Turn Lane, delays and v/c values not correct. Defacto lanes should be taken seriously. It is possible that the v/c ratio for the entire group is acceptable, while the v/c ratio for the turning lane is not acceptable. To correct a defacto turning lane, recode one of the through lanes as a turning lane and turn sharing off for that turn. A defacto left or right turn lane usually indicates the need for an additional exclusive turning lane.
110	SCH	Defacto Right Turn Lane, delays and v/c values not correct. Defacto lanes should be taken seriously. It is possible that the v/c ratio for the entire group is acceptable, while the v/c ratio for the turning lane is not acceptable. To correct a defacto turning lane, recode one of the through lanes as a turning lane and turn sharing off for that turn. A defacto left or right turn lane usually indicates the need for an additional exclusive turning lane.
111	S	Detector Phase is not a phase for the lane group. Normally a movement's detectors should call one or more of the phases serving that movement.
112	S	Detector Phase is blank, but movement does not have maximum recall. If a movement has no detection, be sure to set its phases to maximum recall. It is okay to code a detector phase when no detection exists, but be sure to set the phase's recall to maximum.
122	SH	Protected left without left lane is inefficient. This is a protected left phase with no left turn lane. Left traffic will block through traffic during the through phase. The v/c, delay, and LOS results for this approach may be suspect. If you are using this left phase as a pedestrian only phase at a 'T' intersection, ignore this error.
123	SCH	Possible trapping, lagging left turn with oncoming permitted lefts. This warning points out a potentially hazardous situation of trapped cars. If a car is trying to make a permitted left turn and sees a yellow light, the driver may think the oncoming traffic also has a yellow light. In reality, oncoming traffic continues due to the lagging left turn.
124	CH	Phases must be changed for conversion to single ring timing. Both HCS

Error #	Code	Cause & Resolution
		and CORSIM (pretimed) model signals as a single ring. This intersection's timing cannot be modeled as a single ring without modification. This phenomenon occurs when one phase turns yellow while a phase in another ring is in the middle of a yellow. For example, phase 1 turns yellow at time 20 and phase 5 turns yellow at time 22, and they both have a yellow time of 4 seconds.
126	SC	Minimum Gap is greater than Vehicle Extension. When using volume density controllers, the gap is reduced from Vehicle Extension to Minimum Gap. It is an error if Minimum gap is larger than vehicle extension. CORSIM will give a fatal error with this input.
127	C	Actuated coordinated single ring, CORSIM may trouble when phase 6 not used. CORSIM seems to have trouble modeling actuated signals in coordination unless both phases 2 and 6 are used. The work around is to use both phases 2 and 6 or to use phase 1. ![NOTE] This problem appears to be fixed in CORSIM version 4.32.
128	SCH	All Red less than 0.5. Check the **PHASING** settings.
129	S	Volume Density operation not recommended with long detection zone. The travel time across the detection zone will effectively be added to both the Minimum and Maximum gap times, making the operation less effective. Check the Time to Reduce, Time before reduce, and Minimum Gap settings.
130	C	A coordinated phase is leading, CORSIM may have problems. The FHWA has stated that CORSIM does not support phases 1 or 5 as lagging in an actuated-coordinated signal. It is recommended to model these signals using phase 2 and 6 as the lagging phases even if this means assigning a 2 or 6 to an actuated left turn phase. Another alternative is to model this intersection as pretimed. ![NOTE] This problem appears to be fixed in CORSIM version 4.32.
131	C	Left, Thru and Diagonal together for pretimed. CORSIM does not have pretimed phase codes to fully control traffic with all these movements. Some phase codes may be incorrect. If all movements share the same phases, this configuration will work.
132	C	U-turns cannot be modeled in CORSIM. The U-turn traffic was coded on this link will not be transferred to CORSIM.

Error #	Code	Cause & Resolution
133	C	Too many lane groups, this lane group is dropped. CORSIM is limited to 4 lane groups, Left, Through, Right, and Diagonal. Synchro can model five plus U-turns. In some cases not all Synchro lane groups can be translated into CORSIM lane groups.
134	C	Storage bays for through or diagonal lanes not allowed in CORSIM.
140	S	Lane group did not transfer.
141	S	NBT imported as NBR, check Lane Assignments. If there was a TL lane, it will become a R only lane because right lanes cannot share with left. Either realign the links so the movement is through or change the lane codings. In Synchro version 5, approaches will not be considered diagonal unless they are more than 35 degrees away from an orthogonal direction or the orthogonal direction is used by another approach.
142	S	SBT imported as SBL, check data. You may wish to realign the links to preserve the lane groups from Synchro version 3.2. In version 5, approaches will not be considered diagonal unless they are more than 35 degrees away from an orthogonal direction or the orthogonal direction is used by another approach.
160	H	Grade exceeds X%. The grade was changed when creating an HCS file. The range for grades is +10% to -6% for SIGNAL and +4% to -4% for UNSIGNAL.
170	S	Poor coordination downstream is causing spillback. Node #X (direction) capacity is reduced along and the v/c ratio is increased.
171	S	Lack of coordination downstream is causing spillback. Node #X capacity will be reduced and the delay and v/c ratio will increase.
172	S	Poor coordination upstream is causing starvation. Node #X capacity will be reduced and the delay and v/c ratio will increase.
173	S	Lack of coordination upstream is causing starvation. Node #X capacity will be reduced and the delay and v/c ratio will increase.
174	S	Storage blocking is occurring. Left or right turn pocket is getting blocked by the through movement. Node #X capacity will be reduced and the delay and v/c ratio will increase.

Table 17-2   Synchro Errors

Error #	Code	Cause & Resolution
201	C	Node number for CORSIM exceeds 1000. CORSIM requires all node numbers to be 1000 or less. To perform a CORSIM analysis, change the node number to less than 1001. **NOTE** It is not necessary to code the entry nodes 8000 to 8999 within Synchro. Synchro creates the 8000 series node automatically in the trf file.
202	C	Link Distance is less than 50 feet. CORSIM requires link distances to be between 50 and 4000 feet. Change the distance to be at least 50 feet or combine the 2 intersections. If necessary, the speed can be adjusted to compensate for the change in travel time.
203	C	Link Distance exceeds 4000 feet. CORSIM requires link distances to be between 50 and 4000 feet. Change the distance to be less than 4000 feet or disconnect the 2 intersections. If necessary, the speed can be adjusted to compensate for the change in travel time. To disconnect the intersections, first create two bends in the link connecting the intersections, then delete the middle segment. **NOTE** Prior versions of CORSIM required the distance between coordinates to be within 20% of coordinate distance. CORSIM version 4.32 no longer requires coordinate and input distances to match.
205	C	Too many turning lanes, maximum for CORSIM is 3. CORSIM has a limit of up to 3 left or right turn lanes. Reduce the number of lanes or consider coding a through-shared lane.
205	SCT	Volume sent to intersection, not received. This is a problem with balancing volumes. Volume is put onto a link upstream and no volume exists downstream. This problem may occur due to an uncompleted network. If this is the case, try putting the completed intersections into a zone and perform the analysis on the completed intersections only. CORSIM will give fatal errors if this problem is not corrected. It is possible to have a mid-block traffic sink, in this case add an unsignalized intersection and route all traffic off the link.

Error #	Code	Cause & Resolution
206	SC	Volume received at intersection, not sent. This is a problem with balancing volumes. Volume is not put onto a link upstream and volume exists downstream. This problem may occur due to an uncompleted network. If this is the case, try putting the completed intersections into a zone and perform the analysis on the completed intersections only. CORSIM will give fatal errors if this problem is not corrected. It is possible to have a mid-block traffic source, in this case add an unsignalized intersection and route traffic onto the link.
207	SC	Storage length exceeds link length. The length of the turning bay must be less than the link distance.
208	SC	Leading Detector setting exceeds storage. The detectors for a turning movement must fit within the turning bay.
209	C	CORSIM is limited to 2 lanes in the storage bay. More than 2 storage lanes were coded in Synchro. Card 11 will be coded with 2 pocket lanes, the other lanes will be coded as full travel lanes.
212	SC	No lanes WITHOUT storage are specified. Add a through lane for this approach or set the storage to zero for one of the turning groups.
220	SC	Leading Detector is less than Trailing Detector. Leading detector must be greater or equal to the trailing detector. Remember that leading detector is the detector farthest from the stop bar. Trailing detector is the extension detector closest to the stop bar.
221	SC	Leading Detector exceeds link distance. The detectors must fit within the link distance.
230	SCH	Volume with no green time. The phase indicated has volume and lanes but no green time. Check the **TIMING** settings. For a right turn movement, check the right turn treatment and also make sure there is an overlapping left phase, if applicable.
231	SCH	Volume with no capacity. There is no lane set up to handle this movement. Check lanes and sharings. Remember that turning traffic can use a through lane, but through traffic cannot use a turning lane. Any lane used by two or more movements counts as a through lane. If there is no through movement, shared lanes are left lanes.
232	SCH	Lanes with no green time. There is a lane for this group but no green time. Synchro does not create a phase unless there is actually volume. CORSIM may report errors if there is a link without green time.

Error #	Code	Cause & Resolution
240	SCH	Split less than Minimum Split. Check the **TIMING** settings. The current split should always be greater or equal to the Minimum Split.
241	SCH	Split less than Minimum Initial + Yellow + All Red. Check the **TIMING** settings and the **PHASING** settings. The current split should always be greater or equal to the Minimum Initial time plus Yellow and All Red time. Remember that the split includes the initial interval and yellow plus all red time.
243	SCH	Split less than Yellow + All Red + 3. Check the **TIMING** settings and the **PHASING** settings. The green time should always be at least 3 seconds.
244	SCH	Yellow + All Red less than 3. Check the **PHASING** settings. Yellow + All Red time should always be at least 3 seconds.
245	SCH	Total Lost time less than 3. Check the **LANE** settings. Total Lost time should always be at least 3 seconds, unless there is a study to justify less. Remember that total lost time includes startup lost time and clearance lost time.
246	SCH	Ped timing + Yellow + All Red exceeds Maximum Split. The Walk plus Do not Walk time is greater than the maximum green. Synchro requires the green time to accommodate pedestrian timings, except when actuated uncoordinated.
248	SCH	Ped timing exceeds minimum split. The Walk plus Do not Walk time plus Yellow and All Red is greater than the Minimum Split. Synchro always requires the green time to accommodate pedestrian timings.
250	SCH	Reference phase not assigned. The offset reference phase must be assigned to one or two used phase numbers. Check the offset section of the **TIMING** settings. This error only applies to coordinated signals.
251	SCH	Reference phase not in use. The offset reference phase must be assigned to one or two used phase numbers. Check the offset section of the **TIMING** settings. This error only applies to coordinated signals.
252	SCH	Reference phase assigned to conflicting phases. If the offset reference phase is assigned to two phases, they must appear in the same barrier. Sequential phases appear one at a time. Check the offset section of the **TIMING** settings. This error only applies to coordinated signals.
253	S	Detector Phase is not in use. One of the phases coded for the detector phase is not active.

Error #	Code	Cause & Resolution
260	C	More than 2 phases per ring-barrier, modeled as pretimed. CORSIM' actuated signals are limited to 8 phases, 2 barriers, 2 rings, and 2 phases per ring-barrier.
262	C	X Links are in this network, CORSIM is limited to 1000. This file is too large for CORSIM. Try dividing it into zones and analyzing pieces of it with CORSIM. Remember that external nodes need links also. On average, about 8 links are required for every intersection.
263	C	X Nodes are in this network, CORSIM is limited to 500. This file is too large for CORSIM. Try dividing it into zones and analyzing pieces of it with CORSIM. Remember that external nodes count as nodes also. On average, about 3 nodes are required for every intersection.
264	C	Coordinated phase is not 2 or 6 as CORSIM requires. Actuated signals in CORSIM require phases 2 and 6 to be the coordinated phase. To correctly analyze this intersection with CORSIM, change the main street phase numbers and the reference phase to 2 and 6.
265	C	CORSIM is limited to 3 turning lanes with storage. Recode the lanes with 0 storage length.
266	C	CORSIM does not currently support metric units. Convert the file to feet and miles. TRAF-NETSIM still supports metrics.
267	C	Group Control (Multiple Intersection 1 Controller) will be modeled as pretimed. Synchro does not generate actuated signal cards in this case. CORSIM actuated signals are designed for a single node, although it is theoretically possible to trick CORSIM into operating two signals identically with detectors at both nodes.
268	C	More than 2 barriers used, will be modeled as pretimed. CORSIM's actuated signals are limited to 8 phases, 2 barriers, 2 rings, and 2 phases per ring-barrier.
269	C	More than 2 rings used, will be modeled as pretimed. CORSIM's actuated signals are limited to 8 phases, 2 barriers, 2 rings, and 2 phases per ring-barrier.
285	C	Phase intervals must be less than 120 second.
286	C	Too many turning lanes, maximum for CORSIM is 3. CORSIM has a limit of up to 3 left or right turn lanes. Reduce the number of lanes or consider coding a through-shared lane.

Error #	Code	Cause & Resolution
290	H	This intersection has approaches that will not fit into HCS. HCS is limited to four legged intersections. This message could also appear with multiple diagonal legs.
291	H	NS Phases conflict with EW Phases for HCS. Phases for North and South Streets cannot be concurrent with phases for East and West streets, except for right turns.
292	H	Too many East-West phase intervals for HCS. HCS is limited to 4 stages per side; this timing plan is too complex for HCS.
301	HC	Conflicting approaches have no sign control. This message applies to unsignalized intersections. It could occur at an intersection if both NB and EB approaches had sign control of 'free'. If this intersection is actually a merge of some sort, ignore this message.
302	HC	NB has sign control but SB does not. This message applies to unsignalized intersections. It can apply to 3 way stops. HCS and CORSIM are not good at analyzing 3 way stop signs.
		NOTE The prior version of CORSIM did not model 4-way stops. The latest release of TSIS, does model all way stops.
304	H	All way stops cannot have more than 2 lanes per leg in HCS.
305	H	Two way stops cannot have more than 3 lanes per leg in HCS.

SimTraffic Errors and Warnings

When opening a file, SimTraffic performs a coding error check on the Synchro (*.syn) file. This list describes each error and warning along with suggestions for correcting them.

Warnings indicate likely problems, but they may be acceptable in certain circumstances.

Errors indicate serious problems that require fixing. However, in many cases the simulation may work correctly in spite of the error.

Fatal Errors indicate a serious coding problem. SimTraffic is unable to generate lanes and geometrics until the error is corrected.

The error list will only appear when the input file has been changed or needs recording. If a valid history (*.hst) exists for the current file with no changed data; the error list is not shown.

Table 17-3   SimTraffic Warnings

Code#	Description
126	Minimum Gap is greater than Vehicle Extension. When using volume density controllers, the gap is reduced from Vehicle Extension to Minimum Gap. It is an error if Minimum gap is larger than vehicle extension. CORSIM will give a fatal error with this input.
127	Vehicle extension for phase p should exceed 111% of travel time from trailing detector. Extension detectors should keep phase active while the vehicle travels from the last extension detector to the stop bar. The minimum value for gap time is: Dtrail / (speed * 1.47 * 0.90), when speed is mph Dtrail / (speed / 3.6 * 0.90), when speed is km/h
128	Minimum Gap of phase p should exceed 111% of travel time from trailing detector. Extension detectors should keep phase active while the vehicle travels from the last extension detector to the stop bar.
129	Volume Density operation not recommended with long detection zone. The travel time across the detection zone will effectively be added to both the Minimum and Maximum gap times, making the operation less effective. Check the Time to Reduce, Time before reduce, and Minimum Gap settings.
130	Short Links under 100 feet (30 meters) may have problems. This is not necessarily an error. Pay careful attention to short links because SimTraffic may have modeling problems including stuck vehicles, only 1 or 2 vehicles approved at a time. Short links reduce the opportunities for lane changes.
131	Angle between d1 and d2 approaches less than 25 degrees. Avoid using acute angles between approaches, this causes the interior space of the intersection to be quite large and gives performance problems. If necessary use a bend node before the intersection to give a larger angle between movements.

Table 17-4   SimTraffic Errors

Code#	Description
200	2 input lanes on: Node #X EBT, But only 1 receiving lanes on link: Node #Y EB. There are less lanes downstream than input upstream. This geometry could cause mid-intersection collisions. Try coding a lane drop downstream using a bend node.
207	Storage length exceeds link length. The length of the turning bay must be less than the link distance.
208	Storage length less than right radius.
209	Link distance less than Right Radius plus 80 feet (24 m). The length of the Curb Radius as

Code#	Description
	shown in the **LANE settings** must be less than the link distance minus 80 feet (24 m).
210	Circle Maximum Lanes is 3; Synchro will not allow entry > 3.
211	Circle Inside Radius must be less than Outside Radius.
212	Link distance is too short for lane changes with upstream channelized right. If there is an upstream right turn channel with 1 add lane on a 3-lane link. The vehicles from the right may need to make two lane changes on this link. If the distance is less than 80ft plus curb radius plus the distance for lane changes. The distance for lane changes is 60ft for a single lane change or 180ft per lane change when two or more changes are required.
220	Leading Detector is less than Trailing Detector. Leading detector must be greater or equal to the Trailing detector. Remember that Leading detector is the detector farthest from the stop bar. Trailing detector is the extension detector closest to the stop bar.
222	Leading Detector is too far forward. Leading Detector is the leading detector. If Leading detector is set to 0, vehicles will not reach the detector to place a call.
	NOTE: Do not set the Leading Detector to zero; the minimum value is 5 feet (1.5 m). If there is no detector for this lane group, code a value of 'None' in the setting for Detector Phases and ensure that this is either the coordinated phase, is a pre-timed signal, or 'maximum' is coded for the Recall Mode.
240	Split less than minimum split. Check the **TIMING settings**. The current split should always be greater or equal to the minimum split.
241	Split less than minimum initial + Y + AR. Check the **TIMING settings** and the **PHASING settings**. The current split should always be greater or equal to the minimum initial time plus yellow time plus all-red time. Remember that the split includes the initial interval, yellow time, and all-red time.
243	Split less than Y + AR + 3. Check the **TIMING settings** and the **PHASING settings**. The green time should always be at least 3 seconds.
244	Y + AR less than 3. Check the **TIMING settings**. Yellow time plus All-Red time should always be at least 3 seconds.
246	Ped timing + Y + AR exceeds max split. The walk plus do not walk time plus clearance is greater than the maximum split. Synchro requires the split time to accommodate pedestrian timings. If this signal is coordinated, pedestrians may cause strange results.
250	Reference phase not assigned. The offset reference phase must be assigned to one or two used phase numbers. Check the offset section of the **TIMING settings**. This error only applies to coordinated signals.
251	Reference phase assigned to unused phase. The offset reference phase must be assigned to one or two used phase numbers. Check the offset section of the **TIMING settings**. This error only applies to coordinated signals.

Code#	Description
252	Reference phase assigned to conflicting phases. If the offset reference phase is assigned to two phases, they must appear in separate rings within the same barrier. Check the offset section of the **TIMING settings**. This error only applies to coordinated signals.

Table 17-5   SimTraffic Fatal Errors

Code#	Description
401	X input lanes on: Node #Y EBL but no receiving lanes on link: Node #Z NB. No receiving lanes. Traffic is sent to a link with no lanes. Check upstream traffic volumes and lane assignments. .
402	More than 7 lanes specified. SimTraffic is limited to 7 lanes per link including storage lanes.
405	Distance must be within 30% of coordinate distance. SimTraffic requires the coordinate distance to be close to the overridden link distance, otherwise geometrics cannot be drawn correctly.
406	No lanes WITHOUT storage are specified. Reduce the number of Storage Lanes or set the Storage Length to zero for one side of the approach.
407	Volume with no capacity. Add a lane for this movement or an adjacent lane with sharing.
408	0 travel lanes on bend, but receiving lanes downstream. Caused by setting travel lanes on an end to 0, when lanes are coded downstream.

Data Access Errors

These errors occur when reading data from data file during simulation. These errors are caused by bad or unexpected data in the external data files.

Table 17-6   SimTraffic Data Access Errors

Code#	Description
500	Volume for movement but no lanes. This error is caused if volume exists for a movement but there are no lanes available. In some cases SimTraffic will assume a shared lane for turning traffic, but not if there is zero volume in the initial timing period. SimTraffic will assume a LTR lane is a LR lane if there is no through traffic. Code at least 1 vph of through volume in any LTR lane to insure that SimTraffic creates a through lane.
501	Non-zero split in data file for unused phase. The timing data feature of SimTraffic can not be used to turn phases on and off. Timing data can only be used to change splits, offsets, and phase sequences.
502	Zero split in data file for active phase. The timing data feature of SimTraffic cannot be used to turn phases on and off. Timing data can only be used to change splits, offsets, and phase sequences.

Chapter 18 – CORSIM Analysis

CORSIM is produced by the Federal Highway Administration and their contractors. CORSIM is the successor to the TRAF-NETSIM product. CORSIM is in Settings and has the freeway modeling of FRESIM integrated with the surface modeling of NETSIM.

Before Starting CORSIM Analysis

Before starting a CORSIM analysis, it is important to be aware of all the steps involved. Performing a CORSIM analysis, even with a preprocessor like Synchro can be quite time consuming. Be sure to allow plenty of extra time when performing a CORSIM analysis to allow for unexpected problems. Do not wait until the last minute to perform a CORSIM analysis. Tasks involved with a CORSIM analysis include:

Learning CORSIM: Even though Synchro generates the necessary CORSIM cards, it may still be necessary to edit the cards for special purposes or to correct errors. It should be noted that learning about all the CORSIM card types can take days or even weeks.

Data Collection: If your data is already entered into Synchro this is not an issue. If you are starting a new project from scratch, this may take a large amount of time.

Coding TRF Card File: Synchro will create all the cards automatically, so this should not be an issue. If your project involves advanced features such as multiple time periods or transit vehicles, there may be some card coding required.

Correcting CORSIM Errors: Although Synchro attempts to produce error free card files, CORSIM is very particular about its input. CORSIM is very likely to report errors in the input file. Correcting these errors may take a long time.

Modifying Input data and Rerunning CORSIM: It is very rare to have an entire network coded correctly the first time. Watching the network in simulation may bring up problems with the original coding. Be sure to leave time to make corrections and redo the analysis.

Quality Assurance: Be sure to leave time for checking your work and rerunning the simulation if necessary.

Creating Reports and Summaries: Documenting the findings can also take significant time.

Create a CORSIM File

To use the transfer to CORSIM feature, it is necessary to first create a datafile in Synchro. CORSIM requires that all signal timing information be determined before performing an analysis. It is necessary to optimize splits, cycle lengths, and offsets using Synchro or another software package before using CORSIM. All of the items in the following list should be determined before performing a CORSIM analysis.

Data required for CORSIM:

- Volumes

- Lanes

- Storage Lengths

- Left Turn Type

- Street Names

- Phase Order (lead or lag)

- Cycle Length

- Splits

- Offsets

Data calculated by CORSIM:

- Delay and Fuel Consumption Data

- Data for Simulations

Setting Options

To perform a CORSIM analysis, choose the **Transfer→CORSIM Analysis** command from Synchro. **Figure 18-1** illustrates the CORSIM Analysis dialog.

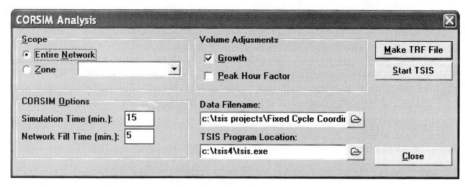

Figure 18-1   CORSIM Analysis Dialog

In TSIS a project is a file that keeps track of all the files in the directory. Before selecting a Data File path, start TSIS and create a project. This project directory can be used to hold the TRF files created by Syncrho.

TSIS Program Location

Enter the location of the TSIS program. Normally this is:

```
C:\Program Files\TSIS\Tsis.exe
```

Data file path

The Data file path is the name of the input file that will be used. By default, it is in the *C:\TSIS PROJECTS* sub-directory and has the same name as the *SYN* file, but with a *TRF* extension.

CORSIM Options

Scope

Select **Entire Network** or specify a zone to simulate. Dividing a Synchro file into zones allows a portion of the file to be analyzed with CORSIM. This can be useful for bypassing CORSIM's limit of 60 intersections.

If you have any bends in your network, be sure to include them in the zone of the adjacent intersections.

Simulation Time: Enter the number of minutes to perform a simulation. The default is 15 minutes. Synchro will round decimal minutes to the nearest minute (e.g., 15.5 rounded to 15).

Network Fill Time: Enter the maximum number of minutes to fill the network before simulation actually begins. CORSIM will start simulating when equilibrium is achieved or this time has elapsed, which ever comes first. The default is 15 minutes.

 Set Simulation Time and Network Fill time to 2 minutes initially. This will significantly reduce the execution time of CORSIM. After you have determined that the network is operating correctly, then set the simulation time back to 15.

Volume Adjustments

Synchro gives the option of adjusting volumes by Growth factors and/or PHF factors. To get similar v/c ratios with Synchro, use both adjustments.

 If the Peak Hour Factor adjustment option is selected, the volumes are adjusted for the PHF even if they are invisible. The PHF is considered to be invisible (set to 1.0 with a hidden value of something else) if the analysis period is set to 30 minutes or greater. To see the actual PHF that is used, set the analysis period (See the **NETWORK SETTINGS**) to 15 minutes.

Synchro with TRAF-NETSIM

Synchro requires CORSIM. If you have not yet upgraded to CORSIM from TRAF-NETSIM, contact the McTrans center for upgrade information.

Synchro is not compatible with NETSIM. It may be possible to modify some of the cards to provide a TRAF-NETSIM compatible file. However, Trafficware is not able to provide technical support for this operation.

As an alternative, you can perform animations with SimTraffic, Trafficware's simulation model. SimTraffic contains most of CORSIM's functionality and is much easier to use.

Run CORSIM

After setting appropriate options described in the previous section, select [**Make TRF File**] and a CORSIM input file is generated.

Select [**Start TSIS**] to execute TSIS.EXE. TSIS can be used to view and edit the TRF files. TSIS can also be used to start CORSIM and TRAFVU. When starting TSIS, open or create a project in the directory with your TRF files.

Fixing Common CORSIM Errors

Many CORSIM coding errors are found by Synchro when creating the TRF file. Refer to the section on **Errors and Warnings** (page 17-1) for a list of errors and their explanations.

Link distances must be between 50 and 4000 feet. If there are any links greater than 4000 feet break them up. If any nodes are closer than 50 feet, move them apart.

The storage bay length must be between 50 feet and the length of the link. Make sure that all turning bays are less than the link distance.

Only links that actually have traffic or lanes are included. Turning receiving nodes on card 11 must be valid links. If traffic is sent to a receiving node and this link has no lanes an error will be created. Do not try to send traffic or lanes to links that have no lanes.

Detector distances must be less than the link length or turning bay link. Make sure that the leading detector entry is less than the link distance or the storage length.

Node Numbers

To see the node numbers used by Synchro and CORSIM, go to the **MAP** view and push the ***Show Node Numbers*** button. The map with node numbers can be printed out for easy reference. Node numbers can be changed by double clicking on the intersection when node numbers are showing.

Lane Groups

Normally Through, Right, and Left movements are coded as the corresponding lane groups in CORSIM. There are some exceptions.

If a diagonal movement has phases within the same barrier, or if a through movement does not exist, the diagonal movement is coded as a CORSIM Through movement. The Through movement, if any, is counted as a Diagonal, Left, or Right movement.

If there are Through, Left and Left 2 movements in Synchro, the Left movement will be coded as Diagonal and Left 2 coded as Left.

If there are Through, Right and Right 2 movements in Synchro, the Right movement will be coded as Diagonal and Right 2 coded as Right.

If there are Through, Left, Left 2, Right and Right 2 movements in Synchro, the Right 2 movement will not be coded.

U-turn information is not transferred to CORSIM.

Actuated Signal Limitations

Synchro will generate CORSIM cards for actuated signals, except for some complex situations. If any of the following exists, Synchro will generate pretimed cards for the intersection:

- Intersection is coded Pretimed.
- Group Control (Multiple Intersections with One Controller)
- More than 2 barriers used
- More than 2 rings used
- More then 2 phases in a ring-barrier
- More than 8 phases used

Synchro phase numbers may be changed to meet CORSIM's phase numbering standard. Only phase numbers 1 to 8 can be used. CORSIM does not support sequential phases, so exclusive phases 4 and 8 would be changed to phases 3 and 4.

CORSIM requires phases 2 and 6 to be coordinated for actuated-coordinated operation. Synchro will not change phase numbers to accommodate coordination. Code the coordinated phases as 2 and 6 in Synchro if you plan to use CORSIM.

Notes on How Synchro Creates a CORSIM Data File

This section explains which cards Synchro creates for CORSIM's data files and what information goes into each card. It is not necessary to know this information to perform an analysis (unless CORSIM returns error messages). However, if you are interested in how Synchro works with CORSIM or if you want to edit the CORSIM input file, this information can be useful. Please refer to the *TRAF User Reference Guide* for detailed description of the input files and specifications for each card 's requirements.

CORSIM is very particular about having the right inputs, and error messages are quite common. If you receive error messages, refer to the message description in the OUT file or the *CORSIM Users Guide*. The following sections can be helpful in correcting the CORSIM errors. Do not be alarmed if CORSIM gives errors, it is quite common. Take some time to research what is causing them and make adjustments to your Synchro file or your TRF file.

The following cards are all entered into the TRF file.

CARD 0 - Run Title

Set to say: "Synchro File: *filename* Date:Apr 11, 2003 00"

CARD 1 - Run Identification

The **user name** is set to the analyst set in the Scenario Manager.

The **date** is set to the current date.

The **run number** is left black

If the Synchro file has a description, the description is included on a comment card after card 1. The file description is set in the **SCENARIO MANAGER settings**.

CARD 2 - Run Control

Entry 1: 1 (One or more Simulation Models)

Entry 2: Blank, FRESIM input and not used for NETSIM

Entry 3: Fill time, user definable, see previous section

Entry 4: 7981, default vehicle entry headway random number seed

Entry 5: 01, in form XY (see CORSIM User Guide)

Entry 6: Blank, FRESIM input and not used for NETSIM

Entry 7: 0, all emission headways are set equal to the uniform headway

Entry 8: Blank, since entry 7 is set equal to 0

Entry 9 to 13: Blank, used for RT-TRACS

Entry 15: 1200 simulations begin at 12:00

Entry 14: 3, to indicate CORSIM

Entry 16: Blank, transitions not used

Entry 17: 7781, default random number for CORSIM

Entry 18: 7581, default random number for CORSIM

CARD 3 - Time Period Specifications

Entry 1: Time period specified by user

Entries 2 to 19: Blank, only one time period used

CARD 4 - Time Intervals

Entry 1: Blank, not used

Entry 2: 60, time interval duration

CARD 5 - Reports and Graphics

Entry 1: Blank, one report

Entries 2 to 10: Blank, reporting periods not used

Entry 11: 1, Turn movement data *is* requested

Entry 12: First six characters of input file excluding the extension

CARD 10 - Link Name Table

For every link that has a street name, an entry is generated.

> If a street only has traffic in one or zero directions, only one or zero links are generated for that link.

CARD 11 - Link Description

A card 11 is generated for every link with lanes. See the *TRAF User Reference Guide* for what constitutes a link. Only one link per segment is generated for one way streets.

Node numbers are the internal node numbers used by Synchro. For external nodes there is an entry node with a number of 8000 plus the regular node number. There is also a dummy node with the regular node number.

Link Length is the distance between intersections as shown in Synchro.

There are **turning pockets** if there is one or more turning lanes and the storage length is not zero. Otherwise the turning lanes are counted as travel lanes. The **turning pocket length** is the storage length and the **number of pocket lanes** is the number of turning Storage lanes. Diagonal and Through lanes cannot be in the pocket and CORSIM only allows two pocket lanes.

The **Grade** is taken from Synchro's data.

Queue Discharge Characteristics is blank for default.

Channelization Codes are coded as zero with the following exceptions:

Turning lanes with no pocket are channelized as Right '4' or Left '1'. If there is no through movement and the left lane is shared with the right lane then the movement has a shared code of '9'

Exclusive through lanes are marked 'T', Through-Right lanes are marked '7', Through-Left lanes are marked '8', Right-Through-Left lanes are marked '9'.

Downstream nodes are the node numbers of the appropriate links. These values are only entered if there really is traffic on that link. See **Lane Groups** section above for information about how Synchro lane groups are coded as CORSIM lane groups

Start-up Lost Time is blank for default

Queue Discharge Headway is blank for default

Free Flow Speed is the speed entered for the link in Synchro

Right Turn on Red is 0 for allowed, and 1 for prohibited

Pedestrian Code is taken from the pedestrians entered in Synchro on the **VOLUME** settings. Note that in Synchro you enter the pedestrians conflicting with turns. These are translated to the appropriate link.

Lane alignment: If there is a right turn lane with no pocket and a through lane, the lane alignment is r+1, 1 (r is the number of exclusive right turn lanes). Otherwise, this entry is blank.

 If you have a turning lane with **storage length** 0, then it will be modeled as a full travel lane. Make sure you enter the storage lengths for all turning lanes if appropriate. Also, make sure that the storage length is less than 90% of the link length.

CARD 21 - Turning Movements

A card 21 is entered for every link.

For entry and exit links, all traffic goes through.

For links at intersections, the turning movements are based on the turning movement counts provided, entered in vph.

If volumes for a link are zero, all valid turns will be assigned 10 vph.

Volumes may be adjusted for PHF and Growth Factors depending on Input Settings.

Turn prohibitions are left blank.

See **Lane Groups** section above for information about how Synchro lane groups are coded as CORSIM lane groups.

CARD 22 - Conditional Turn Movements

Conditional turn movements are entered based on the values in the LINK O-D **VOLUMES** settings.

Values are entered in vph, not percentages.

CARD 35 - Pretimed Signal Control

For Pretimed, Signalized Intersections:

The offset is the beginning time of Phase #1 (or the first used phase).

The upstream nodes are for any approach links with lanes. Note that there is a limit of 5.

The intervals are the times for each phase after converting it to single ring control. Note that if there are concurrent phases that terminate within y seconds of each other (y is yellow + all-red time) they are treated as terminating at the same time and their splits are averaged.

For **Dummy Entry/Exit Nodes:**

The upstream nodes are 8000 plus this node and the adjoining intersection.

The remainder of the card is blank.

For **Unsignalized Intersections**:

The upstream nodes are for any approach links with lanes. Note that there is a limit of 5.

The remainder of the card is blank.

CARD 36- Pretimed Signal Control Codes

For **Pretimed, Signalized Intersections**:

The Control Codes are entered as appropriate as follows:

1 - Green ball. Used when Through and either Left or Diaganol is Green. Also used if Left and Diagonal is green and through is not used.

2 - Red

0 - Yellow ball, yellow left arrow, or yellow right arrow

3 - Right only is green.

4 - Left only is green.

6 - Diagonal only is green.

7 - Through only is green.

8 - Left and Right are green.

9 - Trough and right are green.

 If a link contains Left, Through, and Diagonal movements; it is not possible to display phases for each group independently. This is a limitation of CORSIM. In some cases, right turns will be displayed red when diagonal is green. This is a limitation of CORSIM.

For Dummy Entry/Exit Nodes:

The Control Code is 1 for each approach (green ball).

For **Unsigalized Intersections**:

The Control Codes are entered as appropriate as follows:

0 - Yield sign.

1 - Uncontrolled

5 - Stop Sign

CARD 43 - Approaches for Actuated Controller

For **Actuated Intersections:**

For each approach to this intersection with volumes, an entry is made. The upstream node is the adjacent intersection.

The downstream node is always this node.

The record sequence is always 0.

The micronode code is always left blank so this is not modeled as a micronode.

CARD 44 - Coordination for Actuated Controller

For **Actuated Intersections with Fixed Cycle:**

Cycle Length is Current Cycle Length in Synchro.

Offset is the offset referenced to the end of main street green. This may not be the same offset used within Synchro. If phase 1 or 5 is lagging, the offset is referenced to the first phase (2 or 6) to yield.

Permissive Periods are assigned, as needed to the following phases. Lagging main street phases 1 and/or 5. Leading Cross street phases, usually 3 and 7. Lagging Cross Street phases, usually 4 and 8. Leading main street phases 1 and 5. The start time for the permissive periods is equal to the amount of time from the offset to the time the permissive phase begins, less the main street yellow. Permissive period 1 starts at time 0. The end of the permissive period is the same as the start time plus 1. This means that each phase is given a one second permissive period to begin at the time it would begin if it were pretimed.

A Permissive Period Code of 1 is only given to phases for their own permissive period. If there are not enough permissive periods for all of the phases, the phase is allowed to start in an earlier permissive period.

Force Offs are assigned as the the time between the offset to the end of yellow for each phase. In practice the force offs will not be used because the force off times are based on maximum greens and thus the phases will always max out before, or at the same time, as the Force Off time.

Example of permissive periods and Force Offs.

Phase 2: coordinated phase, offset is 20 referenced to begin of yellow, yellow is 5 s.

Phase 3: max green is 20, yellow is 4

Phase 4: max green is 30, yellow is 3

This will be coded as follows:

Offset = 20

Permissive 1 start = 0, end = 1. Permissive 1 always starts at 0.

Permissive 1 phases: 3 only

Permissive 2 start = 24 end = 25. (Phase 3 green + Phase 3 yellow)

Permissive 2 phases: 4 only

Force Off Phase 3 = 25. (Phase 2 yellow + Phase 3 green)

Force Off Phase 4 = 59. (Phase 2 yellow + Phase 3 green + Phase 3 yellow + Phase 4 green)

CARD 45 - Movements for Actuated Controller

For **Actuated Intersections:**

For each phase 1 to 8 that is in use for an actuated controller, a card 45 is generated.

For each movement of each approach a movement code is entered. Each movement is allowed

Thru Movements: Through movements are allowed on through phases.

Left Movements: Left movements are allowed on left phases. Left movements are also allowed on through phases for permitted, permitted/protected, and split left turn phasing.

Right Movements: Right movements are allowed on the approach's through phase if right turn type includes protected or permitted. Right movements are allowed on the right approaches left phase if the right turn type includes overlap. Right movements are allowed on all phases if the right turn type is free.

Diagonal Movements: Synchro does not set up links with diagonal movements and thus they are never allowed to go.

CARD 46 - Detectors for Actuated Controller

For **Actuated Intersections:**

A card 46 is coded for every lane, in every lane group, for all approaches, unless the lane group has no Detector Phases. If a lane group has two or more detector phases, the card 46 will be created for the first Detector Phase only.

If a lane group has two or more lanes, they may be able to share a detector card. The lane numbers are coded as follows:

        1 to 7: lane numbers as specified in CORSIM documentation

8: all non-pocket lanes

9: all lanes

Detector Group is always 1. All detectors are extension and count detectors. If your approach has calling-only or type-3 detectors at the stop bar, this will be simulated by having no detectors at the stop bar in conjunction with locking calls and extended initial intervals.

Three detectors are used if the distance from the leading to the trailing detector is 200 feet (60 m) or more. Two detectors are used if the distance from the leading to the trailing detector is 100 feet (30 m) or more. Otherwise, only one detector is used.

The leading detector has a leading edge equal to the Leading Detector entry in Synchro. The last detectors trailing edge is equal to the trailing detection setting in Synchro. If three detectors are used the middle detector is placed half way between the first and last detector.

The detector length is 10 feet if two or more detectors are used. Otherwise, the detector is equal to the distance between the first and last detector.

If the distance between detectors is greater than 100 ft (30m), a carryover time of 0.1 s is added for every 5 ft (1.5m) over 100 ft (30m).

If the last detector is within 50 ft (15 m) of the stopbar it is a presence detector; otherwise, it is a passage detector. Upstream detectors are passage.

CARD 47 - Phase Operations for Actuated Controller

For **Actuated Intersections:**

A card 47 is created for every phase used by the actuated controller.

Maximum Green is set to the Maximum Green setting in Synchro. If this is an actuated coordinated controller, then the maximum green is equal to the cycle length minus 10 seconds. This will allow the controller to reach the Force-Off point without early max-out.

Minimum Green is set to the Minimum Green setting in Synchro. (Maximum Split - Yellow - All-Red)

Vehicle Extension is set to the Vehicle Extension setting in Synchro.

Initial intervals are handled in one of two ways. If there is an extension detector within 50 ft (15m) of the stopbar, no initial interval calculation is needed.

With a stop bar detector, initial interval code is 0 or extensible. The Maximum Initial Interval is the same as the minimum green. Yellow and red lock are not set.

With no stop bar detector, initial interval code is 0 or extensible. Yellow lock is set. The time added per actuation is 2.2s and the Maximum Initial Interval is calculated as:

max initial = 2.5 + 2.2 * vehStored

vehStored = LastExt / VehLength

MaxInitial $\leq$ maxGreen

MaxInitial $\geq$ minGreen

Gap Reduction Code is set to 2, time to reduce to minimum. Minimum Gap is set to the Synchro setting. Maximum Gap is set to Vehicle Extension setting in Synchro. Time to Reduce is set to the sum of Time-to-Reduce plus Time-Before-Reduce in settings in Synchro.

Double Entry is always permitted.

Last Vehicle Passage feature is always 0 or off.

Minimum Recall is set if the phase has Minimum or Pedestrian Recall in Synchro.

Maximum Recall is set if the phase has Maximum Recall set in Synchro.

Rest in Red is set if the phase has No Recall set in Synchro.

Lag Code is set to 0 if this phase is leading, 1 if this phase is lagging. If the phase's lead-lag partner is not used, the lag code is 1 for even phases, 0 for odd phases.

Overlap codes are not used.

Red revert time is 2.0 seconds.

Lag Phase Hold is set if there is one lagging phase on the main street and the controller is in coordination. Our tests show that this feature does not work correctly in CORSIM version 4.2.

Simultaneous Gap is always set off.

Dual Service is not used.

Minimum Conditional Service Time is not used.

CARD 48 - Pedestrian Operations for Actuated Controller

For **Actuated Intersections:**

A card 48 is created for any actuated phase that has a pedestrian phase with pedestrian calls. No card 48 is generated if there are 0 pedestrian calls.

Walk Time is the same as the Synchro setting.

Dont Walk Time is the same as the Synchro setting.

Pedestrian Intensity for stochastic arrivals is taken from the Pedestrian Calls setting in Synchro's **PHASING** settings. Deterministic arrivals are not used.

Pedestrian Recall is set on if this phase has pedestrian or maximum recall, and the signal is coordinated.

Pedestrian Rest is set on if this phase has pedestrian or maximum recall, and the signal is uncoordinated.

CARD 50 - Entry Link Volumes

A 50 Card entry is created for every entry node with traffic. The volume is the sum of the arrivals at the intersection. The node number is in the range 8000 to 8999.

Volumes may be adjusted for PHF and Growth Factors depending on Input Settings.

The Percent Trucks is equal to the percent heavy vehicles input on the **VOLUME** settings.

The Percent Carpools is zero.

CARD 51 - Source/Sink Volumes

A 51 Card entry is created for every link where the traffic entering does not match the traffic leaving downstream. There can be quite a lot of 51 cards because the volume counts entered into Synchro typically do not match exactly. This could be due to different times the counts were taken or cars entering/leaving midblock. There is no card 51s for entry and exit links.

The Centriod numbers are in the range 2000 to 2999.

The entry exit volume is the difference between volume arriving at the downstream intersection less the traffic arriving from the upstream intersection.

CARD 56 - Parking Activity

A card 56 is generated when parking movements are specified in the **VOLUME** settings.

The downstream distance is equal to the storage bay distance, if applicable, or zero.

The upstream distance is equal to the link distance minus 80ft (24 m) minus any storage distance.

The number of movements is the total number of parking movements in all lane groups.

For a one way street, distances are also specified on the left side.

No Card 56 is generated for links approaching bends, or exit links.

CARD 140 Turning Speeds

The default turning speeds are 15 mph for left turns and 9 mph for right turns. If the values in the **NETWORK** settings are changed, Synchro will generate a Card 140.

The speeds on the card are those in the **NETWORK** settings. All other values on Card 140 are left blank.

CORSIM has no option to set turning speeds for individual intersections.

CARD 170 Sub-network Delimiter

Indicates end of CORSIM section, a zero is coded for entry 1.

CARD 195 Node Coordinates

For each intersection and each entry/exit node, a card 195 is generated with the appropriate coordinates. The coordinates are expressed in feet. If there are any coordinates less than 0 or greater than 9999999, all the coordinates will be adjusted to be in this range.

CARD 210 Final Card in Time Period

Indicates end of time period

Entry 1 is 1 to indicate the last time period.

All other entries are blank.

Chapter 19 – SimTraffic Introduction

Introduction

SimTraffic is designed to model networks of signalized and unsignalized intersections, including roundabouts. The primary purpose of SimTraffic is to check and fine tune traffic signal operations. SimTraffic is especially useful for analyzing complex situations that are not easily modeled macroscopically including:

- Closely spaced intersections with blocking problems
- Closely spaced intersections with lane change problems
- The affects of signals on nearby unsignalized intersections and driveways
- The operation of intersections under heavy congestion

SimTraffic Features:

- Pre-timed Signals
- Actuated Signals
- 2-way Stop Intersections
- All-way Stop Intersections
- Roundabouts
- Freeways
- Roadway Bends
- Lane Additions and Lane Drops
- Cars, Trucks, Buses
- Pedestrians
- Right Turn Islands
- Curved Links

SimTraffic Measures of Effectiveness (MOEs):

- Slowing Delay
- Stopped Delay

- Stops
- Queue Lengths
- Speeds
- Travel Time and Distance
- Fuel Consumption and Efficiency
- Exhaust Emissions
- Observed Actuated Green Times

At present SimTraffic will not model ramp metering, bus stops, bus routes, bus and carpool lanes, light rail, on-street parking, and short-term events. Many of these features may be added into future versions of SimTraffic.

SimTraffic Quick Start

To use SimTraffic follow these steps:

 To start SimTraffic, simply choose the **SimTraffic** icon from the **Programs→Trafficware** group of the Start Bar.

 Select the **File-Open** button or the **File→Open** command to load a file. SimTraffic uses Synchro style SYN files. Choose one of the sample files that come with SimTraffic and press [**Open**].

SimTraffic seeds the network with traffic; this will take 10 to 40 seconds or more depending on the size of the network and the speed of your PC.

 After the network is seeded, you can begin animating by pressing the **Simulate-While-Playing** button. Vehicles will begin to move through the network.

Further information about using SimTraffic is available later in this Users Guide.

Demo Version

The Demo version can be used to record and playback simulations for the example files located in the Trafficware directory. The Demo version cannot be used to record animations on other files.

The Demo version can also be used to playback prerecorded history files. This allows unlicensed users to view animation files. If you would like to share a SimTraffic animation with a client or colleague who does not own a SimTraffic license, they can view the animations and reports but not make changes using the demo version of SimTraffic. Be sure that the client receives all of the following:

1. The Synchro Data file (SYN)

2. The SimTraffic Parameters file (STN)

3. The History file (HST)

4. Timing or volume data files, if data access is used.

5. The Synchro/SimTraffic 6 demo CD or download file (setup.exe).

Changes to the Synchro file or SimTraffic parameters may mark a history file as 'dirty' or out of date. To test that the history file reflects the current data settings:

1. Close both SimTraffic and Synchro

2. Re-open SimTraffic

3. Make sure the network doesn't re-seed and the animation plays without simulating (green triangle with blue film clip)

4. Do not make any further changes to the Synchro file

Make sure that the same version and build of SimTraffic is used for both playback and recording.

SimTraffic can playback history files marked read-only. This allows for playing history files stored on a CD-ROM, and allows the user to protect history files from accidental rerecording.

Chapter 20 – SimTraffic Operation

SimTraffic Operation

This chapter explains the overall operation of SimTraffic including loading files, recording simulations and playing simulations.

Loading Files

Select the **File-Open** button or the **File→Open** menu command to load a file. SimTraffic 7 uses Synchro 7 style SYN files for data inputs.

 If you are working with a file in Synchro, you can start SimTraffic by pressing the **SimTraffic-Animation** button or pressing **[Ctrl]+[G]**.

Recording and Playback

Seeding Network

After a file is loaded, the network is seeded. Network seeding fills a network with vehicles, so that there will be vehicles in the network when simulation begins. The length of seed time can be changed with **Options→Intervals and Volumes** command.

Simulating	⊠
Seeding Network	

| Current Time: | 6:59:00 A |
| Target Time: | 7:00:00 A |

Vehicle Counts	
Total Entered:	411
Total Exited:	82
In Network:	330
Denied Entry:	42
Stopped:	140
Entered Last Min:	211
Exited Last Min:	64

Stop

Simulation Recording

Simulations can be recorded and subsequently played back. Alternatively, simulations can be created while animating.

 The **Record-Simulation** button or **[Ctrl]+[E]** will perform simulation and record information for animation, reports, and static graphics. The length of time recorded can be changed with the **Options→Intervals and Volumes** command.

 The **Simulate-While-Playing** button (**[F5]**) will simulate traffic while animating (SimPlay). The SimPlay option is useful for quickly viewing traffic. Simulations created with SimPlay cannot be used for reports and static graphics.

In many cases, it is possible to change traffic volumes or signal timings and simulate while playing without re-seeding the network. This makes it possible to simulate many similar timing plans quickly. To change data without reseeding, it is necessary to start SimTraffic from Synchro.

Playback

The **Speed-Control box** shows the current speed and allows the user to change the speed quickly. Click on the center red bar to stop playback or SimPlay. Pressing [**F2**] will also pause playback or SimPlay.

 The **Play** button [1] will play the animation back at 1 time speed. This would be similar to changing the speed with the Speed-Control box.

 The **Stop Simulation** button [**0**] or [**F2**] will stop the simulation playback.

Clicking on the right bars will play or SimPlay at 1/2x, 1x, 2x, 4x, and 8x speed. If simulation data is recorded, it will be played back, otherwise new simulation data will be SimPlayed. The simulation may not actually play at the full speed with a large network or on a slow computer. To speed animations, consider animating a small part of the network.

Clicking on the left bars will play in reverse at 8x, 4x, 2x, 1x, and 1/2x speed.

 The **Go-Back-in-Time-to-Beginning-of-Recorded-History** button or [<] key returns to the start of recorded history.

The **Frame-Reverse** button or [-] key takes the animation back 0.5 seconds. SimTraffic simulates traffic at 0.1 s increments but only records traffic data at 0.5 increments. A frame is therefore 0.5 s.

The **Frame-Advance** button or [+] key takes the animation forward 0.5 seconds. SimTraffic simulates traffic at 0.1 s increments but only records traffic data at 0.5 increments. A frame is therefore 0.5 s.

The **Skip-to-the-End-of-Recorded-History** button or [>] key sets the animation at the end of recorded history.

The **Playback-Time box** shows the starting and ending times of recorded history on the left and right sides. The center number indicates the current animation time. The needle in the playback time box can be dragged to quickly go to a specific time.

3D Simulations

SimTraffic can create a 3D format file for viewing with Trafficware's 3D Viewer program. To create the 3D file, use the command **Animate→Create 3D Graphics File**. A file with an S3D extension will be created in your project directory.

 Use the **3D Viewer** button to launch the 3D Viewer application. Refer to Chapter 25 for full details on using 3D Viewer.

Multiple Simulation Runs

 The **Record-Multiple Runs** button or [**Ctrl**]+[**M**] will perform and record a simulation on multiple runs. A dialog will appear allowing the user to select the number of runs to simulate and record and the starting random number seed. The random number seed will be incrementally increased by one for the simulated runs. For instance, 1, 2, 3, 4 and 5 if starting from 1 with 5 runs.

The **Run Number of Recorded History** will allow the user to load a recorded history file if multiple runs have been performed. Choose the number of the run you would like to animate with the drop down list. The number will be the random seed number that was used. It is possible to have a blank value in the drop-down list. This indicates a simulation run without a run number extension.

In the reports, the user is allowed to have the report generator average the results for some of all of the runs performed.

 The run numbers are used on the same input data and time intervals to get a statistical average of varied random seeds. See page 22-5 for information on random seeds and page 23-3 for creating reports with multiple runs.

History Files

SimTraffic records the animation data into a history file. Normally this file has the same name as the SYN file but has the extension HST. If you have recorded multiple runs (see above), the HST file will be formatted as filename-#.HST. The '#' will indicate the random seed number that was used during the recording. To print the average result of the history files, see the section on Reports, Graphics and MOEs on page 23-3.

This file(s) is preserved so that animations can be displayed later and reports can be created without re-seeding and re-recording.

Sometimes the HST file may need to be destroyed or may require re-recording. The following actions can render a HST file invalid.

- Changing data in the SYN file. Zoom settings are exempt.

- Changing any simulation options or parameters in SimTraffic. MAP View and zoom positions are exempt.

- Changing the data files if volume or timing data is used.

- Use the SimTraffic-Animation button in Synchro to change data without re-seeding.

Making Presentations with Prerecorded Data

If you are planning to make a presentation, it is helpful to have a HST file with the animations pre-recorded. To insure that the HST file is valid and does not require re-seeding, close SimTraffic and restart SimTraffic to verify that the history file can be loaded without re-seeding.

When copying files between computers or directories, be sure to copy the SY7, ST7, and HST files so that all data is transferred. The demo version can play but not record history (HST) files.

Analyzing Part of a Network or a Single Intersection with SimTraffic

SimTraffic analyzes all intersections in a file or network. There is no provision for modeling part of a network or zone within a file.

To analyze part of a network, do the following:

1. In Synchro, select the desired intersection(s) on the map. Multiple intersections can be selected by dragging a rectangle around them.

2. Choose the **File→Save Part** command.

3. Start SimTraffic from the Settings start bar and Open the sub-network file.

Starting More than One Instance of SimTraffic

It is possible to load multiple copies of SimTraffic to display multiple versions of a network at the same time.

Choosing the **SimTraffic-Animation** button from Synchro will not start a second instance of SimTraffic; it simply loads the current file into the already started instance of SimTraffic.

Multiple instances of SimTraffic can be started by choosing the SimTraffic icon on the Settings Start bar.

Map Settings

Use the command **Options→Map Settings** to change the appearance of the map (see **Figure 20-1**). This command can change the color and size of the map elements for the Layout, the vehicle appearance and for static graphics.

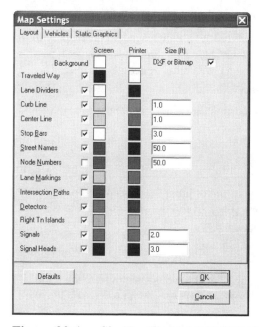

Figure 20-1   SimTraffic MAP VIEW Settings

To change a color, click on the Color box for the desired element (Screen Color or Printer Color) and then select a color from the choices shown. To cancel the selection, use the [Esc] key.

Layout Tab. The sizes for curb lines, center lines, stop bars, street names, and node numbers are in feet (meters). These elements will be scaled when the map is zoomed in and out. The Street Name Height also affects how often the street name is repeated. To have the street names repeat farther apart or closer together, decrease the height of the street names.

For best printing performance, set the printer background color and the printer traveled way color to white.

The checkbox can be selected or de-selected. A check will indicate to show the element and unchecked will make the element transparent.

Use the 'DXF or Bitmap' checkbox to turn off/on the background image. You can import a bitmap or jpeg image into your Synchro file to use as a Map background. In SimTraffic, the network will animate on the background image (DXF or Bitmapped). See the topic on **Background Images** (page 2-22) for details on importing the background image.

Vehicles Tab. The Vehicles tab is used to adjust how vehicles are displayed on the map, with one color, color coded by turn type, color-coded by vehicle type, color coded by driver type or hidden. The Hide Vehicles option is useful for making a printout of the geometrics only. This tab also includes the option to change the pedestrian color.

Static Graphics. The Static Graphics tab is used to change the colors that are used for the Static Graphics display.

Map Zooming and Scrolling

 To scroll around the map, choose the *Pan* button or press the [End] key. To deactivate, select the button again or press [Esc]. In addition, holding the mouse wheel button down will allow you to drag the map.

 The *Pan* button replaces the option to scroll when the mouse is moved to the edge of the Map in older versions of SimTraffic. Using the key pad arrows still scrolls the map.

 To view the map closer, choose the **Zoom-In** button or press [**Page Down**]. It may be necessary to scroll to put the map in the center of the **MAP** view first.

 To view more of the map, choose the **Zoom-Out** button or press [**Page Up**].

 To view the entire map, choose the **Zoom-All** button or press [**Home**].

To view a specific section of the map, use the **Zoom-Window** button or press [**Ctrl**]+[**W**]. Then click on the upper-left corner of the viewing area. Then click on the lower-right corner of the viewing area.

 To view the map at a specific scale, use the **Zoom-Scale** button. Then enter the desired scale to view the map in feet per inch (meters per inch). This command assumes 100 pixels per inch on your screen.

To return to the previous view, press [**Ctrl**]+[**Bksp**].

 The command **File→Print-Settings** for both Synchro and SimTraffic will print to the scale specified by Zoom-Scale. The printout will be centered on the center point of the current screen view. For further details, see **Print Settings** on page 23-3.

To center the view on an intersection, select the Zoom to Intersection button or press [**F8**] and select the intersection from the list.

To center the view, press [**Ctrl**]+[**C**] and click on the map feature to center it.

Signal status

Click with the mouse in the middle of the intersection to display the status of an actuated or pre-timed signal.

```
Int:3  Main Street & 3rd St   CL:110 Clk:40.0
Ph     Dir  Time  Mn  FO  Rcl    Gap   Ped
 4    SBTL  31.0   4  73  Min      X
 8    NBTL  31.0   4  65  Min     3.7
Calls:_23__678       Ped Calls:_____
```

A sample of the signal status appears above. Here is a brief explanation of the signal status.

Table 20-1   Signal Status Description

Int:3	This displays the intersection node number.
Main Street & 3rd St	This displays the street names of the intersection.
CL:110	This is the cycle length for pre-timed and coordinated intersections.
Clk:40.0	This is the cycle counter for pre-timed and coordinated intersections. The cycle counter will be greater or equal to 0 and less than the cycle length. If the offset is 5, the reference phase will be started or yield when the cycle clock is 5.
Ph 4	These are the currently active phase number(s).
Dir SBTL	These are the direction(s) serviced by the currently active phases.
Time 31.0	This is the amount of time elapsed for the currently active phase.
Mn 4	The minimum initial green time for this phase
FO 73	The force off or yield time for this phase. Coordinated and pre-timed only. The phase will yield to yellow or be forced off to yellow when the cycle clock reaches the force off time.
Mx 20	For actuated-uncoordinated only. This is the phase's maximum green time.
Rcl Crd	The recall for the phase if any. This will be Crd for coordinated, Max for Max recall, Ped for Pedestrian recall, and Min for minimum recall.
Gap 3.0	This is gap counter. It is set to the vehicle extension time when a vehicle is on a detector. The gap counter is reduced whenever there are no vehicles on the detectors. When the phase gaps out, the gap counter shows X. The gap counter is blank for pre-timed signals.
Calls:__4__78	This indicates which phases have a vehicle call. Phases with recall always place a call. This information is blank for pre-timed signals.
Ped Calls:_4__	This indicates which phases have a ped call. Phases with ped recall always place a pedestrian call.

To hide the Signal status, press the [**Delete**] button while it is in focus. To move to a different status pane press [**Ctrl**] + [**Up**] or [**Ctrl**] + [**Down**].

Vehicle Status

Click with the mouse on a vehicle to display the status of a vehicle. Vehicle status can be used to help explain vehicle behaviors.

A sample of the vehicle status appears above. Here is a brief explanation of the vehicle status.

Vehicle ID#:	4	Next Turn:	Thru
Vehicle Type:Car2		2nd Turn:	Exit
Driver Type:	9	Speed (ft/s):	71.3
Node:	8	Accel (ft/s2):	2.4a
Upstream Node:	7	Current Lane:	3
Dist to SBar (ft):	27	Dest Lane:	3

Table 20-2   Vehicle Status Description

Vehicle ID#: 4	This is a number that uniquely identifies each vehicle. ID numbers are reused when a vehicle leaves the network.
Vehicle Type: Car2	This identifies what type of vehicle is shown. The **Options→Vehicle-Parameters** shows the characteristics for each vehicle type.
Driver Type: 9	This identifies what type of driver is shown. The **Options→Driver-Parameters** shows the characteristics for each vehicle type. There are 10 driver types from 1 to 10. The smaller numbered drivers are more conservative and courteous. The higher numbered drivers are more aggressive.
Node: 8	This is the node number the vehicle is approaching. While in an intersection, this is the node number of the next intersection.
Upstream Node: 7	This is the upstream node number.
Dist to Sbar (ft): 27	This is the distance from the front of the vehicle to the stop bar.
Next Turn: Thru	This is the next turn the vehicle will make. This field will be Left, Thru, Right, Exit, or Sink. Exit indicates the vehicle is exiting the network. Sink indicates the vehicle is exiting through a mid-block sink.
2nd Turn: Exit	This is the second turn the vehicle will make.
Speed(ft/s): 36.2	This is the current speed of the vehicle in ft/s (m/s).
Accel (ft/s^2): -4.0	This is the current acceleration of the vehicle in feet per second squared. (m/s^2).
Current Lane: 2	The current lane. Lanes are numbered sequentially starting at one for the leftmost lane.
Dest Lane: 2	If a lane change is in progress, this is the destination lane the vehicle is moving into. Otherwise, the Destination Lane will be the Current Lane.

To hide the Signal status, press the [**Delete**] button while it is in focus. To move to a different status pane press [**Ctrl**] + [**Up**] or [**Ctrl**] + [**Down**].

SimTraffic Keyboard Shortcuts

Table 20-3   Keyboard Shortcuts

ZOOM ALL	[HOME]
ZOOM IN	[PAGE DOWN]
ZOOM OUT	[PAGE UP]
ZOOM SETTINGS	[W], [CTRL]+ [W] or [SHIFT]+[W]
ZOOM PREVIOUS	[CTRL]+[BKSPACE]
ZOOM SCALE	[S]
ZOOM CENTER	[CTRL]+[C]
SCROLL MAP	[↑] [↓] [←] [→]
PAGE MAP	[CTRL]+[↑] [↓] [←] [→]
SIMPLAY	[F5]
PAUSE	[F2] OR [0] OR [']
PLAY, SIMPLAY	[1] [2] [4] [8]
REVERSE PLAY	[SHIFT] + [1] [2] [4] [8]
START OF HISTORY	[<] OR [,]
END OF HISTORY	[>] OR [.]
FRAME ADVANCE	[=] OR [+]
FRAME REVERSE	[-]
FILE OPEN	[CTRL]+[O]
PRINT SETTINGS	[CTRL]+[P]
CREATE REPORT	[CTRL]+[R]
REMOVE STATUS PANE	[DELETE]
UP/DOWN STATUS PANE	[SHIFT]+[↑] [↓]

Chapter 21 – SimTraffic Input Data

Input Data

This chapter supplements the topics earlier in this User Guide and places an emphasis on items specific to SimTraffic. Synchro is required for data input for SimTraffic. SimTraffic uses the Synchro files as input.

Map View Data

It is necessary to have the links and nodes laid out on an accurate map. You create your analysis network on the **MAP view** in Synchro. For further information, see the topic on **Mapping Out Links and Intersections** on page 2-3.

The **coordinates** of the nodes are used in the layout of the map and the geometry of intersection approaches.

It is possible to **override** link distances with the **LANE** settings in Synchro. Link distances should match map coordinate distances within 20%.

The **minimum distance** between nodes for SimTraffic is 70ft (20m) for the model to function correctly. Shorter links may have problems drawing paths through intersections, lack space for crosswalks, and prevent lane changes. Consider consolidating several driveways into one for the purpose of simulation.

 When feasible, entry links should be long enough to store a complete cycle of traffic.

Entry (external) links should be about 300 feet long (90 m) to 600 feet (180 m). Very long entry links will increase seed time and the number of vehicles in the network. For high volume roads with long cycle lengths, make entry links approximately 600 feet (180 m). As noted in the Tip above, the entry link should be long enough to store one cycle of traffic when possible. **Figure 21-1** illustrates an internal link, an external link, an intersection node and a bend node.

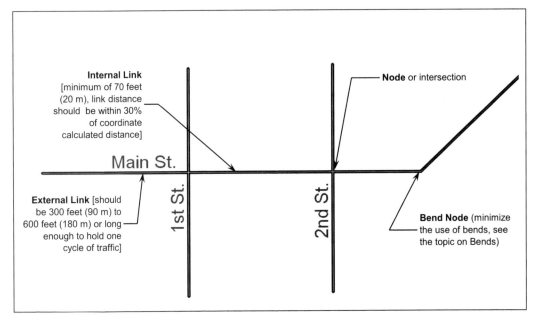

Figure 21-1   Map Data

Roundabouts

SimTraffic can model roundabouts. In the **MAP** view, create the roundabout location as any other intersection. When you select a 'Roundabout' as the Controller Type in the **SIGNING** settings, options will become available for the roundabout.

Node Settings

The **NODE** settings show editing for the following:

- Intersection ID or Node Number
- Zone, not used by SimTraffic
- Cycle Length, Control Type, Lock Timings and Optimize buttons
- Coordinates (X, Y, Z)
- Description Note box

To activate the **NODE** settings in Synchro, double click on an intersection. Or select a group of intersections and pressing [Enter] can activate the **NODE** settings when one or more intersections are selected.

To create an overpass, assign a higher Z coordinate elevation to the nodes of the overpass link.

Control Type determines if the intersection is unsignalized (traditional or roundabout), pre-timed, actuated-uncoordinated, or actuated in coordination.

Cycle Length is used to set the background cycle length.

Offset settings determine the offset used for pre-timed and coordinated signals.

Reference Phase is used to determine the coordinated phase for pre-timed and actuated-coordinated signals. During timing transitions, only pre-timed signals will rest on the reference phase during the transition.

The **Yield Point** affects when the Coordinated Phases will "yield" to side street phases. This setting affects whether there is a single yield point for all phases or multiple yield points. See page 4-15 for a more thorough discussion.

Flexible Yield Points allow the signal to yield any time between the single point and the phases scheduled start time. Flexible Yield Points can be useful with low volume side streets; the side streets have a wider range of time to yield to the signal.

Using a Single Point in conjunction with Inhibit Max makes the most time available for side street phases. By Phase can be helpful when providing coordination to side street phases. It is sometimes possible for the phase to be skipped because its yield time occurs before the platooned traffic arrives.

With low volumes of traffic, using a **Flexible Yield Point** can appear to look similar to a fully actuated signal. This is especially true when using **Coordinated Minimum Recall** for the main street phases.

Sign Control is used by unsignalized intersections to determine the sign control. With SimTraffic, it is possible to model two-way, three-way, and all-way stop or yield control intersections.

Lane Settings Data

For detailed information, see the chapter on the **LANE** settings on page 5-13-1.

Lanes and Sharing determines the number of lanes and the channelization of each lane. The diagrams in Synchro illustrate the use. Remember that shared lanes always count as through lanes (or left lanes at a T).

To code a LR lane at a street transitioning from two-way to one-way, code the lane as LTR with no through traffic. SimTraffic will assume a LR lane.

Street Names can be used to identify streets on the map.

Link Distance can be used to override the link distance taken from the map. The link distance is the distance from center point to center point. Link distances must match map coordinate distances within 20%. The **minimum distance** between nodes for SimTraffic is 70ft (20m). Otherwise, there is insufficient distance between intersections for the model to function correctly.

The link's internal distance is calculated by SimTraffic based on the number of lanes on the cross street, the angle between streets, and the setback distance for the pedestrian crosswalk.

Link Speed is used to control the driver speed on the link. The link speed is the 50th percentile speed for free flowing vehicles. Vehicles may not be able to attain the link speed due to traffic control devices, vehicles ahead, or to slow for turns. The actual speeds will be a range of speeds based on the driver type. The Driver Options of SimTraffic contains a speed factor for each driver type. The speed factors range from 0.75 to 1.27 and are multiplied by the link speed to determine each vehicle's maximum speed.

Travel Time is not used by SimTraffic. It is only used by Synchro.

Ideal Saturated Flow will affect the Headway Factor which will influence headways and Saturated Flow Rates.

Lane Width is used for drawing lanes. It will also change the Headway Factor which will influence headways and simulated flow rates.

Grade will affect the **Headway Factor** which will influence headways and Saturated Flow Rates.

Area Type will affect the Headway Factor which will influence the headways and Saturated Flow Rates.

Storage Length is used to determine whether a storage bay exists and its length. A zero value indicates no bay and the turning lanes are considered travel lanes. Make sure that there is one or more non-storage travel lanes.

Any number of lanes can be in the storage bay including Through lanes. It is also possible to have both storage and travel turning lanes.

 Code storage bays to reduce lane changes.

Storage Lanes are the number of lanes in the right or left storage bay. This value only appears when the storage length is greater than 0. By default the number of storage lanes is equal to the number of turning lanes.

This field can be overridden so that some of the turning lanes are full travel lanes, or so that some of the through lanes can be storage lanes.

The **Lane Utilization Factor**, **Right and Left Turn Factors**, and **Saturated Flows** are not used by SimTraffic. These are Synchro only calculations.

Right Turn on Red determines if right turn on red is allowed. Right turns may also be allowed for overlapping or free style right turns.

Saturated Flow Rate (RTOR) is not used by SimTraffic.

Channelized Right Turns

Right Turn Channelized is active for the rightmost movement. The choices are **None**, **Yield**, **Free**, **Stop** and **Signal**. If this value is changed, it will also be updated for unsignalized analysis.

Curb Radius controls the graphics and layout in SimTraffic. It is measured from center point to curb.

Add Lanes controls how many add lanes are for the right turn movement. Set to zero (0) for a yield or merge. Set to the number of turning lanes for add lanes.

Right turn islands can be used in conjunction with shared right/through lanes, with exclusive lanes or with right turn storage bays. For most situations, a right-turn lane with a storage bay works better than a shared lane. This creates a bigger right island and also gives more space for right turns to bypass stopped through vehicles.

If right channelization is not used, SimTraffic will automatically create add lanes for right turns; if:

- There are enough downstream lanes, and
- There is enough distance for required lane changes.

Slip Lanes for Roundabouts

To code a right turn slip lane at a roundabout for SimTraffic, set the **Right Turn Channelized** to Stop, Yield, or Free. SimTraffic will add additional right turn lane(s) to the roundabout, outside of the **Outside Radius**. The width of the slip lane is determined by the width of the incoming right turn lane group.

The below Input Fields have the following affect:

- **Right Turn Channelized** = **Yield** or **Stop**: Vehicles in slip lane will yield at end of slip lane if there is a merge.
- **Right Turn Channelized** = **Free**: Vehicles in slip lane will merge at end of slip lane if there is a merge.
- **Right Turn Channelized** = **None**: No slip lane
- **Lanes and Sharing**: Controls number of lanes in right turn slip lane, and number of lanes to enter main circle.
- **Curb Radius** (in the **SIGNING** settings): Has no affect; slip lane controlled by Outside Radius.
- **Add Lanes**: Slip lane will add lane(s), provided enough lanes exist downstream.

With a small circle or tight angle between links, the slip lanes will directly connect. With a larger circle or angle, the slip lanes will be additional lanes on the outside of the roundabout with additional radius.

Alternate Method

It is also possible to create a slip lane by coding a multilane roundabout with a Two-Lane Exit (see **Roundabout Analysis**, page 21-9). To get a direct slip lane it is necessary to code two lane exits at both the entry and the exit links. This method works best for creating a slip lane in all directions.

Combining a slip lane with a Two Lane Exit may give a three-lane exit or other strange results. It is usually best to use one or the other.

Volume Settings Data

For detailed information, see the chapter on the **VOLUME** settings on page 6-1.

Traffic volume is used to determine the vehicles entering at external links, the proportion of vehicles turning and also for traffic sinks and sources.

The actual volumes modeled may be adjusted for Peak Hour factor, Growth factor, and/or percentile scaling. The volume adjustments can be set with **Options→Intervals and Volumes** command in SimTraffic.

If traffic between intersections is not balanced, SimTraffic will assume a traffic source or sink. Traffic will appear mid-block or exit mid-block for a source or sink respectively.

It is also possible to use volume data from a **data file** (see the topic on Database Access, page 22-6). In this case the traffic volume in the Synchro (*.syn) file may be ignored.

Conflicting Pedestrians are used to determine the number of pedestrians crossing the roadway. Peds conflicting with a right turn will appear on the link to the right. Peds conflicting with a left turn at a T-intersection will appear on the link to the left. If pedestrian calls are coded for the signal phase, the number of pedestrians will be the maximum of the coded values. See the topic on Coding Pedestrians, page 21-14.

Peak Hour Factor (PHF) can be used to adjust volume data. By default, volumes are not adjusted by PHF. This is set with the volume adjustments in the **Options→Intervals-and-Volumes** command.

Growth Factor can be used to adjust volume data. By default, volumes are adjusted by growth. This is set with the volume adjustments in the **Options→Intervals-and-Volumes** command.

Heavy Vehicles data is used by SimTraffic. The heavy vehicle fleet volume for each movement is equal to the volume multiplied by the Heavy Vehicle percentage. The light vehicle fleet volume is equal to the remaining volume. Heavy Vehicle fleet traffic will be assigned one of the 4 truck types or a bus type. The Light Vehicle fleet traffic will be assigned to a car or carpool vehicle type. The composition of each vehicle fleet can be adjusted with the **Options→Vehicle-Parameters** command. If your network has a mixture of different Heavy Vehicle percentages, SimTraffic may create additional sources or sinks to balance traffic for each vehicle fleet.

Bus Blockages will affect the Headway Factor, which will influence the headways and Saturated Flow Rates. Busses are not explicitly modeled by SimTraffic.

Adjacent Parking Lane and **Parking Maneuvers** will affect the Headway Factor, which will influence the headways and Saturated Flow Rates.

Traffic From Mid-Block can be used to create a traffic source from mid-block. SimTraffic will also assume a mid-block traffic source if necessary to balance traffic flows. The mid-block traffic can be used to create a source larger than needed for balancing and in some cases create a sink as well.

Link OD Volumes allows detailed control over the origin and destination of two adjacent intersections. Volume Balancing can be used to reduce or eliminate certain turn combinations. The most common use is to prevent vehicles from turning left twice at a freeway or wide median arterial.

The **LINK ORIGIN-DESTINATION VOLUMES** setting displays **Movement Weighting Factors** that control how volume is allocated between input and output volumes.

The **Adjusted Flow**, **Traffic in Shared Lane** and **Lane Group Flow** settings are not used by SimTraffic, only Synchro.

Timing and Signing Settings Data

For detailed information, see the chapter on **TIMING** settings on page 7-1.

Phase Templates (**Options→Phase Templates**) allow phase numbers to be set automatically.

Turn Type is used to set the treatment for the left and right turn movements.

Protected and Permitted Phases are used to determine which movements are allowed during each phase.

Detector and **Switch Phases** determine which phases each lane group's detectors are connected to. Calls are placed to the Detector Phases by detectors in the lane group, regardless of the currently active phases. The Switch Phase is a secondary phase that extends the set phase when it is green but does not place a call.

Leading Detector is the distance from the leading edge of the first detector to the stop bar. This value can be ignored for pre-timed intersections and unsignalized intersections.

Trailing Detector is the distance from the trailing edge of the last extension detector to the stop bar.

The Leading and Trailing Detector will be set automatically based on the settings in the **DETECTOR** settings (see page 10-1).

Total Split is used to determine the maximum green time.

It is also possible to load split, cycle length, and lagging information from a data file. Refer to **Database Access** for more information (page 22-6).

Lost Time Adjustment is not used by SimTraffic. The **Total Lost Time** in SimTraffic is dependant on driver reaction time, length of yellow time, yellow deceleration rates, intersection width, and approach speeds.

Signing Settings Data

For unsignalized intersections, **Median Width**, **TWLTL Median** and **Right Turn Channelized** are only used in Synchro to perform the HCM unsignalized two-stage gap analysis. SimTraffic does not model two-stage gap acceptance at this time. The Median Width will be shown in SimTraffic.

Roundabout Analysis

SimTraffic will now model modern roundabouts. The inputs are set in Synchro. The following settings are used.

Control Type should be set to Roundabout.

Inside Radius, **Outside Radius** controls the size of the roundabout. 900' (100m) is the maximum.

# of Lanes is where to set the number of internal lanes within the roundabout, up to 4 lanes.

Speed Limit is the internal speed of vehicles within the roundabout.

Inside Color allows the user to change the inside color of the circle.

Two-Lane Exit controls how many of the internal lanes exit for the subject approach. If you have a multi-lane roundabout and this is set to Yes, two outer-most lanes in the circle will exit as illustrated in **Figure 21-2**. Note the differences in the intersection paths in this two lane roundabout.

If you have a roundabout with a slip ramp, see the topic **Slip Lanes** for Roundabouts (page 5-7).

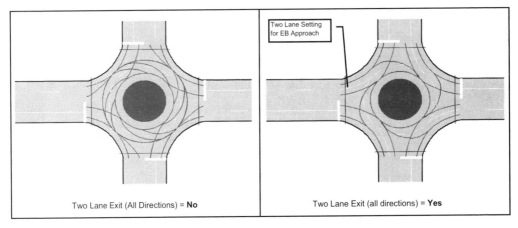

Two Lane Setting
for EB Approach

Two Lane Exit (All Directions) = **No**   Two Lane Exit (all directions) = **Yes**

Figure 21-2   Two Lane Exit Coding

Phasing Settings Data

For detailed information, see the chapter on the **PHASING** settings on page 8-1.

The **Ring and Barrier Designer** allows up to 32 phases to be entered in one of 64 fields. This allows for the modeling of complex phasing strategies. Phase numbers are entered into the appropriate barrier, ring and position (BRP) fields in the four rings and four barriers.

Minimum Initial is used with actuated intersections to determine the minimum initial green time. This is used as the minimum green time.

Minimum Split is not used by SimTraffic.

Maximum Split is used to determine the maximum green time.

Yellow and All Red are used to determine the yellow and all-red times.

Lead/Lag is used to determine the phase order.

Allow Lead/Lag Optimize? is not used by SimTraffic.

Vehicle Extension is used with actuated phases. A vehicle passing over a detector will extend the gap counter by the amount of time specified by the Vehicle Extension time.

Minimum Gap is used with actuated phases for volume-density operation. After Time Before Reduce the gap time is reduced from Vehicle Extension to the Minimum gap. After Time Before Reduce and Time To Reduce, the Minimum Gap time is used as the gap time.

Time Before Reduce and **Time To Reduce** are used with actuated phases for volume-density operation. Set these values to 0 to disable volume-density operation. The Time Before Reduce and Time To Reduce start counting at the beginning of green.

Recall Mode determines the operation of each phase. With **Max Recall**, the phase will always show for its maximum time. With Max Recall, detector information and pedestrian calls are ignored; pedestrian phases will always be serviced. With **Minimum Recall**, the phase will always appear for its Minimum initial time, even with no calls. With **Pedestrian Recall,** the phase will always show a walk and flashing don't walk sequence, even with no pedestrian calls. With No Recall, the phase may be skipped if there are no calls.

C-Max termination is used with coordinated signals only. This option is available for phases selected as the reference phase in the Offset Settings. Phase shows for its maximum time starting at its scheduled start time.

C-Min termination is used with coordinated signals only. This option is available for phases selected as the reference phase in the Offset Settings. Phase shows for its minimum time starting at its scheduled start time.

Pedestrian Phase determines if the phase has a pedestrian phase. This field is used for both pre-timed and actuated intersections.

Walk Time and **Flash Don't Walk** determine the length of each pedestrian interval. Flash Don't Walk is not concurrent with yellow time.

Pedestrian Calls determines how many calls each phase receives. Conflicting pedestrians coded in the **VOLUME** settings will also call an actuated phase. The number of pedestrians is the maximum of conflicting pedestrians and pedestrian calls. Also see the topic on **Coding Pedestrians**, page 21-14.

For an actuated controller, **Dual Entry** affects which, if any, phase shows when there is no call or recall for a ring-barrier sequence.

Inhibit Max is used for Actuated-Coordinated signals only. When set to Yes, a non coordinated phase can show more than its maximum time when it starts early. When set to No, actuated phases will not extend past their maximum times.

Simulation Settings

For detailed information, see the chapter on the **SIMULATION** settings on page 9-1.

Taper Length is used to define the length of the taper at the end of the Storage Lane.

Lane Alignment is used to align the approach lanes with the downstream receiving lanes. See page 9-2 for details.

Enter Blocked Intersection setting controls simulation modeling gridlock avoidance. Checking the box will set this value to Yes. An unchecked box is No. See the topic on page 9-4 for details.

Median Width is the width of the median in simulation. Vehicles will not stop in the median during simulation, regardless of the median width.

Link Offset allows the link to be offset to the right or left of the center line.

Crosswalk Width controls the width of the crosswalk. See page 9-6 for details.

TWLTL Median is a visual setting. Vehicles will not use the TWLTL. Checking this box will show a TWLTL in the median.

Headway Factor is an adjustment to headways on a per movement basis. The Headway Factor can be used to calibrate the Saturated Flow Rates.

Turning Speed determines the speed limit while turning. This is adjusted by driver speed factor. The defaults are 15mph (25 k/h) for left turns and 9 mph (15 k/h) for right turns. For large intersections, these speeds can be increased for improved operation.

Mandatory Distance, **Positioning Distance**, **Mandatory 2 Lane Distance** and **Positioning 2 Lane Distance** controls the distance where vehicles make lane changes. See the discussion on **Lane Choice** and **Lane Changes** on page 24-8.

Detector Settings

For detailed information, see the chapter on the **DETECTOR** settings on page 10-1.

Number of Detectors is the number of longitudinal detector sets, not the number across the lanes. Detectors are numbered from the stop bar back; detector 1 is at the stop bar. You can enter up to 5 detectors.

Detector Phase is the primary phase for this detector. This is the same as the Detector Phase setting in the **TIMING** settings.

Switch Phase is a secondary phase that extends the phase when it is green. This setting does not call the listed phase, and does not call the Primary Detector phase when Switch phase is green.

Leading Detector and **Trailing Detector** are the same settings as in the **TIMING** settings (refer to page 7-8).

Detector Templates are predefined detector layouts. Number, position, size, type and times are included.

Add Template is activated by choosing **Options→Detector-Templates**, or by double clicking on the **DETECTORS** settings. The template allows the user to setup detector templates. There is one column for each detector.

Detector n Position is the distance from the stop bar to the trailing edge (closet to stop bar) of detector n.

Detector n Size is the size of the detector in the traveled direction.

Detector n Type can be **Calling**, **Extend** or **Cl+Ex**. Calling places a call when the phase is yellow or red. Extend places a call when the phase is green. Options for delay, queue, and extend detectors are set by using a non-zero time for these options.

All detectors are presence detectors, not passage.

Detector n Channel is not currently used by Synchro or SimTraffic, but can be imported and exported in UTDF data access. In the future there may be a conversion program to convert counts by detector number into counts by turning movement for use by Synchro.

Detector n Extend is the detector Extend time (e) for detector n. This is sometimes called "carry time". Entering a non-zero value will extend calls from this detector e seconds after the vehicle moves on.

Detector 1 Queue is where to enter the Queue time to have the stop bar detector act as a queue detector (the old name is "Type 3 detector"). A queue detector will extend the phase during the first q seconds, and then be disabled. Queue detection is useful for extending the phase during the queue clearance time, then later allowing the advance detectors to extend the phase.

Detector 1 Delay is the setting to have the stop bar detector act as a Delay detector. A delay detector will not place a call on red or yellow, until the vehicle has been there for at least d seconds.

Bends

Avoid using excessive bends in your street network. Bend nodes can cause performance problems, especially with SimTraffic and CORSIM. Short links can also cause reduced speeds and capacities within SimTraffic. It is not necessary to follow the exact alignment of the street along the centerline. Use curved links instead of bends where possible.

Coding Pedestrians

Pedestrians can be coded by setting **Conflicting Pedestrians** in the **VOLUME** settings or setting **Pedestrian Calls** in the **PHASING** settings.

Each link can have pedestrians crossing its end at an intersection. At a signalized intersection, each link has one or zero **Pedestrian Phases** associated with it. A single phase can be associated with pedestrians on more than one link. Pedestrians waiting to cross a link place calls to the Pedestrian phase. Pedestrian calls are allocated among all links having a phase as their Pedestrian Phase.

The number of pedestrians crossing the link is the maximum of the conflicting pedestrians and the pedestrian calls for the associated Pedestrian Phase. If the Pedestrian Phase serves more than one pedestrian movement, these pedestrian calls are divided among the links.

SimTraffic has smart logic to assign phases to links. This logic takes into account the use of Pedestrian-Only phases, and pedestrians at a T intersection.

Normally links are associated with the phase serving the through movement on the next link to the left, (see **Figure 21-3**). A link may also be associated with a turning movement, (see **Figure 21-4**). To have a phase be used as a Pedestrian Phase, set Pedestrian Phase to *Yes* in the **PHASING** settings. At a 5-leg intersection, SimTraffic will attempt to use a phase from the next left link, before using others (see **Figure 21-5**).

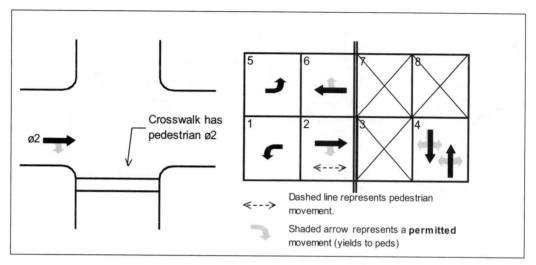

Figure 21-3   Pedestrian Phase Associated with Through Phase

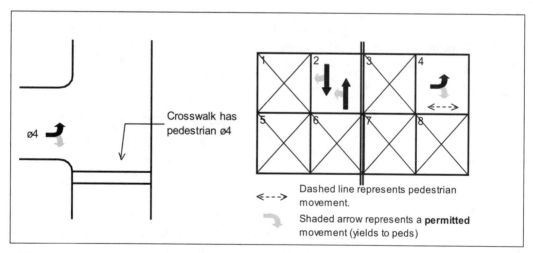

Figure 21-4   Pedestrian Phase Associated with Left Phase

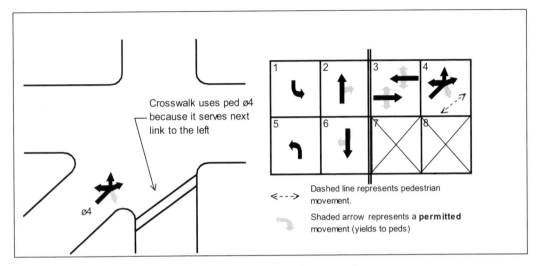

Figure 21-5   Pedestrian Phase at a Five-Leg Intersection

If a phase serves a conflicting, protected right turn movement, the link will try to use another phase. Set the right phase to Permitted to have pedestrians using that phase (see **Figure 21-6**). Set the right phase to protected to use an alternate phase. Similarly, set the left phase for permitted to have pedestrians move with a crossing left movement (see **Figure 21-7**).

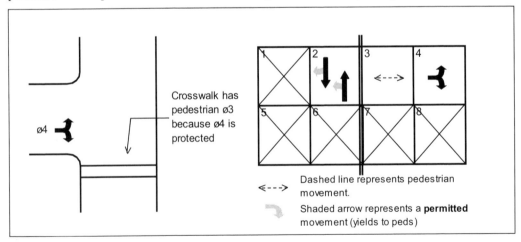

Figure 21-6   Protected Pedestrian Phase

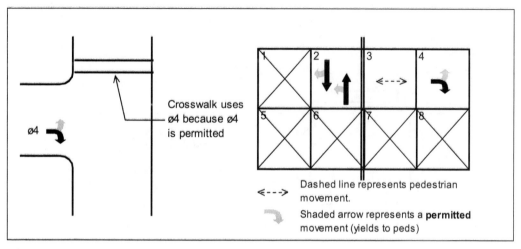

Crosswalk uses ø4 because ø4 is permitted

Dashed line represents pedestrian movement.

Shaded arrow represents a **permitted** movement (yields to peds)

Figure 21-7   Pedestrian Phase with Permitted Left Turn Phase

A pedestrian only phase will be assigned to all links not served by another phase. Setting permitted and protected turning movements can determine which links are assigned to the pedestrian phase. See **Figure 21-8** for use of pedestrian phase with crossing one-way streets.

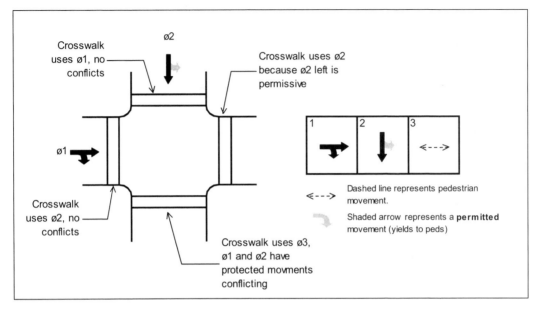

Figure 21-8   Pedestrian Phases for One Way Streets

Chapter 22 – SimTraffic Advanced Parameters

Advanced Parameters

This chapter describes the SimTraffic parameter pages. These parameters are used to allow access to the advanced features of SimTraffic. For many simulations, these parameters can be left at the defaults.

The **Intervals** page can be used to control the seeding time and recording time. The Intervals page can also control the adjustments to volumes and can be used to setup multiple intervals with changing volumes and timing plans.

The **Data Options** page is used to activate the data access feature. Data Access is used to simulate multiple timing plans or changing traffic volumes.

The **Vehicle Parameters** page can be used to view and change the vehicle characteristics. Normally the default parameters are acceptable. This page can be used to change the percentage of cars, trucks, and busses in the fleet. This page can also change the length and width of vehicles, the acceleration rate, and the maximum speed of the vehicle.

The **Driver Parameters** page can be used to view and change the driver characteristics. Normally the default parameters are acceptable. This page can be used to change the driver's reaction rates or to make the driver population more or less aggressive.

All of the parameters and SimTraffic settings are stored in a file with the same name as the Synchro (*.syn) file, but with the extension *.sim. It is possible to copy parameters from one file to another by copying the SIM file. The SIM file is a text file so it is possible to copy some of the parameters using a text editor with cut and paste between two SIM files.

Intervals and Volume Adjustments

The Intervals page controls the length of time recorded, the length of seed time, and volume adjustments. If data files are used, the intervals page is also used to control the timing plan and volume used for each time period. The Interval Parameters page is shown in **Figure 22-1**.

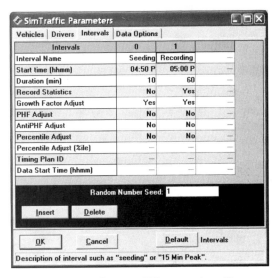

Intervals	0	1	
Interval Name	Seeding	Recording	---
Start time (hhmm)	04:50 P	05:00 P	---
Duration (min)	10	60	---
Record Statistics	No	Yes	---
Growth Factor Adjust	Yes	Yes	---
PHF Adjust	No	No	---
AntiPHF Adjust	No	No	---
Percentile Adjust	No	No	---
Percentile Adjust (%ile)	---	---	---
Timing Plan ID	---	---	---
Data Start Time (hhmm)	---	---	---

Random Number Seed: 1

Insert   Delete

OK   Cancel   Default Intervals

Description of interval such as "seeding" or "15 Min Peak".

Figure 22-1   Interval Parameters Page

Choose the **Options→Intervals-and-Volumes** command to activate the Intervals page.

Intervals

Each column represents an interval. Normally a simulation has a "seed" interval followed by one or more recorded intervals.

The purpose of the **Seed Interval** is to fill the network with traffic. The seed interval should be long enough for a vehicle to traverse the entire network with stop time included.

The **Recorded Interval(s)** follow the seed interval and these intervals are recorded for animation, reports, and static graphics.

For some applications, it may be necessary to have more than one recorded interval. It is possible to have a congested peak interval of, for example, 15 minutes, followed by an off-peak interval to see how quickly the network recovers from congestion.

Multiple intervals can also be used to simulate multiple timing plans and the transition between timing plans.

Each interval has a **Duration** in minutes.

Each duration has a **Start Time** expressed in the format hh:mm. All time periods must be contiguous.

Record Statistics indicates whether statistics and vehicle paths are recorded for each interval. Set this field yes for all intervals after the seeding interval(s). Once recording starts, it remains on for the rest of the simulation.

Setting the Seed Time

The seeding time should be long enough for a vehicle to traverse the entire network between the two most distant points including all stops. The seeding time should also be longer than the maximum cycle length used in the network. After the seeding time, the number of vehicles entering the network per minute should be about the same as the number of vehicles exiting the network per minute. Look at the Vehicle Counts in the Recording Status settings during seeding and recording to see how many vehicles are entering and exiting the network.

If one or more movements are above capacity, the number of entering vehicles will always exceed the number of exiting vehicles, and equilibrium will not be achieved. In this case, the seed time should be long enough so that the number of exiting vehicles per minute stabilizes at a fixed value.

Volume Adjustments

The volumes simulated come from the traffic volumes in the SYN file or from an external data file (refer to page 22-6). These volumes can be adjusted by a number of factors as detailed below.

Set **Growth Factor Adjust** to adjust for growth factors. The growth factors are input in Synchro's Volume settings and are 100% by default.

Set **PHF Adjust** to adjust for peak hour factors. Volumes are divided by the PHF. The PHF are input in Synchro's **Volume** settings and are 0.92 by default. The PHF is the ratio a volume for the entire hour divided by the peak 15 minute period times 4. A common use of PHF Adjust is to model 15 minutes of peaking traffic followed by an interval of off peak traffic.

Set **Anti-PHF Adjust** to **unadjust** for peak hour factors. The PHF increases the hourly count for the peak 15 minute period. The volume for the remaining 45 minutes will thus be decreased from the hourly rate. Volumes are adjusted by the following formula:

$v' = v * (1 - (1/PHF- 1)/3)) =$ volume adjusted for anti phf

> v = unadjusted volume

> PHF = peak hour factor

Set **Percentile Adjust** to create a pulse of traffic based on Poisson arrivals. The percentile adjust can be used to model a 95th percentile queue or to see how a network fares with peaking traffic conditions.

$SD = SquareRoot(v / 60 * d) * 60 / d =$ standard deviation in volume

> v = unadjusted volume

> d = interval duration in minutes

$v' = v + SD * Z =$ adjusted volume

> $Z = Z$ Factor dependant on percentile, some samples are shown below

Table 22-1   Z Factor Table

Percentile	Z
10	-1.28
30	-0.52
50	0
70	0.52
90	1.28
95	1.64
99	2.33

For example, a 5-minute interval has a 95th percentile adjustment and a volume of 300 vph. The percentile adjusted volume will become 384 vph.

$SD = Sqrt(300 / 60 * 5) * 60 / 5 = 60$ vph

$v' = 300 + 60 * 1.64 = 384$ vph

The percentile adjustment in SimTraffic is intended to be used for a short period of time. The 95th adjusted volume would not be observed for the entire hour or even 15 minutes, but maybe for 2 or 3 minutes. It is a quick way to get a high traffic loading without performing a 60-minute simulation. If you want to use the percentile adjustments, the following intervals are recommended:

Interval 0, Seeding: Duration long enough for vehicle to traverse from one side of the network to another, including stops.

Interval 1, Recording: Duration is closest to cycle length, volume is percentile adjusted 95th.

Interval 2, Recording and Recovery: Duration 15 minutes, no volume adjustment.

Database Parameters

The last two rows of the Intervals page are used in conjunction with external data files. SimTraffic can read a Timing.csv and Volume.csv file.

Timing Plan ID is used to specify a timing plan from a timing data file. The timing data file may contain more than one set of timing plans and the timing plan ID specifies which one to use. It is possible to simulate multiple timing plans by using a different Timing Plan ID for each interval. The signals will transition between timing plans at the beginning of an interval with a new timing plan.

Data Start Time is used to identify which volume counts to load from a volume data file. A volume data file may contain multiple volume counts, each marked with a different set of dates, times, and intersection ID numbers. It is possible to load a different set of volume counts for each interval by specifying the data time of the volume count. This time does not need to match the start time listed above.

For details on setting up the database access files, see the topic on **Database Access** on page 22-6

Random Number Seed

SimTraffic uses random numbers to determine when new vehicles and pedestrians enter the network and to choose vehicle paths through the network. The random number seed can be used to generate the same sequence of vehicle entries or to create a new sequence each time.

If **Random Number Seed** is **zero (0)**, SimTraffic will choose a random number seed at random. All simulations with random number seed 0 should be unique from each other.

If the random number seed is non-zero, SimTraffic will use this number as a seed. All simulations with the same file and the same seed will produce the same simulation sequence. By default the seed is set to **one (1)**. The non-zero seed is useful so that simulation results are repeatable.

Using a common non-zero seed cannot be used to generate identical traffic streams for two similar files with different signal timing. The vehicle paths are randomly determined as vehicles traverse the network. If the travel time of vehicles is changed between files, the application of random numbers is changed and the vehicle generation sequence will be changed.

Multiple Runs

For serious simulation applications, it is recommended that multiple runs be performed with different random number seeds. The **Record-Multiple Runs** button or [Ctrl]+[M] will perform and record a simulation on multiple runs. A dialog will appear allowing the user to select the number of runs to simulate and record and the starting random number seed. The random number seed will be incrementally increased by one for the simulated runs. For instance, 1, 2, 3, 4 and 5 if you are starting from 1 with 5 runs.

SimTraffic will combine MOEs from multiple simulation runs. It is also possible to save the reports in text format and import the text reports into a spreadsheet program.

Database Access

The database access feature allows volume counts and timing plans to be read from an external data file. The database feature is useful to model multiple intervals with more than one timing plan or volume count.

The data files are Volume and Timing style comma separated files (CSV). Refer to Chapter 1.

The **Data Options** page (**Figure 22-2**) can be accessed with the **Options→Database-Access** command.

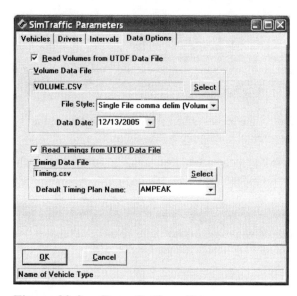

Figure 22-2   Data Options Page

Volume Data Options

To read volume counts from a data file, check the **Read Volumes from UTDF Data File** box. This feature is most useful when two or more counts will be simulated in two or more intervals.

Next, select a Volume **File Style**. This option specifies whether the data format. Volume data can be stored in a single file (Volume.CSV), multiple files (TMC###.VOL) one file per date (Vyymmdd.CSV).

Next, select a **Filename** or **File Directory** depending on the file style using the [Select] button.

If the data file(s) contain counts from multiple dates, select the **Data Date**. On the interval page, select a **Data Start Time** for each count.

The volume counts can either be 15 minute or 60 minute counts. The top of the volume file should identify the duration of the counts. If not specified, SimTraffic will assume 15 minute counts.

It is possible to read TMC style Volume count files. The filename should be in the format TMC###.VOL, where ### is the intersections' node numbers.

Timing Data Options

To read timing plans from a data file, check the **Read Timings from UTDF Data File** box. This feature is most useful when two or more timing plans will be simulated in two or more intervals. This feature can be used to model transitions between timing plans.

Next select a **data filename** for the timing plans using the [Select] button. All the timing plans must be in the same data file.

Select a **Default Timing Plan Name**. This plan name is used when a **Timing Plan ID** (on the **Intervals** tab) is not specified for one or more intervals.

The timing data file should contain one or more complete timing plans for all intersections. Each row contains a single timing plan for a single intersection. An intersection ID or node number, and a **PLANID** identify each timing plan.

The timing data file contains splits, cycle lengths, offsets, and lagging information. These timing inputs are considered variable and can be changed with time-of-day timing plans. All other timing information is considered fixed and cannot vary between intervals.

Vehicle Parameters

The **Vehicle Parameters** page can be accessed with the **Options→Vehicle-Parameters** command.

The **Vehicle Parameters** page can be used to view and change the vehicle characteristics. Normally the default parameters are acceptable. This page can be used to change the percentage of cars, trucks, and busses in the fleet. This page can also change the length and width of vehicles, the acceleration rate, and the maximum speed of the vehicle.

The **Vehicle Options** page is illustrated in **Figure 22-3**.

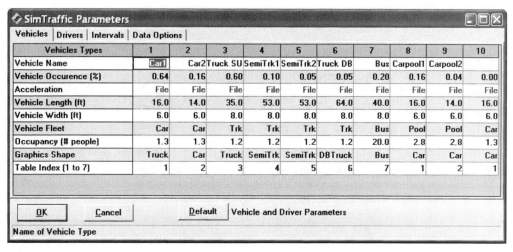

Vehicles Types	1	2	3	4	5	6	7	8	9	10
Vehicle Name	Car1	Car2	Truck SU	SemiTrk1	SemiTrk2	Truck DB	Bus	Carpool1	Carpool2	
Vehicle Occurence (%)	0.64	0.16	0.60	0.10	0.05	0.05	0.20	0.16	0.04	0.00
Acceleration	File	File	File	File	File	File	File	File	File	File
Vehicle Length (ft)	16.0	14.0	35.0	53.0	53.0	64.0	40.0	16.0	14.0	16.0
Vehicle Width (ft)	6.0	6.0	8.0	8.0	8.0	8.0	8.0	6.0	6.0	6.0
Vehicle Fleet	Car	Car	Trk	Trk	Trk	Trk	Bus	Pool	Pool	Car
Occupancy (# people)	1.3	1.3	1.2	1.2	1.2	1.2	20.0	2.8	2.8	1.3
Graphics Shape	Truck	Car	Truck	SemiTrk	SemiTrk	DBTruck	Bus	Car	Car	Car
Table Index (1 to 7)	1	2	3	4	5	6	7	1	2	1

Figure 22-3   Vehicle Options Page

Vehicle Name is used to identify the vehicle type.

Vehicle Occurrence defines what percentage of the vehicle fleet is made up of this vehicle type. When vehicles are created, they are randomly assigned a vehicle type based on the Vehicle Occurrence of each type. This value can be used to change the percentage of trucks, busses, high performance cars, or low performance cars.

New vehicles are randomly assigned a vehicle type based on each vehicles occurrence. New cars are assigned a Car or Carpool vehicle. New heavy vehicles are assigned a Truck or Bus vehicle.

The sum of car types will add up to 1.0. The sum of the heavy vehicle types will also add to 1.0.

 The Heavy Vehicles percentage setting in Synchro determines the proportion of Heavy Vehicles for each link. The Vehicle Occurrence setting adjusts the proportion of vehicles within the Non-Heavy fleets (cars and Car-pools) and the Heavy fleets (trucks and busses).

Acceleration is used to determine the acceleration available at a given speed. The Acceleration is listed in an accels.csv file in the program installation directory. For Version 7, these acceleraltion rates were taken from TSIS version 5, based on FHWA research. This table contains the maximum acceleration in ft/s^2. Each row is a speed in ft/s.

The speed limit for a link is determined by the link speed (page 5-4) in conjunction with the driver's speed factor (see the next section).

Vehicle Length is used to determine the length of each vehicle type. This value is used both for simulation and for graphics. The length is the bumper to bumper length of a vehicle. The SimTraffic model assumes a distance between stopped vehicles of 5 feet (1.5m).

Vehicle Width is used for the width of the vehicle. This value is used for graphics only and has no affect on the simulation model.

Vehicle Fleet is used to assign a vehicle type to a fleet. The fleet can be car, bus, truck, or car pool. The fleet is used to determine which set of fuel and emissions parameters to use for this vehicle. Heavy Vehicles are assigned a vehicle in the Truck or Bus Fleet. Light Vehicles are assigned a vehicle in the car or carpool fleet.

Occupancy is the number of people per vehicle. SimTraffic does not currently use this value but is here for future use.

Graphics Shape is used in with a cars.dat file found in the installation directory. The shapes are Car, Truck, SemiTrk, DBTruck and Bus.

The **Table Index** is used in conjunction with the acceleration, fuel, and emissions tables. These tables are located in csv format in the installation directory. This allows carpools and cars to use the same parameters.

The **Default** button will reload the default parameters for all the vehicles. Defaults are loaded file the file defaults.sim. If you want to setup a standard parameters for your agency, save the file with these settings to DEFAULTS.SIM in the same directory as SIMTRAFFIC.EXE

Driver Parameters

The **Driver Parameters** page can be accessed with the **Options→Driver-Parameters** command.

The **Driver Parameters** page can be used to view and change the driver characteristics. Normally the default parameters are acceptable. This page can be used to change the driver's reaction rates or to make the driver population more or less aggressive.

When vehicles are created, they are randomly assigned a driver type between 1 and 10. Each driver type represents 10% of the driving population with driver type 1 being the most conservative and driver type 10 being the most aggressive.

The **Driver Parameters** page is illustrated in **Figure 22-4**.

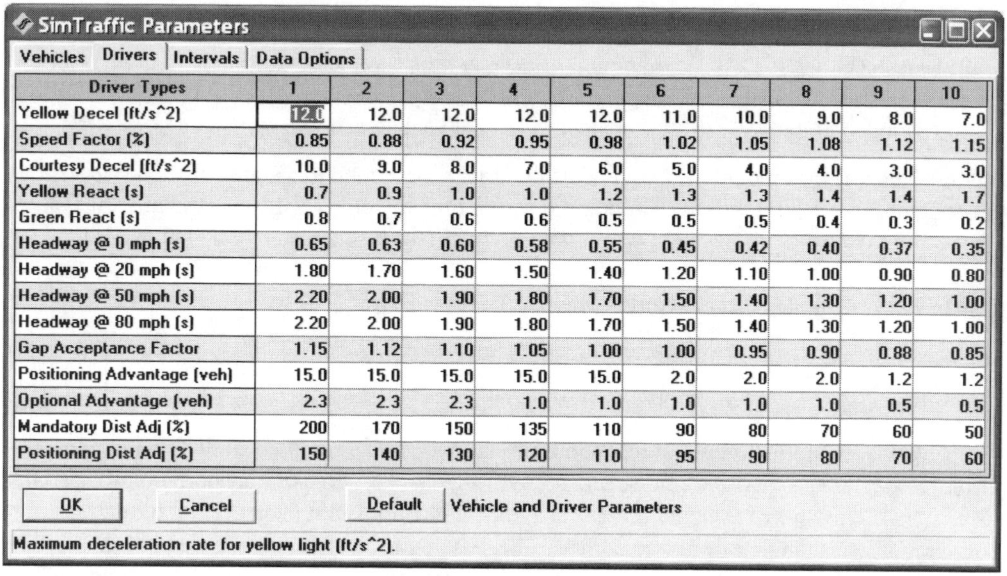

Driver Types	1	2	3	4	5	6	7	8	9	10
Yellow Decel (ft/s^2)	12.0	12.0	12.0	12.0	12.0	11.0	10.0	9.0	8.0	7.0
Speed Factor (%)	0.85	0.88	0.92	0.95	0.98	1.02	1.05	1.08	1.12	1.15
Courtesy Decel (ft/s^2)	10.0	9.0	8.0	7.0	6.0	5.0	4.0	4.0	3.0	3.0
Yellow React (s)	0.7	0.9	1.0	1.0	1.2	1.3	1.3	1.4	1.4	1.7
Green React (s)	0.8	0.7	0.6	0.6	0.5	0.5	0.5	0.4	0.3	0.2
Headway @ 0 mph (s)	0.65	0.63	0.60	0.58	0.55	0.45	0.42	0.40	0.37	0.35
Headway @ 20 mph (s)	1.80	1.70	1.60	1.50	1.40	1.20	1.10	1.00	0.90	0.80
Headway @ 50 mph (s)	2.20	2.00	1.90	1.80	1.70	1.50	1.40	1.30	1.20	1.00
Headway @ 80 mph (s)	2.20	2.00	1.90	1.80	1.70	1.50	1.40	1.30	1.20	1.00
Gap Acceptance Factor	1.15	1.12	1.10	1.05	1.00	1.00	0.95	0.90	0.88	0.85
Positioning Advantage (veh)	15.0	15.0	15.0	15.0	15.0	2.0	2.0	2.0	1.2	1.2
Optional Advantage (veh)	2.3	2.3	2.3	1.0	1.0	1.0	1.0	1.0	0.5	0.5
Mandatory Dist Adj (%)	200	170	150	135	110	90	80	70	60	50
Positioning Dist Adj (%)	150	140	130	120	110	95	90	80	70	60

Figure 22-4 Driver Parameters Page

Yellow Decel is the maximum deceleration rate a driver is willing to use when faced with a yellow light. If the driver is unable to stop using the Yellow Deceleration Rate, they will continue, even if it means entering the intersection on red. By default the Yellow Deceleration Rate varies between 12 ft/s^2 and 7 ft/s^2 (3.6m/s^2 to 2.1m/s^2). To make the drivers' less prone to running red lights, increase the yellow deceleration. The Yellow Decel rates by driver type are listed in **Table 22-2**.

Table 22-2 Yellow Decel Rates by Driver Type

Driver Type	1	2	3	4	5	6	7	8	9	10
Yellow Decel (ft/s^2)	12	12	12	12	12	11	19	9	8	7
Yellow Decel (m/s^2)	3.6	3.6	3.6	3.6	3.6	3.3	3.0	2.7	2.4	2.1

The **Speed Factor** is multiplied by the link speed to determine the maximum speed for this driver. If the link speed is 50ft/s and the speed factor is 1.1, this driver will attempt to maintain a speed of 55ft/s. By default the Speed Factors vary between 0.85 and 1.15. These numbers can be increased or reduced to change the range of speeds.

This is a change in version 7, the speed factor range in version 6 and earlier was 0.75 to 1.27.

Courtesy Decel rate (CDR) is the amount of deceleration a vehicle will accept in order to allow an ahead vehicle in an adjacent lane to make a mandatory lane change. A driver with a CDR of 11 ft/s^2 is much more likely to stop or slow to let in a vehicle than one with a CDR of 4 ft/s^2.

Yellow React is the amount of time it takes the driver to respond to a signal changing to yellow. More aggressive drivers will have a longer reaction time to yellow lights. By default, this value ranges from 0.7 to 1.7 s. The Yellow React times by driver type are shown in **Table 22-3**.

Table 22-3   Yellow Reaction Rates by Driver Type

Driver Type	1	2	3	4	5	6	7	8	9	10
Yellow React (s)	0.7	0.7	1.0	1.0	1.2	1.3	1.3	1.4	1.4	1.7

The yellow deceleration rates and reaction times are based on a research study "Evaluation of Driver Behavior at Signalized Intersections", Wortman and Matthias, Transportation Research Record 904. This study measured driver behaviors at locations in Arizona. This study found deceleration rates ranging from 5 to 24 ft/s^2. The maximum deceleration allowed in SimTraffic's car following model is 12 ft/s^2. This study found reaction times ranging from 0.5 seconds to 3 seconds. The SimTraffic reaction times do not use this full range because the longer reaction times are not necessarily the same drivers as the lower deceleration rates.

Older versions of SimTraffic used lower deceleration rates and shorter reaction times as noted above. The higher deceleration parameters will tend to reduce red light running for higher speed approaches and for vehicles slowing into a turn. However, the longer reaction times may increase red light running at low speed approaches. These changes are consistent with research that shows vehicles accept higher rates of deceleration on high-speed approaches.

Users are encouraged to perform studies of local conditions to determine the behavior of local drivers. An active red light enforcement program may lower the yellow reaction times and increase the yellow deceleration rate. Of most interest is driver type 10, the most aggressive, because they will be most likely to run lights and cause startup delays to the next movement. In the field, these drivers are the most likely to cause accidents.

Green React is the amount of time it takes the driver to respond to a signal changing to green. More aggressive drivers will have a shorter reaction time to green lights. By default, this value ranges from 0.8 to 0.2 s.

Headways are the amount of time between vehicles drivers try to maintain. When traveling at 30 ft/s a vehicle with a 1-second headway will try to maintain 30ft between it and the leading vehicle. SimTraffic accepts headway values for headways at 0 mph, 30 mph, 50 mph and 80 mph (0, 50, 80, and 130 km/h). Interpolation is used to determine headways at other speeds. See **Calibrating Speeds and Headways** on page 22-15 for further details. Note that headways can be adjusted for individual movements using the headway factor in the **SIMULATION** settings of Synchro.

Gap Acceptance Factor is an adjustment to the approach gap times. This is the gap vehicles will accept at unsignalized intersections, for permitted left turns, and for right turns on red. By default, these values range from 1.15 to 0.85. The higher values represent more conservative drivers.

Drivers will make **Positioning Lane** changes to be in the correct lane for future turns. A driver will defer making a Positioning Lane change when there is **Positioning Advantage** more vehicles ahead in the target lane than the current lane. Higher Values are associated with more conservative drivers and cause drivers to line up in the correct lane. Lower Values are associated with aggressive drivers and cause drivers to avoid lining up in the correct lane until reaching the mandatory lane change point. The range of values is 0.5 to 20 vehicles. If all vehicles ahead are moving, they count as a fraction of a vehicle depending on the speed of the slowest vehicle ahead.

Drivers will make desired lane changes to get in a lane with fewer vehicles ahead. A driver will make a desired lane change when there is **Optional Advantage** less vehicles ahead in the target lane than the current lane. Higher values are associated with more conservative drivers and cause drivers to have unbalanced lane use. Lower Values are associated with aggressive drivers and cause drivers to use lanes evenly. The range of values is 0.5 to 20 vehicles. If all vehicles ahead are moving, they count as a fraction of a vehicle depending on the speed of the slowest vehicle ahead.

Mandatory Distance Adjustment is the factor by which the mandatory lane change distances are multiplied. The default values are shown in **Table 22-4**

Table 22-4   Default Mandatory Distance Adjustment Factors

Driver Type	1	2	3	4	5	6	7	8	9	10
MLCD Factor (%)	200	170	150	135	110	90	80	70	60	50

The **Positioning Distance Adjustment** is used to multiple the **Positioning Distance** (see page 9-8) values for each driver type. The default values are listed in **Table 22-5**

Table 22-5   Default Positioning Distance Adjustment Factors

Driver Type	1	2	3	4	5	6	7	8	9	10
PDA Factor (%)	150	140	130	120	110	95	90	80	70	60

For additional details, see the discussion in the topic **Lane Choice and Lane Changes** (page 24-8).

The **Default** button will reload the default parameters for all the drivers. Defaults are loaded from the file defaults.sim. If you want to setup standard parameters for your agency, save the file with your default settings to DEFAULTS.SIM. Save this in the same directory as SIMTRAFFIC.EXE.

Vehicles Entering Intersection at the Beginning of the Red Interval

Some vehicles will enter the intersection into the yellow interval and even the red interval.

When the signal turns yellow, each vehicle decides to stop based on their yellow reaction time and the deceleration required to make a stop. In some cases, a vehicle may enter the intersection up to 7 seconds after the beginning of yellow depending on their speed and position.

If you observe a vehicle running a red light, click on the vehicle and note its driver type. Red light running by driver types 8, 9, and 10 is sometimes normal behavior.

If this is an issue, you may want to consider using longer yellow times, especially on links with speeds above 35 mph. Also, consider increasing the Yellow Decel rate in the driver parameters.

Some red light running may be considered normal. In actual practice, a minority of drivers will not stop, when encountering a yellow light in the dilemma zone.

Consider increasing the turning speed for left and right turns. If a vehicle is slowing for a turn, this can increase the time to enter the intersection and the time to clear the intersection. Use Synchro's **SIMULATION** settings to adjust the turning speeds (see page 9-8). The default turning speeds may be too low for many large intersections.

Calibrating Speeds and Headways

In order to realistically model traffic it is important to have realistic Saturated Flow Rates, headways, and speeds. In some cases it may be necessary to change the default parameters to match local driver parameters. This section gives some guidance on how these parameters interact and suggestions for calibration and field studies.

Consider the following relationship:

$s = 3600 / TV$

s = Saturated Flow Rate (vph)

$TV = HW + L/spd$ = Time per vehicle

HW = headway between vehicles

L = Length of vehicles including stopped distance between

spd = vehicle speed (ft/s)

$L = 19.45$ft using default vehicle parameters

By default the average headway for all driver types are as follows:

$HW0 = 0.5$ s = Headway at 0 mph

$HW20 = 1.3$ s = Headway at 20 mph

$HW50 = 1.6$ s = Headway at 50 mph

$HW80 = 1.6$ s = Headway at 80 mph

Using the above values, the headways can be calculated with interpolation. These values are shown in **Table 22-6**

Table 22-6 Saturation Flow and Headways for Given Speeds

Speed (mph)	Headway (s)	Saturated Flow Rate (vph)
0	0.50	NA
9	0.86	1545
10	0.90	1619
15	1.03	1883
25	1.35	1916
30	1.40	1955
40	1.50	1966
50	1.60	1931
60	1.60	1977
80	1.6	2039

From the above table several features are of interest.

The ideal Saturated Flow Rate of the HCM (Highway Capacity Manual) is 1900vph. The default headways are chosen to give a Saturated Flow Rate similar to the HCM for cruising speeds from 25 mph to 50 mph.

The HCM Saturated Flow Rate for protected right turns is 1900 * 0.85 or 1615vph. The default right turn speed in SimTraffic is 9 mph and the Saturated Flow Rate for 9mph is 1545 vph.

The HCM Saturated Flow Rate for protected left turns is 1900 * 0.95 or 1805vph. The default left turn speed in SimTraffic is 15 mph and the Saturated Flow Rate for 15 mph is 1883 vph.

At low speeds, the Saturated Flow Rate is highly sensitive to small changes in speed. When the speed increases between 9 mph and 10 mph (11% increase) the Saturated Flow Rate increases from 1545 to 1619 vph (5% increase). It is therefore critical that the turning speeds in SimTraffic be entered as realistically as possible. The default speeds of 9 mph and 15 mph for right and left turns are based on small radius urban intersections. With larger sized suburban intersections, the speeds may be significantly higher.

 Be sure to set the link turning speeds as accurately as possible.

Field Studies

To calibrate the model for local conditions, the following data can be collected.

- Speeds within intersections
- Headways between intersections
- Reaction time to green light

The speed data should be collected as the tail of the vehicle crosses the stop bar. Do not count the first few vehicles in queue because they will still be accelerating. The average speed can be used to set the link speed and turning speeds. The range of speeds can be used to set the speed factors in the Driver Parameters page. Note that vehicles following closely may be traveling at less than their desired speed because they may be following a slower vehicle. If there are many closely spaced vehicles, the speeds and the speed factors may need to be skewed upwards to account for the dominance of "slow leaders".

Headway data can be collected with a stopwatch. The headway is the time starting when the tail of the lead vehicle crosses the stop bar until the front of the following car crosses the stop bar. Headways should be grouped by speed if possible since headways are dependent on speed. Any headway over 2 seconds should be discarded since the following vehicle is not in following mode. The headways can be graphed against speed to determine the range of headways for the input speeds of 0, 20, 50, and 80 mph (if applicable).

Reaction time can be measured with a stopwatch. This is the time between when the signal turns green and when the first vehicle starts to move. You may also be measuring the reaction time of the observer, hopefully, the observer will have a similar reaction time to observing the green light and observing the vehicle and they will cancel out. If the vehicles are waiting for a straggling cross vehicle or pedestrian, disregard this observation. The range of green reaction times can be used to set the Green Reaction times.

Calibrating Yellow Deceleration Rates

Calibrating yellow deceleration rates is also important, especially for the most aggressive drivers. Vehicles remaining in the intersection after the end of yellow increase the startup time for other movements. In many cases, the yellow and all-red times are too short to clear vehicles at the prevailing speeds.

Many communities have begun stepped up enforcement of red-light runners. It is unclear how effective these programs are at increasing the acceptable yellow deceleration among the most aggressive drivers.

Here is a simple formula for calculating the yellow deceleration rate for the most aggressive drivers. In the field, you are only observing the most aggressive drivers who do not stop for yellow lights. The data collected is their speed before yellow and the amount of time after the beginning of yellow before they enter the intersection. The times can be collected at the stop bar by simply noting the times of the worst red light runners. Only count the worst offenders, the others may have been beyond the dilemma zone or may be more conservative. Measure the speeds of the fastest drivers, 200 to 400 ft upstream for speed data.

$YD10 = spd90/(2 * (T - 0.5)) =$ deceleration rate drivers did not accept for yellow light.

$spd90 = $ 90th percentile speed

$T = $ time from beginning of yellow till vehicle enters intersection. The Subtracting of 0.5 seconds is for driver reaction time.

YD10 can be used for the deceleration rate for driver type 10. The other drivers will have higher yellow deceleration rates.

Fuel and Emissions Parameters

The fuel and emission parameters control the rate at which vehicles consume fuel or emit exhaust. Fuel and emission parameters are used for calculating the MOEs used in the reports and in static graphics.

Fuel and Emission rates are calculated using tables with entries for a range of speed and acceleration rates. These tables are in comma delimited format and stored in the same directory as the SimTraffic program. The filenames are shown in **Table 22-7**.

Table 22-7   Fuel and Emissions Data Filenames

Filename	Description
fuel_data.csv	Fuel table for all vehicles
hc_data.csv	HC Emission table for all vehicles
co_data.csv	CO Emission table for all vehicles
nox_data.csv	NOx Emission table for all vehicles

There are 7 vehicle types in the first column. There are 70 data rows for each vehicle type representing speeds from 0 to 70 ft/s. There are 21 data columns representing acceleration rates

-10 to +10 ft/s^2. The fuel data is in gallons per second times 10^5. The emissions data is in mg per second. The data must be entered using imperial units, no metric option is available.

The fuel and emission data was taken from the CORSIM simulation software.

The fuel and emissions data can be edited with a spreadsheet such as Microsoft Excel. The data needs to be stored in CSV format and the row and column structure must be preserved.

Notes

Most of the fuel consumption and vehicle emissions associated with a stop occurs during vehicle acceleration. A large part of the acceleration occurs after the front of the vehicle crosses the stop bar and the vehicle becomes associated with the next link. Much of the fuel consumption and emissions will be reported on exit links and intersections links downstream from where stopping occurs.

In some cases network improvements will actually increase fuel consumption and air emissions because vehicles consume more fuel when they are moving than when they are stopped. Increasing the throughput of a network will increase fuel consumption because more vehicles are moving. A signal may increase consumption over a two way stop because some main street vehicles will have to stop at a signal while at a two-way stop no main street vehicles stop or slow.

Controller Interface (CI) Options

The command **Options→CI-Options** will open the Controller Interface options. **SimTraffic CI** and these options are fully documented in Chapter 26.

Chapter 23 – SimTraffic Reports, Graphics and MOEs

Reports, Graphics, and MOEs

To create a report in SimTraffic, select the **File→Create Report** command and the **SELECT REPORTS** dialog will appear. Select the reports desired. The following sections describe the reports available.

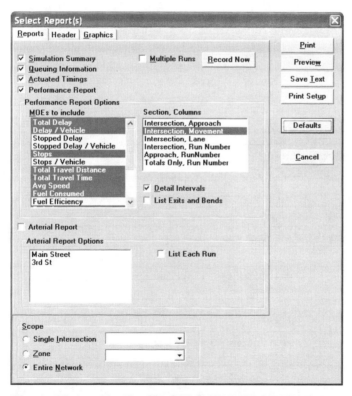

Figure 23-1   SimTraffic SELECT REPORTS dialog

There are four reports available in SimTraffic: **Simulation Summary Report, Queuing Information, Actuated Timings**, and **Performance Report Measures of Effectiveness**. All intervals must be recorded to create reports. SimPlay recordings will not work because the statistics are not recorded (see page 20-1). It is not possible to record statistics with SimPlay because it is possible to go back in time and re-record sections.

If any parameters were changed, the network must be re-seeded. All intervals including seed intervals must be recorded with the current parameters.

The data can be summarized with the groupings listed in the Section, Columns option settings in the **Select Report Window**.

Header and Footer Options

The Header tab controls the report header and footer. Each can have two lines with information on the right and left sides. The eight input boxes control which information appears in each line and each side. The header and footer include macros to display dynamic information. These macros are shown in **Table 23-1**.

Table 23-1   Header and Footer Options

Macro	Description	Notes
%report_title%	Title of Report	Name of the report type being printed
%filename%	Filename	Filename and path of file analyzed or "Multiple"
%page%	Page Number	Starting page number can be changed
%date%	Current Date	Date report was created, not analysis date
%description%	Description	Set in **Options→Scenario Manager**, location of analysis
%alternative%	Alternative	Set in **Options→Scenario Manager**, alternative being analyzed
%analyst%	Name of Analyst	Set in **Options→Scenario Manager**, person or firm performing study
%data_date%	Date of Data	Set in **Options→Scenario Manager**, date of volume counts or projection
%data_time%	Time of Data	Set in **Options→Scenario Manager**, time of volume counts or projection
%planid%	Timing Plan ID	Set in **Options→Scenario Manager**, name of timing plan

The report footer may contain part of the registration key code. This is normal behavior to help Trafficware track the use of product key codes.

Graphics Option

Use the **Graphics** tab to set the line colors, fonts and picture options.

Shade Rows, **Horizontal Lines**, **Section Color**, and **Back Color** control the look of the printed report.

The **Font** buttons allow for editing of the fonts used in the reports. The default font is Arial Narrow 10 for data and Arial 12 for titles. The narrow font of the data is better for separation of the data columns.

Defaults

Press the [**Defaults**] to change the settings back to the user defaults. Refer to page 2-27 for additional details.

Scope

The **Scope** determines which intersections are included in the report.

Choose **Single Intersection** and select an intersection to create reports for a single intersection.

Choose **Zone** and enter a zone to create reports for a group of intersections. To select multiple zones, separate the zones with a comma (i.e., "A, B, C" to print reports for zone A, B and C).

Choose **Entire Network** to report the entire network.

Multiple Runs

Multiple runs can be performed from the **SELECT REPORTS** settings by checking the 'Multiple Runs' box and selecting the [**Record Now**] button. A dialog box will appear prompting for the number of runs and starting seed number. More details on recording can be found in the topic, SimTraffic Operation (page 20-1).

SimTraffic will generate a report that averages the results of multiple runs. Check the 'Multiple Runs' box prior to selecting the [**Print**], [**Preview**], or [**Save-Text**] buttons. A dialog box will appear showing the History (HST) files for each simulation run recorded. The format of the history file will be 'filename-#.hst' where # indicates the random seed number. Select the runs you want to average by holding the [**Ctrl**] key and clicking on the desired filenames. The resulting report will be the average of the files you have selected. To see the results for the individual history files, create a report that selects only the desired history file.

 If your computer is configured to open files on a single click, hold the [Ctrl] key down when selecting the first file. Then hold the [**Shift**] key to select the last file. Clicking a file with the [**Ctrl**] key down can select or deselect a file. Multiple files can also be selected by dragging a rectangle around their names. Start the rectangle to the right of any filenames.

Print Settings

Select the **File→Print-Window** command to print the current settings. Printing the Map has an options settings. The user can setup header and footers and select the font. The scale is also adjustable and there are a number of options including fixed scale or print to fit.

When printing the **MAP** view, this will print to the scale specified by Zoom-Scale. The printout will be centered on the center point of the current screen view.

If static graphics are shown, the static graphics will be printed.

When choosing colors in the **MAP** view settings, there are two sets of colors for each object type. The Printer colors are used in conjunction with printing. Normally a white background is used with printing. A black roadway is used with screen drawing to match real-world colors.

Viewing and Printing Reports

After selecting the desired report options, select [Preview] to view the report, or [Print] to print the report.

Viewing Reports

Select [Preview] from the Report Options settings to view reports. To change pages use the buttons [|<], [<<], [>>], and [>|]. You can also change pages using the [Page Up], [Page Down], [Home], and [End] keys. To move around the current page, click on it and drag with the mouse. You can also move the page with the arrow keys. To return to the **SELECT REPORTS** dialog, use the [Back] button.

Printing Reports

To print the report, select the [Print] button from the Report Options or REPORT PREVIEW settings. To change the printer, select File→Print-Setup command.

Simulation Summary Report

The Simulation Summary report (**Figure 23-2**) lists the intervals and their properties, and some overall statistics about the number of vehicles serviced.

The summary report can be used to keep track of the intervals simulated, the volume adjustments made, and the timing plan(s) used.

SimTraffic Simulation Summary
Baseline   1/24/2006

Summary of All Intervals

Start Time	6:57
End Time	7:10
Total Time (min)	13
Time Recorded (min)	10
# of Intervals	2
# of Recorded Intvls	1
Vehs Entered	2093
Vehs Exited	1902
Starting Vehs	423
Ending Vehs	614
Denied Entry Before	40
Denied Entry After	184
Travel Distance (mi)	1140
Travel Time (hr)	111.2
Total Delay (hr)	77.1
Total Stops	4179
Fuel Used (gal)	612.5

Interval #0 Information Seeding

Start Time	6:57
End Time	7:00
Total Time (min)	3
Volumes adjusted by Growth Factors.	
No data recorded this interval.	

Interval #1 Information Recording

Start Time	7:00
End Time	7:10
Total Time (min)	10
Volumes adjusted by Growth Factors.	
Vehs Entered	2093
Vehs Exited	1902
Starting Vehs	423
Ending Vehs	614
Denied Entry Before	40
Denied Entry After	184
Travel Distance (mi)	1140
Travel Time (hr)	111.2
Total Delay (hr)	77.1
Total Stops	4179
Fuel Used (gal)	612.5

Figure 23-2   Simulation Summary Report

Entire Run Statistics

The first section of the report covers the entire run including all intervals.

The start time, end time, total time, and total time recorded are listed. Total time includes seed intervals; total time recorded includes the recorded intervals only.

Data includes the vehicles entered and exited, total distance, total time, total delay, total stops, and total fuel, track statistics for the recorded intervals of the simulation. Details of the calculations are available under the SimTraffic Performance Report.

Denied Entry vehicles are vehicles that are unable to enter a link due to congestion. These vehicles are waiting to enter the link. These vehicles can either be from an external link or from a mid-block source.

Seeding Intervals

Limited information is available for seeding intervals because statistics are not recorded. The primary purpose of seed intervals is to fill the network with traffic.

The start time, end time, and interval duration are listed.

Any volume adjustments will be listed. If volumes or timings are read from an external file, this information will be listed as well.

Recorded Intervals

The **start time**, **end time**, and **interval duration** are listed.

Any volume adjustments will be listed. If volumes or timings are read from an external file, this information will be listed as well.

The vehicles entered and exited, distance, time, delays, stops, and fuel, track statistics for this interval of the simulation will be listed. Details of the calculations are available under MOEs.

Measures of Effectiveness

The Performance report (**Figure 23-3**) details the measures listed in the MOEs to Include box.

SimTraffic Performance Report
Baseline   1/24/2006

2: Main Street & 2nd St Performance by movement

Movement	EBL	EBT	WBT	WBR	SBL	SBR	All
Total Delay (hr)	0.4	1.0	1.1	0.4	1.4	0.1	4.3
Delay / Veh (s)	45.4	23.2	35.1	40.2	52.3	18.1	35.6
Total Stops	32	83	74	28	102	10	329
Travel Dist (mi)	11.8	51.3	30.3	8.8	10.1	1.2	113.5
Travel Time (hr)	0.8	2.3	1.9	0.6	1.8	0.1	7.5
Avg Speed (mph)	15	22	16	14	6	12	15
Fuel Used (gal)	5.0	20.0	14.3	3.9	6.7	0.7	50.6
HC Emissions (g)	0	3	3	1	0	0	7
CO Emissions (g)	162	1052	963	250	98	19	2544
NOx Emissions (g)	1	11	8	2	1	0	24
Vehicles Entered	35	148	116	33	93	11	436
Vehicles Exited	33	152	104	31	99	12	431
Hourly Exit Rate	198	912	624	186	594	72	2586
Input Volume	200	1000	900	200	500	100	2900
% of Volume	99	91	69	93	119	72	89
Denied Entry Before	0	0	0	0	0	0	0
Denied Entry After	0	0	0	0	0	2	2

Figure 23-3   Performance Report

Total Delay is equal to the total travel time minus the travel time for the vehicle with no other vehicles or traffic control devices. For each time slice of animation, the incremental delay is determined with the following formula.

$$TD = dT * (spdmax - spd) / spdmax = \text{Total Delay for time slice}$$

$dT = \text{time slice} = 0.1s$

$spdmax = \text{maximum speed of vehicle}$

$spd = \text{actual speed}$

The maximum speed may be less than the link speed if a vehicle is within a turn, approaching a turn, or accelerating out of a turn. Total delay also includes all time spent by denied entry vehicles while they are waiting to enter the network.

Delay per Vehicle is calculated by dividing the total delay by the **Number of Vehicles**.

The **Number of Vehicles** is not a fixed number because some vehicles in the area are analyzed before the interval begins and some after the interval ends. Part of these vehicles delay is counted in prior and subsequent intervals and thus it is not fair to count these vehicles in the vehicle count for this interval. The **Number of Vehicles** is thus equal to:

$$nVeh = nX - 0.5 * nS + 0.5 * nE = \text{Number of Vehicles}$$

$$nX = \text{Vehicles Exited this interval}$$

$$nS = \text{Vehicles in area at start of interval}$$

$$nE = \text{Vehicles in area at end of interval}$$

Per vehicle values for a network or arterial will be higher than their intersection components. If all vehicles are delayed at 3 intersections for 5 seconds each, the network delay per vehicle will be 15s.

Per vehicle statistics are not shown in by-lane columns. Because a single vehicle may spend part time in multiple lanes.

The **Stopped Delay** is the sum of all time slices where the vehicles are stopped or traveling at less than 10 ft/s (3 m/s). Normally the Stopped Delay will be less than the total delay. Stopped delay also includes all time spent by denied entry vehicles while they are waiting to enter the network.

Stop Delay/Vehicle is calculated by dividing Stop Delay by the Number of Vehicles.

The **Total Stops** is a count of vehicle stops. Whenever a vehicle's speed drops below 10 ft/s (3 m/s) a stop is added. A vehicle is considered going again when its speed reaches 15 ft/s (4.5 m/s).

Stops /Vehicle is calculated by dividing the number of Stops by the Number of Vehicles.

The **Travel Distance** is simply a summation of the vehicle distance traveled. This distance includes the curve distance within intersections.

The **Travel Time** is a total of the time each vehicle was present in this area. The travel time includes time spent by vehicles Denied Entry.

The **Average Speed** is calculated by dividing Total Distance by Total Time. Average Speed is weighted by volume, and includes stopped time and denied entry time. The time use in calculation for Average Speed does not include time spent by denied entry vehicles while they are waiting to enter the network. Average speed may thus be higher than Total Time divided by Total Distance.

Fuel Used is calculated with the fuel consumption parameters. These parameters are located in a text file that is in the Trafficware directory. The fuel used in each time slice is determined by the vehicle's fleet (car, truck, or bus), speed, and acceleration.

The **Fuel Efficiency** is calculated by dividing the Total Distance by the Fuel Used.

Emissions data are calculated with the vehicle emission parameters. The vehicle's speed and acceleration determine the emissions created in each time slice. There are no emission tables available for trucks and busses. SimTraffic assumes trucks and busses emit exhaust at three times the rate of cars.

Vehicles Entered and **Vehicles Exited** is a count of how many vehicles enter and exit the link or area during the interval(s). If this is a network or arterial summary, the Vehicles Entered and Vehicles Exited do not count a vehicle moving from one intersection to the next within the arterial or network. The Entered and Exited counts for a network or arterial will thus be less than the sum of the counts from each intersection.

The **Hourly Exit Rate** is the Vehicles exited at an hourly rate. If the intersection is above capacity and the input volume is not constrained upstream, this value might be used as the capacity for this movement

Denied Entry is a count of vehicles that are unable to enter a link due to congestion. Denied Entry includes external links and mid-block vehicle sources. The report lists the number of vehicles denied entry at the start and end of the period. This is useful to see if congestion is getting worse or better. Denied Entry can also be used to determine the Network Throughput. In a congested network lower values of Denied Entry indicate increased throughput.

New in Version 7:

Density is the average distance per vehicle over the simulation period. It is only available by-lane, and by-approach but not by-movement; multiple movements can share a lane.

Ocupancy is the average number of vehicles in a lane or approach over the simulation period.

SimTraffic Arterial Reports

The Arterial Report uses origin destination data to only count vehicles that came from the arterial on the next upstream link. This is almost, but not exactly the same as taking the travel time of only those vehicles that travel the entire corridor. This allows the arterial report to be compared with car travel time studies.

Refer to **Figure 23-4**. For a travel time study, the travel time on link 1T is wanted only for those vehicles that started on link 4T. The combined delay for approach (1T) includes vehicles from 2T, 2R, and 2L. The arterial delay only considers the delay and travel time of vehicles from 2T. The signal at node 2 acts as a bit of a mixing and filtering mechanism. The departure profile of vehicle from 2T is nearly the same whether these vehicles came from 4T, 4R, 4L, 3R, or 3L. Note that the arterial delay at 2T will only consider arrivals from 3T.

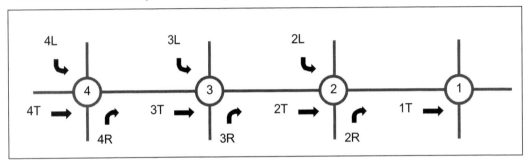

Figure 23-4   Arterial Travel Report Movements

This discussion begs the question: 'why not track only those vehicles that travel the entire corridor?' The data collection for such a process would be difficult. For many corridors, especially with 5 or more intersections, less than 5% of all vehicles drive through the entire corridor. Many valid data points would be thrown away from vehicles that traverse part of the corridor. The SimTraffic vehicles only know 5 turns ahead where they will be going; they do not know in advance whether they will be traversing the entire arterial or not.

Network Totals

The totals section includes MOEs for all vehicles in the network including exit links and bend links. This causes the network totals to be higher than the sum of the intersection links.

 To see the average result of multiple runs, see the topic on Multiple Runs (page 23-3).

Queuing and Blocking Report

The Queuing and Blocking report (**Figure 23-5**) gives information about the maximum queue length for each lane and the percentage of time critical points are blocked.

Queuing and Blocking Report
Baseline   1/24/2006

Intersection: 1: Main Street & 1st St

Movement	EB	EB	EB	WB	WB	WB	NB	NB	SB	SB	SB
Directions Served	L	T	TR	L	T	TR	L	TR	L	T	R
Maximum Queue (ft)	274	468	277	134	241	265	124	656	116	138	110
Average Queue (ft)	274	418	236	104	154	173	107	549	79	64	71
95th Queue (ft)	275	481	304	151	263	300	143	663	113	127	112
Link Distance (ft)		453	453		1767	1767		641		636	
Upstream Blk Time (%)		5						4			
Queuing Penalty (veh)		0						0			
Storage Bay Dist (ft)	250			150			100		100		100
Storage Blk Time (%)	20	3		0	17		11	63	7	2	2
Queuing Penalty (veh)	102	9		0	33		55	63	40	11	5

Intersection: 2: Main Street & 2nd St

Movement	EB	EB	EB	WB	WB	SB	SB
Directions Served	L	T	T	T	TR	L	R
Maximum Queue (ft)	224	245	263	224	267	546	52
Average Queue (ft)	153	167	192	171	193	444	23
95th Queue (ft)	270	303	287	274	284	576	55
Link Distance (ft)		1767	1767	1314	1314	558	
Upstream Blk Time (%)						0	
Queuing Penalty (veh)						0	
Storage Bay Dist (ft)	200					300	
Storage Blk Time (%)		9				25	
Queuing Penalty (veh)		19				25	

Figure 23-5   Queue Report

Each column represents one lane from left to right.

Queues are reported individually for each lane, no summing or averaging is performed between lanes. A vehicle is considered queued whenever it is traveling at less than 10 ft/s (3 m/s). A vehicle will only become "queued" when it is either at the stop bar or behind another queued vehicle.

The **Maximum Queue** is the maximum back of queue observed for the entire analysis interval. This is a simple maximum, no averaging is performed. The maximum queue is calculated independently for each lane. The queue reported is the maximum queue for each individual lane, NOT the sum of all lane queues.

SimTraffic records the maximum back of queue observed for every two minute period. The **Average Queue** is average of all the 2 minute maximum queues.

A standard deviation is also calculated using the sum of squares for each 2 minute interval. The 95th Queue is equal to the Average Queue plus 1.65 standard deviations. The 95th Queue is not necessarily ever observed, it is simply based on statistical calculations.

Vehicles can stop when queued and when waiting for a mandatory lane change. SimTraffic tries to determine whether the stopping is due to queuing or lane changes. In some cases stopping for lane changes will be counted as queuing. Sometimes in SimTraffic and real life, the lane changes and queuing behavior are closely interconnected.

The **Link Distance** is the internal distance of the link from Stop-bar to stop-bar. This value will be less than the link distance defined in Synchro because it is the internal distance after subtracting the widths of the intersections.

Upstream Block Time is the proportion of time that the upstream end of the lane is blocked. There is a hot spot 20ft (6 m) long placed at the top of the lane. Every time slice that this hot-spot is occupied by a queued vehicle counts towards the block time.

The **Queuing Penalty** is a rough measure of how many vehicles are affected by the blocking. The Queuing Penalty is equal to the estimated volume of the lane times the percent of time the lane is blocked. The Queuing Penalty for a storage bay blockage is based on the volume of the adjacent lane. If a through lane is blocking a storage bay, the penalty is based on the volume of turning traffic. The Queuing Penalty is a quick way to quantify the affects of queuing. It can be used to show that Timing Plan A has less blocking problems than Timing Plan B. Queuing Penalty is not calculated for external links.

To see the **hot-spots** graphically, display Static Graphics with the % of Time Blocked option.

Storage Bay Distance is the length of a turning bay.

Storage Block Time is the proportion of time that a lane is queued at the top of the storage. There is a hot spot 20ft (6 m) long placed at the top of the storage bay. Through lanes adjacent to storage bays are also tracked. Queuing in the through lane can block access to the storage bay. Every time slice that this hot-spot is occupied by a queued vehicle counts towards the block time.

B## is a column that is not always present and is used for reports on the queue for a bend link.

If an approach link has a bend upstream, the queue for the bend link is recorded separately. The queue is reported with the downstream intersection because the queue is caused by that intersection. The queue for bend links is recorded separately because the number of lanes can change at the bend.

The Bend queues are normal behavior, although they can be confusing to interpret. To eliminate the reporting of bend queues, remove bends from your networks or move them further upstream.

Many bends are unnecessary (see the topic on **Bends**, page 2-2). If the roadway bends slightly, it may be easier to adjust for the bend by overriding the link distance.

Comparing Queues to Other Models

The maximum queues reported in SimTraffic may vary significantly from the queues reported in Synchro and other models. Here are some reasons why the queues are different and how to get comparable values.

The average vehicle length in SimTraffic (and CORSIM) including distance between is 19.5 ft (6 m). Synchro and other macroscopic models typically use a vehicle length of 25ft (7.5m) in conjunction with queues. When comparing queue lengths to those in other models such as Synchro, keep in mind that these queues in SimTraffic will be 25% less with everything else being equal.

The 50th percentile queues in Synchro are based on traffic adjusted for PHF, adjust SimTraffic traffic for PHF when comparing percentile delays.

The 95th percentile queues in Synchro are based on traffic adjusted for 95th percentile traffic but not for PHF. To get SimTraffic queues comparable to Synchro, create a 3 minute interval with 95th percentile traffic adjustments and no PHF, this interval can be followed by an interval without percentile adjustments. The queues for approaches in the middle of the network may not experience 95th percentile traffic because the surge in traffic dissipates before reaching the center of the network.

An alternate method of observing the 95th percentile queue in SimTraffic is to simulate traffic for an entire hour without adjustments. SimTraffic's volumes will vary over the course of an hour and at some point the traffic will most likely surge to the 95th percentile flow rate.

Queues in SimTraffic may also be higher than Synchro due to conditions that are not reflected in a macroscopic model. Reasons include spillback between intersections, spillback beyond turning bays, forced lane changes, unbalanced lane use for downstream turns, and other subtle traffic flow interactions.

Actuated Signals, Observed Splits Report

The actuated signal report (**Figure 23-6**) displays information about the actual times observed in actuated signals. This report can be used to show how an actuated signal will perform with detailed modeling. This report can be helpful to compare the affects of adjusting gap settings, detector layouts, recalls and so on.

```
Actuated Signals, Observed Splits
Baseline                                                                    1/24/2006

Intersection: 1: Main Street & 1st St

Phase                        1      2      4      5      6      8
Movement(s) Served         WBL    EBT   SBTL    EBL    WBT   NBTL
Maximum Green (s)          16.0   38.0   34.0   22.0   32.0   34.0
Minimum Green (s)           4.0    4.0    4.0    4.0    4.0    4.0
Recall                     None  C-Max   None   None  C-Max   None
Avg. Green (s)             14.1   39.5   34.0   21.8   32.3   34.0
g/C Ratio                  0.14   0.39   0.34   0.22   0.32   0.34
Cycles Skipped (%)           0      0      0      0      0      0
Cycles @ Minimum (%)         0      0      0      0      0      0
Cycles Maxed Out (%)        33    100    100     83    100    100
Cycles with Peds (%)         0      0      0      0      0      0

Controller Summary
Average Cycle Length (s): 100.0
Number of Complete Cycles : 5


Intersection: 2: Main Street & 2nd St

Phase                        2      4      5      6
Movement(s) Served         EBT    SBL    EBL    WBT
Maximum Green (s)          57.0   35.0   16.0   37.0
Minimum Green (s)           4.0    4.0    4.0    4.0
Recall                    C-Max   None   None  C-Max
Avg. Green (s)             57.0   35.0   14.1   39.1
g/C Ratio                  0.57   0.35   0.14   0.39
Cycles Skipped (%)           0      0      0      0
Cycles @ Minimum (%)         0      0      0      0
Cycles Maxed Out (%)       100    100     67    100
Cycles with Peds (%)         0      0      0      0

Controller Summary
Average Cycle Length (s): 100.0
Number of Complete Cycles : 5
```

Figure 23-6   Actuated Signal Report

Each column represents one signal phase.

Movement(s) Served is the lane group(s) served by this phase.

Maximum Green is the maximum green time before this phase will max out. For a coordinated signal this is the maximum time before the signal will yield or be forced off.

Minimum Green is the minimum green time. In Synchro this is called the minimum initial time.

Recall is the recall for the phase. This will be Coord for coordinated, Max for Max recall, Ped for Pedestrian recall, Min for minimum recall, or None for no recall.

Avg. Green is the average of all green times. Skipped phases do not count. Green periods that begin or end in another interval do not count.

g/C Ratio is the observed green time to cycle length ratio. Since there may be green time measured from cycles that fall partially outside this interval, an adjustment is used. The formula for g/C is as follows:

g/C = TotalGreen / TotalCycles * NumCycles / (NumGreens+NumSkips)

Cycles Skipped (%) is the percentage of cycles skipped by this phase. Green periods or permissive periods that begin or end in another interval do not count.

Cycles @ Minimum (%) is the percentage of cycles that show for their minimum time. Normally these phases have gapped out. Green periods that begin or end in another interval do not count.

Cycles Maxed Out (%) is the percentage of cycles that max out. This value also includes all cycles for coordinated phases and phases with Max Recall. Green periods that begin or end in another interval do not count.

Cycles with Peds (%) is the percentage of cycles with a pedestrian call. If this phase has Pedestrian Recall all phases will have pedestrians. Green periods that begin or end in another interval do not count.

Average Cycle Length(s) is an average of the cycle lengths modeled. For a coordinated signal, this is the actual cycle length.

Number of Complete Cycles(s) is a count of the number of complete cycles modeled. Partial cycles do not count, although phases from partial cycles may count for individual phase statistics.

Static Graphics

To display static graphics, choose the **Graphics→Show Static Graphics** command. Select the display desired. The following sections describe the graphics displays available.

All intervals must be recorded to show static graphics. SimPlay recordings will not work because the statistics are not recorded. It is not possible to record statistics with SimPlay because it is possible to go back in time and rerecord sections.

If any parameters were changed, the network must be re-seeded as well. All intervals including seed intervals must be recorded with the current parameters.

Color Legend

A legend appears in the lower right corner of the display showing the colors used. By default, the brighter colors indicate higher congestion on the screen and darker colors indicate higher congestion on the printouts.

The colors can be changed with the **Options→Map Settings** command.

Intervals

If more than one interval is recorded, the static graphics can be created for one interval or the entire simulation. Static graphics cannot be created for seed intervals.

Static Displays

Delay per Vehicle shows the Total Delay per vehicle for each lane group. If a lane is shared between movements, it will be split with a section for each turn. The Total Delay is measures the amount vehicles are delayed by traffic control and other vehicles. See **Measures of Effectiveness** (page 23-7) for the calculation formula. This delay includes time spent by denied entry vehicles.

Stopped Delay per Vehicle shows the Stopped Delay per vehicle for each lane group. The Stopped Delay is the amount of time each vehicle's speed is less than 10 ft/s (3 m/s). This delay includes time spent by denied entry vehicles.

Stops per Vehicle shows the number of stops per vehicle. A vehicle is considered stopped when its speed is less than 10 ft/s (3 m/s). The vehicle is no longer stopped when its speed exceeds 15 ft/s (4.5 m/s).

Average Speed shows the average speed for each movement. The speed is calculated by dividing the total travel time by the total travel distance for vehicles on this link. This speed does not include time spend by denied entry vehicles.

Fuel Efficiency shows the fuel efficiency for each movement. The fuel consumption calculation is described in Measures of Effectiveness. The fuel efficiency is distance traveled divided by fuel consumed.

% of Time Blocked shows queuing and blocking at the "hot-spots". A hot-spot is located at the top of every link and a hot-spot is located at the top of storage bays and in the lane adjacent to storage bays at the top. The hot-spots are 20 ft (6 m) long. The blockage counts the number of time steps with a vehicle traveling less than 10 ft/s (3 m/s) over the hot spots. It is also possible that blockage is counted when a large vehicle is waiting on the other side of the upstream intersection to prevent gridlock.

Vehicles Denied Entry shows the number of vehicles that are denied entry at the upstream end of each entry link and mid-block for each source. The number shown is the number of vehicles at the end of the interval or the entire simulation. Vehicles are denied entry when there is insufficient capacity, when blocking prevents vehicles from entering the network, or when there are no gaps for vehicles to enter mid-block.

Queues shows the Maximum, Average, and 95th Percentile Queue Lengths. Queues are reported individually for each lane, no summing or averaging is performed between lanes. The queues reported are the maximum back of queue during the analysis period. A vehicle is considered to be "queued" when its speed is less than 10 ft/s (3 m/s). A vehicle will only become "queued" when it is either at the stop bar or behind another queued vehicle. The **Maximum Queue** is the maximum back of queue observed for the entire analysis interval. This is a simple maximum; no averaging is performed. SimTraffic records the maximum back of queue observed for every two minute period. The **Average Queue** is average of all the 2 minute maximum queues. A Standard Deviation is also calculated using the sum of squares for each 2 minute interval. The **95th Queue** is equal to the Average Queue plus 1.65 standard deviations. The 95th Queue is not necessarily ever observed, it is simply based on statistical calculations.

Chapter 24 – The SimTraffic Model

The SimTraffic Model

This chapter explains the assumptions and formulas used by SimTraffic. This information is not needed for coding files or using SimTraffic, but it is provided to explain SimTraffic's behavior.

Traffic Generation and Assignment

Trip generation and **route assignment** are based on traffic volumes. These volumes may be adjusted for growth factors, PHF, or percentile adjustments. The volumes may also change between intervals. See Intervals and Volume Adjustments for more information. The adjusted volume is shown on the Performance Report Input Volume.

Trip Generation

Trips are added to entry points based on the volume counts at the downstream intersection.

Trips are also added mid-block if mid-block traffic is specified or a volume source is needed to balance traffic. If balancing and a mid-block source exist, the mid-block entry will be the maximum of the two.

For each 0.1 s slice a vehicle is created when R36000 < vl

vl = hourly traffic volume of link or mid-block source.

R36000 = a random number between 0 and 35999

For example, a link's volume is 500. Over an hour there are 36000 chances to add vehicles (once per tenth of a second). About 500 of the random numbers will be less than 500 and about 500 vehicles will be created. The actual volume generated is shown on the Performance Report Hourly Exit Rate.

For any given time period more or less vehicles will appear. Looking at many time periods, the vehicles will exhibit a Poisson arrival distribution.

Link Volumes are calculated independently for cars and for heavy vehicles. The heavy vehicle volume is equal to the adjusted volume times the Heavy Vehicle percentage. The car volume is equal to the remaining adjusted volume. Entering Heavy Vehicles are assigned to a Truck or Bus vehicle type based on their percentage of the total Heavy Vehicle Fleet. Entering Cars are assigned to a Car or Carpool vehicle type based on each type's percentage of the total Car Fleet.

Denied Entry

Once a vehicle is created it is placed in the network if it is **OK To Enter**. To test if a lane is clear, a **Test Deceleration** is determined between the created vehicle and vehicles ahead and behind using car following formulas. The test decelerations must be less than the normal deceleration (decelNormal).

The trip generator will attempt to place the vehicle in any allowed lane at either full speed, half speed, or stopped.

In some cases it will not be possible for the vehicle to enter due to vehicles on the link. These existing vehicles may be stopped in a queue or simply moving too fast to let the new vehicle in. If it is not possible to place the vehicle, the created vehicle will be placed in denied entry status. Vehicles in denied entry status will be attempted to be placed in later time slices. On a congested link, there may be a back log of **denied entry vehicles**. This usually indicates a capacity problem or other operational problem.

Route Assignment

When a vehicle is created it is assigned a turn at the end of its link and the next eight links. The turns are random based on the turning counts for each direction.

vT = sum of approach traffic

Rv = random number between 0 and vT -1

If Rv < vLeft then

Vehicle turns left

Else If Rv < (vLeft + vThru) then

Vehicle proceeds straight

else

Vehicle turns right

A vehicle may also be assigned to a mid-block sink using similar logic.

vSink = vUp - vT + vMidBlock = sink volume

vUp = volume from upstream intersection

vMidblock = volume entering mid-block, either specified or from balancing.

A vehicle always knows its next ten turns. Whenever a vehicle enters a new link, the tenth turn is assigned.

If Link O-D Volumes are specified, the probability for each turn is determined by the upstream turn of the vehicle. Link O-D Volumes can be used to suppress certain movements such as making two left turns in a row.

Turning Volumes are calculated independently for cars and for heavy vehicles in the same way as link volumes. Cars are assigned turns based on car volumes. Trucks and Busses are assigned turns based on heavy vehicle volumes.

Pedestrian Generation

Pedestrians are generated using logic similar to vehicle generation.

The number of pedestrians is the maximum of either the Conflicting Pedestrians for right turns on the link to the right or the Pedestrian Calls for the through phase on the link to the left (see Coding Pedestrians).

For a 'T' intersection, the number of pedestrians on the link to the left of the 'T' is the maximum of either the conflicting pedestrians with the left turn of the 'T', or the pedestrian calls of the left turn phase for the link itself.

When pedestrians are generated, they wait at either end of the crosswalk until it is safe to cross. While crossing, pedestrians walk at the network walking speed (4ft/s or 1.2 m/s by default). Pedestrians begin crossing when there are no conflicting vehicles in the intersection and there is a walk signal for signalized intersections.

For each link-end there can be up to two pedestrians walking in each direction and a third pedestrian in each direction waiting to start. When the third pedestrian starts, he will replace the second (middle) pedestrian. Because of this simplified model, SimTraffic always assumes there could be additional pedestrians between the two shown pedestrians.

Car Following and Speed Selection

Cruise Speed

Without any impediments, a vehicle will travel at its **cruise speed**. The cruise speed is equal to the link's speed multiplied by the speed factor for the driver type. By default the speed factors range from 0.85 to 1.15.

Acceleration Rates

Each vehicle type has a maximum **acceleration rate**. The acceleration rates vary by speed. The acceleration rates ar stored in the files accels.csv. These rates are taken from TSIS version 5 in ft/s^2.

Deceleration Rates

There are a number of **deceleration rates** used depending on the situation involved.

The maximum possible deceleration rate is 12 ft/s^2 (3.6 m/s^2). This is normally reserved for crisis situations. This is **decelMax**.

When the signal turns yellow, drivers decide whether to stop based on a comfortable level of deceleration for their driver type. The deceleration rates for a yellow light vary between 12 ft/s^2 and 7 ft/s^2 (3.6 m/s^2 to 2.1 m/s^2), and is editable in driver parameters.

To slow for an upcoming turn, vehicles will decelerate at 4 ft/s^2 (1.2 m/s^2). This is **decelNormal**.

The values in the deceleration rate table will be discussed with car following and lane changes.

Table 24-1   Decel Rate Table

Name	Amount	Metric Amount
decelNormal	4 ft/s^2	1.2 m/s^2
decelPlus	6 ft/s^2	1.8 m/s^2
decelHard	8 ft/s^2	2.4 m/s^2
decelMax	12 ft/s^2	3.6 m/s^2
accelMin	2 ft/s^2	0.6 m/s^2

Speed Model

Vehicles will slow or stop for one or more of the following events

- Exceeding Speed Limit
- Turn Ahead
- Vehicle Ahead
- Slow to Start Mandatory Lane Change Start
- Slow to Finish Mandatory Lane Change
- Slow to enter turning pocket
- Slow to allow merging vehicle into lane
- Slow to merge with vehicles in destination lane
- Red or Yellow Signal Ahead
- Stop or Yield sign
- Yield to pedestrians or traffic in intersection
- No Space beyond Intersection
- Any of the above on the next link
- Vehicles within Roundabout

Lane changes, intersection right-of-ways, sign control and signal control will be discussed later in this Chapter.

Car Following

Fast following is used when the leading vehicle is above 2 ft/s (0.6 m/s). **Slow following** is used to track a slow or stopped vehicle or to stop at a fixed point such as the stop-bar or mandatory lane change start point.

The distance between vehicles, or distance to the stopping point is as follows.

$DBv = Xu - Lu - DB - Xv$ = distance between vehicles

Xu = position of lead vehicle (or stopping point)

Xv = position of subject vehicle

Lu = length of lead vehicle (0 for stopping point)

DB = Distance Between = 5 ft (1.5 m)

Stopped vehicles will not start until the leading vehicle has moved at least 5 ft (1.5m). This has the effect of creating a startup reaction time of about 1 second per vehicle. The 10th vehicle in line will not start to move until about 10 seconds after the first vehicle has moved.

Fast Following

SimTraffic's car following model will attempt to have the trailing car following the leading car with 1 second of headway between vehicles. **Fast following** is used when the leading vehicle is traveling faster than 2 ft/s (0.6 m/s). The following formulas are used for fast following:

$DSafe = DBv + min(spdU^2 - spdV^2, 0) / 2*decelNormal - spdV*HW$

spdU = speed of leading vehicle

spdV = speed of trailing vehicle

DBv = distance between vehicles

HW = desired headway = dependant on driver parameters and Link Headway Factor

DSafe is the distance between vehicles, adjusting for speed differential and reduced by the trailing vehicle's desired headway (units are feet). Dsafe is distance above or below desired distance

SF = safety factor = DSafe / (spdV * HW)

SF is unit less. SF has the following characteristics:

SF = 0 vehicle is at correct distance

SF = -1 vehicle is 1 headway too close, unsafe following and maximum deceleration

SF = 1 vehicle is 1 headway too far, accelerate

dV = recommended acceleration (deceleration)

When SF >= -0.3

dV = DecelHard * SF / 1.5

When -0.3 > SF >= -1.0

$dV = decelHard * [-0.2 + (SF+0.3)*8/7]$

-When 1.0 > SF

dV = -decelHard

The acceleration must be greater or equal to -decelMax and less than or equal to the vehicle's maximum acceleration capabilities.

The fast car following model assumes 0.1 second time slices. At 0.5 or 1 second time slices the vehicles are not able to react quickly enough.

Slow Following

For **slow following**, the following methods are used.

DB2 = DBv - 2 * spdU / 10 - 1; new distance after 0.1 second and fudge factor

$dv2 = (spdV + 2 * accelMin / 10)^2 / (2 * DB2)$ = deceleration required after accelerating at 2*accelMin

$dv4 = (spdV + 4 * accelMin / 10)^2 / (2 * DB2)$ = deceleration required after accelerating at 4*accelMin

$dv6 = (spdV + 6 * accelMin / 10)^2 / (2 * DB2)$ = deceleration required after accelerating at 6*accelMin

If dv2, dv4, or dv6 are greater than negative decelNormal then the vehicle will accelerate by 2*accelMin, 4*accelMin, or 6*accelMin respectively subject to the vehicle's maximum acceleration capabilities.

If dv2 < -decelNormal then

$dV = -spdV^2 / (2*DB2)$

If DB2 < 0 then

dV = -decelMax

The acceleration must be greater or equal to -decelMax and less than or equal to the vehicle's maximum acceleration capabilities.

Lane Choice and Lane Changes

There are different types of lane changes in SimTraffic. The lane change values are set in the Synchro **SIMULATION** Settings (see page 9-8). The sections that follow describe the settings.

Single Lane Changes

Refer to **Figure 24-1**.

The **Mandatory Distance** is the distance back from the stop bar where a lane change must commence. If a vehicle is not able to commence its lane change before this point, it will stop and wait for an opening. Vehicles in the next lane will cooperate to allow this vehicle to merge in.

The **Mandatory Distance** is adjusted by the **Mandatory Distance Adjustment** for each driver type. The actual mandatory distance could be 50% to 200% of the distance depending on driver type.

The **Positioning Distance** is the distance back from the Mandatory point where a vehicle first attempts to change lanes. The positioning distance is added to the Mandatory distance. Beyond the positioning distance, vehicles are unaware about upcoming lane change requirements.

The **Positioning Distance** is adjusted by the **Positioning Distance Adjustment** for each driver type. The actual mandatory distance could be 50% to 200% of the distance depending on driver type.

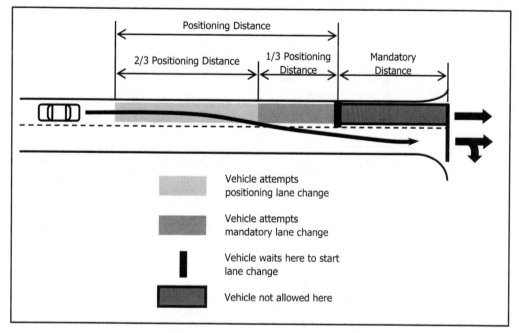

Figure 24-1   Vehicle Turning Right from Left Lane

For the first 2/3 of the distance between the positioning point and the mandatory point, vehicles will attempt a positioning lane change. Aggressive drivers will ignore positioning lane changes and even move the other way to avoid a queue. Some driver types will not cooperate with positioning lane changers.

After the 2/3 point, vehicles will attempt a mandatory lane change. All vehicles are forced to cooperate with mandatory lane changers. In the mandatory zone, vehicles will match the speed of the target lane and merge as soon as conditions are available.

These lane change distances carry through intersections upstream. A vehicle may need to start getting in the appropriate lane several blocks ahead.

Lane change distances can even go around corners through intersections when there are multiple turning lanes. If there are two left-turn lanes and then another turn shortly downstream, vehicles may choose their left-turn lane based on the lane alignments through the intersections.

Two or More Lane Changes

Refer to **Figure 24-2**.

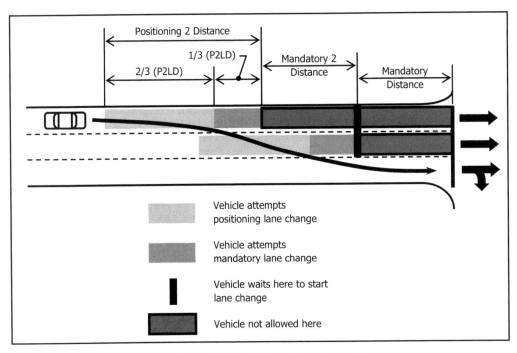

Figure 24-2   Vehicle Turning Right Making Two Lane Changes

Mandatory 2 Lane Distance and **Positioning 2 Lane Distance** are used when a vehicle needs to make 2 or more lane changes on a link with three lanes or more. **Mandatory 2 Lane Distance** is added to **Mandatory Distance** to determine the **Mandatory Point** for commencing the first of two lane changes. **Positioning 2 Lane Distance** is added to both **Mandatory 2 Lane Distance** and **Mandatory Distance** to determine the beginning of the positioning zone for the first of two lane changes.

The space between Positioning 2 Lane Distance and Mandatory 2 Lane Distance is divided into zones, where the first 2/3 is the positioning zone, and the remaining 1/3 is the mandatory zone, similar to the single lane change.

When a vehicle needs to make two lane changes, it is critical that the first lane change is completed early. Especially on high speed facilities. If the vehicle changes late, it can block two or even three lanes of the link. **Figure 24-3** shows a vehicle exiting a 3 lane freeway and waiting to make the first of two lane changes. This vehicle is blocking the left lane and will require a cooperating vehicle to stop in the middle lane. Then this vehicle will require another cooperating vehicle to stop in the right lane. By changing late, this vehicle has caused all three lanes to stop. Two lane change distances should be significantly higher than single lane change distances.

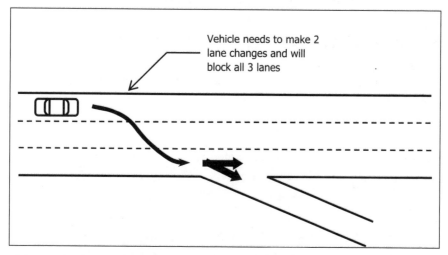

Figure 24-3   Vehicle Making Two Lane Changes

If three or more lane changes are needed. The distances are determined by adding in additional **Mandatory 2 Lane Distances**. **Table 24-2** outlines the distances for one, two, three, or four lane changes.

Table 24-2   Lane Change Distances

Number of Lane Changes	Positioning Point, distance from Stop Bar	Mandatory Point, distance from Stop Bar
1	PD + MD	MD
2	P2D + M2d + MD	M2D + MD
3	P2D + 2 * M2D + MD	2 * M2D + MD
4	P2D + 3 * M2D + MD	3 * M2D + MD

Default Lane Change Distances

Here are the **default lane change values** used by Synchro. Note that these distances are based on casual observations and there is no formal research backing up these parameters. These values may need to be adjusted to meet local conditions.

Table 24-3   Default Lane Change Distances

Value	Default Value, ft	Default Value, m
Mandatory Distance, Intersections	max (200 ft, C/6 * L)	max (60 m, C/6 * L)
Mandatory Distance, Bends	100 ft	30 m
Positioning Distance	max (300 ft, v * 30s)	max (90 m, v * 30s)
Mandatory 2 Lane Distance	max (200 ft, v * 20s)	max (60 m, v * 20s)
Positioning 2 Lane Distance	max (300 ft, v * 40s)	max (90 m, v * 40s)

C = Cycle Length (s)

L = Vehicle Length (ft)

v = Link Speed (ft/s)

The Mandatory Distance for signals is based on Cycle Length so that vehicles will normally get into the correct lane behind the back of queue.

The Mandatory Distance for bend nodes is shorter so that merging for lane drops will occur late.

The positioning and 2 lane distances are adjusted by speed so that lane changes can occur earlier at full speed.

Optional Lane Changes

Optional Lane changes are made to choose a lane with less congestion. Optional lane changes are not made when a mandatory lane change is needed. A lane change is attempted when an adjacent lane has less vehicles ahead and the adjacent lane also feeds the destination link(s) of this vehicle. An optional lane selection is based on the number of vehicles ahead and the speed of the vehicles ahead. Lanes with slow vehicles ahead are avoided. Aggressive driver types are more likely to make optional lane changes. Vehicles will attempt an Optional Lane change if there is an advantage to switching to an adjacent lane.

The lane desirability is determined by Advantage, calculated as follows:

Advantage = nC * (1 – spdCmin/ spdLimit) – nT * (1 – spdTMin/spdLimit) = Desirability of Lane Change

nC = number of vehicles ahead in current lane

nT = number of vehicles ahead in target lane

spdCMin = slowest vehicle ahead in current lane

spdTMin = slowest vehicle ahead in target lane

spdLimit = link speed limit

Vehicles are counted if they lie within 5 seconds at spdLimit. If one or more vehicles are stopped, all vehicles ahead count as a full point. If the ahead vehicles are slowed but not stopped they count for fractional points. Driver type 6 will make an optional lane change for a 1 stopped vehicle advantage. Driver 6 will ignore a positioning lane change if there is a 2 stopped vehicle advantage to staying in the current lane.

A lane change takes at least 1.5 seconds to complete. If a vehicle is traveling slower than the **Lane Change Speed**, 6 ft/s (1.8 m/s), a vehicle will take longer to complete a lane change. This prevents a vehicle from moving sideways with no forward speed and insures that a mandatory lane change can be completed in the allotted space.

A vehicle can start and complete a lane change from a standing queue.

Ok to Enter

A vehicle will start a lane change if the adjacent lane is clear of traffic. To test if a lane is clear, a **Test Deceleration** is determined between the changing vehicle and vehicles ahead and behind using car following formulas. Depending on the type of lane change, the maximum test deceleration must not exceed the following.

Table 24-4   Maximum Test Deceleration

Lane Change Type	Maximum test deceleration
Mandatory Lane Changes	decelHard (8ft/s^2 or 2.4m/s^2)
Anticipatory Lane Changes	decelPlus (6ft/s^2 or 1.8m/s^2)
Optional Lane Changes	decelNormal (4ft/s^2 or 1.2m/s^2)

Yielding to Lane Changers

Vehicles making a lane change will find a "lead" vehicle based on relative speed and position. The vehicle that would reach a matched speed-position first is considered a leader. The changing vehicle will adjust its speed to trail the "lead" vehicle.

Vehicles in a lane also look for merging vehicles to "trail" based on relative speed and position. If the vehicle is a "trail" vehicle, it will adjust its speed to follow the merging vehicle.

The lane change logic above is a change from version 1. This logic allows for high speed merging and weaving in freeway operations. In general the above logic yields higher speeds and flow rates and less disruptive lane changing.

Coding Tips

Mandatory lane changes are inefficient and can block two or more lanes for extended time periods. Code storage bays to reduce lane changes.

Lane Change Applications

For the majority of situations the default lane change distances should work fine. Here are some special situations that may require adjusting the lane change distances.

Signal

Normally vehicles need to be in the correct lane for turning before the back of queue. The drivers won't necessarily know where the back of queue is for any given time, but regular drivers will have a general knowledge of the maximum queue lengths and will be able to see the queues in real time.

The default mandatory distance is set for one vehicle for every 6 seconds of cycle length. This value will somewhat approximate the maximum queue for nearly saturated movements.

To allow vehicles to shift into the correct lane earlier, use a higher Mandatory Distance. To allow vehicles to shift into their lane at the last possible moment, use a lower Mandatory Distance. Generally, large cities tend to have more aggressive drivers who will wait to get in the correct lane if there is a shorter line up, while smaller towns tend to have more courteous drivers implying longer mandatory distances.

 Key Point — Use mandatory distances equal to the maximum back of queue to get most vehicles into the correct lane before queue.

Freeway Off-Ramp

The positioning and mandatory distances can be used to control the point when drivers first become aware of the need to be in the correct lane and the point at which they must be in the correct lane. **Figure 24-4** shows how the mandatory and positioning distances might be related to exit signing.

 Key Point — Use long mandatory and positioning distances at high speeds to get vehicles into the correct lane early and avoid "last chance" stopping.

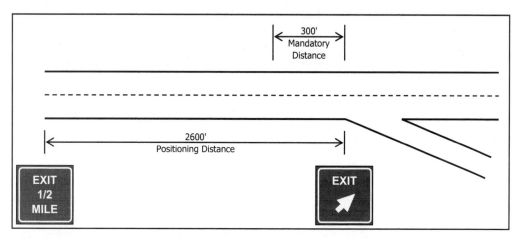

Figure 24-4   Freeway Off-Ramp Lane Change Distances

Three Lane Freeway Off-Ramp

With a **three lane freeway**, it is critical to get exiting vehicles into the right lane early. Making lane changes at the last moment can cause all three lanes to stop, see **Figure 24-5**.

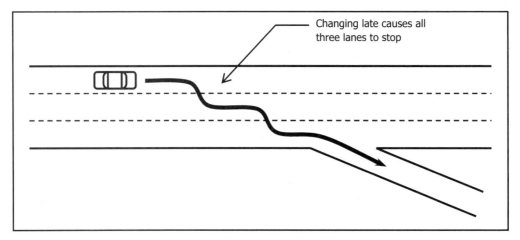

Changing late causes all three lanes to stop

Figure 24-5   Vehicle Making Late Lane Changes

Key Point

Use long two lane mandatory and two lane positioning distances at high speeds to get vehicles into the correct lane early and avoid "last chance" stopping and blocking of multiple lanes.

Figure 24-6 shows how the mandatory 2 and positioning 2 distances are related to exit signing. Higher values can be used if there is more advanced signing.

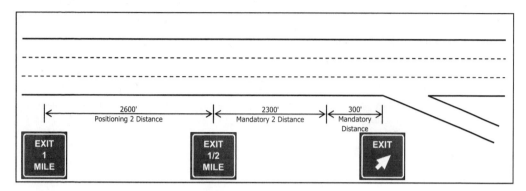

Figure 24-6   Freeway Off-Ramp Lane Change Distances (Three-Lane Freeway)

Lane Drop after Signal

If there is a **lane drop** after the signal it is sometimes desired to have vehicles use the dropping lane though the signal. This may be encouraged with lane use signing. The default positioning distance for 35 mph is 1540 ft. This distance will cause drivers to avoid the drop lane at the signal when the acceleration lane is less than 1500 ft. Lowering the mandatory and positioning distances can get drivers to use all lanes.

Refer to **Figure 24-7**. There is a 300 ft auxiliary lane after the signal. Using a mandatory distance of 100ft and a positioning distance of 200 ft will cause 50% of the drivers (driver types 6 to 10) to ignore the lane drop until after the signal.

 Adjust the mandatory and positioning distances to the length of an auxiliary lane to get balanced lane use before an auxiliary lane drop.

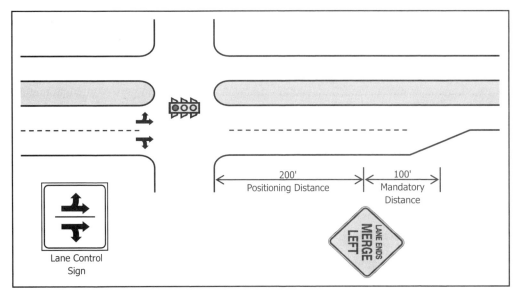

Figure 24-7   Lane Drop after Signal

Controlling Lane Utilization

The **Lane Change distances** can also be used to influence lane utilization. **Figure 24-8** shows an intersection with a lane drop 500 ft after the intersection.

Adjusted Mandatory Distance is the distance from the downstream stop bar where a vehicle must start its lane change. The vehicle will stop and wait for an opening if the lane change has not started. The mandatory distance is multiplied by the driver's **Mandatory Distance Adjust**.

The **Start of Mandatory Zone** is the distance from the downstream stop bar where a vehicle begins attempting a mandatory lane change. The **Start of Positioning Zone** is the distance from the downstream stop bar where a vehicle begins attempting a positioning lane change. The calculations are in the following formulas.

AMD = MD * MDA = Adjusted Mandatory Distance

SMZ = MD * MDA + PD *PDA / 3 = Start of Mandatory Zone Distance

PZ = MD * MDA + PD *PDA = Start of Positioning Zone Distance

MD = Mandatory Distance

MDA = Mandatory Distance Adjustment for driver

PD = Positioning Distance

PDA = Positioning Distance Adjustment for driver

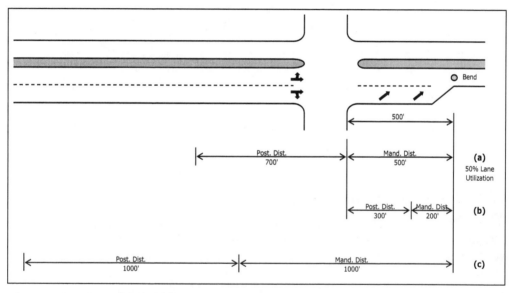

Figure 24-8   Controlling Lane Utilization

In case (a) in the above figure, the mandatory distance is set to 500ft and the positioning distance is set to 700'. **Table 24-5** illustrates how each driver type is affected by these distances. These distances are all measured from the end of the lane drop.

Table 24-5   Case (a) Driver Type Distances

Driver Type	Mand. Adj.	Positioning Adj.	Mand. Dist.	Start of Mand.	Positioning Distance
1	2	1.5	1000	1350	2050
2	1.7	1.4	850	1177	1830
3	1.5	1.3	750	1053	1660
4	1.35	1.2	675	955	1515
5	1.1	1.1	550	807	1320
6	0.9	0.95	450	672	1115
7	0.8	0.9	400	610	1030
8	0.7	0.8	350	537	910
9	0.6	0.7	300	463	790
10	0.5	0.6	250	390	670

Note that the mandatory distance for a driver type 1 to 5 exceeds 500 feet; all of these drivers will be out of the right lane before the upstream intersection. Fifty percent of all drivers will not use the right lane at the upstream signal.

The start of the mandatory zone for a driver type 6 to 8 exceeds 500 feet. These drivers will be very aggressive about making a lane change before the signal, but they will not stop for the lane change until after the signal.

Driver types 9 and 10 have positioning distances exceeding 500 feet. These drivers will attempt to use the left lane if the queue is not significantly longer and they do not need to slow for a lane change. They are not aware of the need to be in the left lane until 790' and 670', respectively.

In case (a) 50% of the drivers are excluded from the right lane, and an additional 30% of the drivers will aggressively avoid the right lane.

In case (b), mandatory is set to 200ft and positioning distance is set to 300'. **Table 24-6** illustrates how each driver type is affected by these distances. These distances are all measured from the end of the lane drop.

Table 24-6   Case (b) Driver Type Distances

Driver Type	Mand. Adj.	Positioning Adj.	Mand. Dist.	Start of Mand.	Positioning Distance
1	2	1.5	400	550	850
2	1.7	1.4	340	480	760
3	1.5	1.3	300	430	690
4	1.35	1.2	270	390	630
5	1.1	1.1	220	330	550
6	0.9	0.95	180	275	465
7	0.8	0.9	160	250	430
8	0.7	0.8	140	220	380
9	0.6	0.7	120	190	330
10	0.5	0.6	100	160	280

In this case no Adjusted Mandatory Distance exceeds 500ft. No drivers are forced to use the left lane.

The start of the mandatory zone for driver type 1 exceeds 500 feet. These drivers will be very aggressive about making a lane change before the signal, but they will not stop for the lane change until after the signal.

Driver types 1 to 5 have positioning distances exceeding 500 feet. These drivers will attempt to use the left lane if the queue is not significantly longer and they do not need to slow for a lane change.

In case (b), no drivers are excluded from the right lane. 10% will aggressively avoid the right lane, and an additional 40% of drivers will passively avoid the right lane.

In case (c), mandatory is set to 1000ft and positioning distance is set to 1000 ft. **Table 24-7** illustrates how each driver type is affected by these distances. These distances are all measured from the end of the lane drop.

Table 24-7   Case (c) Driver Type Distances

Driver Type	Mand. Adj.	Positioning Adj.	Mand. Dist.	Start of Mand.	Positioning Distance
1	2	1.5	2000	2500	3500
2	1.7	1.4	1700	2167	3100
3	1.5	1.3	1500	1933	2800
4	1.35	1.2	1350	1750	2550
5	1.1	1.1	1100	1467	2200
6	0.9	0.95	900	1217	1850
7	0.8	0.9	800	1100	1700
8	0.7	0.8	700	967	1500
9	0.6	0.7	600	833	1300
10	0.5	0.6	500	700	1100

Note that the mandatory distance for a driver types 1 to 10 exceeds 500 feet; all of these drivers will be out of the right lane before the upstream intersection. No drivers will use the right lane at the upstream signal.

Long Turning Bay

Refer to **Figure 24-9**. There is a **long turning bay** for right turns and dual right lanes at the signal. The right turn movement has a lot of volume. The goal is to allow some right turning vehicles to use the left lane and merge right after the start of the storage bay.

In this case the storage bay is 1000 ft. Setting Mandatory Distance less than the storage distance will allow some vehicles to use the left lane and make a late lane change.

Key Point

Set mandatory distance less than the turning bay length to allow lane changes after the start of the turning bay.

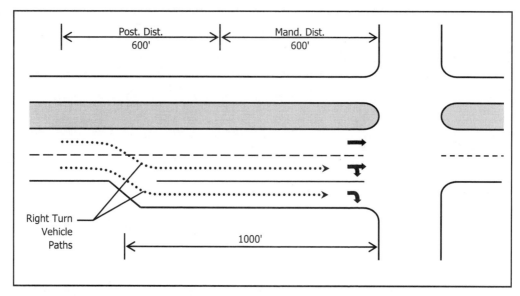

Figure 24-9   Long Turning Bay Example

Lane Selection through Multiple Intersections

Sometimes it is necessary to control lane use through multiple intersections. In **Figure 24-10**, a lane control sign tells motorists to use both lanes before the first signal. There is only 400 ft between the intersections for left turning vehicles to get into the correct lane. The vehicle in the through curb lane must change lanes into the through/left lane after passing through intersection 1. Using lower values for mandatory and positioning can cause the left turning vehicles to use both lanes at the first signal. With default settings, more vehicles would favor the leftmost through lane at intersection 1.

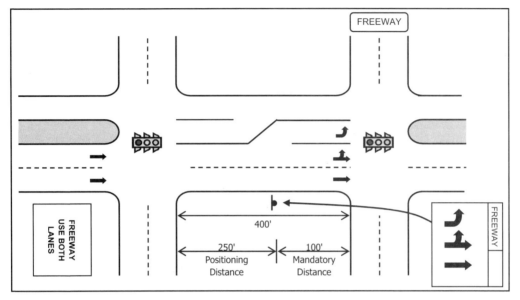

Figure 24-10   Lane Change through Multiple Intersections

Figure 24-11 illustrates a different case. In this case, advanced signing informs motorists to use only one of two left turn lanes for an upcoming freeway on ramp. For this example use the default high values for positioning and mandatory distances. This will cause freeway entering vehicles to use only the single allowed turn lane.

Key
Point

Set mandatory distance low to allow lane changes on a short link. Use higher mandatory distances to force vehicles into the correct lane earlier.

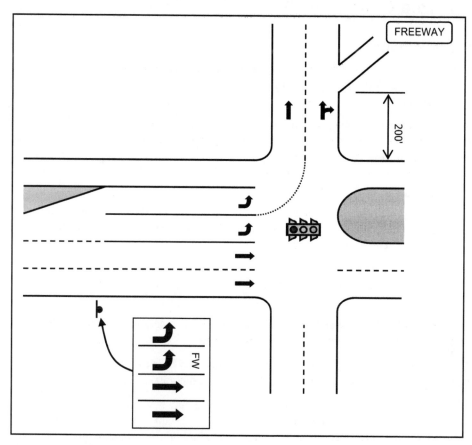

Figure 24-11   Lane Positioning Example

Unsignalized Operation

Collision Avoidance

All intersections, both signalized and unsignalized have **collision avoidance logic**. This logic prevents vehicles and pedestrians from entering an intersection when a conflicting vehicle or pedestrian is present.

Vehicles are given approval to enter the intersection depending on when they are approved by signal or sign control and there are no conflicts. Once approved, other vehicles seeking approval must not conflict or must wait for the approved vehicles to clear. A vehicle can be approved when its travel time is within the Maximum Gap time, which is 7.0 s.

Vehicles can be approved if conflicting vehicles have been approved but their travel time to the intersection is greater than the appropriate gap time. Vehicles can also be approved if conflicting vehicles have completed traversing part of the intersection. The amount of traversal depends on the turn of the subject vehicle and the target vehicle.

For example, the subject vehicle is going through and the target vehicle is from the left going straight, the subject must wait for the target vehicle to clear 80% of the intersection before entering.

If the target was coming from the right and going straight, the subject must wait for the target vehicle to clear only 40% of the intersection before entering.

If a conflicting vehicle is destined to the same link, merge analysis is performed. If target lanes do not cross, there is no conflict. U-turns are not eligible for merge analysis.

Right turn movements will only conflict with merging or crossing streams. If a right turn has its own lane, no collision avoidance is performed and this is a free right. A through movement may also be considered a free movement if there are no links to the right and the through movement has an exclusive target lane.

Pedestrian Vehicle Interactions

Pedestrians cross the street at the **Network Walk Speed** (4 ft/s or 1.2 m/s by default). The internal logic calculates a time until entering and clearing each lane. These times have an extra buffer of 1 s or 4 ft.

For approved vehicles, times to enter and to clear both the near and far crosswalks are calculated based on their current speed, turning speed, distance through intersection, and vehicle length.

The arrival time is underestimated and the departure time is overestimated to allow a factor of safety.

A pedestrian can be approved to start if no currently approved vehicles are scheduled to be in each crosswalk lane when the pedestrian will be in that lane.

A vehicle can be approved to start if no approved pedestrian will be in the near or far crosswalk lane when that vehicle is projected to cross.

If a pedestrian is ready to start, vehicles will not be approved unless they can clear the intersection before the pedestrian would reach their lane. At a signal, waiting pedestrians are only ready when they have a walk indication.

Vehicles in a roundabout will also stop for pedestrians when exiting the roundabout.

Gridlock Avoidance

Vehicles will not be approved if there is not room for them on the next link. Gridlock avoidance is controlled by the **Enter Blocked Intersection** setting in the **SIMULATION** settings. Refer to page 9-4.

Unsignalized Approvals

Vehicles are only approved when there are no conflicting pedestrians or vehicles already approved. At an unsignalized intersection, vehicles are approved in the following order:

1. Through and right vehicles on free approaches.

2. Left vehicles on through approaches.

3. Pedestrians on any approach.

4. Vehicles on next-up signed approach.

5. If any vehicle has been approved, vehicles on non next-up signed approaches.

Entering vehicles will not be approved if they conflict with a pending pedestrian.

Vehicles at stop or yield signs will not be approved if they conflict with a pending main street left turn.

The unsignalized intersection manager tracks the next-up signed approach. When vehicle(s) at the stop bar of the next-up signed approach are served, the next-up approach rotates clockwise to the next signed approach. This ensures that each signed approach has its fair turn at the intersection. Vehicles that are waiting for a stop sign cannot go until their approach is next-up or until a compatible vehicle moves from another higher priority movement. This scheme allows two-way, three-way, and four-way stops to be modeled in a round-robin type fashion.

Stop versus Yield

Stop sign and yield sign operation are very similar. For both control types, the vehicle will come to a stop if necessary and wait until the intersection is clear. The key difference between a stop and a yield is the distance at which vehicles can be approved.

A vehicle approaching a stop sign cannot be approved when it is within 3 ft (0.9 m) of the stop bar. The stopping vehicle will be prepared to stop, and at 5 ft (1.5 m) may be traveling at 6 ft/s (1.8 m/s). SimTraffic assumes "Hollywood" type stops. A vehicle will slow to 6 ft/s (4mph) but not stop when there is no conflicting traffic. When there is conflicting traffic, both stopping and yielding vehicles will stop and wait.

Gap Times

When approving vehicles, the conflict manager will also look at approved vehicles approaching the intersection. The estimated travel time until entering the intersection is calculated for these vehicles. If the **Approach Gap Time** is less than these vehicles' travel time to the intersection, they will not be in conflict.

The approach gap time is not quite the same as the gap times seen in Chapter 10 of the HCM. The gap time in the HCM is the time between vehicles. In SimTraffic, the approach gap time is the currently estimated time it will take approaching vehicles to enter the intersection. The approach gap time in SimTraffic is generally less than the HCM style gap time because SimTraffic's gap time does not include the time it takes for the conflicting vehicles to clear the intersection.

The approach gap times were determined experimentally to match the saturation flow rates found in Chapter 10 of the HCM. In some cases, the gap times are so low that main street vehicles need to almost stop to avoid collision. Even with these low approach gap settings, the resulting Saturated Flow Rates are about 50 to 150 vph less than those predicted by the HCM. The HCM is most likely calibrated based on observations of congested intersections. At these intersections, the cross traffic may be willing to accept tight gaps because they have been waiting a long time. It is also possible that the loss in capacity due to impedance is understated in the HCM formulas. Thus, the resulting approach gaps in SimTraffic are a trade off, giving less than acceptable gap times and lower than predicted capacity.

The required gap times for each movement are summarized in **Table 24-8**. In general, the gap time is equal to the time it will take a vehicle to enter and clear the intersection. The conflicting vehicles may be slowing to make a turn and this will increase their estimated travel time.

Table 24-8   Required Gap Times

Movement	Approach Gap	Nominal Time (s)
Main Through or Right	3.0 s	NA
Main Left	3.6 s	3.6 s
Cross Left	3.9 s	3.6 s
Cross Thru	3.4 s	1.9 s
Cross Right	2.9 s	4.6 s

When determining a gap time, the travel time though the intersection is calculated using the curve distance and the curve or link speed. If the travel time is longer than the nominal travel time, the gap is increased by the difference.

$$\text{GapX} = \text{Gap} + \max(0, (\text{Dist} + \text{L})/\text{CurveSpeed} - \text{NomTime}) = \text{adjusted gap time}$$

Gap = Approach Gap Time

Dist = distance of path through intersection

L = Vehicle Length

NomTime = nominal time

CurveSpeed = speed limit for turn or link

This distance adjustment results in longer gaps for large intersections or slow turns.

Pre-Timed Signal Operation

The operation of pre-timed signals is mostly straightforward. Each phase operates in sequence as defined in Synchro. During animation, the current state of the signal can be viewed by clicking with the mouse in the middle of the intersection.

Vehicle Approvals

These rules determine when vehicles are approved, both for actuated and pre-timed signals.

The signalized intersection manager can approve the first unapproved vehicle in each lane. For each 0.1-second time-slice, vehicles and pedestrians are approved in the following order:

1. Permitted left turns beginning their sneak at the beginning of red.

2. Pedestrians with walk phase.

3. Vehicles with green light moving through and right.

4. Vehicles turning left with a green ball or a green arrow.

5. Right turn vehicles on red, if RTOR is allowed.

In addition:

- No vehicles or pedestrians are approved if conflicting vehicles or pedestrians are already approved.

- New vehicles will not start if a pedestrian is waiting and has a walk light.

- RTOR vehicles will not start if a vehicle is waiting with a green light.

- When a signal turns green, the driver does not react until after their Green Reaction time.

- When a signal turns yellow, approved vehicles may be unapproved if they can stop at their Yellow Deceleration Rate. The Yellow Deceleration Rate is dependent upon the driver type.

Left Turn Sneakers

When the signal is yellow it is possible for permitted left turn vehicles to complete their left turn movement by sneaking. If the vehicle's distance to the stop bar at the beginning of the yellow is less than the Yield Approve Distance (30 ft or 10 m), it will be marked for sneaking. This normally allows two vehicles per cycle to sneak on each permitted left turn movement.

The sneaking vehicles are allowed to enter the intersection during yellow and the beginning of red, if the intersection becomes clear. Normally oncoming through traffic will clear the intersection during yellow and the sneaking vehicles will be approved. It is possible that an oncoming through vehicle will "run" the yellow light and the sneakers will not be able to start until the signal turns red. If you observe vehicles sneaking during red, this may indicate that longer yellow and/or all-red intervals are needed, or that the yellow deceleration rate is too low.

Pre-Timed Signal Transitions

If multiple timing plans are used in conjunction with data files and multiple intervals, it is possible to have the signal transition between timing plans. **Pre-timed signals** will transition with the following steps:

1. Transition begins

2. Signal reaches the sync point. The sync point is the first point where all coordinated phases are green.

3. New timing plan is loaded.

4. Signal rests on coordinated phases until sync point in new timing plan is reached. Transition is now complete.

Signal transitions with pre-timed signals can be quite disruptive. It may take nearly an entire cycle to reach the sync point, then the signal may rest on the main street phases for up to a full cycle in addition to the normal main street green time. This operation is intended to mimic the operation of electromechanical pre-timed signals. To get more efficient transitions, use coordinated signals.

Actuated Signal Operation

The operation of **actuated signals** is quite complex compared to pre-timed signals. Actuated signals have detectors and gap counters, and can skip phases. The current state of the signal can be viewed during animation by clicking with the mouse in the middle of the intersection.

Detectors

Detectors are placed per the settings in the **DETECTOR** settings. Full details can be found in Chapter 10.

If a phase has a pedestrian signal and does not have max or ped recall, a pedestrian button is assumed. Whenever a pedestrian is generated, a ped call is generated.

Gap Counters

Each actuated phase has a **gap counter**. The current state of the gap counter can be seen in the signal state settings. Every time a vehicle is over a detector, the gap counter is reset to Vehicle Extension, or to a calculated gap for volume density operation. Once the gap counter reaches zero, the phase has gapped out and the counter remains at zero.

The signal will not gap-out during the minimum initial interval.

At a fully actuated or semi-actuated signal, the gap counter will not start counting until there are calls on conflicting phases. If a detector has extension time (e), it will place a call for e seconds after actuation.

Phase Sequences

Phase sequences are served in the order determined by the Ring and Barrier Designer in Synchro. Normally each phase is serviced in order as expected for a dual ring controller.

With lagging operation, the even phase will appear before its odd phase partner. For example, phase 2 will show before phase 1.

SimTraffic assumes dual service. If phase 1 has calls, but no calls are present on phase 3 or 4, phase 4 will still appear so that a phase in each ring will show. It is always the even phase that shows for dual service in the absence of calls.

If the leading phase of a phase partner gaps out and there is no call to the lagging phase, the leading phase will remain on. For example:

- Phases 1 and 5 are showing.

- Phase 1 gaps out and phase 5 still has time left and there are no calls for phase 2.

- Phase 2 will be skipped and will not reappear until all other phases have had a chance to display.

Coordinated Phase Sequences

In an actuated-coordinated signal, each phase has a start time and an end time. The end time is the force-off point for actuated phases and the yield point for coordinated phases.

When the coordinated phases reach their first yield point, the phases enter the Ready to Yield state. While in the Ready to Yield state, the signal can yield to any actuated phase when its start time appears.

Once all the coordinated phases yield, the signal enters Yielded State. In Yielded State, all actuated phases are serviced in turn until the actuated phases reappear. SimTraffic can operate with "Inhibit Max" operation. Any unused time from actuated phases can be used later by other actuated phases. Each actuated phase is terminated when it gaps out, or at its yield point, whichever comes first. An Actuated phase can also be terminated at its max time if Inhibit Max is not used.

When both coordinated phases come back, the signal enters Display Main State. The signal remains in Display Main State until the first yield point. No actuated phases can be displayed during this state.

Signal Transitions

If multiple timing plans are used in conjunction with data files and multiple intervals, it is possible to have the **signal transition** between timing plans.

If the new timing plan is fully actuated or uncoordinated, the transition occurs immediately.

If the new timing plan is coordinated, the transition will occur with the following steps:

1. New timing plan is loaded and cycle clock is set based on time from midnight.

2. Cycle Clock for current state is calculated based on current phase durations and their start times.

3. The calculated cycle clock is compared to the target cycle clock. If the calculated cycle clock state is ahead by less than half a cycle, the controller will attempt to regain coordination by using shortened phases. Otherwise, the controller will attempt to regain coordination by using longer phase times.

4. The transition maxtimes are calculated by increasing or decreasing the phase max green times by 17%. No green times will be shortened below the pedestrian walk plus flashing-do not-walk times or the minimum initial time. If shortening is unable to reduce the cycle length by at least 10%, the transition will occur using longer green times.

5. The signal will continue to time using the shortened or extended phase times. No force off or yield points are used.

6. At the beginning of each barrier transition, the calculated cycle clock is compared to the actual cycle clock. When the calculated cycle clock is a little bit behind, the transition is complete and the signal will begin operating coordinated with the new timing plan.

The transition is complete when the calculated cycle clock is less than this amount behind:

Long Way, Coordinated Barrier 30%

Long Way, Non-Coordinated Barrier 20%

Short Way, Coordinated Barrier 50%

Short Way, Non-Coordinated Barrier 30%

When a phase order switches from leading to lagging, it is possible that a phase may be shown twice within the barrier, or skipped. SimTraffic contains special logic to prevent a phase from being skipped or shown twice. Note that actual controllers may not contain this logic and it is possible that real-world controllers will skip phases or service phases twice during a timing plan transition.

Consider the following example:

Old Order: $1 - 2 \mid 4$

New Order: $2 - 1 \mid 4$

Case 1

State at transition start: ph 1 green

Normal order $4 \mid 1 \mid 4$

Adjusted order $4 \mid 1 - 2 \mid 4$

Case 2

State at transition start: ph 1 yellow, committed to phase 2

Normal order $4 \mid 1 - 2 - 1 \mid 4$

Adjusted order $4 \mid 1 - 2 \mid 4$

Case 3

State at transition start: ph 2

Normal order $4 \mid 1 - 2 - 1 \mid 4$

Adjusted order $4 \mid 1 - 2 \mid 4$

Case 4

State at transition start: ph 4 yellow, committed to phase 1

Normal order $4 \mid 1 - 2 - 1 \mid 4$

Adjusted order $4 \mid 1 - 2 \mid 4$

Case 5

State at transition start: ph 4 yellow, not committed to new phase

Normal order	$4\,|\,2-1\,|\,4$
Adjusted order:	No adjustment necessary

In order to display overlaps, the new phase may be committed during yellow time, if it is part of an overlap.

Corner Points and Curb Radii

The center line for each link is offset to the left and right based on the median widths and widths of the lanes. The lane widths are the widths of through and right lanes. Left lanes are part of the median which is calculated as described above.

The **Right Width, wR**, is equal to 1/2 the median width plus the widths of through and right lanes.

The **Left Width, wL**, is equal to 1/2 the median width plus the number of departure lanes. The departure lanes include all lanes except for storage lanes.

The offset lines for adjacent links are crossed to create corner points (ptL and ptR). These corner points are used to determine the location of crosswalks, stop-bars, and curb line curves.

Refer to **Figure 24-12**. Each link is given two points ptL and ptR where the link intersects at the intersection. When the angle is obtuse ($\geq$ 90 degrees), these points are set where the curb lines intersect. See ptRB and prLC in the diagram.

When the angle is acute (< 90 degrees), these points are set based on the minimum curb radius (w). See ptRA and prLB in the diagram. If there is a right turn island or no right turn path, the points are set the same as an obtuse intersection

At a 'T' intersection, these points are based on the location of the points across the street, ptRC is across from ptLC and ptLA is across from ptRA.

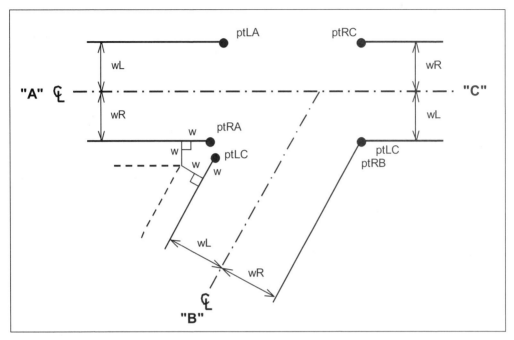

Figure 24-12 Corner Points

Once the corner points are located the stop bar points can be found. Refer to **Figure 24-13**. Each link connects its ptR and ptL and this line is offset by the crosswalk width, 16 ft or 2.4 m. The crosswalk width is the same as the minimum curve radius. This offset line represents the stop bar, the edge of the crosswalk and the boundary of the intersection. Stop bar points ptSBR and ptSBL are located at the intersection of the curb line and the stop bar line. These points also represent the beginning of the Curb Corner Curves. These curves are created by fitting Bezier curves to these points. The Curb Corner curves always start at the stop bar and crosswalk; with the exception of right turn islands.

The **Pedestrian Path** is located 1/3 the crosswalk width beyond the stop bar. The path starts and ends 4 ft outside the extended curb lines so that the path will be outside of the curb corner curve.

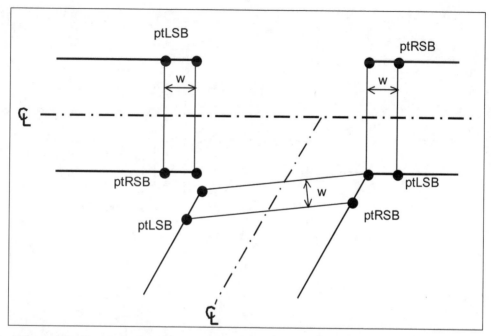

Figure 24-13   Stop Bar Points

Right Turn Islands

Figure 24-14 shows how a right turn island is laid out. With a **right turn island** there can be two right widths (wR and wR') and two left widths (wL and wL'). The widths wR and wL include the full width with all lanes, while wR' and wL' do not count lanes dropped for the island and lanes added by the island.

The outside curb lines are offset by the curve radius to find a center point ptC. Also the points of curvature and tangency (PC and PT) are found along the outside curb lines. The inside curb lines are crossed to find the corner points (ptL, ptR, and ptIX). The inside radius of the right turn curve is intersected with the inside curb lines to find the corners of the island (points I1 and I2).

The Stop Bar points are based on the inside curb lines and are found in the same manner, as illustrated in **Figure 24-12**. The stop bar and crosswalk extend to the island only.

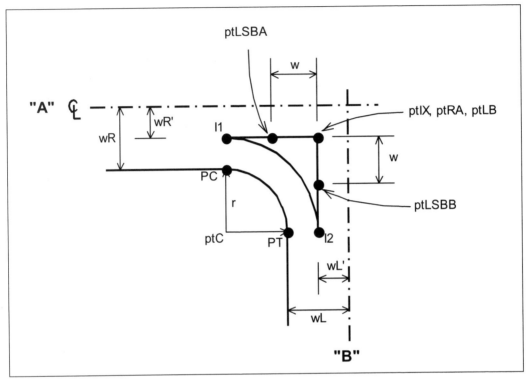

Figure 24-14   Right Turn Island

Roundabouts

Figure 24-15 shows how corner points and stop bar points are located for a **roundabout**. Normally the corner points (ptL and ptR) are set where the curb line crosses the outer radius of the circle (point A in diagram). When two links have curb lines crossing outside the circle the corner point is set at the curb line intersection (point B in diagram).

The stop bar points are found by offsetting the corner points by the crosswalk width (w = 16 ft or 2.4 m).

The point where the Corner Curb Radius meets the circle is found by rotating around the circle by the crosswalk width. Point C in the diagram is found by rotating the crosswalk width from point A. The entry and exit curves for vehicles are found in a similar manner.

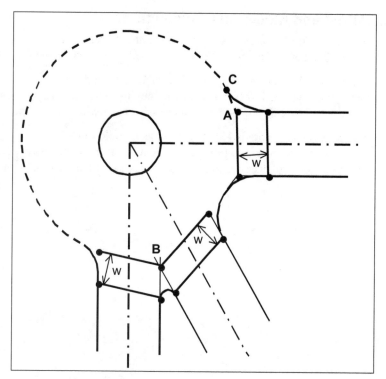

Figure 24-15   Roundabout

Delay, Fuel and Emissions Considerations

SimTraffic reports two delays, total delay and stopped delay.

Stopped delay is the sum of time that the vehicle is stopped or moving slower than 10 ft/s.

Total delay is the difference between the actual travel time and the time it would have taken to clear the network without any signals, signs or other vehicles.

Total delay is comparable to the signal delay in Synchro and the delay reported in TRANSYT and HCS.

If one or more links are congested, SimTraffic delays can get quite large. The longer the analysis period, the larger the delays will grow. Each model makes different assumptions about what happens during congestion. This makes it difficult to compare delays for congested movements.

Stopped Vehicles and Fuel and Emissions Calculations

In some cases fuel and emissions in SimTraffic can increase while stops and delays decrease. This seems counterintuitive since fuel and emissions should be proportional to stops and delays.

In a congested network, many of the vehicles may be stopped and are not reaching their destinations. Stopped vehicles emit and consume less per second than moving vehicles. It is possible that by improving traffic flow, more cars are moving and emissions increase.

To check the results look at the miles per gallon and divide the emissions by miles traveled. Most fuel is consumed when accelerating from a stop to full speed. The fuel and emissions may be reported on the exit link since the majority of acceleration occurs after crossing the stop bar.

Chapter 25 – 3D Viewer

3D Viewer is a simple, easy-to-use tool for three-dimensional modeling of SimTraffic simulations. Users can create rich visualizations by adding buildings and scenery, then produce a digital video for presentations using fly-thru and drive-thru animation.

3D Viewer uses a SimTraffic simulation to create a Scene. A Scene is a three-dimensional rendering of a SimTraffic network. A scene is generated when the user creates a 3D graphics file using SimTraffic. See page 20-3 for recording a 3D graphics file.

Getting Around 3D Viewer

The User Interface

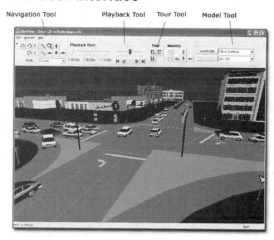

| Navigation Tool | Playback Tool | Tour Tool | Model Tool |

Navigation Tool	Allows the user to move through the scene.
Playback Tool	Controls the animation of the scene.
Tour Tool	Enables creation of virtual scene tours and digital video.
Model Tool	Enables the user to customize the scene with buildings, trees, signs, etc.

Navigation Tools

3D Viewer provides navigation tools for moving through a scene. The navigation tools are located on the upper left of the toolbar. The keyboard can also be used for screen navigation.

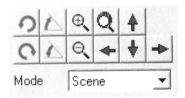

Pan

Pan control moves the scene left, right, forward, and backward.

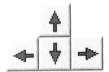

The **[Left]**, **[Right]**, **[Up]**, and **[Down]** keys can be used to do the same. Holding down the **[CTRL]** key while pressing the arrow keys will increase the pan speed. Increasing the pan speed is useful for moving across large areas of the scene quickly.

The user may also move through the scene using the mouse. By left-clicking on the scene, the user can move the scene left, right, backwards, and forwards by moving the mouse left, right, up, and down respectively. Similarly, holding down the **[CTRL]** key while moving the mouse will increase the rate at which the scene moves.

Rotate

The user can click the rotate buttons to pivot the scene clockwise or counterclockwise about the center of the scene window. To rotate the scene, click and hold down the ⟳ button to rotate counterclockwise, or the ⟲ button to rotate clockwise. The user may also press the **[Insert]** key to rotate counterclockwise, or press the **[Delete]** key to rotate clockwise.

The user may also rotate the scene using the mouse. By right-clicking on the scene, the user can move the scene counterclockwise, clockwise, tilted up, or tilted down by moving the mouse left, right, up, and down respectively.

Tilt

The user can click the tilt buttons to adjust the "camera" angle up or down. The ▲ button will raise the camera angle. The ◢ button will lower the camera angle. The user may also press the **[Home]** and **[End]** keys to respectively raise and lower the viewing angle.

Zoom

The user can click the zoom buttons to enlarge or reduce the screen size. The ⊕ button zooms into the scene. The ⊖ button zooms out of the scene. Likewise, the **[Page Up]** and the **[Page Down]** keys can be used to zoom in and zoom out.

The user can also zoom the scene such that the entire simulation fits within the window by clicking the 🔍 button.

Mode

3D Viewer has 3 different modes for moving through the scene.

Mode   [Scene   ▼]

The first mode, **Scene** mode, enables the user to navigate through the scene using the above mentioned navigation tools. Selecting **Scene** in the **Mode** combo box or pressing **[S]** will put the application in scene mode.

The second mode, **Ride** mode, enables the user to select a vehicle and move through the scene from the driver's point-of-view. To put the application in **Ride** mode, click on a vehicle, then choose **Ride** in the Mode combo box or press **[R]**.

The third mode, **Track** mode, enables the user to select a vehicle and move through the scene as an observer over the vehicle, following its movement throughout the scene. To put the application in **Track** mode, click on a vehicle, then choose **Track** mode in the **Mode** combo box or press **[T]** button.

Home Position

The user can set "home" position of the scene. The home position is a saved location and viewing angle. To set the home position, navigate to the desired location and orientation in the scene. Next, press **[CTRL][7/HOME]** (the **[7/HOME]** key on the numeric keypad). To return to the home position, press the **[7/HOME]** key on the numeric keypad at any time.

Playback Tool

3D Viewer animation tools playback the vehicle and signal activity according to the simulation generated in SimTraffic.

Timeline

The timeline control enables the user to move to any point within the simulation time window.

The timeline control displays the total time contained in the simulation. The current time marker shows the relative position within the simulation timeline and displays the current time offset in the middle of the control.

The user can step through the scene in extremely slow motion by using the keyboard in conjunction with the timeline control. First, left-click on the position indicator on the timeline control, then hold down either the left or right arrow keys to step through the scene.

Playback

The playback control manipulates the animation rate and direction.

The user can animate the scene at 1 to 8 times real-time speed by clicking and dragging the playback control to the left or right. When the playback control moves to the right, the application animates the scene forward in time. When the playback control moves to the left, the application animates the scene backward in time.

Frame Skip and Playback

The Frame Skip buttons advance the timeline to the end or return the timeline to the beginning.

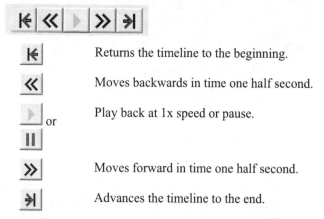

⏮	Returns the timeline to the beginning.
⏪	Moves backwards in time one half second.
▶ or ⏸	Play back at 1x speed or pause.
⏩	Moves forward in time one half second.
⏭	Advances the timeline to the end.

Tour Tool

The Tour Tool enables the user to create virtual tours of the simulation environment for later playback or digital video creation.

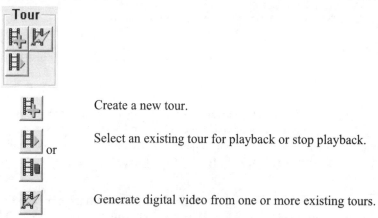

	Create a new tour.
or	Select an existing tour for playback or stop playback.
	Generate digital video from one or more existing tours.

Model Tool

The Model Tool enables the user to add buildings and other scenery to the scene.

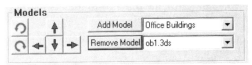

Model List

The model list contains the inventory of available buildings, signs, trees, shrubs and other items.

The combo box at the top lists the model categories. The combo box on bottom lists the models contained within each category. To add a model, select the category, then select the model within the category. Then click **Add Model** to add the model to the scene. To remove a model, select a building, tree, or other item from the scene and click **Remove Model**.

Model Position Tool

The model position tool helps the user place the model exactly in the desired location.

Models may be moved left, right, forward, and backward. Models may also be rotated clockwise and counterclockwise. To position a model, select a building, sign, tree, or shrub from the scene. Next, click the model position buttons to place and orient the model as desired. Additionally, the user may use the **[Insert]**, **[Delete]**, **[Up]**, **[Down]**, **[Right]**, and **[Left]** keys to manipulate a model once it is selected.

The user can also position a model by using the mouse. To move a model with the mouse left-click on the model then move the mouse left, right, up, or down. This will move the model left, right, backward, or forward. The user can increase the speed at which the model moves in the scene by holding down the **[CTRL]** key while moving the mouse.

To rotate a model using the mouse, right-click on the model and move the mouse left or right.

After adding, removing, or changing model placement, be sure to select the **File** menu and choose **Save**.

Using 3D Viewer

Create a New Scene

Once the user creates a 3D graphics file from within SimTraffic, the user can then launch 3D Viewer Version 7 directly from SimTraffic by clicking on the 3D toolbar button.

Ride in a Vehicle

Users can navigate through a scene from the perspective of a driver in a vehicle. To "ride" in a vehicle, click on a vehicle in the scene, then choose **Ride** in the **Mode** combo box on the toolbar or press **[R]**.

While "riding" in a vehicle, users can click on other vehicles to jump to another driver's perspective.

To "get out" of a vehicle, choose **Scene** in the **Mode** combo box or press **[S]**.

While 3D Viewer is in **Ride** mode, the scene navigation functions rotate, tilt, zoom, and pan are disabled.

Track a Vehicle

Users can follow a vehicle through a scene as an observer. To follow, or "track" a vehicle, click on a vehicle in the scene, then choose **Track** in the **Mode** combo box on the toolbar or press **[T]**.

While "tracking" a vehicle, the user can click on other vehicles to follow their movement through the scene.

To discontinue tracking a vehicle, choose **Scene** in the **Model** combo box or press **[S]**.

While 3D Viewer is in Track mode, the use can tilt and zoom the scene, but the rotate and pan functions are disabled.

Create Digital Video

3D Viewer can be used to create digital video in .AVI format. Digital video can then be copied to other computers for playback, even if 3D Viewer is not installed.

3D Viewer generates digital video are based on "Tours". Tours can then be used as input to the video generation process.

To create a tour, navigate to the point in the scene where you would like the tour to begin, then click the ![button] button. 3D Viewer will present the Tour Save dialog:

The file name defaults to the current scene name with the extension ".s3t". If you desire, you may type a different name. Click the **[Save]** button. The application is now in "Tour" mode. 3D Viewer is now recording the camera angle in time. You may navigate through the scene and change the scene mode if as you like to create the tour through the simulation environment. To end the tour, click the ![button] button.

To playback a saved tour, click the ![button] button. 3D Viewer will present the Open Tour dialog:

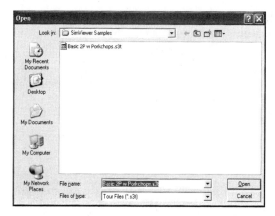

Select a tour file and click "Open". 3D Viewer will automatically start playing the tour. To end tour playback, click the 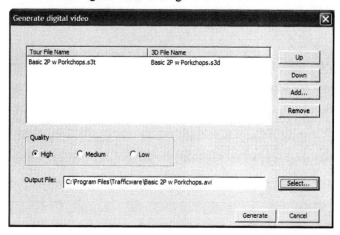 button.

Finally, to generate digital video from a tour file, click the button. 3D Viewer will present the Generate Digital Video dialog:

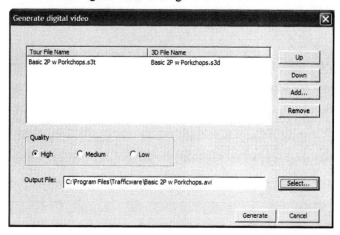

3D Viewer can generate digital video from one or more tour files. To select a tour file, click the [Add...] button and choose a tour file. You may add as many tour files as you wish. 3D Viewer will generate the digital video from the tour files in the order that they appear in the listbox. Click the [Up] or [Down] buttons to move tour files up or down in the listbox.

The "Quality" radio button controls the quality of the video and the corresponding size of the resulting .AVI file. Higher quality files have the best appearance, but take the longest time to generate and create the largest video file.

Choose the output file for the digital video by clicking the **[Select...]** button.

The output file name will default to the name of the simulation followed by a ".AVI" extension. You may choose to use a different name. Click [Save] to begin establish the digital video file.

The user can then click the [Generate] button to start the video compression engine, which is used to create the digital video.

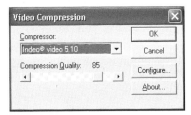

Windows offers multiple forms of video compression. The relative quality of each varies. Note that not all systems have the same compression engines. Therefore, selecting an Indeo or Windows Media Player compressor is usually a preferred choice since they are among the most widely available compressors. Click **[OK]** to begin generating the digital video.

While the application is generating the digital video, the application will display a progress bar indicating the percentage of the digital video processed.

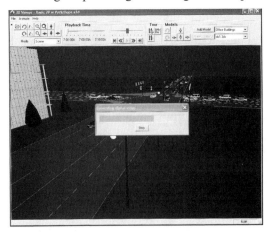

Users can interrupt the digital video generation by clicking the **[Stop]** button. To view the resulting digital video, navigate to the directory where the simulation file is located and double-click on the file with the "Video Clip" type. Windows will then open Media Player and begin playing the file. The video clip file can then be copied to

Add Buildings and Scenery

Users can add buildings and scenery to 3D Viewer scenes to create realistic simulations. To add a building, tree or other model, navigate to the location in the scene near the point where the model is to be placed. Select the model from the model list. Choose the model category then select a model from the list below. Next, click ___Add Model___. The model will be placed at the location near the center of the window.

To adjust the model location and orientation, left-click on the model in the scene, the user can then use the keyboard, mouse, or toolbar to move the model. To use the mouse, left-click on the mouse and hold down the button, then move the mouse. Right-clicking will rotate the model.

To use the keyboard, use the arrow keys to move the model. Holding down the **[CTRL]** key while pressing the arrow keys will move the model more quickly. Holding down the **[Insert]** and **[Delete]** keys will rotate the model.

To remove a model, click on the model in the scene then click ___Remove Model___.

Chapter 26 – SimTraffic CI

This chapter provides instructions for using SimTraffic CI. SimTraffic CI interacts with a controller interface (CI) device connected to a controller to simulate the operation of the controller with simulated traffic.

Setup

Before using SimTraffic CI, connect the controller interface (CI) device (sold separately), controller, and PC as shown in the following diagram.

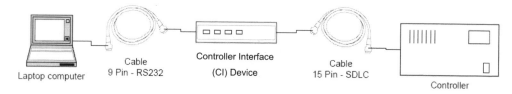

Before proceeding, confirm the port used for the CI testbox for your PC. From your PC's *Control Panel*, choose **System**. From the *System Properties*, select the **Device Manager**. Expand the *Ports* option and confirm the port used for the CI device.

Turn on all of the devices after connecting the cables. Open SimTraffic after initializing the CI device.

After opening SimTraffic CI, choose the command **Options→CI-Options**. **Figure 26-1** illustrates the CI Options dialog for SimTraffic CI setup.

Select the port which is connected to the CI device. In the **Settings for Selected Port**, choose the intersection which will run through the CI device. In **Controller Type**, choose the type of controller that is being used. Check on the **CI Active**. Close the CI options window. Create your simulation (see 20-1 for details on creating a recording a simulation).

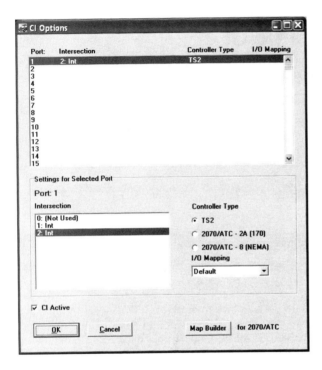

Figure 26-1   CI Options Dialog

When opening or recording a file, SimTraffic CI scans the system for an active controller connection. Click on the intersection to see status. If the CI device and SimTraffic CI are configured correctly, a CI signal status box will appear as shown below.

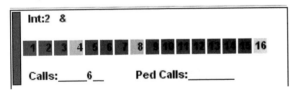

If the intersection is not connected to the CI or not configured properly, the standard SimTraffic signal status box will appear as shown below.

```
Int:1  &                    CL:80 Clk:0.0
Ph   Dir  Time   Mn   FO   Rcl   Gap   Ped
 2   EBT  10.9    4   54   Crd
 6   WBT  10.9    4   54   Crd
Calls:_2_4_6__        Ped Calls:_____
```

I/O Mapping

The purpose of the controller interface (CI) device is to emulate cabinet functionality. In the TS2 standard, the functionality of the BIU pins are defined; however, in ATC/2070 applications, the functionality of the FIO pins is variable. Therefore, the IO **Map Builder** utility is provided for defining the functionality of the IO Pins in a 2070/ATC FIO.

In order for SimTraffic CI to operate properly, it must know the correct pin to apply the detector call on. The IO Map Builder allows the user to assign a physical pin to a functional signal. For example, controller application 'A' may use FIO input 1-1 as Detector #1, while controller application 'B' may use FIO input 4-1 as Detector #1 input. The user can create an IO Map for each controller application. This will allow multiple controller applications to run in the same system.

Map Builder

To launch, select the *Map Builder* button from the **CI Options** dialog. The **Map Builder** dialog is llustrated in **Figure 26-2**. The IO Map Builder also provides default FIO maps based upon the 2070 TEES specification. The default map can not be modified.

The map builder allows you to define 20 maps beyond the default maps (10 2070-8 maps, and 10 2070-2A maps).

To define a new map, you first select the FIO **Map Type** for which the map will be defined. Your choices are either a **2070-2A** for 170 style cabinets, or a **2070-8** for NEMA style cabinets. You next choose a **Map Number** of each map you wish to edit. It is this instance number, 1 through 10, that will be identified in the INI file to tell the CID which map it will be using. The **Description** field can also be modified for each map, as a reminder of the controller application to which it applies.

Once the map type and number are selected, you can then assign functionality to the input and output pins. To add a function to a pin, you highlight the pin number and the function you wish to assign to it, and press the [Assign] button. You may reassign a pin's function without removing the current function. To remove functionality from a pin, you highlight the pin and press the [Remove] button.

Once you are satisfied with the changes, you may press the save button. If you wish to exit, press the exit button. If you have not saved, then upon exiting it will give you the option to keep or discard your current changes.

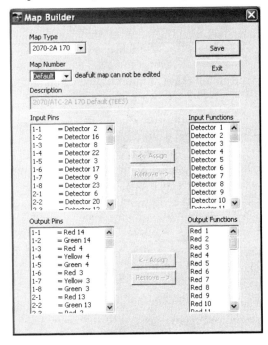

Figure 26-2   Map Builder Dialog

Input Data

Input data requirements for SimTraffic CI are the same as regular SimTraffic, except as noted in the following sections.

Timing Data

SimTraffic CI does not use the timing and phasing data from Synchro. The external controller determines signal timing.

However, it is necessary to code **Phase Numbers** (page 7-5), **Left Turn Type** (page 7-3), and **Right Turn Treatment** (page 7-4).

Code **Pedestrian Calls** (page 8-11) or **Conflicting Pedestrians** (page 6-2), to have CI place pedestrian calls to the controller.

The CI device software uses phases 13 to 16 as pedestrian phases for phases 2, 4, 6, and 8. These phases are not available for vehicle use.

Detector Data

If modeling actuated control, detector information is necessary. SimTraffic CI will use the detector information listed in the **DETECTOR** settings (refer to page 10-1).

Interval Parameters

Interval Parameters work the same as in regular SimTraffic CI.

Loading timing plans for a UTDF data file has no effect on the test box signals since they are controlled externally.

Operation

Data is exchanged between SimTraffic CI and the CI device software 10 times per second.

SimTraffic CI simulates vehicles and simulates detector operation. These detector calls are sent to the CI device and the Hardware Controller. The Controller operates as though it has real traffic. The current phase information is returned to SimTraffic CI through the CI device.

Record and Simulation Speed

SimTraffic CI can only simulate or record traffic at real time speed. The hardware controller is not capable of operating at an accelerated rate.

Stopping and **restarting** the simulation can give strange results. A hardware controller can not be "paused" or sent back in time. Resuming simulation will start with the controller at its new current state. It is possible that "approved" vehicles will now find a red signal but continue through. It may take 10 seconds or more to return to normal operation.

To record MOEs, it is necessary to perform a complete simulation in real time including the seed time. To perform a 15-minute simulation, it takes 15 minutes to record.

To reduce analysis time, try simulating first with regular SimTraffic to insure that traffic and geometric data is coded correctly.

Signal Status

Click on the center of an intersection to obtain signal status.

If the CI device (or CI Test) is operating correctly with a controller matching this intersection ID, a CI status box will appear.

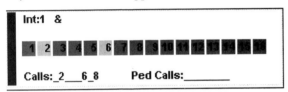

If no CI device is attached for this intersection, SimTraffic CI will create a virtual controller, the standard SimTraffic signal status will appear.

Int:1 &				CL:80 Clk:0.0			
Ph	Dir	Time	Mn	FO	Rcl	Gap	Ped
2	EBT	10.9	4	54	Crd		
6	WBT	10.9	4	54	Crd		
Calls:_2_4_6__			Ped Calls:_____				

If the CI device software is loaded after SimTraffic CI, or a problem is corrected, re-Open the SimTraffic file. SimTraffic CI will search for the connected CI device when opening the data file.

Using Overlaps

Operating SimTraffic CI with overlaps can be a bit tricky. An overlap is a movement served by two phases, often used for right turn phases.

Example: NBR is served by phases 2 and 3. The controller has this programmed as Overlap A and uses output channel 9.

In Synchro code the following for the NBR:

> Protected Phase: 9

> Detector Phases: 2

Switch Phase: 3

It may be necessary to add phase 9 to the ring and barrier sequence. This file can not be used for analysis in Synchro and can not be used in SimTraffic, except with the Controller Interface. Remember to code the Permitted and Protected phases to match the output channel and code Detector phases to match the phase number used. If Protected Phase is coded as 2 plus 3, the simulation will display yellow between phases 2 and 3, using output channel 9, will maintain a continuos green.

Modeling a Diamond Interchange

SimTraffic models multiple intersections using one controller and it is possible to use SimTraffic CI in conjunction with a controller setup for a diamond interchange.

The file **Diamond For CI.syn** is setup with a basic diamond interchange for SimTraffic CI and a Naztec controller set to 4 phase diamond mode.

First, set the controller into 4 phase diamond mode. Refer to the controller manual for details.

This mode uses phases 4 + 12, and 8 + 16 for the offramp movements. These overlaps are setup to use output channels 4 and 8 so no special phase coding is needed. Notice the phase coding within Synchro. The interior through movements use phases 1+2, and 5+6. These are setup as overlaps A and B, using output channels 9 and 10. Notice that the protected phase numbers for these movements is set to 8 and 9.

The controller number is equal to the lowest node number of the intersections, 1 in this case.

Index